Diversity and Motivation

Culturally Responsive Teaching in College

Second Edition

Margery B. Ginsberg
Raymond J. Wlodkowski

JOSSEY-BASS
A Wiley Imprint
www.josseybass.com

Published by Jossey-Bass
A Wiley Imprint
989 Market Street, San Francisco, CA 94103-1741   www.josseybass.com

Jossey-Bass books and products are available through most bookstores. To contact Jossey-Bass
directly call our Customer Care Department within the U.S. at 800-956-7739, outside the
U.S. at 317-572-3986, or fax 317-572-4002. Jossey-Bass also publishes its books in a variety of
electronic formats. Some content that appears in print may not be available in electronic books.

Library of Congress Cataloging-in-Publication Data

Ginsberg, Margery B., 1954-
    Diversity and motivation : culturally responsive teaching in college / Margery
B. Ginsberg, Raymond J. Wlodkowski. – 2nd ed.
        p.   cm.
    Includes bibliographical references and index.
    ISBN 978-0-7879-9611-6 (cloth)
        1. College teaching—United States.   2. Motivation in education—United States.
    3. Minority students—Education (Higher)—United States.   4. Multiculturalism—
    United States.   I. Wlodkowski, Raymond J.   II. Title.
    LB2331.G57   2009
    378.1'25—dc22
                                                                    2009001137

Printed in the United States of America
FIRST EDITION
HB Printing   10 9 8 7 6 5 4 3 2 1

The Jossey-Bass

Higher and Adult Education Series

Contents

Preface

Motivation is a concept that is intended to explain one of life's most elusive questions: Why do we do what we do? Implicit in seeking to answer this question is the intention that educators might better understand motivation in order to support student learning. Conventional wisdom as well as research indicates that "motivated students" will surpass "unmotivated students" in learning and performance. Knowledge about motivation can improve classroom pedagogy to support student learning.

This book responds to the question: How can postsecondary instructors more consistently support student motivation across diverse student groups? When we define motivation as the natural human capacity to direct energy in the pursuit of a goal, an undergirding assumption is that human beings are purposeful. We constantly learn, and when we do, we are usually motivated to learn. We are directing our energy through attention, concentration, and imagination to make sense of our world. With learning defined as an active and volitional process of constructing meaning from experience and text, there is substantial evidence that motivation is consistently and positively related to educational achievement.

At the same time, the task of supporting student motivation in diverse classrooms is a highly nuanced endeavor. Who we are culturally and how we interact with the world is an intriguing intersection of language, values, beliefs, behaviors, and experiences that pervades every aspect of a person's life and continually changes and evolves. What culture is not is an isolated, mechanical aspect of life that can be used to explain phenomena in the classroom or can be learned as a series of facts, physical elements, or exotic characteristics (Banks, 2006; Gay, 2000; Kitayama and Markus, 1994). Neither is culture an experimental science in search of a law. Rather, it is a highly interpretive one in search of meaning (Geertz, 1973). Across cultural groups, all students are motivated, even when they are not motivated to learn what an instructor has planned.

This second edition builds on the first by updating global demographic shifts, elaborating on approaches that support the success of linguistically diverse students, and expanding the pedagogical repertoire and related theory of our earlier volume. Further, the concluding chapter provides ways to implement global trends in professional learning. Colleges and universities have more students than ever before whose perceptions and ways of making meaning vary from one another and from the instructor. Influenced by global forces and unprecedented patterns of migration and immigration, skillful postsecondary teaching requires skill and humility. In the United States alone, almost 30 million people were born in other countries. Forty-eight percent of students in New York City's public schools come from immigrant-headed households that represent more than one hundred languages. In California, 1.5 million students are classified as English language learners (Suarez-Orozco and Suarez-Orozco, 2002). The implications of these statistics for higher education are significant.

This book proposes that teacher awareness of and respect for cultural diversity influence student motivation to learn. Ultimately it provides a theory and a set of practices that can help postsecondary educators develop a clear focus on intrinsically motivating instruction for all students. From literature and research that spans academic disciplines, we offer a motivational framework for culturally responsive teaching. It is an instructional compass that has been generative for over a decade as it has been used to develop new ideas and directions for lessons and courses.

As important as motivation is to student learning, scholars differ on their assumptions about motivation, in part because it cannot be directly observed or precisely measured. Psychology, a dominant historical lens for understanding student behavior, provides an important yet incomplete understanding of this remarkable intricacy. With the pernicious effects of racism still at work and the connection between economic status and academic performance in need of considerable attention, scholars and practitioners are turning to an interdisciplinary approach for more flexible and interpretive ways to understand motivation.

The essentials of this motivational framework are that it (1) respects diversity; (2) engages the motivation of a broad range of students; (3) creates a safe, inclusive, and respectful learning environment; (4) derives teaching practices from across disciplines and cultures; and (5) promotes equitable learning. This book specifically illustrates a pedagogical response to these essentials. Our goal is to create learning experiences that allow the integrity of every learner to be sustained while each person attains relevant educational success and mobility. Among the reasons we embrace this goal, we believe that a primary purpose of higher education is the intellectual and moral empowerment of learners to achieve personal goals that matter not only for themselves but for a pluralistic and just future.

To accomplish this, we provide extensive examples and illustrations of flexible teaching approaches. These are organized as a set of integrated norms and practices. Norms are explicit assumptions, values, and purposes that are shared among the instructor and learners. Practices are instructional strategies that can be adapted and applied across disciplines and programs. Finally, we provide specific ways faculty can collaborate to extend their own learning. The examples range from how to design a lesson with the motivational framework to how to adapt the Japanese lesson study process to the context of higher education in the United States.

Audience

College teaching and learning center directors, as well as faculty, are primary audiences for this book. However, the ideas here can be adapted to contribute to the instructional repertoire of high school teachers as well. In recent years, important pipeline partnerships between high school and college faculty have emerged to create seamless academic mobility for diverse groups of students. We hope this book will support this crucial work so that educators at all levels of a system can align and advance instructional knowledge based on principles of intrinsic motivation.

Finally, we hope this book will be useful to student services personnel. The motivational framework is easily adapted to the unique contexts and interactions that these indispensable professionals provide. Advisors and counselors can apply the motivational framework to create a counseling environment in which students feel included, positive, engaged, and able to succeed.

Context

The enterprise of instruction as a primary influence on student learning operates within the shifting context of local, state, national, and global politics. Furthermore, we know firsthand the demands on faculty time. While instructors have an enormous influence on student learning, we work within a larger policy environment and continuously negotiate competing commitments. Nonetheless, we believe that the instructional approaches in this book are pragmatic and offer concrete alternatives to entrenched conventional teaching.

Terms

It is always a challenge to determine how to use language in ways that are accessible and meaningful to others. We therefore briefly explain our choices. When referring to issues related to race, ethnicity, or culture, we frequently use the term *cultural diversity*. We realize that this term is sometimes criticized for subsuming and homogenizing racial, ethnic, economic, sexual, physical, and age-related identities, among others. Our work has been primarily in colleges and universities that serve diverse student populations, where there are many ethnicities and linguistic groups, first-generation college students, recent immigrants, and working adult learners. With a focus on practical, macrocultural applications of cultural theory, using language that accommodates a broad range of students has been useful to connect with faculty regarding the need for change. We know, however, that language choice not only represents how we think; it influences how we think, and we struggle with the imperfections of our choices.

We use *culturally responsive teaching* to mean understanding and constructing culturally respectful and motivationally aligned instructional practices. We use the terms *instruction* and *pedagogy* interchangeably, as we do *students* and *learners*. *Instruction* to some implies an approach to teaching that undermines the emancipatory potential of higher education and encourages passivity. We tend to prefer it, however, because it is widely used in academic and local communities within which colleges reside. It is accessible to the audiences we engage.

Overview of the Contents

Because many of the ideas in this book are complex, the book follows a narrative flow. By that, we mean that not all major ideas are identified or defined in the first chapter. They are presented and discussed as we introduce the conditions of the motivational framework.

Chapter One, "Understanding Relationships Between Culture and Motivation to Learn," provides an overview of the intersections between culture and motivation. Our concern is that what seems to have once worked for classroom teaching is now inadequate. We elaborate on this idea by offering a rationale for teaching that intentionally supports intrinsic motivation among a range of learners.

To use intrinsically motivating instruction requires an understanding of learners' perspectives and prior knowledge. Their responses to learning activities reflect their cultural backgrounds. Social scientists today regard the cognitive processes as inherently cultural.

Prior to introducing the motivational framework for culturally responsive teaching, readers will have an opportunity to examine some of their cultural values. Chapter One concludes with a graphic model of the motivational framework and a teaching example that illustrates the four motivational conditions for enhancing student motivation to learn.

Chapters Two through Five define, illustrate, and provide instructional strategies for the motivational conditions. Each of these chapters is devoted to one of the four conditions: "Establishing Inclusion" (Chapter Two), "Developing Attitude" (Chapter Three), "Enhancing Meaning" (Chapter Four), and "Engendering Competence" (Chapter Five). These chapters pragmatically and theoretically describe how each motivational condition embodies two related criteria, following this order: respect and connectedness for inclusion, volition and relevance for attitude, challenge and engagement for meaning, and authenticity and effectiveness for competence. Readers will find theoretical and pragmatic descriptions of each motivational condition, plus useful classroom norms and teaching practices that can be easily adapted to a range of academic disciplines.

Due to our own backgrounds and professional experiences, examples from the social sciences, education, and language acquisition are most frequent. However, whenever possible, we illustrate pedagogical strategies that colleagues from other disciplines have used. Our intention is that faculty in the science professions, general education, and all other areas of study can adapt the strategies in this book to their discipline-specific goals.

Chapter Six, "Implementing a Culturally Responsive Pedagogy," provides ways for faculty to independently implement the motivational framework. It also provides detailed descriptions of activities for faculty development. These include a comprehensive set of all the instructional norms and practices that correspond to the motivational framework, a narrative example of a course that supports student intrinsic motivation, a syllabus that is revised based on the ideas in this book, cooperative learning and reciprocal peer coaching for instructors, how to develop research lessons by adapting the Japanese lesson study process, how to facilitate a book study based on this text, and a collaborative approach to reading articles for faculty development in a brief period of time.

In the Resources, we provide specific tools for instructional planning, peer coaching, and faculty development, including agendas for a one- or two-day faculty retreat on the ideas in this book.

Although our goal is to help faculty transform their instructional plans into intrinsically motivational plans for all students, there are tools throughout this text that can be integrated into teaching repertoires, regardless of an instructor's beliefs about the relationship of cultural diversity, intrinsic motivation, and student learning. Ultimately we want to provide a cohesive instructional ecology that integrates vital constructs of motivation from many disciplines: psychology, philosophy, sociology, education, economics, linguistics, anthropology, political science, and cultural and spiritual studies. We realize that a sufficiently complex but cohesive pedagogical focus is needed to improve instruction for today's students. Without a deliberate approach to lesson planning, enhancing student motivation too often becomes a process of trial and error that lacks cohesion and continuity. With a cohesive plan, there tends to be greater commitment to creating lessons with a well-coordinated range of motivational strategies.

The learning environment provides a meaningful context for addressing and redressing the ways in which bias occurs. The task of understanding, talking about, and working against racism and its consequences may seem formidable. Having the courage to challenge ourselves as cultural beings and skillful professionals is essential. We believe that all students, at all educational levels, can learn in a motivating way. In this book, we seek to provide a realistic approach toward that goal.

February 2009

Margery B. Ginsberg
Seattle, Washington

Raymond J. Wlodkowski
Seattle, Washington

Acknowledgments

This book is the result of numerous conversations and the generosity of friends, colleagues, and students who have shared resources and perspectives. In this regard, we are particularly grateful to those who work closely with us. In particular, Margery would like to thank the core faculty team of the executive-level educational leadership preparation program at the University of Washington College of Education, known as Leadership for Learning. Watching these extraordinary educators communicate with students and teach in ways that are public and collaborative has significantly elevated our understanding of intrinsic motivation in practice. Margery's UW colleagues are Kathy Kimball, Mike Knapp, Brad Portin, Marge Plecki, Meredith Honig, Mike Copland, Brieanne Hull, and, more recently, Doris McEwen.

We also thank David Brightman, senior editor of the Higher and Adult Education Series at Jossey-Bass, whom we regard as a true colleague for his patience, support, and critical insights.

We are eternally grateful to friends who have influenced this work: Suzanne Benally, Lois LaShell and Alan Guskin, Anita Villareal, Cathy Thompson, and Marianne Rubiner.

Finally, we thank Matthew Aaron Ginsberg-Jaeckle and Daniel Mark Ginsberg-Jaeckle. Their connections across generations and international communities are deeply rooted. They continuously teach us that possibility more than probability makes idealism both necessary and joyful.

M.B.G.
R.J.W.

*To Kathy Kimball—educator,
artist, and friend*

The Authors

Margery B. Ginsberg, with a background as a teacher on two Indian reservations, university professor, and Texas Title I technical assistance contact for the U.S. Department of Education, directs Leadership for Learning, a doctoral program for aspiring superintendents and system-level leaders at the University of Washington-Seattle. She also works nationally and internationally to provide support for comprehensive school reform. Her work has been the foundation for several comprehensive school reform designs.

Ginsberg's publications include *Motivation Matters: A Workbook for School Change* (Jossey-Bass, 2003), *Creating Highly Motivating Classrooms for All Students: A Schoolwide Approach to Powerful Teaching with Diverse Learners* (Jossey-Bass, 2000), and *Educators Supporting Educators: A Guide to Organizing School Support Teams* (Association for Supervision and Curriculum Development, 1997). In addition, her work provides the foundational material for two video series, Encouraging Motivation Among All Students (1996) and Motivation, the Key to Success in Teaching and Learning (2003). She has a Ph.D. in bilingual/multicultural/social foundations of education from the University of Colorado-Boulder.

Raymond J. Wlodkowski is professor emeritus at Regis University, Denver, where he was the director of the Center for the Study of Accelerated Learning and the executive director and founding member of the Commission for Accelerated Programs. He is a licensed psychologist who has taught at universities in Denver, Detroit, Milwaukee, and Seattle. His work encompasses adult motivation and learning, cultural diversity, and professional development. Wlodkowski lives in Seattle.

He received his Ph.D. in educational psychology from Wayne State University and is the author of numerous articles, chapters, and books. Among them are *Enhancing Adult Motivation to Learn*, which received the Phillip E. Frandson Award for Literature for its first edition. Three of his books have been translated into Spanish, Japanese, and Chinese. Wlodkowski has worked extensively in video production. He is the author of Motivation to Learn, winner of the Clarion Award from the Association of Women in Communication for the best training and development program in 1991. He has also been the recipient of the Award for Outstanding Research from the Adult Higher Education Alliance, the Award for Teaching Excellence from the University of Wisconsin-Milwaukee, and the Faculty Merit Award for Excellence from Antioch University, Seattle.

1

UNDERSTANDING RELATIONSHIPS BETWEEN CULTURE AND MOTIVATION TO LEARN

In recognizing the humanity of our fellow beings,
we pay ourselves the highest tribute.
—Thurgood Marshall

How can culturally diverse people in higher education learn well together in ways that are relevant and stimulating? For postsecondary educators, the response to this question can be examined through the lessons of history, linguistics, the arts, and any number of other disciplines. As each of us grapples with complicated notions about fairness, respect, or, for that matter, what it means to learn, this book offers forms of pedagogical action that are widely considered to enhance student motivation and learning. Our premise is that educators who seek to support learning among diverse groups of students need to be increasingly intentional and imaginative about instructional practice. Colleges and universities have more learners than ever before whose perceptions and ways of making meaning vary from one another and from the instructor. Influenced by global forces and unprecedented patterns of migration and immigration, skillful postsecondary teaching has become a highly nuanced endeavor.

In the United States, alone, almost 30 million people were born in other countries. Forty-eight percent of students in New York City's public schools come from immigrant-headed households that represent more than a hundred languages. In California, 1.5 million students are classified as English language learners. In Dodge City, Kansas, more than 30 percent of public school students are the children of immigrants (Suarez-Orozco and Suarez-Orozco, 2002). The implications of these statistics for higher education are significant.

Although high school graduation rates have steadily improved in the United States, students from low-income families continue to perform significantly lower on assessments of literacy and mathematics achievements before they even start kindergarten. These differences tend to persist as students progress through school and raise considerable equity concerns (Lee and Burkham, 2002). Nearly half of black Americans have a high school diploma or less, according to 2005 data from the U.S. Census Bureau. In contrast, more than seven in ten Asian Americans ages twenty-five to sixty-four and more than six in ten European Americans have completed some college (EPE Research Center, 2007).

Yet in the twenty-first century, a college degree has become more important than ever before. A college graduate in the United States earns on average $23,441 more per year than a high school graduate and $31,595 more than a high school dropout (Olson, 2007). And while only 7 percent of twenty-four-year-olds from low-income families had earned a four-year college degree in 1999–2000, 52 percent of those from high-income families had completed a postsecondary degree. Making learning more accessible at every level is not only a matter of equity. It has significant pragmatic value.

This book does not attempt to address the larger policy environment of postsecondary education in the United States and throughout the rest of the world. Although we are deeply concerned with broader issues and their influence on educational concerns, this book's contribution is in the detail of daily teaching and ongoing program development. It is serendipitous that it comes at a time when colleges and universities are beginning to experience the same scrutiny on graduation rates and demonstrating what students have learned as elementary and secondary education. Our primary interest is, and has long been, to assert that there is more that each of us can do as educators and educational leaders to redress disparate learning conditions. This book offers perspectives on and ideas for strengthening pedagogical skill through the lens of intrinsic motivation.

Motivation is a topic that concerns most educators. Within our own teaching environments, we understand that students' concentration, imagination, effort, and willingness to continue are powerfully influenced by how they feel about the setting they are in, the respect they receive from the people around them, and their ability to trust their own thinking and experiences. People who feel unsafe, unconnected, and disrespected are often unmotivated to learn. This is as true, if not more so, in college as it is in prekindergarten through twelfth grade. Such a conclusion does not explain all the issues and barriers related to the progress of people of color and low-income students in postsecondary educational settings, but it is fundamental to what happens among learners and teachers wherever they meet. In education, the day-to-day, face-to-face feelings matter tremendously with respect to whether people stay or leave and whether they are willing to direct their energy toward learning.

This book offers concrete ideas about how students and teachers can create a milieu that promotes learning. In our opinion, to do so means that those with the most power in the classroom, those often in the majority, must take the greater responsibility for initiating or participating in the process. The task is a difficult one. As Lisa Delpit (1988) eloquently states, "We do not really see through our eyes or hear through our ears, but through our beliefs. To put our beliefs on hold is to cease to exist as ourselves for a moment—and that is not easy. It is painful as well, because it means turning yourself inside out, giving up your own sense of who you are, and being willing to see yourself in the unflattering light of another's angry gaze.... We must learn to be vulnerable enough to allow our world to turn upside down in order to allow the realities of others to edge themselves into our consciousness" (1988, p. 297).

In other words, this task requires raising questions about discrimination or scrutinizing one's own power, even if that power stems merely from being in the majority. Certainly what follows in this book, when taken in the light of what typically occurs in many learning settings in postsecondary education, invites that kind of questioning.

Making direct suggestions for change was a challenge for us because we do not pretend to know what is best. Clearly we have very strong beliefs about what might be better. These beliefs are informed by research and experiences, both of which lead us to ask readers to keep in mind at least two sensibilities while reading this book. First, acknowledge what can and should be done on a personal level as soon as possible, and earnestly pursue it. Second, identify the larger long-term and institutional changes that require resources and collective action, and begin to discuss these with others to create the means to make them happen.

This book is not a blueprint. What is considered motivating varies across cultures and among individual human beings. People are experts on their own lives. Using a multidisciplinary approach that includes but is not limited to philosophy, anthropology, communications, critical theory, feminist theory, adult learning theory, multicultural studies, and linguistics as well as psychology, we offer an interpretive and process-based approach that is more in keeping with the metaphor of a compass than a map. There are essential directions to take because all people are intrinsically motivated to learn and share a common humanity. But the cultural terrain of each individual's life so varies that the path to understanding another person is beyond the precision of any modern mental cartographer.

The Influence of Culture

The cultural composition of today's postsecondary learners differs markedly from that of thirty years ago, when many of today's college educators were beginning their careers or were still in school. If we look only from the perspective of ethnicity and language, we realize that the wave of immigration absorbed by the United States during the 1990s was the largest in seventy years and that today at least one out of every four people in this country speak a language other than English in their home. (For a more extensive discussion on factors influencing migration to the United States, see Suarez-Orozco and Suarez-Orozco, 2002; Adams, Bell, and Griffin 2007.)

In addition, 73 percent of all college students today can be identified as nontraditional learners (National Center for Educational Statistics, 2002). They possess one or more of the following characteristics: delayed enrollment into postsecondary education, part-time attendance, financial independence, a full-time job, dependents other than a spouse or domestic partner, single parent, or nonstandard high school diploma. Interestingly, the majority of adult college students age twenty-five or older are women—approximately 65 percent (Aslanian, 2001).

It is not surprising that the topic of motivation and cultural diversity is of interest to so many teachers. For more than might care to admit it, the convergence of multiple and, at times, far-ranging perspectives among students contributes to a binary classroom dynamic with chaotic or laissez-faire exchanges, on the one hand, and majority cultural dominance on the other. For students armed with academic self-confidence and hierarchical connections, certain approaches to instruction may be uncomfortable. But we would argue that it is even more daunting for the increasing number of postsecondary students whose success relies on instructional interactions in the classroom. Their instructor's attention to teaching is essential. Taking a closer look at the concept of culture can help educators understand why culturally diverse classrooms frequently challenge the resources of educators, even those who are earnest and experienced. Quite simply, what seems to have once worked for classroom teaching may now be clearly inadequate, whether in the area of encouraging motivation, initiating humor, or helping students to learn effectively.

As a society, we are two generations removed from legally sanctioned educational segregation, yet despite efforts to integrate urban schools through busing, many of us who now teach grew up in what appeared to be monocultural schools and communities. It is likely that we were socialized in our formative years with an unexamined set of traditions and beliefs about ourselves and a limited knowledge about others. In addition, as members of human communities, our identities have been fundamentally constructed in relation to others (Rogoff, 2003; Tatum, 2007). Being socialized and living in the dominant culture often lessens awareness that beliefs and behaviors reflect a particular racial group, ethnic heritage, sexual orientation, or gender affiliation. This is especially so if we are white, European American, heterosexual males. For many educators, it is not a stretch to think of these attitudes and norms as universally valued and preferred.

A dominant group can so successfully project its way of seeing social reality that its view is accepted as common sense, as part of the natural order, even by those who are disempowered or marginalized by it (Foucault, 1980; Freire and Macedo, 1987). We may not imagine that we hold negative assumptions or stereotypes toward people with other values or beliefs (Adams and Marchesani, 1992; Butler, 1993). In fact, for some, it may feel like heresy to acknowledge that Anglo Americans and dominant Western norms enjoy a position of privilege and power in this country's educational system that has diminished other norms as valuable as cooperation (versus competition) and interdependence (versus independence).

Although culture is taught, it is generally conveyed in ways that are indirect or a part of everyday life (Anzaldua, 1987; Young, 1990; Schein, 1992). That is one of the reasons that it is difficult for most of us to describe ourselves culturally in explicit terms. The times we are likely to experience uniqueness as cultural beings occur when we are in the presence of those who appear different from ourselves. As an example, a person from a family and community that is emotionally demonstrative and sees this as a sign of open communication may embarrass or concern a person whose own traditions view public modesty as a mark of respect for that which is greater than oneself. When we meet others whose family or community norms vary from our own, it is akin to holding up a mirror, provoking questions we might not otherwise think to ask. Contrast and dissonance can be disturbing in spite of the opportunity they present to examine assumptions, making it possible to more deeply understand who we are in relation to one another.

The most obvious cultural characteristics that people observe are physical. On the surface, race, gender, age, and other observable characteristics signal social group membership. Clearly, however, physical characteristics provide only cursory insight into another person. In fact, it is interesting to note who is not typically defined by physical characteristics in media and everyday conversation. To be blunt, white men are rarely defined by whiteness and maleness. The idea about what is "normal" can be so psychologically ingrained that it is entirely possible to overlook one's own assumptions about people whose physical characteristics or repertoire of behaviors fall outside a familiar sphere. Of course, even within the supposedly unitary majority culture, there is tremendous variation (Said, 1993; Lobo and Peters, 2001; Banks, 2001). A clear perspective on anyone's interior landscape is remarkably complicated.

Educators who seek to be highly responsive to students are often puzzled by how to pedagogically enact their respect for diversity. Personal histories and psychological traits interact dynamically and distinguish human beings as individuals. The subtle complexity of who we are makes it difficult to define a person by a set of narrow or static characteristics. The primary point here is that the variation and distinction among cultural groups transcend a single set of cultural norms. When we accept norms as universal, we are likely to see deficit rather than difference. One common example occurs in classrooms where the teachers rely heavily on the Socratic seminar, one of several instructional methods that, in the absence of adequate student preparation, tends to favor those for whom assertive public discourse is a part of everyday life. Should an instructor perceive this form of active participation as evidence of being smart, entire groups of students may find themselves at risk of failure.

Certain forms of discourse in higher education are commonly viewed as a sign of preparation and analytical skill, and students with public reserve may be misjudged as underprepared, linguistically or cognitively limited, lacking in initiative, easily intimidated, or even arrogant. The presumption of deficit in human beings who fail to conform to expectations and standards that are commonly associated with a dominant culture is one of the key factors accounting for dropout rates from kindergarten through postsecondary education. Throughout the literature on retention and attrition, this phenomenon is attributed to a broad range of institutional barriers that fail to take into account the expectations and experiences of students from a host of cultural backgrounds, many of which may differ from those of the majority culture (Adams, 1992; Yosso, 2005; Hebel, 2007). It is our hope that there will always be ambiguity and nuance in understanding ourselves and others as cultural beings, learners, community members, and world citizens. However, being aware of and responsive to cultural variation is an essential aspect of equitable instruction.

In diverse postsecondary classrooms, we believe that opportunities for pluralistic discourse on issues of race, ethnicity, and a host of civic issues ought to occur across disciplines. The ability for human beings to engage respectfully with different belief systems extends well beyond the social sciences and humanities. All of academia must accept a share of responsibility. This matter is important to the educational quality of instruction, and the moral implications are vast.

If university-educated adults know little about their classmates and even less about the rest of the world, the impact of a university education as it relates to democratic values will remain largely theoretical (Galston, 2006). Today, more than ever before, discourse about tensions that arise from cultural pluralism in classrooms and global contexts is all too easily trumped by knowledge that can quickly be converted into utility (Engell and Dangerfield, 2005).

Culture is the deeply learned confluence of language, values, beliefs, and behaviors that pervade every aspect of a person's life, and it is continually undergoing changes. What it is not is an isolated, mechanical aspect of life that can be used to directly explain phenomena in the classroom or that can be learned as a series of facts, physical elements, or exotic characteristics (Ovando and Collier, 1998; Valenzuela, 1999). Cultural awareness takes into account that human beings are suspended in webs of significance that we create. Drawing from Geertz (1973), an analysis of culture is "not an experimental science in search of a law but an interpretive one in search of meaning" (pp. 5, 29).

Geertz's perspective is fundamental to this book. There are few hard-and-fast rules about entire groups of people. Similarly, there are few hard-and-fast rules about the ways in which human beings work and learn together. As teachers, being aware of our own beliefs and biases and being open to the meaning that is created through authentic interactions with diverse students is fundamental. Without such awareness, stereotypes and biases that reside within learning environments become agents of historic patterns of marginalization.

Stereotyping is rooted in our assumptions about the "average characteristics" of a group. We then impose those assumptions on all individuals from the group. In fact, some of the characteristics commonly associated with European Americans—for example, Christianity, individualism, and social conservatism—have become so pervasive that these traits have become a form of taken-for-granted national "commonsense" (Sue, 1991; Blum, 2005). Indeed, a great deal of heterogeneity exists within as well as across all cultural groups. "Seek first to understand" is a bit of wisdom whose genesis lies within many ethnic and faith communities.

Educators as well as students have beliefs and values regarding learning and the roles of teacher and learner. These are culturally transmitted through history, religion, media, family, mythology, and political orientation. The ways in which we experience a learning situation are mediated by such cultural influences. No learning situation is culturally neutral. If we are European American and teach as we were taught, it is likely that we sanction individual performance, prefer "reasoned" argumentation, advocate impersonal objectivity, and condone sportslike competition for testing and grading procedures. Such teaching represents a distinct set of cultural norms and values that for many of today's learners are at best culturally unfamiliar and at worst a contradiction of the norms and values of their gender or their racial and ethnic backgrounds. In a Socratic seminar, many learners find themselves in a dilemma if they have been socialized toward a value of cooperation in their families and communities but are expected to be highly competitive within educational settings.

Few of us in postsecondary settings would care to admit that the way we teach compromises the learning of members of certain cultural groups. And many would agree that higher education has a responsibility to safeguard against a majority rule that functions oppressively for a minority. Yet in spite of new instructional technologies, teaching centers, and the language of learning styles, the tension between a serious examination of teaching practices and research is real.

This issue, as well as our concern that colleges and universities have moved too far away from involvement with the broader social communities in which they reside, exceeds our emphasis on pedagogy in this book. But our commitment to educational access and opportunity requires us to acknowledge that colleges and universities implicitly and explicitly perpetuate larger systems of inequality. We encourage educators to examine policy and structural issues in higher education and in local communities that undermine the conditions for change within classrooms. (On the themes of commercialization, student civic disinterest, and a desire to increase faculty involvement with their surrounding communities, see Galston, 2006, and Engell and Dangerfield, 2005.)

We also encourage educators to become familiar with various interpretations of the term *diversity*. It is a word whose meanings are dependent on the context in which it is being understood. An anthropological approach to diversity would provide a comparative view of human groups within the context of all human groups. A political approach would analyze issues of power and class. Applied to a learning situation and the purpose of this book, diversity conveys a need to respect similarities and differences among human beings and to move beyond simply developing sensitivity to active and effective responsiveness. This requires constructive action to change ideas and attitudes that perpetuate the exclusion of underserved groups of students and significantly challenge their motivation to learn.

In addition to the various academic connotations of the word *diversity*, some view its general use as platitudinal or euphemistic. Although we use the words *diversity, cultural diversity,* and *cultural pluralism* interchangeably, there is the belief that language associated with cultural differences must acknowledge issues of racism, discrimination, and the experience of exclusion. This argument implicates *diversity* as a way to dilute or skirt critical issues by implicitly representing all forms of difference—including individual differences and heterogeneity—within personal identities (Nieto, 2004; Geismar and Nicoleau, 1993; Adams, Bell, and Griffin, 2007). Some see the term *cultural diversity* as more closely connected to issues of racial, economic, and political marginalization. Our point here is to acknowledge that each of us has beliefs and understandings that guide and challenge our work within a pluralistic society. Despite the earnestness with which we use language, we are frequently implicated through the meanings we are trying to express.

Although we use the term *diversity* throughout this book, we are advocates for social justice education that includes an understanding that social inequality is structured and maintained in ways that protect privileged interests. By *privilege*, another common term in this book, we mean unearned access to resources and social power, often because of social group membership.

With respect to cultural diversity, this book offers a macrocultural pedagogical framework. Our framework is built on principles and structures that are meaningful across cultures, especially with students from families and communities that have not historically experienced success in higher education. Rather than comparing and contrasting groups of people from a microcultural perspective—one that, for example, identifies a specific ethnic group and prescribes approaches to teaching according to assumed characteristics and orientations—our approach emerges from literature on and experience with creating a more equitable pluralistic framework that elicits the intrinsic motivation of all learners. The complicated interaction of history, personality, cultural transmission, and cultural transformation is yet another worthy area of exploration outside the scope of this book. A macrocultural framework can provide instructional guidance without reducing dynamic groups of people to sets of stereotypical characteristics. Our emphasis is on creating multiple approaches from which teachers may choose in order to more consistently support the diverse perspectives and values that learners bring to the classroom. This does not, of course, preclude the need for ongoing examination of one's own socialization, cultural identity, and related practices.

Personal Appreciation of the Concept of Culture

Unless we as educators understand our own culturally mediated values and biases, we may be misguided in believing that we are encouraging divergent points of view and providing meaningful opportunities for learning to occur when we are in fact repackaging or disguising past dogmas. It is entirely possible to believe in the need for change and therefore learn new languages and techniques, and yet overlay new ideas with old biases and frames of reference. It is possible to diminish the potential and the needs of others at our most subconscious levels and in our most implicit ways without any awareness that we are doing so. Mindfulness of who we are and what we believe culturally can help us examine the ways in which we may be unknowingly placing our good intentions within a dominant and unyielding framework—in spite of the appearance of openness and receptivity to enhancing motivation to learn among all students.

One of the most useful places to begin the exploration of who we are culturally and the relevance of that identity is to ask what values we hold that are consistent with the dominant culture. This question allows us to be cognizant not only of our dominant-culture values but also of the distinctions we hold as members of other groups in society. This is particularly important for fourth-, fifth-, and sixth-generation Americans of European descent. For many descendants of European Americans, one's family's country or countries of origin can be only marginally useful in understanding who we are now as cultural people in the United States. The desire and ability to assimilate, as well as affiliations with numerous other groups (religious, socioeconomic, regional, and so forth), can create confusion about the cultural origins of personal beliefs and values. Furthermore, culture is a dynamic and changing concept for each of us, regardless of the country of our geographical origin. Our cultural identities are constantly evolving or changing, and consequently values, customs, and orientations are fluid. Because we as educators exert a powerful influence over classroom norms, it is important to make explicit those values that are most often implicit and profoundly affect students in our classrooms.

Several approaches can help to personalize the concept of culture. One way to gain insight into the elusive concept of culture is to consider the research of sociologist Robin M. Williams Jr. (1970). Williams identified cultural themes that tend to be enduring reflections of dominant values, which in the United States have been northern European. These themes may or may not be operative in a classroom, but because belief systems influence teaching practices, the selected themes, condensed by Locke (1992), may provide a useful source for reflecting on prevailing rhetorical, cultural, and political norms in a classroom. In the list that follows, each theme, in italics, is accompanied by at least one alternative perspective. The alternative examples are meant to invite a conversation about counterbeliefs and values that students and teachers bring to a learning environment:

1. *Achievement and success:* People emphasize rags to riches in stories.

   Alternatives: Personal generosity is the highest human value; conspicuous consumption represents greed and self-interest; "rags to riches" is rooted in cultural mythology that overlooks the social, political, and economic forces that favor certain groups over others. Thus, achievement has at least as much to do with privilege as do personal desire and effort.

2. *Activity and work:* People see this country as a land of busy people who stress disciplined, productive activity as a worthy end in itself.

   Alternatives: People believe that caring about and taking time for others is more important than "being busy"; discipline can take many forms and should be equated with respect, moral action, and social conscience; a means-ends orientation has been the justification for such things as cultural genocide and environmental disaster; sustenance is a higher value than productivity.

3. *Humanitarian mores:* People spontaneously come to the aid of others and hold traditional sympathy for the underdog.

   Alternatives: Human beings are selective about whom they will help; for some, personal gain takes precedence over kindness and generosity; for others, human emotion is to be avoided because it makes them feel vulnerable and inept.

4. *Moral orientation:* People judge life events and situations in terms of right and wrong.

   Alternatives: People feel there is no objective right or wrong and that such a perspective tends to favor and protect the most privileged members of society; finding meaning in life events and situations is more important than judging.

5. *Efficiency and practicality:* People emphasize the practical value of getting things done.

   Alternatives: People believe that process is just as important as product and that it makes the strongest statement about what an individual values; living and working in a manner that values equity and fairness is both practical and just.

6. *Progress:* People hold the optimistic view that things will get better.

   Alternatives: People believe that the idea of progress assumes human beings can and should control nature and life circumstances; instead, we ought to acknowledge, respect, and care for that which we have been given, that which is greater than ourselves, and that which is, like life, cyclical. (Interestingly, many languages in the Americas and around the world do not include a word for *progress*.)

7. *Material comfort:* People emphasize the good life. Conspicuous consumption is sanctioned.

   Alternatives: People believe that a good life is defined by sharing and giving things away. The idea that life will be good if one owns many possessions leads to insatiable behavior and greed.

8. *Freedom:* People believe in freedom with an intensity others might reserve for religion.

   Alternatives: People believe that freedom without justice is dangerous; limiting freedom is necessary for equality; accepting the limitations of personal freedom is a sign of respect for others.

9. *Individual personality:* People believe that every individual should be independent, responsible, and self-respecting; the group should not take precedent over the individual.

   Alternatives: People believe that sharing and humility are higher values than ownership and self-promotion; self-respect is inseparable from respect for others, community, and that which is greater than oneself. Individualism can promote aggression and competition in ways that undermine the confidence and self-respect of others; independence denies the social, cultural, racial, and economic realities that favor members of certain groups over others.

10. *Science and secular rationality:* People have esteem for the sciences as a means of asserting mastery over the environment.

    Alternatives: People believe the earth is a sacred gift to be revered and protected. The notion of scientific objectivity is based on the mistaken presumption that human beings are capable of value-neutral beliefs and behaviors.

11. *Nationalism-patriotism:* People believe in a strong sense of loyalty to that which is deemed "American."

    Alternatives: People believe that, functionally, "American" has meant conformity to Anglo European values, behaviors, and appearances; the way in which the word *American* is commonly used to describe a single country on the continent of the Americas is presumptuous and arrogant; "American" needs to be redefined in the spirit of pluralism and with respect for other global identities.

12. *Democracy:* People believe that every person should have a voice in the political destiny of their country.

    Alternatives: People believe that democracy is an illusion that perpetuates the domination of society's most privileged members; people must have the means and capacity to use their voices—this requires access to multiple perspectives on issues and confidence that speaking up will not jeopardize one's economic and personal security.

13. *Racism and related group superiority:* People believe that racism represents a value conflict in the culture of the United States because it emphasizes differential evaluation of racial, religious, and ethnic groups. They argue for a color-blind ideology based on the assumption that social and economic advantage in contemporary life is the consequence of merit and hard work.

    Alternatives: People believe that racism combines prejudice with power and is personal, institutional, and cultural. It has been used for over four hundred years as a way to secure the psychological, educational, and material dominance of a select group. Without acknowledgment of its existence, it is impossible for members of a society to examine the implications of advantage and power and develop practices that level the playing field.

When we clarify our own cultural values and biases, we are better able to consider how they might subtly but profoundly influence the degree to which learners in our classrooms feel included, respected, at ease, and generally motivated to learn. The range of considerations found in Williams's cultural themes can be helpful as we think of questions to ask ourselves about our own assumptions and as we construct reflective questions to enhance the learning experiences. We offer the following examples, with related ideas:

- *Are classroom norms clear, so that if they are different from what students are used to at home or in their communities, they are able to understand and negotiate alternative ways of being?* It may be important to model behavior, provide visible examples of expectations, and elicit information through student polls or written responses to such questions as, "Do you prefer to work in a cooperative group? individually?" Some students are embarrassed to identify what they do not understand. The anonymity of writing, or conferencing with peers and then sharing the information with an instructor, can facilitate communication. One additional consideration is clarity about time. For students from communities where time is not a commodity that can be spent, wasted, or managed and is experienced more in relation to natural patterns, expectations about punctuality require thoughtful clarity.

- *Have I examined the values embedded in my discipline that may confuse or disturb some students?* Ask questions that encourage students to represent alternative perspectives; with students, construct panels that can discuss key issues from diverse perspectives and help students organize discussion groups for collaborative dialogue and knowledge sharing.

- *Are the examples I use to illustrate key points meaningful to and respectful of students?* Give one example from your own experience, and then ask students to create their own examples to illustrate different points, providing an opportunity for group discussion. Acknowledge the experiences of people from different backgrounds, and be aware of nonverbal language and voice. For example, there is some evidence that a voice with less modulation connotes authority and knowledge, while an approachable voice invites thinking. Regardless, seeking feedback through regular anonymous surveys can be instructive.

- *Do I have creative and effective ways to learn about my students' lives and interests?* You might want to incorporate a photo board, artistic representations, occasional potluck meals, regularly scheduled discussion topics (including current events), acknowledgment of birthdays and cultural holidays, open sharing about yourself, a coffee urn at the back of the classroom as a site for informal discussion, and other similar opportunities.

- *Am I aware of nonverbal communication from a multicultural and cross-cultural perspective?* For many students socialized within the dominant culture of the United States, physical proximity has little effect on emotional safety or academic effectiveness. Similarly, a well-modulated voice signals authority and knowledge. But this varies considerably across cultures (Gudykunst and Kim, 1992; Remland, 2000), and a well-modulated voice, for example, is not necessarily one that is approachable or invites thinking. Although research on communication tends to be painted with a fairly broad brush, attention to voice, proximity, and other kinetic characteristics can determine who gets the floor, whose perspective is respected, and who enjoys learning (Goldin-Meadow, 2003; Andersen and Wang, 2006).

We believe it is important to keep in mind that although individualism has been argued to be the backbone of democracy, it is also considered to contribute to crime, alienation, loneliness, and narcissism. A good place to begin is to consider our own repertoire of behaviors in relation to whom we are teaching, with the understanding that status influences perseverance in spite of how we teach (Bourdieu, 1986). A small focus group of diverse students can contribute to a more nuanced understanding of learner needs.

Peggy McIntosh (1989) has poignantly written: "As a white person I had been taught about racism as something which puts others at a disadvantage, but had been taught not to see one of its corollary aspects, white privilege, which puts me at an advantage.... I was taught to see racism only in individual acts of meanness, not in invisible systems conferring dominance on my group" (p. 10).

Many of us have been socialized, regardless of racial group membership, to think of the United States as a just society. It is hard to imagine that each of us is responsible for everyday actions that can render people as impotent as overt and intentional acts of racism can. The learning environment provides a meaningful context for addressing and redressing the ways in which bias occurs. Learning about who we are culturally, as individuals and as educators, can create a consciousness that is personally, professionally, and socially empowering.

Culturally Responsive Teaching and the Challenges of Cultural Pluralism

Amid great challenge, the United States is moving from the philosophy of an assimilationist melting pot to the philosophy of cultural pluralism, in which members of diverse cultural, social, racial, or religious groups are free to maintain their own identity and yet simultaneously share a larger common political organization, economic system, and social structure (Banks, 2006). Some of this is by will. Undoubtedly some changes can be attributed to significant demographic shifts. In 1970, more than 60 percent of the nation's 9.6 million immigrants originated in Europe, 19 percent in Central and South America, 9 percent in Asia, and 10 percent in other parts of the world. By 2000, only 15 percent of the 28.4 million immigrants in the United States originated in Europe (U.S. Census Bureau, 2002; Passel and Suro, 2005). This change has resulted in a new U.S. landscape, one in which many members of immigrant communities have moved beyond port-of-entry cities to suburban metropolitan areas and rural communities (Hernandez, Denton, and Macartney, 2007). With such changes, the idea of monocultural community and educational norms becomes increasingly preposterous.

Although the promise of a peaceful coexistence among people with diverse lifestyles, language patterns, religious practices, and family structures has long been espoused along with other democratic values, the philosophical position of multiculturalism has been slow to manifest itself in educational institutions. The premise of a pluralistic democracy presumes that there is equal respect for the backgrounds and contemporary circumstances of diverse learners, regardless of individual status and power, and that there is a design for learning processes that embraces the range of needs, interests, and orientations to be found among them.

For the pedagogy of the educational system of a society espousing cultural pluralism, the challenge is to create learning experiences that allow the integrity of every learner to be sustained while each person attains relevant educational success and mobility. Meeting this challenge is transformative as well as integral to a major purpose of higher education: the intellectual empowerment of all learners to achieve equity and social justice in a pluralistic democratic society (Weaver, 1991; Hill, 1991; Marable, 1992).

The whole activity of education is ethical and political in nature. History is replete with examples of the ways in which racism persists over time, often in virulent forms (Lipsitz, 1998; Marabel, 2002; Winant, 2004). The legacy of the United States includes the appropriation of Native American land, the enslavement of African peoples, and the exploitation of Japanese, Chinese, Filipino, and Latino labor. White power and privilege are maintained through law, politics, property ownership, economic rights, and immigration, as well as organizational policy and social structures (Foner and Frederickson, 2004; Katznelson, 2005).

Questions about the consequences of learning to the individual can always be asked in reference to society as a whole (Freire, 1994; Merriam, Caffarella, and Baumgartner, 2007). Whether or not teachers and learners acknowledge the pervasiveness of politics in their work, politics is inherent in the teacher-learner relationship (authoritarian or democratic), the readings chosen for the syllabus (those left in and those left out), and the course content (a shared decision or the teacher's prerogative).

Ethics and politics also reside in the discourse of learning (which questions get asked and answered and how deeply they are probed), the imposition of standardized tests, grading and tracking policies, and the physical conditions of classrooms and buildings, which send messages to learners and teachers about their worth and place in society (Shor, 1993). Politics certainly can be found in the attitude toward nonstandard English reflected in the curriculum and in the way schools are unequally funded depending on the economic class of students served. Most important, as Shor has written, "Education is politics because it is one place where individuals and society are constructed. Because human beings and society are developed in one direction or another through education, the learning process cannot avoid being political" (p. 28).

A pedagogy respectful of multiculturalism and ethics begins not with test scores but with questions. What kinds of citizens do we hope to create through postsecondary education? What kind of society do we want, and how can we reconcile the notions of difference and equality with the imperatives of freedom and justice (Giroux, 1992)?

In spite of significant accomplishments in civil rights laws, community activism, and institutional statements and positions committed to racial equality, a far-reaching agenda for democratic pluralism remains elusive. We live at a time when geographical, cultural, and ethnic borders are giving way to shifting configurations of power and community. Education is a global enterprise that requires new forms of solidarity between academic rigor and broader social concerns that affect how people live, work, and survive. From a purely motivational perspective, experience and research teach that motivation to learn among people is vitally released by a vision of being connected to a larger social purpose and a hopeful future (Ogbu, 1987; Tatum, 2003; Yosso, 2005).

From an educational perspective, achieving a pluralistic democratic society that meets its ideal of equity and social justice is inextricably linked to the pedagogical practices of its educational institutions. An approach to teaching that meets the challenge of cultural pluralism and can contribute to the fulfillment of the purpose of higher education has to respect diversity; engage the motivation of all learners; create a safe, inclusive, and respectful learning environment; derive teaching practices from principles that cross disciplines and cultures; and promote justice and equity in society. Whether we are discussing numerical, linguistic, or social equations, it behooves us to recall that Germany was one of the most educated and literate nations in the world when its leaders presided over the extermination of 12 million Jews, Catholics, Roma, people with disabilities, and people who were gay, lesbian, or transgendered. The struggle for a pluralistic democracy requires consciousness in political chambers, on street corners, and in classrooms. In his "Letter from the Birmingham Jail," Martin Luther King Jr. (1964) wrote, "Injustice anywhere is a threat to justice everywhere" (pp. 2–3). This is as true for pedagogical practice as it is for global economics.

Educational scholars with the philosophical position of multiculturalism have long advocated for the gender, ethnic, racial, and cultural diversity of a pluralistic society to be reflected in classrooms (Johnson McDougal, 1925; DuBois, 2005; Dewey, 1933; Takaki, 1993; Banks and McGee Banks, 1993). Their conversations have focused on moral values, equitable hiring practices, and the content of curriculum. Teaching practices have also become the subject of attention. These instructional practices, known as *culturally responsive* or *culturally relevant teaching*, attempt to apply theories about equitable social power or cultural wealth within the context of classroom interactions. Just as cultural wealth in everyday life generates the opportunity to leverage personal interests, in the classroom it enhances the opportunity for academic success.

Culturally responsive teaching occurs when there is respect for the backgrounds and circumstances of students regardless of individual status and power, and when there is a design for learning that embraces the range of needs, interests, and orientations in a classroom. In other words, an educational system that espouses cultural pluralism also seeks to create learning experiences that protect the knowledge, skill, and experience that learners possess and supports academic attainment and mobility by finding ways for students to develop their strengths. Rising to this challenge is integral to a frequently espoused goal within academia: the intellectual empowerment of all learners to achieve equity and social justice in a pluralistic democratic society (Weaver, 1991; Hill, 1991; Marable, 1992).

These are the essentials of culturally responsive teaching. They foster effective learning for a range of students with attention to the collective good of society, so that systems of oppression, whether they are conceptual or institutional, cannot proliferate. Culturally responsive teaching is guided by a vision of justice and a pedagogy that seeks to transform as well as inform. How to arrive at the essentials of this pedagogy and put them into practice is the narrative of the rest of this book.

Understanding a Motivational Perspective That Supports Culturally Responsive Teaching

Teaching that is inclusive, relevant, challenging, and perhaps even transformative for a range of students has intrinsic motivation as an essential feature. Intrinsic motivation provides a view of teaching and learning that is historically well documented although not widely practiced in college teaching. Researched and advocated within a number of disciplines, it is a cornerstone of cross-cultural studies (Csikszentmihalyi, 1988), education (Vansteenkiste, Lens, and Deci, 2006;

Elliot and Dweck, 2005), bilingual education (Cummins, 1986; Cummins, Brown, and Sayers, 2006), adult education (Wlodkowski, 2008), and work and sports (Frederick-Recascino, 2002).

An analysis of the procedural and structural components of college teaching reveals that they largely follow an extrinsic reinforcement model. Teach-and-test practices, competitive assessment procedures, grades, grade point averages, and eligibility for select vocations and graduate schools are aspects of a system of interrelated elements that most students experience in their pursuit of a college education. This system is based on the assumption that human beings will strive to learn and achieve when they are externally rewarded for such behavior. Strongly supportive of this network of incentives is the implied value that individual accomplishment merits academic and social rewards.

Three major issues cause us to question whether an extrinsic motivation model should dominate in college teaching. The first is the well-documented fact that colleges retain and successfully educate a disproportionately low number of low-income and ethnic minority students. Since motivation strongly influences learning, it may be that an extrinsically based approach to teaching is not effective for many students and across many cultures.

The second issue is that because we as college teachers govern the system of structured external rewards, we are unlikely to change our teaching practices. Consequently it is difficult for colleges to shift from monocultural education, an education largely reflective of one reality and usually biased toward the dominant group, to an education responsive to cultural diversity (Nieto, 2004; Alfassi, 2004). From the tendency to (1) reward those who think like ourselves, (2) rely on our own background and education for determining subject matter, and (3) secure the comfort of the controlled, the familiar, and the predictable in our classes, we have little reason to change these habits. They pervade how we specify the content, process, and assessment of what we teach. As educators, we are gatekeepers who hold the educational rewards for students in our own hands. In terms of our own teaching performance, student evaluations have proven to be inadequate catalysts for change, and few of us are directly evaluated based on the actual learning of our students (Astin, 1993b; Tagg, 2003).

The third issue is that using extrinsic goals to promote learning encourages more shallow conceptual understanding and less persistence while learning than does the use of intrinsic goals (Vansteenskiste, Lens, and Deci, 2006). The negative effects of such extrinsic motivators as grades have been documented with students of different ages and from different cultures (Kohn, 1999). Although this matter is more complex than regarding all extrinsic rewards as controlling or diminishing learning, we agree with Richard Ryan and his colleagues (1999) that people across different cultures are likely to express more satisfaction with their lives when their primary goals and aspirations are intrinsic (being connected, helpful, and self-accepting) rather than extrinsic (being wealthy, famous, and socially attractive).

Another consistent research finding is that when a learning activity is undertaken explicitly to attain some extrinsic reward, people respond by seeking the least demanding and perfunctory way of ensuring the reward (Brophy, 2004). Cramming for tests is an example of this phenomenon that easily comes to mind. Since there are three decades of evidence that dominating instruction with a system of controlling external rewards may contribute to inferior learning, using a pedagogy based on theories of intrinsic motivation appears to be a more reasonable and effective approach to enhancing learning among culturally diverse students.

For these reasons, this book explores and applies theories of intrinsic motivation, finding them to be more informative alternatives for developing an approach to teaching that supports cultural diversity. These theories also promote the creation of teaching and assessment procedures that are open to the voices of students and enhance their learning and involvement.

We can more easily comprehend intrinsic motivation as a foundation for culturally responsive teaching by understanding the relationship of learning to motivation. William Blake believed that thought without affection separates love and wisdom as it separates body and soul. So it is with learning and motivation: they are inseparable. To discuss one without considering the other or to attempt to force them apart ruptures any intelligent discourse and leads to a fragmented notion of what being human might actually mean. Learning is a naturally active and normally volitional process of constructing meaning from information and experience (McCombs and others, 1993). Motivation is the natural human capacity to direct energy in the pursuit of a goal. Although our lives are marked by a continuous flow of activity with an infinite variety of overt actions, we are purposeful. We constantly learn, and when we do, we are usually motivated to learn. We are directing our energy through the processes of attention, concentration, imagination, and passion, to name only a few, to make sense of our world.

In education, psychology continues to dominate the literature about motivation. Yet why people do what they do—the focus of any motivational query—is well within the realm of cultural studies, critical race theory, anthropology, religion, philosophy, physics, and biology. We emphasize this because too often psychology and empirical evidence—using mostly Eurocentric assumptions and values—have become the final arbiters and major decision makers regarding how to teach and, unfortunately, how to label those who have difficulty learning a particular way (Merriam and Associates, 2007). Today's emphasis on and requirements for evidence-based practices throughout education are an evolutionary outgrowth of this perspective and its values. The literature documenting modern psychology provides an incomplete understanding of the many cultural groups that live within the United States (Pedersen, 1994; Hays, 2001). The influences of ethnicity, age, religion or spiritual orientation, socioeconomic status, sexual orientation, indigenous heritage,

national origin, and gender require forms of pedagogical innovation that encompass and build on the diversities and similarities
within classrooms and communities.

Certainly this is a generative process. As one of many
examples of complexity of motivationally anchored instruction, motivation is governed to a large extent by emotion. A
person working at a task feels frustrated and stops. Another person working at a task feels joy and continues. But what elicits a
response of frustration or joy may differ across cultures, because
cultures differ in their definitions of novelty, hazard, opportunity,
gratification, and so forth. It is also quite possible for another
person with a different set of cultural beliefs to feel frustrated at
a task and yet continue with further determination. Depending
on the cultural groups with which a person identifies, illness,
for example, may be understood from the perspective of germs,
God, anxiety, chance, or one's moral failure, and a person's
emotional response to illness will reflect these beliefs. Cultural
groups vary in their beliefs about the meaning of emotional
experiences, expressions, and behaviors (Treuba and Delgado-
Gaitan, 1985; Oishi, 2003; Adams and Markus, 2004; Sternberg
and Grigorenko, 2004). Since the socialization of emotions is so
culturally influenced, the motivational response a student has to
a learning activity reflects this influence and its associated complexity. Although we seek to understand, we must admit to only
a partial understanding of this remarkable intricacy.

Because there is no science of human behavior with underlying, consistent, unifying principles that leads to predictable
results, we advocate that at the very least, teachers accept that
each learner represents her or his own reality, especially when
it comes to what that individual finds motivating. This form of
constructivism does not preclude the existence of an external
reality; it merely claims that each of us constructs our own reality through interpreting perceptual experiences of the external
world based on our unique set of experiences with the world and
our beliefs about them (Jonassen, 1992; Chiu and Hong, 2005).

Given that culture is an influential part of anyone's world, it is rare, perhaps even impossible, for any human being to behave without responding to some aspect of it (Hays, 2001; Tatum, 2003).

Motivation is culturally fused and embedded. Generic motivational goals such as success or achievement and more personal traits such as ambition or initiative may not only have different meanings to different people but may also be undesirable. In this light, influences such as religion, myth, ethnicity, and regional and peer group norms have powerful motivational force. In general, the internal logic as to why a person does something may not correspond to one's own set of assumptions, but it is present nonetheless. Being an effective teacher requires the willingness to understand that perspective and to construct with learners a motivating educational experience. Rather than knowing what to do to the learner, successful educators seek to understand and strengthen the potential for shared meaning. Motivationally effective teaching has to be culturally responsive teaching.

With this orientation, we are less likely to intervene, establish, or determine the learner's motivation to learn and more likely to elicit, affirm, or encourage the learner's natural capacity to make meaning from experience. From this perspective, motivation is seen as intrinsic rather than extrinsic. People are naturally curious and enjoy learning. To be active, to originate behavior, to be effective at what we value is part of human nature (Deci and Ryan, 1991). When one's actions are endorsed by oneself with a sense of integrity and cohesion, authenticity blends with personal values, and intrinsic motivation occurs. When people are feeling insecure or worrying about failure, ridicule, or shame, extrinsic rewards such as money and items that afford power probably have their greatest motivational influence. This understanding lies at the core of the carrot-and-stick metaphor for motivational manipulation. When people are powerless; when they need jobs, promotions, and money; when they are merely surviving, holding on, stopping a downward spiral, or making themselves less expendable, they may seem less intrinsically motivated to learn. Yet even in these circumstances, it is not uncommon to witness humor, insight, and creativity (Mills, 1991; Ratey, 2001). All human beings have the capacity to make meaning, to become more effective at what they value, and to integrate themselves within, with others, and with the world. With specific reference to communities of color and from a critical race perspective, Yosso (2005) asserts that there are at least six forms of cultural wealth that positively influence learning. Referring to these attributes as "community cultural wealth," she delineates forms of capital that allow communities of color to persist amid some of the most oppressive circumstances:

- Aspirational capital—"the ability to maintain hopes and dreams for the future, even in the face of real and perceived barriers" (p. 77).
- Linguistic capital—"the intellectual and social skills attained through communication experiences in more than one language and/or style" (p. 78).
- Familial capital—"cultural knowledge nurtured among *familia* (kin) ... in a way that engages a commitment to community well being and expands the concept of family to include a more broad understanding of kinship" (p. 79).
- Social capital—"networks of people and community resources" historically accessed by people of color to attain opportunity (p. 80).
- Resistant capital—"knowledge and skills fostered through oppositional behavior that challenges inequality" (p. 80).

How to support and elicit the natural desire to learn that all human beings possess is discussed intensively in the chapters ahead. At this point, however, it is important to acknowledge that motivation is a human characteristic that can be vastly underestimated and, as with the carrot-and-stick metaphor, is easily manipulated. One of the greatest problems with this metaphor of control is that it is ineffective as a method to enhance motivation for learning. It objectifies people and reduces their humanity. It also contributes to the idea of people "motivating" other people. In our opinion, the question, "How do I motivate these people?" implies that "these people" are in an inferior position—somehow less able and certainly less powerful than ourselves. This kind of thinking not only diminishes acceptance of their perspective but also takes away their ownership of being intrinsically motivated. The attitude of such a "motivator" violates personal determination and tends to keep learners "less than"—dependent and in need of help from a more powerful other.

Replacing the carrot-and-stick metaphor with the words *understand* and *elicit* changes the idea of motivation from one of manipulation and control to one of communication and respect. In the latter case, we may certainly influence the motivation of people, but it happens through understanding another's perspective and inviting or drawing forth natural and culturally embedded sources of strength. In this way, people are likely to feel empowered, unique, and potentially active. As teachers we may affirm, support, or encourage motivation, but students are in charge of themselves. Through combining our resources, we can together create greater energy for learning. Such a learning environment is neither teacher centered nor learner centered but more community centered, with the teacher serving the agreed-on leadership role.

Since motivation and learning are inseparable, it stands to reason that those who are motivated to learn will learn more than those who are not so motivated. When Uguroglu and Walberg (1979) analyzed 232 correlations of motivation and academic learning, they found that 98 percent of the correlations were positive. Although the sample included only students from the first through the twelfth grades, the researchers found that the relationship between motivation and learning increased along with the age of the students, with the highest correlations occurring in the twelfth grade. Motivation is not only the energy within learning but also the feeling that mediates learning and the attitude that is a consequence of learning. People work longer and more intensely when they are motivated than when they are not. They are also more cooperative and open to what they are experiencing. Time spent actively involved in learning is positively related to achievement, memory, and recall (Fisher and others, 1980; Zull, 2002).

Because motivation plays such a key role in learning, teaching methods and educational environments that motivationally favor particular learners to the exclusion of others are unfair and diminish the chances of success for those learners discounted or denied in this situation. For example, a teacher who grades students on the basis of participation during discussions and calls mainly on voluntary respondents may unwittingly, yet clearly, favor students who are socialized to request personal attention and offer opinions in front of groups of unfamiliar people.

Any educational or other system of professional learning that ignores the history and perspective of its learners or does not attempt to adjust its teaching practices to benefit a range of learners is contributing to a system of advantage for those who have been socialized to "act smart." When we understand motivation to learn as a developing trait that influences life-long learning, we see how insidious such bias in teaching can be. People who eventually find reading, writing, calculating, and expanding their stores of information interesting and satisfying are likely to be lifelong learners (Merriam, Cafferella, and Baumgartner, 2007). The tendency to find such processes meaningful and worthwhile is considered to be the trait of motivation to learn, a propensity for learning, often narrowly conceived as "academically inclined," that gradually develops over time (Brophy, 2004). This trait appears to be related to a sense of self-efficacy while learning (Bandura, 1997). Such self-confidence grows from perceiving personal responsibility for learning, accepting challenge through personal volition, and receiving informative feedback, as opposed to arbitrary grades or competitive peer comparisons (Zimmerman and Kitsantas, 2005). Such insights suggest that traditional teach and test methods based on the assumption that people can be motivated by external pressures and sanctions are unlikely to work for large segments of our population. Such practices may also deny many people the satisfaction of a life in which learning is a compelling joy as well as the means to a better future.

The Motivational Framework for Culturally Responsive Teaching

An effective model for culturally responsive teaching has to have enough breadth to accommodate the range of diversity found in postsecondary education. It also has to integrate the variety of assumptions from different disciplines. But most of all, it has to explain how to create compelling learning experiences through which learners are able to maintain their integrity as they attain relevant educational success. In this respect, the framework is inseparable from the broader issue of how to construct a world in which democratic ideals are a reality for all.

We offer the motivational framework for culturally responsive teaching as a heuristic to provide this understanding. It combines the essential motivational conditions that are intrinsically motivating for diverse learners (see Figure 1.1). It also provides a structure for planning and applying a rich array of teaching strategies. Each of its major conditions is supported by theories aligned with intrinsic motivation. Each condition's influence on learner motivation is also substantiated by research from the social sciences and neurosciences (Wlodkowski, 2008).

The motivational framework for culturally responsive teaching is a way to plan for and reflect on teaching that is respectful of

Figure 1.1 The Motivational Framework for Culturally Responsive Teaching

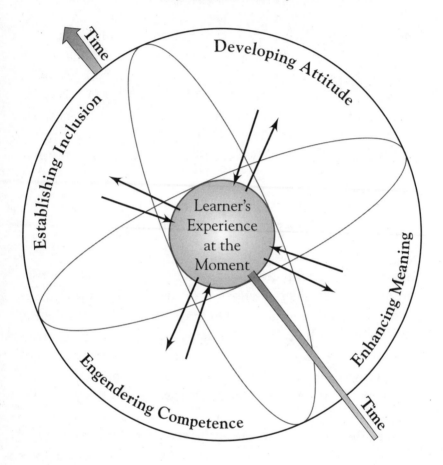

different cultures and capable of creating a common culture that all learners in the learning situation can accept. It is a holistic and systemic representation of four intersecting motivational conditions that teachers and learners work together to create or enhance:

1. *Establish inclusion:* Norms and practices that are woven together to create a learning environment in which

learners and teachers feel respected and connected
to one another

2. *Develop attitude:* Norms and practices that create a favorable
disposition toward the learning experience through personal
relevance and volition

3. *Enhance meaning:* Norms and practices that create challenging and engaging learning experiences that include learners'
perspectives and values

4. *Engender competence:* Norms and practices that help learners
understand how they are effectively learning something they
value and is of authentic value to their community

The chapters ahead explain and exemplify each of these four
motivational conditions in detail. Each of these conditions contains an initial verb as a way of emphasizing its dynamic existence. The conditions are interrelated and reciprocal, affecting
one another simultaneously. As shown in Figure 1.1, they work
in concert influencing the learner in the moment. However,
their effect is usually more continuous and experienced by the
learner as an emotional state such as interest or boredom. In an
analogous sense, these conditions function like the neuronal
networks in our brains.

People experience emotions and motivational influences as a
very rapid (in milliseconds) integration of intersecting processes
occurring both consciously and unconsciously (Winkielman,
Berridge, and Wilbarger, 2005). Imagine, for example, that you
run into a friend you have not seen for several years. As you
greet each other, many emotions occur simultaneously—joy,
sorrow, love, perhaps regret. In that moment, your perceptions
of your friend intersect with the recollection of past events. A
number of feelings arise from this dynamic interaction. How
many of them affect you at this or any given moment? No one
really knows.

From Buddha to Bateson, theorists have understood life and learning to be multidetermined. Researchers in the cognitive sciences view cognition and emotion as neurophysiological processes, occurring either individually or socially, that integrate the mind, the body, the activity, and the ingredients of the setting in a complex interactive manner (Lave, 1997; Scherer, 2005). Meeting your friend alone in an airport might be a very different emotional experience from meeting this same person in her home, surrounded by family.

Human beings frequently act without deliberation. Much of the time we experience life as a jazz musician might experience music, improvising with a band. We hear different sounds at the same time, some of which are reciprocal and distinct, a symmetry through diversity. Perception and action are co-creative, each contributing to the construction of the other. Much of the time, we compose our lives in the moment.

There is evidence that in matters as profound as perspective transformation and cultural identity, many people change through immediate action in response to intercultural challenges, with little deep rational reflection and planned action (Taylor, 1994, 2005). Thus, the four conditions found in the motivational framework are an evolving system that reciprocally interacts with and is a part of learning to influence motivation and learning at any given moment.

Applying the Motivational Framework for Culturally Responsive Teaching

Let us take a look at this framework in terms of the teaching-learning process. In this example, the teacher is conducting the first two-hour session of a semester-long introductory course in research. It is a diverse group of students ranging in age from twenty to fifty-five. The teacher's plan contains the four motivational conditions with each indicated as a motivational goal with a related teaching practice:

Motivational Goal	Teaching Practices
Establishing inclusion	Randomly assigns small groups in which learners exchange concerns, experiences, and expectations they have about research
Developing attitude	Asks learners to choose something they could immediately research among themselves
Enhancing meaning	Assigns research partners who will develop a set of questions to ask volunteers that will make a prediction about them
Engendering competence	After the predictions have been verified, asks learners to create their own statements about what they learned regarding research from this process

The scenario might go like this. After the teacher has handed out the syllabus and had a dialogue with the learners about its contents, she explains that much research is conducted collaboratively and it is important to get to know each other better in order to create such teams as the course continues. For a beginning activity, she randomly assigns learners to small groups and encourages them to discuss any experiences they may have previously had in doing research as well as their expectations and concerns for the course (*establishing inclusion*). At the end of this activity, each group has a volunteer report a summary of its experiences, hopes, and concerns. In this manner, learners are beginning to establish rapport and trust with one another.

The teacher relates her belief that most people are researchers much of the time and asks the group what they would like to research among themselves at this very moment (*developing attitude*). After a stimulating discussion, the consensus is to investigate and predict the amount of sleep some members of the class had last night.

Five people volunteer to serve as subjects, and research partnerships form among the rest of the learners. Each team is asked to devise a set of observations and questions to ask the volunteers, but no one can ask them how many hours of sleep they had the night before (*enhancing meaning*). After the questions have been asked, the teams rank the volunteers from the most to the least amount of sleep. When the volunteers reveal the amount of time they have slept, the class discovers that none of the research teams was correct in ranking more than two people among the five volunteers. The volunteers then tell the researchers questions they might have asked to increase their accuracy, such as, "How much coffee did you drink before you came to class?"

After further discussion, each learner is asked to write a series of statements about what this process has taught him or her about research (*engendering competence*). In small, randomly assigned groups, learners exchange these insights, which include such comments as, "Thus far, I enjoy research more than I thought I might," and "Research is more a method than an answer."

This scenario shows how the four motivational conditions constantly influence and interact with one another. Without the establishment of inclusion (small groups to discuss concerns, experiences, and so on) and the development of a positive attitude (learners choosing something to research), the enhancement of meaning (research teams devising a set of questions for volunteers) may not have occurred with equal ease and energy, and the self-assessment to engender competence (what students learned from their experience) may have had a dismal outcome. Also, the future patterns of inclusion (future research teams) have been prepared for, because learners now have a positive common history.

This learning experience, like all other learning experiences, is holistic as well as systemic. It can be imagined that removing any one of the four motivational conditions would have affected the entire experience and each condition's link to the rest of the course. In fact, from this viewpoint, once a course has started, there is not really a beginning or an end to learner motivation. Rather, there is a set of experiences connected through time in which teachers and learners can enhance or reduce the motivational conditions for eliciting intrinsic motivation and for improving learning for everyone.

Criteria, Norms, and Practices for Using the Motivational Framework

Because it is possible to create conditions that suppress motivation and inhibit learning, one can see that care, planning, and sensitivity are important with something as dynamic as motivation. There are no formulas for using this framework because it is a heuristic that is intended as a tool for continual reflection. The questions and ideas that correspond to the framework are intended to suggest and stimulate. With reflection, teachers can use these to redesign their courses, daily instructional plans, and individual pedagogical strategies, such as structuring small groups for problem solving among students.

Returning to the metaphor of a compass, we offer a set of two criteria or attributes for each motivational condition so that teachers and learners can be reasonably sure they are moving in the direction they desire. By using criteria rather than rules, we develop a more multidisciplinary and interpretive approach to creating the appropriate motivational conditions. For example, for establishing inclusion, the criteria are respect and connectedness. People generally believe they are included in a group when they feel respected by and connected to the group. How inclusion is established may vary greatly, but the teacher realizes that the students' awareness of respect and connectedness is the distinctive feature that determines whether inclusion has actually occurred within the class.

This framework focuses more on the relationship between teachers and learners and less on either of them as individuals. Learning and teaching are understood as reciprocal and co-creative acts. The following four questions that correspond to the framework in Figure 1.1 are essential to beginning and sustaining culturally responsive teaching:

- What do we need to do to feel respected by and connected to one another? (*Establishing inclusion*)
- How can we use relevance and volition to create a favorable disposition toward learning? (*Developing attitude*)
- How do we create engaging and challenging learning experiences that include learners' perspectives and values? (*Enhancing meaning*)
- How do we create an understanding that we are effectively learning something we value and perceive as authentic to our real world? (*Engendering competence*)

These four questions or motivational conditions work together to support intrinsic motivation among diverse student groups. We refer to this as *pedagogical alignment*. We have all been in learning situations where some but not all motivational conditions were met. For example, recall a classroom where there was an exhilarating feeling of inclusion and all students felt safe to take academic risks, yet there were very few challenges to engage these students. Similarly, there are instructors who work with students to build a learning community in which students are collaborative but use competitive grading that builds distrust and ultimately undermines motivation. A congruent set of norms and practices creates the symmetry to evoke intrinsic motivation to learn.

Norms are the explicit assumptions, values, and purposes espoused by a learning group. An example of a norm is, "Everyone has a right to speak from her or his own experience and perspective about what is being learned." Norms work in two fundamental ways. First, they provide an atmosphere and a shared understanding that elicits intrinsic motivation among learners; second, they are the core constructs held in common to build community among learners. Norms not only support certain behaviors but create expectations for those behaviors.

Practices are the teaching and learning strategies the teacher and learning group use to work together in order to accomplish the desired learning targets. They are not prescriptive. Rather, they are a variety of approaches, each of which has a theoretical, ethical, and research-supported history of being an exceptionally useful means to engender the identified motivational condition. Because the four motivational conditions work as motivational goals to accomplish while teaching, the terms *motivational condition* and *motivational goal* are used synonymously. The motivational goal serves as a broad, thematic category in which to organize practices to meet its essential criteria. Each practice is a form of deliberate action. By reflecting on it, teachers and learners can think of specific activities that lead to learning as well as to the intended motivational goal. For example, to establish inclusion, the learning group may use the practice of cooperative learning to generate an activity, such as forming dyads, to create a short biography emblematic of both students' cultural backgrounds. A practice may be used for a small fraction of a course or for the majority of its learning experiences in combination with other practices. The larger the variety of relevant and effective practices teachers and learners know, the greater flexibility they have to support differences among themselves and the topics to be studied.

A congruent set of norms and practices creates the symmetry that enables culturally responsive teaching to evoke and develop student motivation. Because norms support practices and vice versa, all students have a better chance to learn. By following the general example offered below, both novice and seasoned college teachers can peruse the norms and practices found in this book to ascertain their potential application to their own teaching.

A teacher in an urban university begins to plan for an upcoming course. The teacher knows from previous experience that the diversity in the class will approximate a group of students coming from low- to middle-income families, representing a variety of ethnicities, of whom 40 percent will probably be people of color. Age is likely to range from twenty-one to fifty-five. About half the students will be women. There will be a few students with disabilities.

Reflecting on the rich diversity among these students and on the question for establishing inclusion, the teacher studies the criteria, norms, and practices found in Exhibit 1.1 and aims to:

- Make collaboration an expected way of proceeding throughout the course (a norm to build a sense of community among such a diverse group)
- Create a number of learning activities using cooperative learning groups (a practice consistent with the above norm and effective as a method for enhancing motivation and learning)

- Establish participation agreements with the students for the discussion of sensitive and controversial material (a practice to maintain safety and respect while engaged in dialogue)

Exhibit 1.1 Criteria, Norms, and Practices for the Motivational Goal of Establishing Inclusion

Question: What do we need to do to feel respected by and connected to one another?
Criteria: Respect and connectedness

Norms
1. Course work emphasizes the human purpose of what is being learned and its relationship to the learners' personal experiences and contemporary situations.
2. Teachers co-construct knowledge that is inclusive of the ideas, perspectives, and experiences of learners.
3. Collaboration and cooperation are the expected ways of proceeding and learning.
4. Course perspectives assume a nonblameful and realistically hopeful view of people and their capacity to change.
5. There is equitable treatment of all learners with an invitation to point out behaviors, practices, and policies that discriminate.

Practices
1. Introductions
2. Collaborative and cooperative learning
3. Writing groups
4. Peer teaching
5. Opportunities for multidimensional sharing
6. Focus groups
7. Reframing
8. Participation agreements
9. Learning communities
10. Cooperative base groups

Thinking about the question for developing attitude, the teacher examines the criteria, norms, and practices found in Exhibit 1.2 and decides to:

- Conduct the course in ways that encourage learners to make choices about class topics and assignments based on their experiences, values, needs, and strengths (a norm to increase the relevance of the course for such a diverse group of learners)
- Use problem-solving goals and learning contracts (practices to accommodate student choice and to respect their voice in determining topics and assignments)
- Create some learning activities suited to different profiles of multiple intelligences (a practice to more equitably match learning experiences to the wealth of diverse intellectual strengths surely to be found among this multicultural group of students)

Exhibit 1.2 Criteria, Norms, and Practices for the Motivational Condition of Developing Attitude

Question: How can we use relevance and volition to create a favorable disposition toward learning?
Criteria: Relevance and volition

Norms
1. Teaching and learning activities are contextualized in the learners' experience and knowledge and are accessible through their current thinking and ways of knowing.
2. The entire academic process of learning, from content selection to accomplishment and assessment of competencies, encourages learners to make choices based on their experiences, values, needs, and strengths.

Practices

1. Learning-goal procedures
   a. Clearly defined goals
   b. Problem-solving goals
   c. Expressive outcomes
2. Fair and clear criteria of evaluation
3. Relevant learning models
4. Goal setting
5. Learning contracts
6. Approaches based on multiple intelligences theory
7. Sensitivity and pedagogical flexibility based on the concept of style
9. Experiential learning—the Kolb model
10. Culturally responsive teacher-learner conferences

Continuing with a similarly reflective approach based on the question of how to enhance meaning, the teacher studies the criteria, norms, and practices found in Exhibit 1.3 and decides to:

- Make challenging experiences that critically address relevant real-world issues essential to learning throughout the course (a norm likely to engage the involvement of such a diverse group of students and to benefit from their backgrounds and experiences)

- Use critical questioning, posing problems, authentic research, and case studies for classwork and assignments (practices that allow learners to construct and delve into real-world issues and to use their strengths, experiences, and values to deepen understanding)

- Suggest projects as the main way for students to acquire course credit (a practice with the flexibility and range to accommodate in-depth learning experiences with real-world issues)

Exhibit 1.3 Criteria, Norms, and Practices for the Motivational Condition of Enhancing Meaning

Question: How can we create challenging and engaging learning experiences that include learners' perspectives and values?
Criteria: Engagement and challenge

Norms

1. Learners participate in challenging learning experiences involving deep reflection and critical inquiry that address relevant, real-world issues in an action-oriented manner.
2. Learner expression and language are joined with teacher expression and language to form a "third idiom" that enables the perspectives of all learners to be readily shared and included in the process of learning.

Practices

1. Critical questioning for engaging discussions
2. Posing problems
3. Decision making
4. Authentic research
    a. Definitional investigation
    b. Historical investigation
    c. Projective investigation
    d. Experimental inquiry
    e. Action research
5. Invention and artistry
6. Simulations, role playing, and games
7. Case study method
8. Projects
9. Problem-posing model

Finally, with the consideration of assessment and the question related to engendering competence, the teacher peruses the criteria, norms, and practices found in Exhibit 1.4 and decides to:

- Make self-assessment part of the overall assessment process (a norm for understanding the acquisition of competence through the unique and informative perspective of the learner)

- Use documentation of learning based on emerging and completed projects (an alternative to paper-and-pencil tests and a practice that accommodates opportunities to integrate formative feedback and opportunities for students to apply their unique profiles of intelligences)

- Use contracts for grading (a practice that allows for some self-assessment and that can reconcile the many interests, strengths, and needs of this diverse group of students with a fair assessment of their competence)

Exhibit 1.4 Criteria, Norms, and Practices for the Motivational Goal of Engendering Competence

Question: How do we create an understanding that we are effectively learning something we value and perceive as authentic to our real world?

Criteria: Authenticity and effectiveness

Norms

1. The assessment process is connected to the learner's world, frames of reference, and values.
2. Demonstration of learning includes multiple ways to represent knowledge and skill.
3. Self-assessment is essential to the overall assessment process.

Practices

1. Feedback
2. Alternatives to pencil-and-paper tests: contextualized assessment
   a. Comparing personal assessment values with actual assessment practice
   b. Generating creative alternatives to tests

(continued)

3. Well-constructed paper-and-pencil tests
4. Self-assessment
5. Effective grading: example, contracting for grades

With the use of these exhibits, the teacher now has an integrated set of norms and practices for creating an overall approach to teaching that is responsive to the diversity of students. In the chapters ahead, we take each motivational goal (condition) and illuminate its social and academic value as we illustrate how to accomplish it with various subjects and in different learning situations. These chapters contain discussions of the criteria for the motivational goals and their relationship to diversity and intrinsic motivation. We will explain and exemplify the norms and practices that contribute to meeting each of the motivational goals, which will provide a comprehensive overview of a motivation-based approach to culturally responsive teaching.

Fear, Conflict, and Resistance

Although the motivational framework is comprehensive and detailed, we know from experience and the literature that not all of the ambiguities, conflicts, and dilemmas that emerge during culturally responsive teaching can be completely resolved. This is as true from the perspective of the student as it is from the view of the teacher. Yet this reality is often more understandable than we might imagine. In the rest of this section, we present insights and cite references that offer pragmatic ways of reckoning with many of the issues that may result from addressing diversity in the classroom.

Knowing that teacher and student resistance is predictable and often legitimate can reduce our feelings of discomfort and help us remain effectively engaged and less reactive in challenging situations. By finding concepts useful for understanding our own as well as our students' reactions, we can be less personally threatened and more open to learning. Let us begin with fear of conflict:

You are teaching a literature course in a large university. You have been careful to include in your syllabus authors from historically underrepresented racial and ethnic groups. At the moment, a lively discussion is taking place in class. You make a remark about the irony contained in a particular author's novel. After your comment, a student who is of the same ethnicity as the author responds, "You don't know what you're talking about. That's a typical white middle-class interpretation." You look up, surprised, but before you can comment, another student calls out to the student who has just spoken: "That's very rude! You really have no right to tell anybody what they know or don't know. Just because you're a minority doesn't mean your perspective is right, either." Immediately four other students jump into the controversy.

■ ■

This scenario illustrates just a few of the reactions that a teacher who seeks to be culturally responsive may encounter when learners are dealing with situations that touch their lives. Anxiety among teachers about potential conflict can seem overwhelming. Gerald Weinstein and Kathy Obear (1992) speak for many educators when they say:

Our socialization has taught us how important it is to be in control. Our worst fantasy is that the whole situation will go up in flames. There have been a number of times ... when I have felt totally helpless in dealing with certain interactions. A participant may say something that stimulates great tension and anxiety, and a dense silence overtakes the group. The instructor becomes upset and somewhat paralyzed. All eyes are upon us, waiting to see what we will do, expecting us to take care of the situation. I cannot think of any helpful intervention. We are too upset to think clearly. It's a fearsome moment, one that we may anticipate with dread [p. 47].

The intrapersonal emotional dynamics of teachers who deal with bias and conflict are common, expected, and shared—in other words, normal. Those of us willing to assume some of these risks can support one another, teach one another, and reduce some of the misconceptions. Paradoxically it is not uncommon for hope to emerge after an honest discussion about collective moments of despair.

After asking a group of twenty-five university faculty from different disciplines to anonymously respond to the question, "What makes you nervous about raising issues of racism in your classroom?" Weinstein and Obear (1992, pp. 41–42) grouped their findings along with those found by others (Katz, 1983; Noonan, 1988; Cones, Janha, and Noonan, 1983) who had raised similar questions. With subsequent literature in mind, such as considerations for "teaching against the grain" in an institutional context (Cochran-Smith, 2004; Ouellett, 2005), many of the concerns that were initially documented persist. Generally faculty concerns about raising issues of racism tend to revolve around these issues:

1. Confronting one's own multiple identities and inner conflicts, for example:

    Having to further probe my own attitudes regarding my group memberships and multiple identities

    Feeling guilty, ashamed, or embarrassed for behaviors and attitudes of members of my own group

2. Having to confront or being confronted with one's own bias:

    Being labeled racist, sexist, classist, or homophobic

    Having to question my own assumptions

    Being corrected by members of a targeted group

    Facing my own contradictions

3. Responding to biased comments:

    Responding to biased comments from a member of a targeted group

Hearing biased comments from members of a dominant group while targeted members are present

Responding to biased remarks from members of my own social group

Responding to hurtful comments or interactions in ways that oversimplify complicated systems of oppression

4. Doubts and ambivalence about one's own competence:

Having to expose one's own struggles with an issue

Not knowing the most current language being used by those who consider themselves to be "culturally competent"

Speaking about equity while participating in a system that perpetuates hierarchical stratification

Feeling unable to sufficiently unravel the complexities of issues concerning social justice

Having inadequate time and getting sidetracked

5. Need for student approval:

Making a mistake for which some students may be unforgiving

Making students frustrated, frightened, or angry

Leaving students shaken and confused and not being able to fix it

Worrying about rocking the boat

Having discussion blow up

Having anger directed at me

Being overwhelmed by strong emotions engendered by a discussion

Being stereotyped as a bleeding heart

Responses to Biased Expressions

How we approach bias when it is articulated in a learning environment is a theoretical as well as practical issue. Theory offers a way to anchor consciousness for continual reflection on and interpretation of experiences. An established theory for how people learn in tense situations is similar to any cohesive theory of learning. It acknowledges the importance of safety and legitimizes feelings, and presents the situation as a learning opportunity with important tensions that can lead to understanding. On such occasions, students work collectively to define the tensions—for example, through individual writing and then partnering with another person for sense making. Finally, this sort of experience offers a way to explore emerging issues with other students, colleagues, or perhaps networks using the skills of inquiry. Without a theory, skills and methods that might prevent or diffuse a troubling situation can amount to little more than temporary safety.

Our own theory of action for difficult situations that may arise is the foundation for Exhibit 1.1. In that exhibit, we discuss the need for an environment that promotes respect and connectedness among students as well as between students and instructors. How to understand and promote respect and connection among diverse learners is a question that requires an insatiable quest for understanding students as individuals, ideas about cultural nuance, and willingness to co-construct with students new ways to create a safe space for learning.

In the twenty-first century, many people in the United States believe the playing field has been leveled. In spite of data from education, employment, housing, politics, and health care professionals, there is a pervasive belief that the United States is a meritocracy in which hard work and talent are equitably rewarded. Within multicultural postsecondary classrooms, the contrasts in daily lives among students can vary tremendously. Members of historically targeted student groups often have a long history of dealing with negative cues. A person's reluctance to participate in public discourse on controversial racial issues can be nested in an elaborate understanding of the roots and effects of racism and the threat it poses within daily life and globally. Although there are certainly exceptions, the color-coded division of communities makes it possible for racially and economically privileged students to make comments with little awareness of its offense. These statements, known as *cues*, signal triggers.

Triggers are recurring phenomena in classes. These are words, phrases, or concepts usually communicated by members of historically privileged student groups about a targeted group or individuals that signal the onslaught of highly charged issues. Some are blatantly obvious, for example, "the Jewish media," and others are a bit more subtle, for example, "I don't see people as black, brown, red, yellow, or white" or "They're just not as qualified."

Triggers may immediately stimulate the defenses of the person whose group is being commented on, or an ally of that group, and can elicit intense emotional reactions. Responses to triggers can be especially volatile in a setting of diverse student groups that includes students who are at the preliminary stage of examining white advantage and privilege. What often occurs is that one person makes the statement that triggers another student to respond in a confrontational or defensive manner. The original "trigger giver" will argue for the truth of what was said or state that it was never his or her intention to give offense and that the respondent seems to be "overly sensitive." This comment becomes another trigger. The exchange typically continues with a painful and unproductive debate of increasing intensity. It can sometimes lead to a stifling silence or barely controlled frustration—a situation that is troubling for the instructor and difficult to mediate.

While it is important to raise this as an issue that many instructors will experience, this situation does not lend itself to easy answers. Nor should it. Racism and other forms of bias are perpetuated through individual, social, institutional, and global structures. Because it is not merely individual, conversation, even artful conversation, is insufficient. This is one of the reasons we believe it is important to raise the general issue of triggers at the outset of a course, describe what they are, and describe how they may be experienced differently by members of the dominant and targeted groups.

It is important to handle the discussion of triggers so that the members of both dominant and targeted groups are validated as individuals. Targeted members have a right to ask that others be sensitive to their own language. Members of dominant groups need to understand that their socialization included systematic institutional messages that are larger than themselves or their families. They did not seek to be raised in a racist, sexist, classist, homophobic, or anti-Semitic society. They do not need to be assisted in castigating themselves but instead encouraged to explore, in generative ways, their own origins and beliefs. One measure of success may be the extent to which individuals can self-monitor potential triggers for different groups.

One way to anticipate discussions about racism and social justice even in courses where the subject is not specific to such explorations is to establish communication agreements on the first day of class. For example, many instructors find it useful to introduce the concept of triggers and ask students to supply their own examples before any arise spontaneously. A useful communication agreement might be: "Anytime someone feels triggered, including myself, we can write the example on a sticky note and place it on a piece of newsprint on an entryway door. If we are not able to review the example in the moment, we will save time before the class concludes for that purpose." Not having to deal with the trigger at that moment creates some distance between the person who sent the trigger and an analysis of the response it evoked. The focus can then be on understanding the concept rather than personalizing the issue in ways that might lead to additional vulnerability.

Let us return to the literature class scenario that introduced this section. Without knowing the people or the immediate history of the course, we can say that the teacher at the very least can (1) give everyone a brief time-out, (2) ask students to record their own immediate responses in their notebooks, (3) provide time for each member of the class to share responses with one other person, and (4) ask for any suggestions or ideas from the group concerning what happened (Weinstein and Obear, 1992). Such a procedure might lead to setting new communication agreements for further discussion and a host of other possibilities that contribute to group awareness and cohesion. We examine this issue in the next chapter.

Stages of Racial Identity Development

Concerning matters of race, a possible way of understanding tension and conflict in the classroom is that it results from the collision of developmental processes that are necessary for the racial identity development of the individuals involved (Tatum, 1992). Although space allows only the summarization of one theory of racial identity development theory, a number of models have been specifically formulated regarding black, white, Asian, Latina/o, American Indian, and mixed-race students (Tatum, 1992; Cross, 1991; Helms, 1990; Phinney, 1990; Sung, 2002). There are also a number of identity development theorists who address issues such as sexual orientation, religion, gender, and geographical and institutional affiliation (Goldschmidt and McAlister, 2004; Sanlo, 2004; Jackson, 2001).

Each assumes that a positive sense of one's self as a member of specific and various groups (which are not predicated on any assumed superiority) is vital to psychological well-being. Furthermore, in a society where racial group membership is fundamentally an implicit or explicit influence on one's lens or worldview, the development of a racial identity will occur in some form for everyone. Most of the theories are stage theories, meaning that they describe metaphorical states of consciousness or worldviews that are developmental in nature. These are metaphorical because none of us is ever in a stage. We continuously change and grow in ways that are complex, fluid, and braided (Adams, 2007; Cochran-Smith, 2004; Lee and Bean, 2003). Our beliefs, values, and behaviors are always being shaped. This is complicated by the multiple memberships and identities we possess. Metaphorically, however, people usually move from one stage to another when they recognize that their current way of seeing things is illogical or contradicted by new experience and information, detrimental to their well-being, or no longer serving an important self-interest.

Using this paradigm, Hardiman and Jackson (1992, 1997) have created a synthesis from their evolving work on the development of racial identity in black and white Americans. They use racial/color designators rather than ethnic terms such as *African American* to highlight the discrimination aspect of the interactions implied by the model. The following discussion summarizes their developmental framework:

Stage One–Naive

The naive stage of consciousness describes the consciousness of race in childhood when there is little or no social awareness of race per se. Members of both dominant and target groups are vulnerable to the logic system and worldview of their socializing agent such as parents, teachers, and so forth.

Stage Two–Acceptance

In the transition from naive to acceptance children begin to learn the ideology about their own racial groups as well as other racial groups. They begin to learn there are formal and informal rules that permit some behaviors and prohibit others in terms of how the races relate to each other.

The stage of acceptance represents the absorption, whether conscious or unconscious, of an ideology of racial dominance and subordination which touches upon all facets of personal and public life. A person at this stage has accepted the messages about racial group membership, the superiority of the dominant group members and the dominant culture, and the inferiority of target group people and cultures.

Stage Three—Resistance

The transition from acceptance to resistance marks a period that can be confusing and often painful for both targets (Blacks) and dominants (Whites). The transition generally evolves over time and usually results from a number of events that have a cumulative effect. People begin to be aware of experiences that contradict the acceptance worldview. The contradictions that initiate the transition period can arise from interactions with people, social events, information presented in classes, stories in the media, or responses to so-called racial incidents on campus.

The initial questioning that begins during the exit phase of acceptance continues with greater intensity during the third stage, resistance. The worldview that people adopt at resistance is dramatically different from that of acceptance. At this stage members of both target and dominant groups begin to understand and recognize racism in many of its complex and multiple manifestations—at the individual and institutional, conscious and unconscious, intentional and unintentional, attitudinal, behavioral, and policy levels. Individuals become painfully aware of the numerous ways in which covert as well as overt racism affects them daily as members of racial identity groups.

Resistance can manifest itself as active or passive. For example, for Whites, active resistance may show itself as indiscriminately challenging racism in many spheres and distancing themselves from White culture and people, and simultaneously "adopting" or borrowing the traditions and cultural expressions of communities of color. An example for Blacks of active resistance might be challenging and confronting Whites, especially those in positions of authority, and challenging or writing off Black faculty and administrators who are seen as not Black enough or as colluding with the White system. Passive resistance appears more unlikely for Blacks than for Whites and usually manifests itself as some form of withdrawal or "dropping out." Among traditional college-age students, there will be at least some White students and Black students who enter college at the acceptance stage and experience primarily the resistance stage during their college years.

Stage Four—Redefinition

The transition from resistance to redefinition occurs when members of both racial groups realize that they do not really know who they are, racially speaking, or what their racial group membership means to them. At resistance, they recognized that their sense of themselves as Whites or as Blacks has been denied for them in a White racist environment, and they actively sought to question it or reject aspects of it. Now they are no longer actively consumed by rejection, but the loss of prior self-definition of Blackness or Whiteness leaves them with a void.

Whites during the redefinition stage often redirect their energy in order to define Whiteness in a way that is not dependent on racism or on the existence of perceived deficiencies in other groups. There is recognition that all cultures and racial groups have unique and different traits that enrich the human experience, that no race or culture is superior to another. They are all unique, different, and adaptive.

The redefinition stage is the point in the development process at which the Black person is concerned with defining himself or herself in terms that are independent of the perceived strengths or weaknesses of Whites and the dominant White culture. It is here that Black people shift their attention and energy toward a concern for primary contact and interaction with other Blacks at the same stage of consciousness. They find that many elements of Black culture that have been handed down through the generations still affect their lives, and the uniqueness of their group becomes clearer. They come to understand that they are more than victims of racism, more than just people who are not the same as the dominant group—in ways that engender pride.

Stage Five–Internalization

The transition from the redefinition stage to the internalization stage occurs when an individual begins to integrate some of their newly defined values, beliefs, and behaviors in all aspects of life. When the redefined sense of racial identity is fully integrated, the new values or beliefs occur naturally and are internalized as part of the person.

Indicators of internalization for Blacks include: recognition that their Black identity is a critical part of them, but not the only significant aspect of their identity; and the ability to consider other identity issues and other issues of oppression. Indicators of internalization for Whites include: a clear sense of their own self-interest as members of the White group in ending racism; acting on that self-interest; and not seeing others as "culturally different" and Whites as normal, but rather understanding how White European-American culture is different as well [pp. 24–34].

Racial identity development models can be viewed as roughly outlined maps of a journey from an identity in which racism and domination are internalized to an identity that is affirming and liberated from racism. We strongly agree with Hardiman and Jackson (1992) when they caution against using this model simplistically to label or stereotype students or others. Most people are in several stages simultaneously, holding different perspectives on the complex range of issues that relate to their racial identity. Such models can assist us in recognizing our own racial identity issues and how they may influence our teaching and response to students. They can also help educators to be less surprised or threatened by the strength and variety of student attitudes, as well as their heightened emotions as they react to cultural issues. By appreciating these developmental processes, we are more likely to learn ways to avoid prematurely stifling, artificially hastening, or unfairly condemning the behavior of students as they grapple with topics and themes that confront their differences.

For courses that address multicultural issues, sharing models of racial identity development with students provides a useful framework for understanding others' reactions. This can normalize their experience and reduce their fears, resistance, and potential resentment. As Beverly Daniel Tatum (1992) writes:

> In a course on the psychology of racism, it is easy to build in the provision of this information as part of the course content. For instructors teaching courses with race-related content in other fields, it may seem less natural to do so. However, the inclusion of articles on racial identity development and/or class discussion of these issues in conjunction with other strategies ... can improve student receptivity to the course content in important ways, making it a very useful investment of class time. Because the stages describe kinds of behavior that many people have commonly observed in themselves, as well as in their own intraracial and interracial interactions, my experience has been that most students grasp the basic conceptual framework fairly easily, even if they do not have a background in psychology [p. 20].

Returning to the classroom incident that introduced this section, if a racial identity development framework were understood by the teacher and students, this altercation might have been less likely to occur. And if it did happen as stated, the teacher would have been more likely to recognize the aggressive accusation as part of a pattern of active resistance by the student, been less surprised by it, and been better able to respond to it effectively. In addition, the student who yelled, "That's very rude," might not have done so in the first place, making the entire interaction less inflammatory. There is no guarantee this revision would occur, but an understanding of racial identity development theory does lessen the lack of awareness that can so easily lead to blame and anger.

Different Ways of Knowing

Conflict can also occur because of the different ways in which people construct what they know. Based on their interviews of students as they moved through their undergraduate years at Harvard, William Perry (1970) documented a scheme of intellectual development that described how students give meaning to their experience and understand themselves as knowers. Perry traced a progression from an initial position he called *basic dualism*, where the students view the world in polarities of right/wrong, we/they, and good/bad. The final stage of this hierarchical sequence is *full relativism*, when the student comprehends that truth is relative—that the meaning of an event depends on the context in which the event occurs and on the framework that the knower uses to understand the event. Students are also able to see that relativism pervades all aspects of life, including and beyond the academic world. Students at the lower positions are understood to be more likely to view teachers as authority figures who dispense knowledge. These students tend to understand their role as filtering out the right answers from the material presented. Those at the higher end of the hierarchy are more likely to see their teachers as experts who guide them through a search for the relationships among ideas and information. Educators have used the Perry scheme as a developmental framework to guide educational practice.

Building on Perry's scheme but realizing the limitations of its perspective—interviews with a relatively homogeneous group of men at an elite university—Belenky, Clinchy, Goldberger, and Tarule (1986) studied the ways of knowing with women who represented widely different ages, life circumstances, and backgrounds. From their in-depth interviews with 135 women, they found that the developmental stages Perry outlined are far less obvious. Belenky and her colleagues grouped women's perspectives on knowing into the following five major categories (1986, p. 15). These groupings are not fixed, exhaustive, or universal, and similar categories can be found in men's thinking:

> "*Silence*, a position in which women experience themselves as mindless and voiceless and subject to the whims of external authority." They have little awareness of their intellectual capabilities and believe people such as experts and teachers know the truth.

> "*Received knowledge*, a perspective from which women experience themselves as capable of receiving, even reproducing, knowledge from the all-knowing external authorities but not capable of creating knowledge on their own." Other voices and external truths prevail, and the sense of self is often embedded in sex-role stereotypes or in identification with an institution. Their perception of the world tends to be literal and concrete, good or bad.

> "*Subjective knowledge*, a perspective from which truth and knowledge are conceived as personal, private, and subjectively known or intuited." For women, this often means a turning away from external authority with the locus of truth shifting to the self. There is a tendency to value intuition over conventional forms of logic and abstraction. It is here women begin to gain a voice.

"*Procedural knowledge,* a position in which women are invested in learning and applying objective procedures for obtaining and communicating knowledge." Women often feel a greater sense of control and seek real-life opportunities to exercise their own authority.

"*Constructed knowledge,* a position in which women view all knowledge as contextual, experience themselves as creators of knowledge, and value both subjective and objective strategies for knowing." In this stage there is the integration of personal knowing with knowledge learned from others as well as the development of an authentic voice.

As they conducted their study of women's ways of knowing, Belenky and her colleagues documented two distinctive forms of procedural knowledge. Referring to the work of Gilligan (1982) and Lyons (1983), they called these orientations *separate knowing* and *connected knowing.* Separate knowing is based on impersonal procedures for establishing truth, such as the scientific method. It is an orientation where critical thinking, doubt, and rational argument are essential procedures. In connected knowing, truth emerges through care. It is a perspective based on the conviction that the most trustworthy knowledge comes from personal experience. Knowing comes from empathy and reception when people open up to receive another's experience into their own minds. In connected knowing, people understand others' ideas in the other people's terms rather than in their own terms. These researchers believe that connected knowing comes more easily to many women than does separate knowing.

Frequently, as teachers we assert our intellectual authority by referring to research. "Research suggests ..." and "A study has found evidence that ..." are expressions as natural to us as saying hello. Often, for some of our students, what the "research says" is questionable based on their personal experience (connected knowing). When these learners offer their conflicting perspective, a question can emerge within the class as to which position exerts greater authority. Because of different ways of knowing, debate will not usually settle this issue. Also, in a contentious atmosphere, questions from the teacher such as, "Do you have any research to support that opinion?" often only frustrate or silence rather than enlighten the discussion. To avoid discounting students' voices and encourage constructed knowledge and dialogue, we can ask learners to use their experience to inform our opinions and research-based generalizations as we present them. This approach is likely to lead to a more balanced, and perhaps more truthful, understanding for all of us.

Different Belief Systems

Societies throughout the world differ in their belief systems. Social roles, codes of behavior, and what is considered to be true can vary remarkably among a group of diverse learners, often more so when international students are present. The status of teachers may be much higher in one society than in another. Some students may see important and knowledgeable remarks as forthcoming only from the teacher and not from other students. The roles of men and women may be firmly denied. Even with such a short list of possibilities, one can see how questioning the intellectual authority of the teacher or a procedure like cooperative learning could lead to tension, resistance, or conflict for some students. By studying patterns of values based on belief systems, Geert Hofstede (1986) has found characteristic dimensions that are more strongly present in some countries as compared to others. For example, uncertainty avoidance is the extent to which people within a culture are made nervous by situations that they perceive as unstructured, unclear, or unpredictable. These cultures tend to be characterized by strict codes of behavior and belief systems anchored in absolute truths. To illustrate, on Hofstede's continuum, Japan is considerably stronger in uncertainty avoidance than is Hong Kong.

Although the unit of analysis to arrive at these characteristic dimensions has been a country, theoretically they might apply to any number of specific populations, including religious or occupational configurations. Different people see and react to the same thing differently for many reasons that are beyond their immediate awareness or control. When we consider racial identity development processes, different ways of knowing, and different belief systems, we see how profound the influences of culture are and how legitimate the sources of conflict within a class of diverse students may be. This is why students must learn to succeed in classes that appreciate diversity. Cultural diversity is central to their future, and they must be able to learn and work with knowledge and skills that accommodate its complexity.

The assumptions we bring as teachers about how people know and how to know are crucial in determining the atmosphere and discourse of learning in our courses. Most interpersonal conflict is caused by different perceptions or understandings of an event, a person, or an idea. When arguments are based on culturally different assumptions such as religious beliefs, two or more persons may disagree without one being right and the other being wrong (Pedersen, 1994). The issues of controversy can range from the morality of capital punishment to the value of particular scientific inventions.

Truth in a multicultural world is not entirely indeterminate. There are facts. Nurturing freedom of expression in a learning environment does not have to be confused with an obligation to facilitate every point of view. But purpose plays a pivotal role. If the goal of a learning group is to deepen its understanding of what the truth may be rather than to find out who knows the truth, then a real dialogue, a "thinking together," is more likely to occur. Under such circumstances, the group has a much better chance to discover insights not attainable individually (Senge, 2006).

Certainly no single strategy works best in all situations of conflict, especially when that conflict is multicultural. There are numerous models for confronting, mediating, and resolving conflict. Most have to do with helping the parties involved find common ground among their purposes and expectations. A well-planned approach and a proactive stance in matters of cultural relations can prevent highly dysfunctional conflict, which threatens to erode the consensus that brings a group together. This is one of the main reasons that our approach to culturally responsive teaching is organized within an integrated set of norms and practices. They form a symmetry that respects diversity while establishing and maintaining a common classroom culture that all students can relate to with integrity.

Resistance

In addition to a complex variety of beliefs, there are many apprehensions toward issues of diversity and culturally responsive teaching that can lead to resistance. However, what appears to be resistance may also be a response to methods of teaching, assignments, and other aspects of pedagogical practice.

From her teaching in predominantly European American college classrooms, Tatum (1992) documents that students frequently consider race a taboo topic for discussion, especially in racially mixed settings. She also finds that many students, regardless of racial group membership, are uncomfortable with an understanding of racism as a system of advantage for European Americans over people of color because it contradicts their socialization to think of the United States as a just society where rewards are based on merit. Gale Auletta and Terry Jones (1994) have found that some students and faculty believe that acts of racial bias must be mean-spirited or conscious to signify racism. They suggest that some portion of the racial uneasiness that may be felt in college classrooms is due to differences in perception about what constitutes racism.

Educators as well as students may remain silent or unresponsive to issues of diversity because of fear of being misunderstood, anxiety about disclosing too much and becoming too vulnerable, memories of former bad experiences of speaking out, fear of creating anger the group cannot manage, confusion about level of trust, and resentment for having to prove one is not "the enemy." One's own personal and fragmentary understanding of such matters and academia's prevailing interest in empirical data can create a quagmire for instructors who lack a nuanced understanding of power as a social, political, and institutional construct. In spite of significant scholarship and frameworks from the social and political sciences (Ladson-Billings, 1996; Lipsitz, 2006; Marabel, 2002; Bonilla-Silva, 2003; Foner and Frederickson, 2004), personal merit in many college classrooms is seen as color-blind, and a discussion to the contrary is viewed as more likely to mislead than liberate ideas.

We agree there are times when history, context, the presenting issues, and the orientations of people reveal the inadequacy of a reasoned perspective. At issue here is not the rejection of reason but the notion that common notions about reason are inadequate. Art, insight, creativity, humor, intuition, and the spiritual may not be rational, but they may approach a greater wisdom. In certain matters, heeding resistance, putting analysis and the quest for solution aside, and moving on to other ways of knowing and learning may lead to an understanding not otherwise accessible.

Seeing resistance from a number of perspectives helps us to realize that as a human process, it has many forms—that it can be self-protective and personally and socially restrictive—but also that it can reflect perceptiveness and socially beneficial strivings. Most resistance appears to stem from apprehensions about vulnerability or control. Although the advocacy of this book is clearly to change conventional teaching practices, we realize things hardly ever go easily during change efforts. Most college students have gone through secondary schools where teaching methods still mimic those used in universities. They may not be thrilled about how they were taught, but they adapted, were generally successful by the standards applied, and have formed habits and expectations that may run counter to some of the suggested teaching approaches found in this book. To label their fearfulness, reluctance to participate, complacency, or failure to recognize the need for change as resistance is usually ineffectual. It can divert attention from such real concerns as inadequate teaching skills, dubious assessment practices, or the need for more clarity regarding learning goals. Such labeling tends to be blameful, places more of the responsibility for the solution on the students, and leads to thinking that immobilizes creativity.

We prefer an understanding of resistance as a concern about facing difficult realities that is expressed indirectly. For example, if some students maintain that there is not enough time to discuss a controversial topic when the time is actually available, they are probably being resistant. However, if there really is not enough time for an adequate discussion, they are judiciously expressing a realistic concern.

We do not have a formulaic set of guidelines for dealing with resistance. We have found it to be so contextually determined (who, where, when, what, and so forth) that a recommended series of steps flies in the face of the complexity and variation inherent in this reaction. We believe, however, that presupposing a positive intent of students is vastly more informative to our teaching than focusing on the negative. For example, the perception "Indirectly, we are being told to proceed more slowly and cautiously, to make the situation safer, to provide concrete results" is more constructive than "They only want to avoid; they are cynical; they don't want to do the work." Listening respectfully and soliciting information about the nature of learner concerns usually provides insights. We often ask for examples and evidence of the problem as well as suggestions for other courses of action. We have found that making simple syntactical changes can make a conversation more open. For example, the use of exploratory language such as, "Suppose we . . . ," "Is it possible . . . ," or "It seems that . . . ," suggests a wider range of ideas and reduces the need for the implied correct response. In addition, using plural forms such as, "ideas, solutions, some factors ..." invites thinking as well.

■■

In general, gradually shifting toward a more culturally responsive pedagogy involves new and flexible approaches to teaching and intense personal learning. Both teachers and students need to assess such change for its genuine possibilities and to comprehend its effect on their self-interest as well as what they collectively value. Initially there may be little certainty about the kinds of processes or outcomes that may ensue and less assurance that they will be any better than the status quo. These are legitimate issues that deserve careful attention. The chapters that follow are mindful of this inevitable and salubrious scrutiny.

2

ESTABLISHING INCLUSION

Education can never be merely for the sake of
individual self-enhancement. It pulls us into the
common world or it fails altogether.

—Robert Bellah

Although he has been interested in the reading material, Wayne Johnson is thinking about dropping the sociology course taught by Dr. Robert James. Academic learning generally comes easily to him, but he wonders why he is socially isolated and has become disinterested in the course. Dr. James's enthusiasm and sincerity are compelling. He expects that no one will fail the course, all assignments will be clear, and he will be available to help anyone who needs it. Thus far, these are promises he has kept, laid out like a map: read Chapter Six, make appropriate notes in your journal, pass the quiz on Friday, complete a small-group assignment, and it will be all right. However, the group of students with whom Wayne Johnson has been assigned for the small-group assignment are bothered by the amount of work they have in other classes. Their goal for an otherwise interesting assignment is, as one student expressed, "Get the grade and move on. You won't even think of this course two weeks after it's done." Wayne feels trapped. Successful completion of a course assumes a certain level of learning has occurred, yet to push himself and the members of his group to a higher level of expectation would contribute to significant discomfort. In addition, Wayne is the only African American student in his predominantly European American group.

Wayne wishes some of his classmates had taken Marginality and Mattering, a student services workshop (Schlossberg, 1989) that was offered last quarter. One of the initial exercises was for students to remember a moment in the recent past (a week to a month) when they felt marginal, excluded, or discounted—"the only one like me in a group, not understood or, perhaps, unaccepted." After they reflected on this, students paired off and discussed the following questions: How did you know? How did you feel? How did you behave? Next, the instructor asked students to recall a moment when they felt that they mattered, were included, or were regarded as important to a group. Once again, they were provided time to reflect and then paired off to discuss the questions: How did you know? How did you feel? How did you behave? Finally, students were asked to reflect on both situations and discuss the patterns of thinking, feeling, and behaving that emerged, the influence of those patterns on their motivation and enthusiasm, and how the changes in motivation and enthusiasm might relate to learning and teaching. Within this multicultural workshop, Wayne and most of his classmates were able to see for themselves how motivation across cultural groups is constantly influenced by an acute awareness of the degree of a person's inclusion in a learning environment. Together they were able to develop awareness of how when human beings do not feel safe, complex information is often blocked from passage to higher cortical functioning and memory storage, slowing learning and increasing frustration, aggression, or withdrawal.

With the road to success otherwise clear, Wayne is not sure what to do. In some ways, it would be easier to address his concerns if Dr. James's requirements were not so easy to complete. But with limited direction on group work and limited motivation among his peers, completing the course feels like a surrender of sorts, which in a deeper sense could contribute to a feeling of professional estrangement. Wayne doesn't want and can't afford the luxury of a free ride. But to speak up is to invite additional alienation from his peers and perhaps from Dr. James.

From a motivational perspective, this scenario highlights a fundamental need that most learners share: to become part of an environment in which they and their instructors are respected by and connected to one another. This is the challenge of the first condition of the motivational framework: establishing inclusion. It asks college instructors and adult educators to consider how we can help students know they are part of a learning community that supports social and academic risk taking. Inclusion is the result of instructional practices that ideally occur throughout every lesson of every session of every course. Although in education the concept of emotional safety is frequently an introductory activity or warm-up, a mere strategy rarely creates a milieu in which students from a range of backgrounds are comfortable as learners.

Anyone who seeks to be culturally responsive as a teacher simultaneously embraces two challenges: to create with learners a genuine sense of community and to promote justice and equity in the society at large. An undergirding assumption of this chapter is that the impetus for various approaches to a supportive learning community lies as much in their capacity to promote learning about creating a more cooperative world as it does in their instructional effectiveness for the individual learner. Feelings of cultural isolation generally erode student motivation to learn. In a classroom, as in civic life, a sense of community with which all students can identify establishes the foundation for learning and participation.

The ability to create community is prompted and supported by natural human traits and qualities. We are community-forming beings. Our capacity to create and recreate social coherence is enduring and irrepressible (Gardner, 1991). It is in community that we find security, identity, shared values and people who care about one another. This is where the ideals of justice and compassion are nurtured. We do not live ethical lives by merely following the precepts of intellectual philosophies. Experience is a vital influence. This premise can be traced to any number of academic traditions and global communities (Dewey, 1938; Anyon, 1980; Kolb, 1984; Tippeconnic Fox, Lowe, and McClellan, 2005).

The word *community* has its roots in two Latin words: *communitas*, the association of people on mutually equal and friendly terms, and *communis*, belonging to all. A visual image of community as well as its root meaning set the context for how the motivational goal of establishing inclusion can be established in a learning environment. In such a setting, learners and teachers know they are included because they are respected by and connected to one another. In other words, in real communities, there are likely to be norms and experiences that allow people to feel respected and connected. To hear a person say, "I feel a sense of community in this class," is a compliment of the highest order to every member of the group. Let us now look at why the criteria of respect and connectedness are foundational to the intrinsic motivation of diverse learners.

Feelings of cultural isolation often cause adult motivation to deteriorate. In a course or seminar, a sense of community with which all learners can identify establishes the foundation for inclusion. The challenge of instructors is to create a successful learning environment for all learners that respects different cultures and maintains a common culture that all learners can accept. We are fortunate, because adults are oriented toward community. The ability to construct mutual connections is ever present (Gardner, 1990). Within community we have the time and the ease to become acquainted, find common ground, and extend our goodwill. As more and more adults sandwich their education between work and family, an adult education setting may provide one of the few opportunities to experience community and a sense of belonging. But mere contact between people does little to enhance intercultural appreciation. Mutual respect and appreciation evolve from the nature of our contact. The norms we set as instructors and the strategies we use to teach will largely determine the quality of social exchange among our learners. Those norms should be supportive of equity, collaboration, and the expression of each learner's perspective (Wlodkowski and Ginsberg, 1995). It simply makes sense to set a tone in which learners can come together in friendly, caring, and respectful ways.

The strategies that follow contribute to establishing a climate of respect. In this atmosphere, intrinsic motivation is more likely to emerge because learners can voice what matters to them. Their well-being is more assured. They can begin to develop trust. Neurologically and socially, we have set the table for a relaxed and alert social environment. Relevant learning is possible.

Respect, Connectedness, and Intrinsic Motivation

Many educators believe that classes should be conducted in an atmosphere of mutual respect. But what does this really mean? One way to think about what respect means in a learning environment is to imagine an environment in which the integrity of each person is valued. This environment, within reason, welcomes each person's sense of worth and self-expression without fear of threat or blame. In such an atmosphere, people know they are respected because they feel safe, capable, and accepted. They feel respected because they know their perspective matters.

In a climate of respect, intrinsic motivation emerges easily because people are able to be authentic and spontaneous and to accept full responsibility for their actions. These are the qualities of self-determination, which is a hallmark of intrinsic motivation; they are qualities that fear and alienation quickly suppress.

Connectedness in a learning group provides a sense of belonging for each individual and a felt awareness that one is cared for and cares for others. A shared core purpose is to support each other's well-being. In such an environment, people experience trust, some degree of community, and emotional commitment to others; because of this, a spirit of tolerance and loyalty allows a measure of uncertainty and dissent.

Feeling connected elicits intrinsic motivation in people not only because basic social needs are being met but also because our authentic selves are endorsed. It is possible to freely enter into meaningful discussions and relevant action. When we are in a group in which we do not feel included, we are far more likely to guard our resources, strengths, and weaknesses to protect ourselves from others. Feeling related to others helps human beings recognize individual concerns as collective issues rather than simply the problems of those who directly experience them. Not accidentally, we are much more likely to feel connected to those who respect us.

Inclusion is at the core of empowerment and agency. True agency means more than knowing how and being able to attain learning outcomes; it means feeling free enough to make authentic and relevant choices with respect to those outcomes (Ryan and Deci, 2002). We seldom do this in the absence of learning in groups in which we feel included, where some degree of harmony and community exists. Even the approximation to such unity is a powerful force for engendering learning and motivation.

Norms for Establishing Inclusion

For each of the motivational goals presented in this book, we offer a set of norms. Norms help to create an ethos with shared understanding that elicits intrinsic motivation among learners. They are the core constructs held in common that act to build community among learners. Norms not only support certain behaviors but also create expectations for behaviors. For the specific motivational goal of inclusion and the broader purpose of culturally responsive teaching, these conditions are essential. Respect for cultural differences among learners and the explicit integration of issues related to diversity and power in the study of any subject matter heighten the potential for dissonance and conflict. Norms can provide the scaffolding that allows highly charged feelings and responses to be acknowledged and considered by the group. In such an environment, motivation, learning, and teaching are greatly enhanced. Based on experience and study we offer the following norms to promote inclusion in any learning setting:

1. *Course work emphasizes the human purpose of what is being learned and its relationship to the learners' personal experiences and contemporary situations.* People can feel a part of something that is relevant to them. We adhere to a group because it meets our personal needs. A human goal is one that every learner can potentially share, care about, and work in common to achieve. A relevant academic goal is one that authentically connects to the learner's world and frames of reference. A learning goal with this kind of salience and purpose has the potential to become a shared vision among all class members. It can inspire participation, responsibility, and action.

Anything that is taught bears a relationship to a human need or interest. Otherwise why would we teach it? For teachers, the essential question is, "What are the human implications of what we are helping learners to know or do?" Once we have an answer to this question, the relevance to learners of what we teach will be clearer, especially if we can find a way to relate it to the range of daily lives in any classroom. As an example, learning about health care in general is one thing. But learning about health care to improve the quality of our daily lives or the lives of members of our immediate community is quite another kind of task. In the same vein, studying a set of health topics in order to assist our own families makes this learning an obvious shared value.

When a community of learners understands that they are examining something connected to real-world issues, it becomes obvious that different perspectives can lead to different viewpoints. Under such circumstances, the diversity in a community of learners has the potential to contribute to a way of perceiving the complexity and depth of these issues. When topics lie more in the realm of the physical and natural sciences such as biology, chemistry, physics, and geology, showing how these courses of study and their knowledge can be applied to challenges faced by humanity or how they can make life more understandable and peaceful for everyone helps to unite learners in a common cause. Using human problems to learn and practice skills from disciplines as divergent as math and medicine can inspire teamwork and a sense of solidarity among learners.

McMaster University in Ontario, Canada, has developed a problem-based program in medical education in which learners focus on real-life issues and challenges. This program has fundamentally altered this frequently competitive arena into a cooperative venture, a teaching practice now implemented in numerous other universities (Baptiste, 2003). In the Freirean approach (McLaren and Leonard, 1993) a student-centered dialogue occurs in the first hour of class around problems posed from everyday life as well as topical issues from society and the academic subject matter. Students have equal speaking rights in the dialogue, as well as the right to negotiate the curriculum. Taking a critical attitude toward discrimination and inequality, the students codevelop a process to inquire into the problems posed and seek an action outcome whenever feasible. As teachers, the closer we bring the purpose of our course to the humanity we hold in common with our learners, the more we can share a hope for a better world. Ultimately it is the hope that binds us in a peaceful search for understanding, wisdom, and skill.

2. *Teachers use a constructivist approach to create knowledge.* This is a value that establishes the dynamic to encourage all

learners' understanding of their own construction of meaning and the integrity of their own thinking (Lave, 1997; Donovan, Bransford, and Pellegrino, 1999). It undergirds a deeply shared responsiveness to each class member's oral, written, and artistic self-expression. According to this norm, the thoughts, feelings, interests, and needs of every learner in the community are invited, listened and responded to, acted on, and honored. This condition embraces the notion of voice, which in the view of feminists and critical theorists expresses one's innermost knowing and feeling (Gilligan, 1982; Lather, 1991; Apple, 1982; Freire, 1994).

From this perspective, truth is a process of construction in which the knower participates (Belenky, Clinchy, Goldberger, and Tarule, 1986; Zull, 2002). Epistemological confidence and the ability to trust one's own thinking is related to intrinsic motivation. How many times have we heard, "Those students just don't like to think"? If it is not our own thinking, if we do not agree, and we cannot say we see things differently without fear of rejection or threat, then thinking deeply about an issue can certainly lack appeal.

Telling and hearing our stories is essential to human nature. It is personal. It is the way we make sense of things. And it compels. To know we are using our own powers of mind to transcend what we know, to play with ideas, and to realize clearly what was once vastly incommunicable is for many a form of ecstasy.

Perry (1970) found in a study of predominantly male students that those who moved from a view of knowledge as absolute to a view of knowledge as mutable and as subject to multiple perspectives were able to affirm their own personal identities. Belenky, Clinchy, Goldberger, and Tarule (1986) found the personal construction of knowledge to be a salient feature in cognitive development. When learners know that having and sharing ideas, assumptions, and hypotheses is a sincerely respected way of being in a learning environment, they will be more likely to expose their thinking. In fact, this is one of the few ways that students come to realize that there are multiple viewpoints on any issue and to appreciate how others also use the process of construction for their own learning and grasp of knowledge and truth.

3. *Collaboration and cooperation are the expected ways of proceeding and learning.* Learners often work together and can help each other. There is mutual concern that everyone makes relevant progress in learning. The fundamental orientation of the group is to get along. Learners are encouraged to see themselves as a community of learners.

There is a tendency to see an inherent tension between autonomy and community. However, when we reflect on many of our most vulnerable experiences in life, we often find a good deal of evidence for autonomous interdependence, that is, a willingness to depend on others and a desire to authentically provide care for them, realizing that by having their emotional needs met, they have the emotional freedom to meet the needs of others. It is through relationships and support that most people meet their individual hopes, and it is often through freedom of individual expression that many groups find ways to remain cohesive and strong.

When learners work within a competitive framework, communication is often more difficult and more easily misleading. Helping may be viewed as cheating, and there is frequently an aura of suspicion (Johnson, Johnson, and Smith, 1991). Competitive and individualistic learning environments detract from seeing learning goals as having a collective purpose. In such situations, many learners, especially those from supportive and interdependent ethnic minority communities, feel isolated (Cuseo, 1993). Extensive research at the postsecondary level indicates that higher individual achievement, intrinsic motivation, and more positive interpersonal relationships result from cooperative than from competitive or individualistic learning (Johnson and Johnson, 2006; Astin, 1997). People in the process of cooperative learning more accurately take the perspective of others, understanding more precisely how a situation appears to another person and how that person is reacting to the situation (Johnson and Johnson, 2003).

Educators as well as students live in a complex, interconnected world in which many ethnic and cultural groups continuously interact and where dependencies limit the flexibility of individuals and nations. With an increasingly fragile planet, the implications of this are vast. We need to learn the constructive competencies involved in managing interdependence and making shared meaning from conflicts. Skills as well as caring relationships come from mutual accomplishment and the bonding that results from joint efforts. Willingness to listen and to influence and be influenced by others is a consistent finding in cooperative learning situations (Johnson and Johnson, 2003). It is also the foundation of democratic discussion (Brookfield and Preskill, 2005), unity and diversity as global citizens (Banks, 2006), and constructive discourse in general.

Never before in the history of postsecondary education has there been a more diverse body of learners (Attewell, Lavin, Domina, and Levey, 2007). Within roughly eight years of their high school graduation, 80 percent of these graduates will go to college. Adults twenty-five years and older represent nearly 40 percent of college students (National Center for Educational Statistics, 2002). In addition, we are in the midst of the largest immigration in the history of this country. Between 1991 and 2001, approximately 10.2 million people immigrated to the United States (Constitutional Rights Foundation, 2006), and this trend continues. Immigrants and the children of immigrants will increase the ethnic diversity in our colleges. There has never been a greater need to make higher education accessible and successful for all students.

Today's students are likely to be commuters who juggle a college education with family and work, cycling in and out to earn money and meet the responsibilities of a working life. Less than a quarter of today's undergraduates are made up of full-time residential students between ages eighteen and twenty-two. As Paul Attewell and David Lavin (2007, p. B16) emphasize, "A college education is something that has to be fitted into the rest of life. College is no longer a phase of youth to be enjoyed before real life begins."

With larger numbers of students sandwiching their education between work and family, the curriculum and the forum in which learning occurs may provide critical opportunities to experience community and a sense of belonging. Diversity within such a transient and demanding milieu is likely to be overwhelming for everyone. Short-term exposure of underserved members of ethnic minority communities to a system dominated and administered bureaucratically by middle-income European Americans may exacerbate historical mistrust and personal experiences of alienation. Mere contact with those different from oneself does little to foster interracial or intercultural appreciation (Putnam, 2007). Mutual appreciation and respect evolve from the nature of the contact. Most human beings—European Americans, people of color, women, international students—favor learning experiences that are collaborative and participatory. It simply makes sense to establish a tone in which learners can come together in friendly, caring, and supportive ways.

Without a set of cooperative values firmly embedded in the learning environment, there is little chance for diversity to become a pedagogical asset and for the occurrence of cross-cultural dialogue and learning experiences that reduce bias and transform higher education from a privileged system to an institution that is a living conduit for justice, equity, and global peace. Alexander Astin's remarks (1993a) underscore this perspective:

I am convinced the only hope for the future is a cooperative world view. I believe that all significant human progress has come as a result of cooperation.... . And if we really believe that cooperative endeavor is the best solution to the human dilemma, then we have to exemplify that belief in the way we run our institutions.

That is why I believe that higher education has great power to change the world for the better. We can multiply our effectiveness by exemplifying in everything that we do the values we feel represent the most noble side of human nature. What I am saying is that we are not powerless; we all have the freedom to decide—even in our daily work on a campus—which world view we will see prevail [p. 5].

4. *Course perspectives assume a nonblameful and realistically hopeful view of people and their capacity to change.* Justice and equity inhabit a hopeful consciousness. They do not reside in cynicism and accusation. The fate and faith of multiculturalism lie in a belief in a better and more peaceful world where different human beings have essential common bonds. Unless education in the classroom, at its most fundamental level, reflects this perspective, students may learn to ridicule rather than to embrace such a conviction. This is not to advocate the free reign of romantic ideals. Rather, our perspective is similar to what Dewey (1955) called *democratic faith.* Our attempts to construct a world that is inclusive, meaningful, and satisfying are always a work in progress. As instructors, we can teach ridicule for that which is imperfect or incomplete or grapple with tensions in ways that allow learners to develop imagination and concern for the pain of others. Human beings can be selfish and narcissistic, but also decent, empathic, and creative. Many would say it is as natural to help as it is to hurt (Kohn, 1990).

In teaching, a realistically hopeful view of human nature respects this possibility and, from a motivational perspective, affirms learners' assets and strengths, recognizing that it is the action founded on this belief that will lead to ethical and relevant accomplishments. This is not "positive thinking" or the superficial mentality of buttons and bumper sticker clichés. A realistically hopeful view of people is not a mask or an analgesic to smother problems and difficulties in phony feel-good affirmations. Human suffering is not ignored. This is a way of thinking that pays attention to opportunity, gives the benefit of doubt, expects learners to do well, and finds joy in the process of working toward the solution of human problems.

From this point of view, a learning environment is a place (filled with people) in which multiple worlds of experience exist. Individuals will change their behavior when changes in the interactions in this system allow them to perceive different behaviors as appropriate and possible (Molnar and Lindquist, 1989). Within this milieu, a cultural misunderstanding between people is an opportunity for learning rather than a reason for estrangement.

While this norm acknowledges how compelling the need to blame is, it does not condone the act of blaming. In our experience, of all human propensities, blame is among the most damaging to relationships among people, especially culturally different people. Blame frequently provokes and sanctions our inhumanity to one another. Once blame occurs, a cycle of attitudes and actions can emerge whose reciprocal destruction is often surpassed only by the mutual incomprehension of those involved.

Yet we must acknowledge how extremely powerful the grip of blame is for most of us. The act of blaming releases three highly desirable states of consciousness. The first is a sense of control over whatever the situation is. Life is less chaotic. We can find fault. We can, at the very least, accuse. The second is the reduction of guilt. Our misery is not of our own making. It's not me; it's them. The third is the arrogant belief we do not have to change. "They" (usually the other person, racial or ethnic group, gender, and so on) have to change. In a single thought, blame can relax us or set off the fission of righteous indignation. It is an insidious and explosive tonic.

The blame cycle in Figure 2.1 represents the series of outcomes that seem to emerge automatically and then recur, with devastating impacts on the relationship of the people involved. In this instance, the cycle occurs in the relationship between a teacher and a student.

Let us say that in this case, there is a difference in perspective between the teacher and the student regarding required assignments. It could be a series of papers or small projects. At the top of the cycle, the teacher wants to help because the student appears to be struggling with attaining a competent performance on the assignments. The teacher's normal procedure is to encourage persistence, greater effort, and a series of study

Figure 2.1 The Blame Cycle

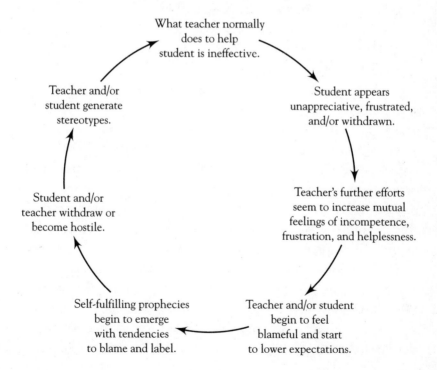

What teacher normally does to help student is ineffective.

Student appears unappreciative, frustrated, and/or withdrawn.

Teacher's further efforts seem to increase mutual feelings of incompetence, frustration, and helplessness.

Teacher and/or student begin to feel blameful and start to lower expectations.

Self-fulfilling prophecies begin to emerge with tendencies to blame and label.

Student and/or teacher withdraw or become hostile.

Teacher and/or student generate stereotypes.

habits that might include reviewing notes, outlining chapters, and making revisions. The student sees the issue as the irrelevance of the tasks. The assignments seem contrived, unnecessarily analytical, and unrelated to the reasons the student took the course. As they talk, the teacher responds to the student's comments with little empathy or validation. The teacher continues to emphasize previous advice, giving more detail and explanations as to why it should help. Upon departure, the student's frustration is noticeable.

When the student's performance on the next assignment has not improved, the teacher does what many people do in circumstances where we feel responsible and see our actions fail: gives a variation of the previous advice, telling the student to join a study group to see how other students are preparing their assignments. Because the student's performance still does not significantly improve, both teacher and the student feel more incompetent and frustrated. Now each feels justified in blaming the other. Once this occurs, the rest of the cycle rapidly advances. As their relationship deteriorates, the student's continued poor performance on assignments confirms the lowered expectations teacher and student have for each other.

Both teacher and the student are now in a frame of mind to search for labels—"unfair," "insensitive," "lazy," "unprepared," and so on. Hostility, withdrawal, and stereotyping are likely to emerge, and if they do, both will feel more compelled not to change—to maintain a sense of not having been intimidated or not having lost their integrity. Unless there is some sort of profound interruption, this cycle will tend to maintain itself. In this way, blame is both a consequence and a catalyst. Listen to faculty talking about students who do not learn in their classes and to students in those classes who talk about the faculty with whom they are not learning. They mirror each other's frustration and blame.

At this point, one might ask what the teacher or student should have done to avoid falling into this cycle of events.

Although that is an appropriate question, the purpose of this example is not to offer an intervention. The point of this illustration is to emphasize how quickly blame can emerge. Our experience is that in difficult matters between people who do not know one another, blame often occurs after only one negative encounter. A norm that prevents blaming is much more effective than interventions that are applied in hindsight.

Blame is a classic trap, something that uses normal behavior or instincts to entangle or immobilize even the best of intentions. Although it can be a symptom of deeper issues such as dominance or prejudice in a relationship, it can sabotage efforts toward positive change even in more equitable circumstances. This is one of the primary reasons that some school improvement programs, such as the one pioneered by James Comer (1993), have a "no-fault" approach. Meeting time is not used to blame others. The focus is on solving problems and taking advantage of opportunities first.

In a seminal article about teaching her course, *The Psychology of Racism*, Beverly Daniel Tatum (1992) explicitly provides the view to students that because prejudice and racism were inherent in our environments when we were children, we cannot be blamed for learning what we were taught intentionally or unintentionally. She points out that we all have a responsibility to interrupt the cycle of oppression and that understanding and unlearning prejudice and racism is a lifelong process. She acknowledges that each of us may not be at the same point in the process and should have mutual respect for each other regardless of where we perceive each other to be.

Ridding a learning environment of blame does not mean giving up our critical reasoning or confronting that which may seem unethical or contradictory. Since many things cannot be changed until they are faced, telling the truth and living with some degree of confrontation is essential to promoting collaboration in a learning community. This means knowing that the general purpose of the disagreement or other viewpoint is to provide information that leads to shared understanding, the resolution of a mutual problem, and a clearer path for communication and community; that even though I may see it differently from you, I do not withdraw my support from you as a person. This form of confrontation is the expression of a differing opinion with the consideration of the other person's welfare. The means to accomplish such communication are considered in the section of this chapter that describes the practices for establishing inclusion.

5. *There is equitable treatment of all learners with an invitation to point out behaviors, practices, and policies that discriminate.* Even in classes where establishing inclusion is an explicitly stated goal, the attitudes and dispositions people have developed in informal settings can penetrate the learning environment and manifest themselves within well-intentioned learning groups.

An enduring example is the way in which women sometimes find themselves in traditional gender-stereotyped roles within learning groups. In addition to Sadker and Sadker's seminal research (1990) that found men to be twice as likely to dominate class discussions and women twice as likely to be silent, there is also a tendency for male students of color to assume a more modest participative role than white males in postsecondary classrooms (Wilson, 2000).

The ability to alter well-established patterns, especially as they influence learning, is not only a pedagogical issue but a vehicle for uniting students from many different backgrounds in a shared understanding of each other's strength, resilience, and experience. Classroom pedagogy provides a unique opportunity to draw attention to the possibilities of a world collectively responsible for everyone's well-being (Dewey, 1932; Anzaldua, 1987; Gutman, 2003). Imagine, as a start, the power of this introductory statement from an instructor: "This class provides an occasion to discuss characteristics of empowerment and elicit specific examples of what everyone in a class can do to ensure that multiple voices and perspectives are equally engaged."

A collective conscience in these matters is important. Many theorists believe that of all educational venues, bias is most pronounced in postsecondary settings—from hiring practices to pedagogical decisions. Instructors, however, regardless of gender, race, or ethnicity, report that they are often unaware of inequitable interaction patterns. When shown videotapes of their discussions or when a colleague comes into a class and systematically records interaction, they are often surprised by evidence of unequal treatment (Sadker and Sadker, 1992). The same could be said when faculty are presented with evidence of what hooks (1994) refers to as the "collective professorial investment in bourgeois decorum" (p. 186). This orientation judges "smartness" according to a set of elaborate linguistic patterns that can cause low-income students, as one of several examples, to feel like unsophisticated imposters in the academic world. The motivational influence of this is obvious. It includes self-doubt, self-censorship, and the veneer of cynicism about all things intellectual (Brookfield, 2006).

Gender, racial, ethnic, classist, heterosexist, and ability bias in postsecondary classroom interactions has been documented from a number of perspectives (Adams, 1992; Frankenberg, 1993; hooks, 1994; Orfield, Marin, and Horn, 2005; Aronson and Steele, 2005). The ways in which socially constructed expectations of students manifest themselves in pedagogical practices include greater nonverbal attention to men in general, longer wait time for white males to answer, more eye contact with white men, and a greater likelihood of remembering their names. Power imbalances also occur in who receives attention from peers, who is interrupted, and other subtle interactions such as whose experiences are honored. For many students, equitable opportunity for public voice facilitates self-confidence and academic motivation. This is especially likely for people who have been historically underserved in education (Tannen, 1991; Luke, 1994).

One easy norm to implement is an agreement to teach each other in the moment when a person's voice is being diminished or underrecognized for its contribution. An instructor's own gentle reminders—for example, simple statements such as, "Let's hear from someone who has not yet spoken"—can cue everyone to resist dominance in patterns of public discourse.

An idea we have also found helpful in both small and large interactive groups, especially when they are newly formed, is to distribute a small number of coins to each learner in the group as a symbol of social currency. With the idea that in order to talk, students need to deposit a coin in the center of the group, group members are asked to "spend" their coins as they speak. Once they have used their currency, they are encouraged to make note of additional thoughts for later discussion. This sets the tone for group work and helps more garrulous learners to think about their comments and screen their perspective for those that seem more significant. These students simply make note of additional thoughts and contributions to share later.

This process also tends to prompt more reserved learners to become increasingly aware of their role as participants in a pluralistic classroom. While instructors will want to safeguard against formulas and easy solutions to complicated interactions, small reminders such as the examples previously offered can lead to more robust academic interactions from a broader range of students.

We have also found that when learners are allowed to form seating clusters that consistently reflect gender, ethnic, or racial segregation, there are some possible negative consequences: within-group perspectives are narrowed, teachers tend to focus attention toward groupings of students with the most social capital (Bourdieu, 1986), and lack of response among other groups is perceived as hostility. There are a variety of ways to intervene, from predetermined seating, to open discussion about seating patterns and their impact, to integrating through cooperative learning groups. These researchers have also noted that teachers who become aware of their inequitable interactions with learners want to change (Treisman, 1992; Kuh and Associates, 2005). They tend to be sensitive to the irony of contributing to bias against others while in the pursuit of knowledge.

■■

As postsecondary educators pursue ways to accept greater responsibility for integrating multicultural content into course work, there is a need for a climate and a community that engages everyone in learning and deals with the social and personal contradictions at hand. Shared norms and expectations build the cohesiveness that allows people to feel validated and confirmed as they learn—and sometimes to persist in spite of doubts and discomforts.

Norms can be implemented in a group in several ways. One is to clearly communicate them at the beginning of the course along with information about attendance, assignments, and assessment procedures. Students often appreciate having them in written form so they can be reviewed and emphasized periodically.

When participation agreements (discussed in the next section) are established, this is a good opportunity to make these norms explicit. Some teachers prefer to incorporate norms in a consensual decision-making process in order to heighten volition and significance to learners. Certainly they should be discussed and clearly understood. The degree to which they are modeled by the teacher, in both tone and practice, formally and informally, also establishes their credibility. Certainly norms, in and of themselves, are insufficient. Classroom practices reenact and support them. In general, the more clearly learners see how these norms lead to the accomplishment of salient goals to which they are committed, the more readily they accept and internalize them.

Practices for Establishing Inclusion

For each of the motivational conditions presented in this book, we offer a set of practices. These are the motivation and learning strategies and processes that educators and students use to accomplish agreed-on learning goals. The practices associated with the motivational goal of inclusion are those that foster *respect* and *connectedness*. These practices include a host of ways in which students become familiar with and support one another as well as the instructor. Since motivation and learning are influenced by culture, the most effective teaching strategies can vary for different learners. We invite you to consider the following practices as possible extensions of your teaching and to apply them in ways that are increasingly responsive to nuance. Csikszentmihalyi (1997) reminds us that it is how we choose what we do, and how we approach it, that will determine whether the sum of our days adds up to a formless blur or to something resembling a work of art.

Introductions

Most veteran instructors make time to introduce themselves, but there are quite a few who fail to extend this courtesy. Thus, no matter how obvious this suggestion may seem, it is worth the reminder. By all means, say a few things about who you are, where you are from, and why you are conducting the course or seminar, and welcome the group. This is a good opportunity to also speak about something you sincerely appreciate. It might be about your own history as a learner, the opportunity to work with this particular group, distinguishing aspects of this course, or other possibilities that make the situation distinct or important. This introduction need not take more than five to ten minutes.

It is also wise to provide a chance for learners to introduce themselves. This part of introductions emphasizes their importance and your interest. It helps people start to learn each other's names (name tents are a valuable supplement to this strategy) and significantly reduces the tension that is often present at the beginning of most courses. Scores of books (McDonald, Mohr, Dichter, and McDonald, 2003; Brookfield and Preskill, 2005; Johnson and Johnson, 2006) describe a host of exercises to help people get acquainted in new learning contexts. We provide several as well in this chapter.

Learning environments that are intellectually and socially inclusive require time to build relationships. Relationships can develop through significant pedagogical encounters such as collaborative and cooperative learning. Although there is impressive research to support the learning value of collaborative ventures, we devote significant space to the topic for philosophical reasons as well. Many of life's most important goals require cooperation. The nurturing of children, the quest for peace, and the safeguarding of the environment rely on mutual goodwill. The achievement of significant global aspirations is profoundly related to the way we learn in groups.

Collaborative and Cooperative Learning

Although there are many *collaborative learning methods*, most emphasize learners' exploration and interpretation of course material to an equal or greater extent than they do the instructor's explication of it. The process of working as partners or in small groups to generate questions and face challenges together energizes group activity. Instructors who use collaborative procedures tend to think of themselves less as singular transmitters of knowledge and more as colearners and co-constructers of knowledge.

As highly evolved social beings, most people naturally want to know what others are thinking and feeling (Brothers, 2000). In collaborative and cooperative learning activities, teachers act as empathic guides, helping to compose compelling learning experiences. This orientation creates active learner participation and engagement. Such involvement in learning with other students and faculty has historically and consistently made a significant impact on student retention and success in college (Astin, 1997; Tinto, 1998; National Survey of Student Engagement, 2006). As Alexander Astin (1993a) pointed out more than fifteen years ago, many postsecondary reform efforts are unsuccessful because they fail to address the implicit values of relentless individualism and competition in higher education. Collaborative and cooperative learning represent another value system—one that holds cooperation and community to be as important as academic achievement. These approaches invite learners to offer their perspectives and listen to the voices of others, deliberate and build consensus, and find academic learning a model of an equitable means to civic life.

Elizabeth Barkley, Patricia Cross, and Claire Major (2005) indicate abundant evidence that nontraditional students—underserved racial and ethnic groups, working adult students, commuters, and reentry students—are learners for whom collaborative learning seems to be a particularly effective and motivating format. From their review of the research on collaborative and cooperative learning in higher education, they note that "almost everyone" (p. 22) seems to benefit from group learning situations. In their estimation, collaborative learning is also an instructional method where all students can learn from diversity, benefiting from the linguistic and cultural perspectives that are possible to be experienced in this format. Among their conclusions, the following sums up our own experience teaching with collaborative learning strategies: "The evidence ... is so strong that collaborative learning has multiple advantages if done well, that it would be folly not to learn how to operate collaborative learning groups productively" (p. 24).

Amid the many collaborative learning possibilities, cooperative learning represents the most carefully organized and researched approach (Cranton, 1996). Although some scholars see cooperative learning as more teacher centered and discouraging of individual dissent (Bruffee, 1995), we suggest that teachers implement cooperative learning in a manner that respects individual differences in perceptions and constructions of knowledge (Barkley, Cross, and Major, 2005). Our treatment of cooperative learning in this book serves this purpose.

More than one-third of all studies comparing cooperative, competitive, and individualistic learning have been conducted with college and adult learners. David Johnson and Roger Johnson (1993) have found in an analysis of 120 of these investigations that cooperative learning significantly promotes greater individual achievement than do competitive or individualistic efforts. A meta-analysis of 375 relevant experimental studies (Johnson, 2003) in which research participants varied in age, economic class, and cultural background supported this finding as well. When students learn cooperatively, they tend to develop supportive relationships across multiple sociocultural and linguistic groups. The following list of learning achievements is compiled from two sources: the first eight achievements are from Johnson (2003); the last achievement is from Rendon (1994). Cooperative learning groups create a setting in which learners can:

- Construct and extend understanding of what is being learned through explanation and discussion of multiple perspectives.
- Use the shared mental models learned in flexible ways to solve problems jointly.
- Receive interpersonal feedback as to how well they are performing procedures.
- Receive social support and encouragement to take risks in increasing their competencies.
- Be held accountable by peers to practice and learn procedures and skills.
- Acquire new attitudes.
- Establish a shared identity with other group members.
- Find effective peers to emulate.
- Discover a voice to validate their own learning.

As practitioners and researchers strenuously empha-size, cooperative learning is more than merely placing learn-ers in groups and asking them to work together. According to Johnson and Johnson (2006), cooperative learning is a rigorous procedure where five fundamental components are necessary: positive interdependence, individual accountability, promotive interaction, social skills, and group processing. To organize les-sons so learners do work cooperatively requires an understanding of these five basic elements and their conscientious implementa-tion in the group and the lesson. It is also of paramount impor-tance that a significant amount of cooperative learning take place within the learning environment to permit monitoring by the instructor and allow groups to initially establish themselves while they can receive needed support.

Positive Interdependence. When learners perceive that they are linked with groupmates in such a way that they can-not succeed unless their groupmates do (and vice versa) or they must coordinate their efforts with the efforts of their partners to complete a task (Johnson & Johnson, 2006), they are positively interdependent: they sink or swim together. Each group mem-ber has a unique contribution to make to the group because of her or his resources, role, or responsibilities. For example, in the popular jigsaw procedure (see Exhibit 2.1), a reading assignment is divided among the group, with each member responsible for comprehending a separate part and explaining or teaching that part to all other members of the group until the entire group has a coherent understanding of the total reading assignment.

The following three approaches are additional ways to create positive interdependence within a cooperative learning group:

1. *Positive goal interdependence:* The group is united around a common goal, a concrete reason for being. It could be to create a single product, a report, or an answer, or it could be general improvement on a task so that all members do better

Exhibit 2.1 Jigsaw Procedure

When you have information you need to communicate to students, an alternative to lecturing or assigning the same reading to every student is a procedure for structuring cooperative learning groups called jigsaw (Aronson and others, 1978). First, think of a reading assignment you will give in the near future. Then proceed through the following steps for structuring a jigsaw lesson:

1. *Cooperative groups:* Distribute a set of reading materials to each group. The set needs to be divisible into the number of members of the group (two, three, or four parts). Give each member one part of the set of materials. This activity assumes at least four groups.

2. *Preparation pairs:* Assign students the cooperative task of meeting with someone else in the class who is a member of another cooperative group and has the same section of the material. They are to complete two tasks: (1) learning and becoming an expert on their material and (2) planning how to teach the material to the other members of their groups.

3. *Practice pairs:* Assign the pair of students the cooperative task of meeting with another pair who have learned the same material and share ideas as to how the material may best be taught. These practice pairs review what and how each plans to teach her or his group. The best ideas of both pairs are incorporated into each student's presentation.

4. *Cooperative groups:* Assign students the cooperative tasks of (1) teaching their area of expertise to the other group members and (2) learning the material being taught by the other members.

5. *Evaluation:* Assess the students' degree of understanding of all the material.

Source: Adapted from Johnson, Johnson, and Smith (1991).

this week than they did last week. Outcomes might include a skill demonstration, a media product, an evaluation summary, a problem solution, an action plan, or just about anything else that leads to greater learning and that a group can produce and hold each other responsible for.

2. *Positive resource interdependence:* Each group member has only a portion of the resources, information, or materials necessary for the task to be accomplished, and the members' resources have to be combined in order for the group to achieve its goals. The metaphor for this approach is a puzzle, for which each group member has a unique and necessary piece to contribute to reach its solution. For example, for an upcoming exam, each member of a group is responsible for a different study question. When the group convenes, that member shares her or his knowledge of the question and checks to make sure all groupmates have satisfactorily comprehended this knowledge.

3. *Positive role interdependence:* Each member of the group selects a particular role that is complementary, interconnected, and essential to the roles of the other group members. For example, consider the learning goal as the development of some form of skill, such as interviewing. One person is the skill practicer (the interviewer), another person is the recipient of the skill (the interviewee), and a third person is the observer or evaluator. In this manner, each person has an essential contribution to make in terms of skill practice or feedback. Roles can easily be rotated.

In all cooperative learning groups, it is extremely important that the learners are clear about the assignment, goal, and role. Especially with diverse groups of learners, checking for this kind of understanding can make the difference between a satisfying or a confusing learning experience. Positive interdependence works best when all group members realize each person has a part to do, all members are counting on them, and all members want to help them to do better.

Individual Accountability. This is present when the learning of each individual in the learning group is assessed, the results are shared with the learner and the group, and the learner is responsible to groupmates for contributing a fair share to the group's success. One of the main purposes of cooperative learning is to support each member as a vital, competent individual in his or her own right. Individual accountability is the key to ensuring that all group members are strengthened by learning cooperatively and that they have a good chance to effectively transfer what they have learned to situations in which they may be without group support. Sometimes texts emphasize individual accountability as a means to prevent "hitchhiking," the situation in which a learner contributes little of worth to the total success of a group's learning experience and overly benefits from the contributions of other group members. Our experience is that this seldom occurs when cooperative norms are well in place and competitive assessment or grading procedures are eliminated.

Individual accountability can be fostered in these ways:

1. Keep the size of the group small (two to four members) and the role of each learner distinct.
2. Assess learners individually as well as collectively.
3. Observe groups while they are working.
4. Randomly request individuals to present what they are learning to you or another group.
5. Request periodic self-assessments and outlines of responsibilities from individual group members.
6. Randomly or systematically ask learners to teach someone else or yourself what they have learned.

7. If the effort will be graded, assess and assign a grade for individual contributions as well as the group's performance or product.

A simple and positive way to support individual accountability and prevent related conflict among group members is to brainstorm with the learning groups and ask, "How would we like to find out if someone in our cooperative learning group thought we were not doing enough to contribute to the total group's benefit? What are some acceptable ways of letting us know?" Then write the possible actions for all to see and discuss them. Such a procedure helps avoid unnecessary suspicion or shame.

Promotive Interaction. When group members encourage and assist each other to reach the group's goals, they are engaged in promotive interaction (Johnson and Johnson, 2006). Often there is the sharing of information, resources, and emotional support, as well as challenge and deliberation to achieve the relevant goals. Mutual care should permeate this interaction as it does, for example, when someone in a cooperative writing group hears a group member read her own words and offers sincere and helpful suggestions to improve the piece. This sort of interaction allows different perspectives and commitments to take hold.

Social Skills. Cooperative work depends on communication skills that help groups reach goals, get to know and trust each other, communicate accurately, accept and support each other, and resolve conflicts constructively (Johnson and Johnson, 2006). Although people want to cooperate, they may not be able to effectively because interpersonal skills vary.

Our experience with diverse groups of learners is that when the four norms cited earlier in this chapter are present and participation agreements (discussed later in this chapter) are established, there is far less need for teaching learning skills such as active listening, which often feel contrived and ridiculous to many people, especially those who do not strongly identify with the dominant culture. It is appropriate for a teacher to intervene in a group when necessary to suggest more effective procedures for working together. Yet we agree with Johnson and Johnson (2006) that teachers should not intervene in a group any more than is absolutely necessary. We often find that with patience, cooperative groups work their way through their problems and construct not only timely solutions but also methods for solving similar problems in the future. Sometimes simply asking a group to set aside their task, describe the problem as they see it, and generate a few solutions and then a decision as to which one to try first is enough to help a group persist.

Group Processing. Cooperative learning benefits from group processing: reflecting on an experience or series of events to describe members' actions that were helpful and unhelpful and to make decisions about what actions to continue or to change (Johnson and Johnson, 2006). When groups with the same members continue over longer periods of time (more than a few hours) or are significantly diverse, discussing group functioning is essential (Adams and Marchesani, 1992).

Learners need time to have a discussion about the quality of their cooperation, reflect on it, and learn from how they work together. This processing time gives them a chance to receive feedback on their participation, understand how their actions may be more effective and cohesive, plan for more helpful and skillful interaction for the next group session, and acknowledge mutual success.

It is important to reserve time for this activity to take place and to provide some basic structure for it—for example, suggesting the group discuss a few things it is doing well and one thing it could improve. Instructors should also clearly communicate the purposes of such an activity and at appropriate intervals conduct whole-group processing to better understand how the learning group is working together.

In general, the more heterogeneous the groups, the better (Cohen, 1994). Many experienced practitioners believe in the importance of mixing groups by age, gender, and ethnicity. However, sometimes practical reasons override the attributes of heterogeneity. Examples include interest in a specific topic, accessibility for meetings outside class, broad variation in skill levels, or language learning issues. We strongly believe, however, that diversity in group work should be encouraged to the extent possible. For projects or activities with significant assessment consequences (for example, if they represent a large portion of a course grade), we usually accept individual completion as an option. In addition, for some activities (usually quite informal), we find that asking students to form their own groups (ranging from two to four members) allows smaller groups and a greater comfort level for students who are less at ease with cooperative learning.

Once cooperative learning groups gain skill and confidence in their group work, the role of the teacher is one of colearner, observer, advisor, and consultant. In the initial stages, however, it is a good idea to observe the groups in action. Certain groups need clarification or guidance. Throughout the process, however, we remain accessible and encourage learners to see themselves as the major resources for support and assistance to one another.

In Exhibit 2.1 we have adapted the jigsaw procedure from Johnson and Johnson's informative text, *Active Learning* (Johnson, Johnson, and Smith, 1991), to provide a descriptive example for conducting cooperative groups. A Cooperative Lesson Worksheet is provided in Resource H to use as a possible model for planning cooperative learning activities. A continuing resource, especially for teachers working with ethnically and linguistically diverse students, is the International Association for the Study of Cooperation in Education. This professional organization publishes a newsletter and is dedicated to educators who research and practice cooperative education and demo-cratic social processes.

Writing Groups

Whether explicitly organized as cooperative learning groups or arranged less formally as peer response groups or reflection circles, writing groups have a long history in postsecondary education (Lander, 2005). This format may involve working in small groups at every stage of the writing process. With peers, students formulate ideas, clarify positions, test arguments, focus theses, or probe the authenticity of their characters before or while they are in the process of writing. Collaboration allows learners to exchange written drafts and receive feedback; read, listen, and communicate with insights and helpful suggestions; and experience firsthand the rich and creative force that diversity can be.

In addition, writing groups can make the process of composing and revising less lonely and alienating. In a supportive milieu, people who have different perspectives and values can safely explore with their peers the vision for their work and reflect. Several researchers claim that the quality of thinking exhibited in the compositions of those in peer writing groups exceeds the quality of thinking of those in more conventional writing formats (Hillocks, 1984; Moore Howard, 2000). As an example of how peer writing groups can be part of the transformation of students as well as their writing, Anne Herrington and Marcia Curtis (2000) eloquently describe the personal and intellectual development of four culturally diverse students at the University of Massachusetts, Amherst, in which peer writing groups and multiculturalism are common denominators. In their writing courses, they often use inter-student exchanges of drafts and completed papers to foster self-refection during the composing process and simultaneously extend the students' sense of audience beyond the teacher alone. In this way, their students as well as other educators are able to see that writing is a social process in which "the personal is seldom absent from the public," and students yearn to address a kindred group capable of identifying with them (p. 5).

It is interesting and often beneficial for students to share writing strategies across groups. Two of many ways to facilitate such a conversation is to ask students to complete and discuss the following sentence starters:

- "Something I try to do to work against self-criticism and procrastination on assignments is ..."
- "Artificially constructed barriers I try to keep in mind as I work on my written assignments are individual (attitudes and beliefs) cultural (broadly accepted stereotypes), and institutional (policies and power structures). A strategy I use to get past these barriers is ..."

Peer Teaching

One of the oldest forms of collaborative learning is peer teaching—today often referred to as *reciprocal teaching*. It is the process of learners teaching learners (Boud, Cohen, and Sampson, 2001). Peer teaching approaches have expanded in postsecondary education under many names and structures. We present two of the most successful and widely adapted models of this genre, both of which depart from forms that focus on a remediation or rescue orientation toward learners.

The *supplemental instruction approach* was developed by Deanna Martin at the University of Missouri, Kansas City, and has been adopted at hundreds of colleges in the United States and abroad. The emphasis of the approach, which began in the health sciences and later was used in general arts and science classes, was not on the at-risk student but on the at-risk class where more than 30 percent of the students were either withdrawing or failing (Blanc, DeBuhr, and Martin, 1983). The university invited undergraduates who had done well in those classes to become "SI leaders." These students were paid to attend the class and to convene supplemental instruction sessions at least three times a week at hours convenient to students in the class. All the students in the class were welcome to attend the SI sessions.

In this model, the instructor works closely with the SI student leaders to develop ways to help students master the content of the class. The SI leader is presented as a student of the subject, not an expert on the subject—an approach meant to reduce perceptions of hierarchical status. Evaluations of this approach have shown that if students attend SI sessions consistently, their grades and their persistence in college are significantly higher regardless of whether they are perceived as strong or weak academically (Center for Academic Development, 1991).

The second peer teaching approach is the *intensive mathematics workshops program* developed by Uri Treisman (1985) at the University of California at Berkeley. This program assumes the orientation of an honors program rather than a remedial program. By emphasizing the development of strength rather than the remediation of weakness and peer collaboration rather than solo competition, Treisman completely reversed the prevailing patterns of failure in calculus classes by Latino and African American students.

Bonsangue (1993) conducted a longitudinal study of the effects of participation in this workshop model on the persistence and achievement of underrepresented minority students enrolled in mathematics, science, and engineering (MSE) majors at California State Polytechnic University, Pomona. Meeting in small groups twice a week for two-hour sessions to work collaboratively on calculus problems, the students were facilitated mainly by upper-division ethnic minority undergraduate MSE students. These facilitators meet weekly with the course instructors, who conduct the regular lecture and discussion sections to ensure the relevance of the material presented in workshop sessions and discuss specific academic issues related to individual students. Among the 320 students studied, 85 percent were Latino, and the rest were African American and American Indian, with approximately 25 percent of the total population being women.

Bonsangue found that within three years after entering school, 40 percent of the nonworkshop students had withdrawn or been academically dismissed from the institution compared to fewer than 5 percent of the workshop students. Moreover, 91 percent of the workshop students still enrolled in MSE after three years had completed their mathematics requirement, compared to only 58 percent of the nonworkshop students. Persistence and mathematics completion were highest among women participating in the workshop, all of whom remained in the university. Bonsangue concluded:

> This research ... has demonstrated that programs such as the calculus workshop, which promote academic excellence through well constructed opportunities for peer interaction, can significantly improve student performance in technical majors, and particularly, the performance of women and members of ethnic minority groups regardless of precollege academic measures. Achievement in mathematics, science, and engineering disciplines among historically underserved students may therefore be less associated with precollege ability than with in-college academic experiences and expectations [1993, p. 20].

After conducting an extensive review of peer teaching in higher education, Whitman (1988) concluded that providing students with opportunities to teach each other may be one of the most important educational services a teacher can render. In addition to a collaborative, small-group learning process, both of these programs employed "near-peers"—peer teachers who are slightly more advanced than the main body of learners. This provides not only a linguistic advantage—language and exemplification relevant to the learner's own understanding and perspective—but also connectedness and a vicarious sense of competence, the awareness by the learners that similar students perform successfully and that therefore they too possess capabilities to meet comparable challenges. Whitman suggests that faculty and student involvement in the recruitment, selection, and training of peer teachers is a key to academic success.

Although learning communities are often categorized as forms of collaborative learning, because of their complexity we discuss them later in this section under a separate heading. By structure and tone, collaborative learning invites us as teachers to be colearners, to establish procedures that model what it means to question, to learn, and to understand in concert with others. Let us now consider a basic procedure that is often not directly subject matter related yet helps to establish inclusion and a spirit of unity in a learning group. We refer to this process as the opportunity for multidimensional sharing.

Opportunities for Multidimensional Sharing

Opportunities for multidimensional sharing are those occasions, from introduction exercises to personal anecdotes to classroom celebrations, when people have a better chance to see one another as complete and evolving human beings who have mutual needs, emotions, and experiences. These opportunities give a human face to a class, break down biases and stereotypes, and support the identification of oneself in the realm of another person's world.

There are many ways to provide opportunities for multidimensional sharing, depending on the history, makeup, and purpose of the group. If there is a caution we have, it is to be more gentle than intrusive. Especially to students from backgrounds that value modesty, such activities may seem contrived and psychologically invasive. At the risk of overstating the case, "Let's all share about one person who made it possible for us to be here," or "What is a gift from our heart that we bring to this group?" are examples of what not to ask.

Meals and extracurricular activities usually offer people ways to be themselves and to reduce self-consciousness. Potluck meals, recreational activities, drinks after class, and picnics are always popular ways for learners and teachers to relax and get to know one another. Anything that helps people learn each other's names and laugh together deserves attention as a possible activity. For teachers, a little self-deprecating humor, not taking ourselves too seriously, suggests that we have some perspective on life and that the way we teach encompasses the vitality of other feelings and views. We have used the following introductory activities successfully. They range in the directness with which they consider cultural difference. They are conducted in a relaxed, trustful and enjoyable manner.

Our Stories is an example of multidimensional sharing that can occur at the start or conclusion of a class. It is especially useful for cohorts of students who are together for an extended period of time as they pursue a degree based on a common course of study. In programs such as the Ed.D. program at the University of Washington-Seattle, students in the Leadership for Learning program meet about once a month on weekends over approximately three years. In the first year, the *our story* format at the beginning of each weekend provides an opportunity for everyone to tell how they found their way to this program and to share their aspirations for educational leadership further. As part of this ongoing series of introductions, students sign up with a partner for a fifteen-minute block of time. Although students will eventually present their own story for roughly seven minutes, they begin the first meeting by briefly introducing their partner. This provides an occasion for students to become well enough acquainted with their partner to create a thoughtful introduction and for the entire group to become better acquainted.

Among faculty and students, the *our story* narratives have taken a variety of forms. Students have created elaborate PowerPoint presentations with photos ranging from grandparents and early family celebrations to world travel. The diversity of approaches has been as intriguing as the stories. One student shared a collection of textiles that represent significant memories, for example, a childhood quilt and a kitchen tablecloth. Another student used the theme of places where he had learned. His presentation included his elementary school, the naval ship where he learned about racism in job assignments, and the school where he currently serves as a principal. A particularly significant influence was his childhood home, where he learned lifelong values from a mother who had played a pivotal role in reparation to Japanese American families interned during World War II. Through "our stories," cohorts laugh together, listen to music, watch simulations, learn of global partnerships, and discover a variety of lives and perspectives. In addition to the ways in which Our Stories creates a stronger sense of community, it provides insight into the ways in which students' personal and cultural experiences can be woven into the curriculum. It has also contributed to an environment primed for risk taking and collaboration, setting the stage and creating a human safety net for rigorous academic challenge.

We offer a few suggestions for assisting students in their preparation. Ask students to (1) prepare the set in advance to maximize time, (2) provide visuals to illustrate their stories, and (3) be careful not to shy away from diversity in ways that one's life and experiences are distinct, in values held, and the creative ways experiences and values can be shared.

We remind students that good stories are memorable, personal, simple, and powerful. They have emotional appeal and inspire others. Like good teachers, good storytellers use symbols and analogies to bring stories to life. They rarely rely on just one method of communication.

This kind of opportunity for multidimensional sharing requires time. One of our goals in describing it is to explore how multidimensional sharing differs from many icebreakers in that it is less gamelike and intrusive. For adults from backgrounds where modesty is a significant value, introductory activities that require self-disclosure or the sharing of deeper emotions may seem contrived and psychologically invasive. Our stories require self-disclosure, but the students control the content and format. The following additional examples of multidimensional sharing work effectively within a small- or large-group format.

In this example, each person (1) introduces herself or himself; (2) names one, and up to five, of the places he or she has lived; and (3) offers one expectation, concern, or hope he or she has for this course.

In a variation of the previous example, each person introduces himself or herself and recommends (1) one thing he or she has read (such as an article, short story, or book), (2) one thing he or she has seen (such as a piece of art, TV program, film, or real-life experience), or (3) one thing he or she has heard (such as a speech, record album, or song) that has had a strong and positive influence on his or her life. The student states the reason for the recommendation.

A third possibility begins with the instructor posting a Venn diagram as a visual graphic (Figure 2.2) and asks students to divide themselves into triads. Next, the instructor asks the class to think broadly about the concept of culture and the qualities, characteristics, and experiences that might influence their cultural identity. People typically suggest such possibilities as gender, socioeconomic class, ethnicity, or geography. Some mention jobs they have had, the number of members in their family, and so forth. The goal is to create an orientation toward examining influences on cultural identities rather than a comprehensive list. It is important to explicitly state that culture is a complex concept that cannot be reduced to a simple list of nouns and adjectives. We also explain that the purpose of the exercise to begin to get to know one another.

After the instructor elicits five to ten examples and contributes a few to stimulate thinking, she asks the class to break

Figure 2.2 Venn Diagram

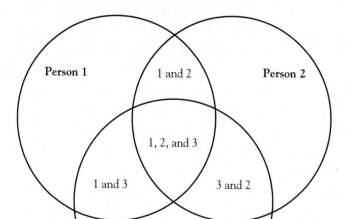

into triads and distributes a large printed Venn diagram to each group. Each member of the three-person group selects one of the circles to represent himself or herself, and group members work together to locate and write on the diagram the words that identify how they understand themselves culturally. As they do this, they observe that all three of them have certain aspects of their lives in common—perhaps gender or occupation. These are entered in the center of the diagram, where all three circles intersect the space.

Some characteristics or experiences will be shared by only two team members, and in different pairs—for example, marital status for persons one and two and perhaps region of birth for numbers two and three. These are entered in the space intersected by the two circles belonging to the two people who share that particular characteristic.

Finally, there will be qualities unique to each member of the triad, such as ethnicity or languages spoken. These are entered in the portion of each circle that does not overlap.

The instructor's primary goal is to make the process clear but to leave the learners as much discretion as possible as to what they enter into each section of the diagram. The instructor encourages learners to share what they are comfortable making public, to get to know each other, and to enjoy themselves. After fifteen to twenty minutes, each person reflects on whatever comes to mind related to the group's discussion. Some participants prefer to discuss this collaboratively. The teacher then conducts a whole group discussion and records the generalizations. Generalizations that occur most frequently are, "We realized we immediately tried to find out what we had in common," or "We spent the entire time talking about one of the many possible ways to discuss influences on our lives and perspectives." There is no limit to what might be said.

We developed this activity as a means to enter into a conversation about culture from a reasonably safe perspective and found that it contributes to deeper discussions about cultural difference and institutional racism. Pedagogically it signals a willingness to learn about students and share the discursive process. Although we always provide the option for groups to eliminate the diagram if it seems to impede conversation, working from a diagram tends to focus people, encourage greater participation, and lessen self-consciousness.

In general, we believe introductions are most inclusive and motivating when they help people learn each other's names, validate individual and collective experiences, relieve the normal tension that most new groups feel at the beginning of a workshop or class, and establish a sense of affiliation. Learning about each other is a continuous process. The more natural and appropriate such opportunities feel, the more likely a genuine sense of community will evolve. At the beginning of a course, these activities can contribute to the initiation of sustainable relationships for personal and academic growth.

Focus Groups

Focus groups are meetings of learners and teachers assembled as representatives of a larger group and organized for the purpose of obtaining information, generating ideas, and assessing course materials, activities, assignments, and social climate. A focus group can serve as a vehicle for collecting sensitive feedback about a class as well as offer a means for creating and improving how a given course evolves (Katz and Williams, 2001). Focus groups provide not only a way to acknowledge the range of diversity in a learning group, but a direct means of enhancing the inclusion, adjustment, and refinement that differences among learners may require for a culturally responsive learning experience. For large classes where learners frequently feel anonymous and distant, focus groups can be especially useful.

Because postsecondary courses vary dramatically, focus groups can range from informal to formal contexts for addressing something as narrowly defined as classroom participation to something as broadly encompassing as the entire operation of a course, including required texts and student assessment. In all cases, planning is essential. We have found it helpful to decide early on about how frequently and regularly the group will meet. This will influence who can participate and how dependable that participation can be. It is important that the group represent the diversity within the class. Four to eight members usually make adequate discussion possible. When appropriate and desirable, each focus group member can meet with a designated number of learners from the entire class to elicit their reactions and exchange information.

A carefully considered agenda with learner input and guidelines on how to work effectively together makes an immeasurable difference in how successfully a focus group operates. We suggest making clear to the members which aspects of the course they can expect to influence. If there are areas of the course that are not open to discussion, explain this. By encouraging all learners in the course to seek out focus group members and offer suggestions, appreciations, and questions, teachers further enhance what is discussed at the focus group meetings. In addition, such an invitation creates an opportunity for participation from learners who might feel vulnerable expressing feelings, ideas, or concerns directly. Allowing class time for members to report to the class can help to validate the focus group and increase cohesiveness within the class. The questions that follow are some that we have found helpful in eliciting culturally sensitive information in a focus group:

- How do the learning experiences and assignments build on what learners know and value? What avenues have been overlooked? What should we emphasize more?

- How do the learning experiences, materials, and assignments allow all learners to use their talents and preferred ways of learning? How do they inhibit?

- Do all learners in our course believe they can successfully accomplish what is required? If not, why? If so, what is being done that helps?

- How are we progressing as a community of learners where there is mutual respect and a sense of connection for everyone? What more could be done?

We have sometimes found that learners need to warm up before they can address questions as complex as the ones we propose. Often we begin by asking participants to think about and discuss a course they have enjoyed and in which they felt valued and challenged. Beyond this, we agree with Cross and Angelo (1988) that any teacher who uses this process must commit to taking learner suggestions seriously.

Reframing

The next practice we recommend for the motivational goal of establishing inclusion is directly intended for teachers. We know only too well how we can remain in a blameful and problematic relationship with a learner where whatever we do seems of no avail. Reframing has helped us and other teachers, and therefore students, in such circumstances. This technique is based on the ecosystemic view that human behavior can be legitimately interpreted in a variety of ways and that people tend to view their behavior as appropriate to the situation as they perceive it (Molnar and Lindquist, 1989).

Consider a simple example. A teacher regards a learner as too aggressive and sees this person's repeated blurting out of comments and answers in class as proof. The learner considers it necessary to blurt out answers because he believes the teacher tends to ignore him. Their perceptions are mutually reinforced when the learner suddenly raises his voice to get the teacher's attention and the teacher deliberately ignores the learner in an attempt to discourage his behavior. And on it goes, with the likelihood of consequent labeling and stereotyping from both parties.

One generative way of promoting change in such problematic patterns of behavior is to formulate a positive alternative interpretation of the behavior and begin acting in ways that are consistent with this new interpretation. This technique is called *reframing*. For a teacher, reframing means finding a new perceptual frame for what is considered to be the problem behavior—one that is positive, fits the facts of the situation, and is plausible to the individual personalities and congruent with the cultures of the people involved. The process of reframing will also suggest how to act differently in the situation when it reoccurs. If the teacher in our example were able to interpret the learner's blurting out answers as impassioned involvement in the learning experience instead of a hostile act to gain attention, then responses other than ignoring the learner would suggest themselves, along with a change in voice, demeanor, and perhaps even a chance for some disarming humor.

Reframing is not a trick or manipulation. It stems from realizing that people hold multiple ideas about the world they experience. Often these are different from the instructor's. With this in mind, we can view the behavior of others positively and then sincerely act toward them accordingly.

We have found that teachers who are familiar with and can embody the norms explored in this chapter have the most ease in using reframing with integrity. If you are not clear about these norms, you may want to review them before proceeding. This procedure is not meant to eliminate talking to someone about a sensitive matter (see the discussion of culturally responsive teacher-learner conferences in Chapter Three). Reframing is a creative alternative.

The process of reframing has the following elements (Molnar and Lindquist, 1989, p. 61):

1. Awareness of your current interpretation of what you consider to be the problem behavior
2. Creation of positive alternative interpretations of the behavior
3. Selection of a plausible positive interpretation
4. Formulation of a sentence or two that describes the new positive interpretation
5. Action that sincerely reflects this new interpretation

We have found that using these elements to reflect on problematic student behaviors is an excellent process for generating creative and effective solutions.

Participation Agreements

Participation agreements or collaboration guidelines are the specific and explicit assumptions that govern the operation of the class. When the teacher clearly identifies the kinds of interactions that will be encouraged and discouraged, participants can create a climate of safety that promotes a disposition toward openness, initiative, and intellectual rigor.

The first class meeting is a prime opportunity to present a set of draft guidelines and to clarify and negotiate them, with the goal of shared commitment. Participation agreements can be entirely constructed in a collaborative manner with learners. However, courses whose primary purpose is to diminish social injustices such as racism and sexism usually report greater chances for mutual respect among learners and teachers when the teacher suggests ground rules and assumptions (Brookfield and Preskill, 2005; Adams, Bell, and Griffin, 2007). For example, if the course holds a committed perspective that learners will be using as they study, such as a feminist viewpoint or a value system that favors change toward equality in society, this should be clearly communicated. Therefore, the idea of striving for equality is not up for debate, although what equality means and how best to achieve it are issues that require thought and discussion. Such clarity about operating assumptions helps learners know what to expect and how it will be framed, reducing the emergence of unnecessary conflict. As an example, Beverly Daniel Tatum (1992) sets out the context and working assumptions in her course on the psychology of racism.

Using a consensus decision-making process, where everyone has to agree, we have found the following guidelines to be acceptable as well as extremely beneficial to establishing inclusion (Adams and Marchesani, 1992; Tatum, 1992, Griffin, 2007).

1. Avoid using put-downs, even for comic relief.

2. Respect the confidentiality of the group.

3. Speak from one's own experience, for example, "I think ..." or "In my experience I have found ..." rather than generalize our experience to others, as in, "People say ..." or "We believe ..."

4. Diminish the tendency to blame.

5. Take responsibility and maintain a problem-solving disposition when conflict arises.

6. Carefully listen.

7. Offer honest expressions and opinions.

8. Share airtime.

9. Be responsible for the quality of the discussion.

10. Acknowledge that racism, sexism, class discrimination, and stereotypes exist and try actively to combat them.

Although we do not use a specific conflict negotiation model, a method that we have found effective when a serious disagreement emerges is to request that before stating an opposing opinion, the individual must be able to state the position of the other person in a way that will satisfy that person. This usually helps to defuse careless arguing.

Most learners easily accept and generate these guidelines because they reduce feelings of awkwardness, embarrassment, and a sense of being threatened. They also provide a framework for critical discourse, an essential component of challenging learning and an equitable society. Leaving participation agreements open to further additions and referring to them as necessary keeps the boundaries of the class clear and dynamic.

Learning Communities

To establish inclusion, we have encouraged the idea of building community among learners. Although learning communities as planned structures take many different forms in postsecondary education (Kuh and Associates, 2005), we use *learning communities* to describe the intentional design of a curriculum to link together courses or different disciplines around a common theme. That way students find greater coherence in what they are learning and have increased interaction with faculty and peers inside and outside of class (Smith, MacGregor, Matthews, and Gabelnick, 2004).

Most learning communities are found in undergraduate programs. They usually teach with highly active, collaborative learning experiences, build community by enrolling students in cohort groups or large blocks of coursework, and provide intellectual coherence for students by developing relationships between various subject areas, or by teaching a skill such as writing in the context of a subject area. For example, a course for a learning community might teach science with religion or emphasize writing through the use of a literary perspective to understand psychology. Teams of faculty representing these different disciplines would teach these courses. In general, where learning communities have been well developed and administratively supported, institutional research indicates that they contribute to increasing student persistence and degree completion (Kuh and Associates, 2005).

As Emily Decker Lardner (2003) points out, learning communities can attract underserved students as well as help them persist and be successful by (1) focusing on a specific group of learners, (2) acting as a means for transforming curriculum, and (3) creating instructional practices that support diverse students. The University of Texas–El Paso serves as an illustrative example. At the University of Texas–El Paso, a commuter campus where 70 percent of the students are Hispanic and 55 percent are first generation college students, the goal was to increase access for students of color to science, math, and engineering. In the late 1990s, after taking placement tests in math and English, students joined learning communities organized around their mathematical skills. In the learning community program, for students entering science, math, or engineering, the retention rate was 80 percent after one year. Such success contributed to an increase in learning communities across many disciplines, including science and engineering as well as the arts and social sciences. As of fall 2003, almost all entering students enrolled in a learning community (Kuh and Associates, 2005).

According to Tinto (1987) retention is a function of three strategies, all of which can be incorporated into the design of learning communities and all of which influence the primary concern of this chapter, establishing a community of learners who are respected and connected to each other and to faculty:

1. Integrating social and academic activities, formally and informally
2. Addressing issues of academic preparedness, making sure that students have the skills they need in order to be academically successful once they are admitted to our campuses
3. Engendering a sense of belonging to a community on campus

In general, learning communities have the potential to provide joint enterprise, mutual engagement, and shared repertoire among faculty (Wenger, 1998). Because of their interdisciplinary nature and orientation toward innovation, they can serve as a context for ongoing curriculum transformation and exploration of new pedagogical practices that respect and respond to diverse student groups. Learning communities are a useful model for how postsecondary institutions can construct the kind of educational setting in which diverse students will want to become involved. (For a comprehensive discussion of learning communities that addresses their conception, implementation, and learning processes, we suggest Smith, MacGregor, Matthews, and Gabelnick 2004 and Fogarty and others, 2003.)

Cooperative Base Groups

Another possible practice to enhance inclusion is cooperative base groups. These are heterogeneous, cooperative learning groups with stable membership that last for the duration of a course or longer, depending on how a college creates its calendar. For members in this kind of group, Johnson and Johnson (2006, p. 497) outline these essential responsibilities. "To 1) provide one another with support, encouragement, and assistance in completing assignments; 2) hold one another accountable for striving to learn; and 3) ensure that all members are making good academic progress." Cooperative base groups meet regularly, usually at least once a week, inside or outside of class. The larger the class or the more complex the subject matter, the more base groups can provide a sense of connectedness and reduce feelings of alienation and anomie. Such groups also increase the probability that diverse perspectives will be shared, adding richness and intrinsic value to the learning experience.

Based on our own experience and the guidelines we've adapted from the work of Johnson, Johnson, and Smith (1998), we suggest the following ideas and goals. To effectively establish base groups:

1. Use cooperative learning groups from the beginning of the course for class activities and instructional purposes until the five essential components (see the section on cooperative learning in this chapter) are understood and some expertise in using cooperative learning is evident among the learners before assigning base groups.

2. Have a reasonable awareness of your students, and wait for class membership to stabilize before assigning base groups.

3. Set base groups at three to five members to allow diversity and lessen the pressure of initial interdependence.

4. Schedule frequent meetings of the base groups during class time. The beginning or ending of class often works best.

5. Ensure that the students understand the purposes of the base groups.

We suggest the following goals for base groups, which can be modified according to course and learners' profile:

1. To provide assistance, support, and encouragement for mastering course content and skills and to offer feedback on how well the content and skills are being learned

2. To provide assistance, support, and encouragement for thinking critically about course content, understanding what one learns, engaging in intellectual controversy, getting work done on time, and applying new learning to one's own life and other contexts

3. To provide comradeship throughout the course and a means for trying out collaborative learning procedures and skills

4. To provide a structure for managing course procedures, such as homework, attendance, and assessment

5. To enjoy one's success and help other groups to be successful until all members of the class are successful. This serves as an opportunity to share the rewards of the members' talents and experiences

It often helps to provide an agenda for base group meetings, especially in their beginning phase—for example:

1. Checking in, using such questions as, "How are people doing, and are we all prepared for this class period?" "Has everyone read the assignment [done the problems]?"

2. Focusing on academic support by checking the assignments each member has and what help he or she may need to understand or complete them, preparing for tests and reviewing them afterward, and sharing expertise and helping each other to practice skills (during or outside class).

3. Summarizing, reviewing, or critiquing what students have read and sharing resources they have found regarding course content and assignments.

4. Getting to know each other better by asking such questions as, "What are some good things that have happened to us this week? Have we had any challenges or problems that we might help each other with?"

Some base groups face relationship challenges. Some take longer to cohere. Teacher patience and the suggestions offered in the earlier discussion of group processing in this chapter apply to base groups as well. Periodically using a short survey to assess how base groups are functioning, as well as being available to meet with them to enhance relationships, are typical ways to ensure the success of this practice from the beginning to the end of a course. (For information about college base groups—those lasting from a year to four years—and advisee base groups, see Johnson, Johnson, and Smith, 1998.)

Conclusion

In this chapter we have discussed norms and practices to create a learning environment with attendant experiences and consequences that foster a critical motivational condition—in this case, inclusion. Although the four conditions of the motivational framework—establishing inclusion, developing a positive attitude, enhancing meaning, and engendering competence—work in concert and are mutually dependent, our goal was to share specific teaching practices, such as cooperative learning, that contribute to the first condition of the motivational framework.

What we believe and how we act are inextricably bound. Until we espouse norms and attempt to put them into practice, there will be little chance for genuine transformation in postsecondary teaching. Nowhere is this truer than in the area of inclusion. In the vignette at the start of this chapter, Wayne Johnson recalled a classroom where he (but not his classmates) was able to see for himself the importance of being included as a learner. A mere teaching technique is not foundation to such a faith. It is the result of an intentional symmetry between explicit ideals and practices.

The commitment to helping students feel acutely aware of their inclusion in a learning environment throughout a learning experience requires a certain amount of vulnerability among instructors. This attribute involves a refusal to allow personal contradictions to thwart a vision of humanity that is just and kind. Inclusion is the result of complicated interactions.

We end this chapter with the following checklist to use as a guide in the ongoing challenge to create the conditions in which every student feels respected and connected.

Establishing Inclusion

- Routines and norms are apparent, and the students understand them:
  - ☐ Routines and norms are in place to help everyone feel that they belong in the session (class).
  - ☐ Students have opportunities to learn about each other.
  - ☐ Students and instructors have opportunities to learn about others' unique backgrounds.
  - ☐ Participation agreements and guidelines are negotiated.
  - ☐ Everyone understands the system of personal and collective responsibility for agreements.
- All participants equitably and actively participate and interact:
  - ☐ The instructor directs attention equitably.
  - ☐ The instructor interacts respectfully with all learners.

☐ The instructor demonstrates to all learners that she or he cares about them.

☐ Students share ideas and perspectives with each other and the instructor (this includes peer participation in a range of peer interactions).

☐ Students know what to do, especially when making choices.

☐ Students assist each other.

3

DEVELOPING ATTITUDE

"I sure did live in this world."

"Really, what have you got to show for it?"

"Show? To who? Girl, I got my mind. And what goes on in it. Which is to say, I got me."

"Lonely, ain't it?"

"Yes. But my lonely is mine. Now your lonely is somebody else's. Made by somebody else and handed to you. Ain't that something? A secondhand lonely."

—Toni Morrison, *Sula*

Although she has been getting above-average test scores, Maria Sanchez feels her positive attitude fading in the geology course taught by Dr. Beverly Kubiak. Maria ruminates over why her opinion of this class has changed, remembering that it seemed to get off to such a good start. Dr. Kubiak began the course with cooperative small group experiments that were authentic representations of what geologists do in their field studies. Although she finds it difficult to explain, Maria knows what bothers her most: she's finishing, not learning. At first the experiments were novel, but now Dr. Kubiak seems to be running out of active learning strategies. The learning is beginning to reflect the huge introductory textbook—lots of information and facts but very little that seems relevant to Maria. She reads and memorizes to pass the tests, but she knows that what she's memorized will evaporate like a mist into thin air once the course is completed.

When she suggested to Dr. Kubiak that she'd like to substitute a couple of different experiments for the ones assigned and that she'd prefer to do the semester's project on geological formations native to the region where she grew up, Dr. Kubiak said she had good reasons why Ms. Sanchez could not do this: the course had specific standards of performance, and there was a related sequence of skill and knowledge acquisition. To alter the assigned pattern would interrupt these objectives and unfairly increase Dr. Kubiak's work load. With a smile, end of conversation.

Maria resisted. She felt as if she had stepped onto a train and didn't like where it was going. She knew Dr. Kubiak's course was better than a few others she'd already passed. Yet somehow she felt indifferent, like the course didn't matter that much. There seemed to be very little room in it for what she might find interesting.

Some people might say that Maria has a bad attitude. She's doing well in a course with a teacher who seems to be fair and uses cooperative and active learning methods. The path to success is clear. Yet from Maria's perspective, the course content is becoming irrelevant. Dr. Kubiak, for reasons that uphold standards of performance and make her workload manageable, will not alter the assigned project to one that is more interesting for Maria. The students who find the given assignments interesting, who are motivated to receive a high grade, who are at ease with benevolent authoritarian teachers, or who possess cultural values that accept and prepare them for this routine would probably find Dr. Kubiak's requirements acceptable, if not typical. For Maria, completing the assignment may be at the very least a boring project done in acquiescence to Dr. Kubiak's authority, and possibly, in a deeper sense, a further step along the path to cultural suicide (Brookfield, 2006).

Yet from Dr. Kubiak's perspective, the rationale she has given Maria is probably legitimate. Her workload may be overwhelming. She may think Maria does not like the assignment because its similarity to the procedures other students must follow forces a comparison between the quality of her work and theirs. Dr. Kubiak may also fear that making an exception for Maria is unfair to the other students, possibly requiring her to individualize assignments for many other students. From each of their viewpoints, Maria and Dr. Kubiak have arguments to support their stance. However, by allowing so little flexibility in the procedures of learning and topical choice, Dr. Kubiak has eliminated opportunities to make learning relevant to the social identities and academic strengths of all her students and inadvertently denied the impact of important cultural influences on learning and motivation.

Many students, especially those whose families and communities have traversed institutionalized racial, class, and gender inequality, have histories and daily encounters that call into question the significance of school. Yet a favorable disposition toward a learning environment, an instructor, or a course is a significant influence on academic success (Tinto, 1998; Rendon, Garcia, and Person, 2004; Allen, 2005). Historically, however, the very notion of human nature has been addressed in terms of an implicit standard that is predominantly white, male, Christian, and Western (Minh-ha, 1989; Hayes & Flannery, 2000; Jackson, 2005; Tatum, 2007). The opportunity for marginalized or historically underserved learners to be heard in their own way and on their own terms, reflecting their own interests and ways of knowing and learning, is institutionally inconceivable in most college classrooms. These conditions are not coincidental. They reflect the ability of those in power to create the terms according to which social reality will be encountered (Lipsitz, 2006).

To deny these political aspects of education is a serious mistake. It is also why, in part, the two most important criteria for developing a positive attitude among learners are relevance and volition. Because attitudes help people to make sense of their world and give cues as to what behavior will be most helpful in negotiating it, irrelevant learning can startle, annoy, and at times frighten. Not only does such a learning experience seem unimportant or strange, we implicitly know we are doing it because of someone else's domination or control. This triggers or develops a negative attitude. We are wasting our time or participating in potentially destructive compromises because of someone's power over us. In such instances, volition would act as a means of avoiding or altering irrelevant learning to better fit our perspectives and values. The absence of voice invites alienation.

Relevance, Volition, and Intrinsic Motivation

Personal relevance is not simply familiarity with a learning activity based on the learner's prior experience. Because of media inundation, a person could be familiar with a particular television program or magazine and find it totally irrelevant. *Personal relevance* is the degree to which learners can identify their perspective and values in the course content, discussion, and methods of inquiry. In other words, the learning processes are connected to who students are, what they care about, and how they perceive and know. In its most comprehensive dimensions, relevancy occurs when learning is contextualized and anchored in the personal, communal, and cultural meanings of the learner; allows the learner's voice to remain intact; and reflects the learner's construction of reality. In this process, the teacher and the learner figuratively become coauthors, taking neither their own view nor the view of the other to be specially privileged but entering into a genuine dialogue, with each standpoint having its own integrity (Clifford, 1986).

Once learners can be spontaneous and authentic, acting from their deepest and most vital selves, they naturally strive for coherence among the aspects of themselves and their world that are in their awareness (Hodgins and Knee, 2002). Their natural curiosity emerges; they want to make sense of things and seek out challenges that are within their range of capacities and values. All of this leads to what human beings experience as interest—the emotional nutrient for a positive attitude toward learning.

When we feel interested, we begin to determine what to do to follow that interest, which leads to volition, the second criterion for developing a positive attitude among learners. Volition, depending on one's cultural orientation, can range from free choice or self-determination to voluntary or valued compliance. In the latter case, learners tend to follow suggestions or directives because such assignments adhere to their socially approved standards. For example, Chirkov, Kim, Ryan, and Kaplan (2003) suggest that in some East Asian societies, people comply with choices that significant others make for them. The genesis of this orientation may be familial, religious, or other cultural beliefs about collective values. When the process of learning—thinking, practicing, reading, revising, and studying—is desirable or enjoyable, learners see themselves as personally endorsing their own learning.

Psychological research and global history merge to support this observation: people consistently struggle against oppressive control and strive to determine their lives as an expression of their beliefs and values. For educators, the question is not whether we should but how we can provide students with relevant learning options while initiating learning with respect for students' perspectives, values, strengths, and needs. The consideration of the role of language as it relates to learners' attitudes can deepen our understanding of how to approach some of the answers to this multifaceted question.

Language and Attitude

Integral to relevance and the development of a positive attitude toward learning is the learner's ability to identify with the values of the learning context and to negotiate inconsistencies for social, intellectual, emotional, creative, and spiritual growth. Data from several studies about the experiences of immigrant students suggest that students enter U.S. schools with a highly positive attitude toward education (Fuligni, 1997; Suarez-Orozco & Suarez-Orozco, 2002). But these attitudes are difficult to maintain amid identity threats and various forms of disparagement, both subtle and direct. In fact, under such circumstances, it is not uncommon for students to direct their energy (that is, their motivation) toward protecting their emotional and cultural well-being.

Language is perhaps the strongest influence on whether a student believes that what is happening in the classroom is relevant to his or her own beliefs, needs, and interests. In fact, Wetherall and Potter (1992) propose that because language manifests values and shapes reality, words are deeds. Language significantly contributes to the common ground that supports the capacity to accept and negotiate differences between people. Under such circumstances, purposes, interests, values, and outlooks among people become mutually understandable and trusted. Although culturally respectful communication skill is too large and complex a topic to be adequately discussed in a book with our focus, we briefly suggest two fundamental concerns: (1) negotiating language with learners to remove inaccurate and demeaning labels and (2) understanding how language can be used to promote participation among bilingual or multilingual students who are in the process of developing English proficiency with academic language.

Negotiating Terminology

As many instructors in culturally diverse classrooms quickly discover, certain words or terms have connotations that make them acceptable or objectionable to different people. Literal definitions interact with connotations, and ultimately connotations may be the most significant reason that a word is accepted or rejected. In addition, words and terms change periodically with new rationales. For example, *American Indian* is a term that has been reclaimed by many native people. *Native American*, a term once preferred among many American Indian activists, is sometimes criticized for its nonspecific reference to all native people—including native Hawaiians, members of indigenous Alaskan communities, Aleuts, and people whose families originate from the part of the United States that was once Mexico. Although *American Indian*, which connotes residence on the U.S. mainland, is sometimes preferred to the more generic *Native American*, many Indian people prefer reference to their specific tribal affiliation when possible.

Another term that is commonly used but is criticized by some for subsuming vast numbers of distinct peoples under a single rubric is *Hispanic*, a term originally created by the U.S. government. Hispanic people can originate from several global communities, including countries such as Cuba, Puerto Rico, Mexico, Spain, and Portugal and nations in Central *or* South America. Some people prefer *Latino*, which connotes identification with Latin or Meso-America, which comprises several indigenous languages. Some people prefer *Chicano*, a term that was reclaimed by people from Mexico to stress the strong and unique culture that has been continuously developing in the United States. In that *Latino* and *Chicano* are masculine terms, many people encourage the use of *Latina* and *Chicana* in reference to women. The evolution of group names and ethnic identities is a reflection of ever-changing politics. Culture and cultural identity are not static concepts. Thus, language and even name identification evolve over time.

Native American and *Hispanic* are but two examples of the possible variations and personal preferences of identification within ethnic groups. Seeking to understand in a respectful dialogue rather than attempting to be "correct" can lead to deeper cross-cultural relationships. As other words arise in conversation, it may be necessary or desirable to ask for other perspectives. This can be easy and enjoyable—especially when, early on, students have had experience identifying potentially problematic words, considering alternatives, and selecting language that conveys the greatest degree of respect. Different classes may elect different words of which to be cognizant. There is not a perfect solution to words that seem outdated, inaccurate, or pejorative. Even if this were so, we do not want to be so self-conscious as to inhibit all forms of communication out of fear of making a mistake. The experience of openly learning together and appreciating that language strongly influences our ability to be heard and to be fair is foremost. We have known verbal purists who rarely make a mistake with language but who thwart rather than invite sincere dialogue. Our goal is greater appreciation for each other and the diversity of meaning we convey.

The process of negotiating language can take many forms. Our preference has been, when appropriate, to initiate a conversation early on with a class about terms or language that could jeopardize the ability to be heard and to hear others. We ask learners to think for a moment about words that cause self-consciousness when used or heard. We also ask learners to think of words that can trigger resentment. Students pursue this process in concert with a partner, recording words and related concerns. Working in partnership enhances the involvement of all class members and creates a less reactive alternative to a large-group discussion. We then ask partners to identify other words that may be more acceptable. Finally, we come together as a class to compose a list of awkward or problematic terms and expressions and to identify alternatives. Even if different preferences for certain terms are expressed within a group, the experience of negotiating language sets the stage for greater understanding and latitude later when words might otherwise create obstacles. In fact, we often invite deliberation about a protocol or norm that can increase the likelihood and comfort among a class for teaching each other in the moment when a learning opportunity regarding language use presents itself.

Promoting Participation for Nonnative Speakers of English

The scholarship of Jim Cummins (1981) has greatly influenced methods that teachers of English language learners use. Distinguishing between language used for social and academic purposes, Kate Kinsella's consolidation (1993) of Cummins's theory offers college teachers a number of insights.

Basic interpersonal communications skills (BICS) is the social language that enables language learners to participate in everyday conversation. Social language is acquired naturally in daily interactions at school, at work, and through socializing with peers. Therefore, the more opportunities learners have to communicate in a variety of contexts in English, both in and away from school, the faster they tend to become fluent in social English. Most of the common activities in college classes require not only a strong foundation in BICS but an equally high proficiency in cognitive academic language proficiency (CALP). CALP is the academic language that enables learners to deal with more cognitively demanding and context-reduced communicative situations and materials, such as formal lectures, lengthy class discussions, standardized tests, textbooks, and other educational media.

Research suggests that it takes English learners approximately two years to become proficient with BICS and five to seven years to acquire competence with CALP. Academic language proficiency is largely developed through extensive reading in a variety of academic contexts and through years of repeated exposure to academic terminology during class. However, many English learners enter the U.S. school system or advance to mainstream secondary and postsecondary content-area classes with limited academic literacy in English. In fact, learners who speak social English fluently may have academic reading and listening skills that are in the initial stages of development.

To further clarify the distinction between BICS and CALP, Cummins has proposed that language uses be located on a quadrant with two continua. The horizontal line in Figure 3.1 distinguishes between context-embedded communicative situations, which offer a variety of contextual clues to assist in the comprehension of language (for example, facial expressions, gestures, real objects, and feedback from the speaker or listener), and context-reduced communicative situations, which offer few clues (for example, a formal lecture, a textbook page, a calculus equation). The vertical line in Figure 3.1 extends from cognitively undemanding to cognitively demanding communicative situations. The distinction between these two may be explained as the difference between a more automatic subconscious control of the routines of everyday life (undemanding) and a conscious deliberate focus on comprehending new language, concepts, and material (demanding).

Although, at a theoretical level, the distinction between BICS and CALP is not without controversy (Edelsky and others, 1983; Wiley, 1996), it is fair to say that common academic activities within college classes are both cognitively demanding and context reduced, making comprehension and retention of material extremely challenging for learners who have not yet achieved full English language proficiency. Instructors across all

Figure 3.1 Range of Contextual Support and Degree of Cognitive Involvement in Communicative Activities

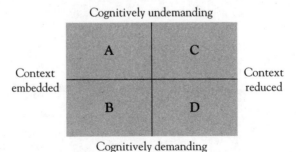

Source: Kinsella (1993, p. 12). Used by permission.

disciplines can greatly enhance learning and participation for English language learners by adding linguistic and contextual support to their lessons, thereby moving the cognitively demanding curriculum from quadrant D (context reduced) to quadrant B (context embedded). For example, students learning another language with the use of audiotapes (context reduced) would much prefer learning the same language in conversation with fluent speakers of the language in real-life settings (context embedded).

One can immediately see the advantages of collaborative, experiential, and active learning procedures that tend to be context embedded and rich with communication cues. In Resources E and F, we have provided Kinsella's suggestions for increasing the effectiveness of discussions and lectures that involve English-language learners.

Norms for Developing a Positive Attitude

With an awareness and expectation that learning will be consistently relevant and volitional, we offer two norms that help learners develop a positive attitude toward learning. These norms create an awareness and an expectation that within the educational community, learning will include their suggestions and relate to what they view as important based on their experience. The first norm is: *Generally, all teaching and learning activities are contextualized in the learners' experience or previous knowledge and are accessible through their current thinking and ways of knowing.* Principles and abstractions can be related to the everyday world of the learners (Tharp, 1989). Personal and community-based experiences can be elicited to provide a foundation for developing skills and knowledge. However, there are many ways to demonstrate openness to learners' knowledge, experience, values, and preferences. When application of learning is considered, for example, we encourage instructors to be especially alert to the interests and cultural perspectives of the learners. When learners' previous circumstances and current knowledge have not allowed the development of personal interest in the topics and concepts to be examined, it is wise to create experiences where students see for themselves how new opportunities are relevant (see Chapter Four).

A pedagogical approach to fostering this norm is offering learner choice and teaching to a range of profiles of intelligences and cognitive strengths (Gardner, 2006). Postsecondary educators, however, may want to keep in mind that not all students equally value the opportunity to make choices. Some find following a prescribed approach to learning more comfortable. Many postsecondary educators learn quickly that although the opportunity for choice bears a relationship to significant social and motivational purposes, it is wise to offer suggestions or guidance to students when introducing such opportunities. An important goal is to identify and respond to the variation within any group of students.

Pragmatically, the second norm, *learner volition*, enables teachers to establish relevance in multicultural classrooms. From a purely functional standpoint, educators cannot possibly be aware of all the experiences and backgrounds of all students. We need ways to hear a range of voices, and unless there are meaningful choices for learners about how and what to learn, their voices have little chance to be genuinely expressed about academic matters. Also, the process of colearning requires acceptance of the learners' prerogative. This norm means the educational community accepts and understands that *the entire academic process of learning, from content selection to accomplishment and assessment of competencies, encourages learners to make choices based on their experiences, values, needs, and strengths.* In general, students enjoy thinking about what, how, how well, and why they learn.

Choosing what to learn is usually a fairly direct process. Choices include the actual topic, the types of materials dealing with the topic, the skills or questions of concern relative to the topic, or the types of assignments and learning goals based on the topic. How teachers frame topics and assignments usually determines the degree to which learners may be autonomous.

Consider this wording: "After you have read the assigned story, select one of these two artists and exemplify how you imagine she would render an expression of the story's protagonist." Another possibility is, "Select a story by one of your favorite authors, and consider an artist whose work has passionately affected you. Then exemplify how that artist might render an expression of what you find most vital about the story." Each assignment offers choice, but the degree of potential choice and relevance varies considerably between the two possibilities.

Issues about how to learn relate to learner choice. Among them are whether to work alone, in small groups, or as an entire class. There is also the matter of where to learn: in class, in the community, on a class trip, and so on. If practice reflects theory, most postsecondary educators apparently believe that all students learn in similar ways. College classrooms continue to use the lecture and the textbook as their main staples of instruction. However, our understanding of individual learning tells us that learners who are motivated to learn but whose own learning styles and profiles of intelligence are not in tune with prevailing instructional practice are frequently casualties of this system (Gardner, 1991). The norm for learner volition means that schools and teachers make efforts to provide instruction and resources compatible with the variety of capabilities and preferred ways of learning among students. For example, some people may be better able to remember and understand a quantitative concept in biology if it is approached numerically and with deductive reasoning (abstract quantitative, as in an analysis of reported research), while others may be more likely to excel by dealing directly with the materials that experientially embody or convey the concept and its numerical considerations (concrete-quantitative, as in a field study). Making these choices available to learners increases their chances of learning in an engaging way that is relevant to their characteristic learning modes.

Conventional postsecondary teachers may see offering learners opportunities to decide how well they have learned something as the most radical set of academic choices to make available to learners. Yet this is probably the kind of decision making that provides the greatest sense of control over one's learning. Determining the criteria by which work will be judged and then playing a role in assessing work against those criteria makes one's personal sense of responsibility for learning self-evident, catalyzes motivation to be autonomous and competent, and is a terrific learning experience in itself. Learners can derive immense intellectual benefits from considering what makes an essay well written, a problem solution creative, or an example conceptually clear. When learners help to decide what a test should include and how it should be given, that they are determining their own learning is evident. (We address this issue more thoroughly in Chapter Five.)

For learners, choosing why they are learning something gets at the philosophical heart of their own education. Cultural values are bound to enter into the creation of the purposes that direct learning. Consider, for example, that when learners believe in why they are solving a problem or developing a project, their learning has a chance to attain deep personal significance as well as intellectual insight. Do we conduct a research study only to find an answer, or also to elevate our minds with a fuller understanding of an important phenomenon? Do we decide on an environmental project because it is a convenient way to complete a course, or because it might offer an insight about something we believe ought to remain on this earth? When courses align their purposes with the deeply held beliefs of their learners, something quite powerful and lasting for learners and teachers is possible.

Resistance to the norm of learner volition is not uncommon among students. Schooling frequently socializes us to accept a posture of passivity. Schooling has also created conditions in which a mistrust of authorities who offer choice can be a response to a history of feeling manipulated or used for "experimental purposes." Furthermore, some learners have found schooling to be so oppressive and difficult that they believe the locus of causality in learning is outside themselves. Choice only increases their sense of apprehension.

It is also important to respect the authoritarian and hierarchical orientation toward sustained learning held, for example, by some international students. These learners may find too much choice to be a disorienting and uncomfortable option. Therefore, we recommend that this norm be established as a flexible set of assumptions where learners still find among their choices some of the more conventional alternatives. Where those do not exist, we recommend establishing a support system to help learners evolve toward a more volitional approach to learning. For example, a learner might prefer to take a test based on a standard textbook in order to convey her or his grasp of a set of concepts rather than to create a project in a collaborative learning group that offers a robust display of similar knowledge. If such a preference can be accommodated without destroying the integrity of the course, this or a similar option should be made available. With each subsequent set of choices, learners can be encouraged to try other approaches. Admittedly at times, this is a tightrope we must carefully walk.

Practices for Developing a Positive Attitude

The process of teaching and learning is complicated and, when done well, intricate and subtle. As we begin to discuss practices for developing a positive attitude toward learning, we see more clearly the shift from conventional instructional practices that emphasize discrete, competitive, academic goals to acquiring competence where understanding and relevance are of primary concern (Dweck and Molden, 2005). If educators desire to provide equitable motivational options for diverse learners in postsecondary education, we have to offer complex and meaningful academic experiences that present a variety of performance opportunities across multiple profiles of intelligences. These opportunities should include student preferences as well. In this manner, we can increase the possibilities for the motivated learning of all students, not simply of historically high achievers. Table 3.1 offers a comparison of conventional teaching and culturally responsive teaching.

Table 3.1 Comparison of Conventional Teaching and Culturally Responsive Teaching

Key Elements	Conventional Teaching	Culturally Responsive Teaching
Source of knowledge and skills	Simple, one way, from teacher to learners or textbook to learners. Perceived value is teacher centered.	Complex, teacher-learner interactive, allowing individual search and reflection—frequently with integrated subject matter. Perceived value is amalgam of teacher and learner preferences.
Dominant perspective	Teacher determined.	Learning content inclusive of relevant learner experience and diversity.
Learning environment organization	Hierarchical and linear. Teacher directed. Competitive.	Complex. Thematic, integrative, cooperative, open, and individualized. Teacher-learner controlled.
Preferred outcomes	Specified and convergent. Emphasis on memorized vocabulary, concepts, and skills. Ability-oriented performance.	Complex. Emphasis on understanding and competence, as well as reorganization of knowledge and skills in unique ways. Both predictable and unpredictable outcomes. Divergent and convergent thinking. Learning demonstrated in varied and relevant contexts. Authentic, application-based goals.

Learning Goal Procedures

Supporting learner volition requires minimizing teacher control and using interaction with students to determine their preferences. It also requires making available the information they need for decision making and reaching the agreed-on learning goal (Deci, Vallerand, Pelletier, and Ryan, 1991). As soon as people know the goals and procedures of a course, they begin to form a personal theory about the choices and competencies necessary for accomplishing those tasks (Dweck and Molden, 2005). They ask themselves questions like these:

"What do I already know about this?"

"Is this worthwhile?"

"Where do I start?"

"What can I do to do this well?"

"Am I able to do this?"

"Is the evaluation system used fair and reasonable?"

From this sort of reflection, they hypothesize how much control they can exert and how effective they will be in learning. The conclusions they reach very much influence their attitude toward learning.

Clearly Defined Goals. When specific skills or competencies are appropriate and meaningful, as in technical subject areas such as medicine and engineering, clearly defined goals can heighten learners' conscious awareness of control and competence. These goals let learners know the skills they need to acquire, opening a window to achievement. With clear goals, confusion is less likely, and learners can discuss and negotiate what is expected of them. For English learners, this may be crucial.

Three essential elements (Caffarella, 2002) for constructing a learning objective or goal are who (the learners), how (the action verb), and what (the contents)—for example, "As a result of this lesson in life skills, students (*the learners*) will write (*the action verb*) the section of their résumé that describes their important work experiences (*the contents*)." Dick, Carey, and Carey (2004) suggest two more elements of specific learning objectives: conditions under which the learning is to be demonstrated and the standards or criteria for acceptable performance. An example of combining all five of these elements for a learning goal is: "Working independently (*condition*), each student (*the learners*) will create (*action verb*) a word problem reflecting diverse populations and requiring computation of a correlation coefficient (*the contents*) including the correct solution (*criteria for acceptable performance*) for classmates to solve."

We should not feel compelled to abandon educational aims that cannot be reduced to measurable forms of predictable performance. Unnecessarily standardizing knowledge often devalues critical and intellectual work, trivializing the deeper meanings of relevance and volition. It is through meaningful problem solving, expressive outcomes, or other complex tasks that learning often becomes rigorous and engaging.

Problem-Solving Goals. Much—perhaps most—of what we aspire to and cherish as human beings is not amenable to uniform and prespecified description. Language is a substitute for experience. We try to say in words what we know in nonlinguistic ways. How could one convincingly define integrity or describe how water tastes? As Elliot Eisner (1985) has stated, "For much of our experience, discursive language performs rather well. But for the subtleties of human experience, for our knowledge of human feelings, for modes of conception and understanding that are qualitative, discourse falls far short . . . . The point here is not an effort to inject the mystical into educational planning but rather to avoid reductionistic thinking that impoverishes our view of what is possible. To expect all of our educational aspirations to be either verbally describable or measurable is to expect too little" (p. 115).

The problem-solving goal differs in a significant way from the conventional instructional objective. In the problem-solving goal, the learners formulate or are given a problem to solve. In a social science course, for example, students might be asked how to reduce homophobia on campus, and for an architecture course how to design a paper structure that will hold two bricks sixteen inches above a table. In these examples, a problem is posed, and goals that need to be achieved to resolve the problem can be made fairly clear. But the forms of its solution range from many to infinite (Eisner, 1985; Schön, 1987). Relative to homophobia, some learners might design a conference, addressing topics, format, speakers, and interaction strategies; others might create a course, outlining its syllabus, readings, and learning activities; and another group might develop a survey, research the campus with it, and as a result of the data gathered submit a proposal that best reflects the opinions and suggestions of those interviewed.

The idea here is that the kinds of solutions and the forms they take are highly variable. Alternative solutions to problem-solving goals can be shared in class so that learners can appreciate different perspectives and related outcomes. This enhances relevance and volition and simultaneously affirms the value of multiple perspectives and different ways of constructing meaning.

Problem-solving goals are common in the design field, science laboratories, media arts and technology, and local and national politics. Designers, for example, are typically given a set of criteria or specifications and asked to generate a creation that will satisfy those criteria. Often they are asked to create several alternatives so that the client can decide which of these options best suits his or her needs.

With problem-solving goals, the potential answers are not definite or known beforehand. The problem is a genuine one. The solution learners reach has the possibility of being a genuine surprise for them. Problem-solving objectives place a premium on intellectual exploration and higher mental processes while supporting different cultural perspectives and values. Because this approach encourages ingenuity, it breeds interest for students from a variety of cultures.

Expressive Outcomes. Another type of educational aim, identified by Eisner (1985, 2002), focuses on expressive outcomes—learning goals that emerge as the result of an intentionally planned activity. In these instances, learning goals do not precede educational activity; they are formulated in the process of action itself. They are what we and the learner construct, intended or not, after some form of engagement. How many times have we read a book or seen a film, the brilliance of which becomes a source of new questions and forms of inspirations for us? To limit learners to only clearly defined goals may potentially confine their imagination and academic outcomes. From a personal perspective, when we as educators encourage expressive outcomes, we become more conscious of the reciprocal nature of learning.

Again, this approach supports the preeminence of learner volition and perspective in defining relevant learning goals. To exemplify two of the many forms of open-ended, participative outcomes, we are reminded of two very different courses: an adolescent psychology class and a course on leadership for school change. The adolescent psychology course began by watching and discussing five films mutually selected with students. In each film, adolescents were the main characters. After these viewings and dialogue, students participated in constructing the course topics, the selected reading list, and personal projects that would provide significant evidence of learning. The experience was so successful that the following semester, two seniors from a local high school participated as coteachers.

The Leadership for School Change course was intended to teach about action research, school change, and professional learning that supports adult and student motivation to learn. From a process perspective, a primary goal was to create the same motivational conditions for postsecondary graduate students that these students were seeking to collectively support in a local high school embarking on a significant improvement effort. Graduate students regularly participated in practices to which the school had committed: collaborative classroom visits with teams of teachers, visits with high school students' families in their homes, and the design of lessons with teachers based on the school's instructional priorities. Interactions led to the creation of unique final products that included a digital media representation of a classroom visit process known as "data-in-a-day," a tool that provides a short, intensive opportunity for a school to gather data about issues that both student and staff view as important (Northwest Regional Educational Laboratory, 2008; Ginsberg, 2001). Students also created "funds of knowledge" charts (Gonzalez, Moll, and Amanti, 2005) to represent some of the cultural experiences and forms of knowledge that exist in all families. Finally, some students cocreated lessons with teachers to integrate insights from data-in-a-day, developed culturally relevant curricular ideas from home visits, and constructed content knowledge based on state standards. Their final products varied according to interests and included a photographic journey of the process of planning, implementing, and critiquing original lessons; a conference proposal and paper on the topic; and a portfolio of sample lessons to demonstrate how to integrate cultural knowledge with learning targets. In all instances, the learning goals for the course evolved and became increasingly personalized as students engaged in and reflected on their field-based experiences.

Fair and Clear Assessment Criteria

Assessment is comprehensively discussed in Chapter Five. However, because learning goals and evaluation procedures go hand in hand in most postsecondary courses, we pay some attention here to criteria of evaluation as an attitudinal issue. The outcomes of assessment in the form of grades and quantitative scores powerfully influence volition, self-efficacy, and the access of learners to careers, further education, and financial aid such as scholarships and grants. Therefore, evaluation criteria are highly relevant to developing or inhibiting a positive attitude toward learning.

Our goal is for students to be clear about what assessment looks like and the merits on which their work will be appraised. If we want students to succeed, they should not have to guess what is expected of them. When learning goals are formulated, evaluation procedures and criteria should be simultaneously addressed.

If the criteria for evaluation are clear and agreed to as fair by learners, they know which elements of performance and creativity are essential. This makes it possible for them to more realistically self-evaluate and self-determine their learning as they proceed. This approach fosters learner motivation, because it becomes possible to anticipate the results of personal learning and regulate options for studying, writing, practicing, and so on with greater certainty.

In general, we advocate the importance of demonstrating how we or students, or both of us, will go about assessing the quality of their learning: What are the learning targets? What does "success" look like? What are the grading policies? Common understanding and agreement about indicators of learning are especially important for students for whom higher education is an uncharted experience.

The less mystery there is about assessment, the more it is possible to be self-determined. Even when final products vary, as we noted in the section on expressive outcomes, it is possible to provide examples of what counts as rigorous as well as relevant. For example, past tests, papers, projects, and media offer realistic examples of how evaluation criteria have been and will be applied. These products serve the additional purpose of providing inspiration. They signal that peers from across cultural backgrounds and with a range of skills have accomplished similar goals (Wlodkowski, 2008).

Relevant Learning Models

When learners witness people similar to themselves (in age, gender, ethnicity, class, and so on) competently performing the desired learning goal, their self-confidence is heightened, because they are more likely to believe that they too possess the capabilities to master comparable activities (Bandura, 1997). People whom learners can identify with also convey information more likely to be relevant to the perspectives and values of the learners themselves. This further increases learners' trust in using the strategies they see or that are being suggested to them. Observing similar people successfully perform a learning task is a powerful teaching strategy that extensive research demonstrates is effective. Students who learn vicariously and adapt their model's methods to their own learning are more successful and motivated than those who rely solely on individual means to learn (Zimmerman and Kitsantas, 2005).

Film and video technology provide creative and economical ways to offer learners pertinent and realistic examples. Past students or graduates are an excellent source for live modeling sessions.

Goal Setting

As postsecondary pedagogy becomes more flexible and teaches for relevance across multiple perspectives and abilities, learning goals will more frequently take the form of projects and complex tasks. The process of setting goals can help learners consider their current and future choices related to their learning goals and to become more aware of what is necessary to have an effective learning experience. This prevents learners from creating unrealistic expectations and gives them a chance to anticipate obstacles to learning. Learners realize more clearly that they can determine their own learning and can gauge their probability for accomplishment before even beginning the learning task.

There are many methods of goal setting (Locke and Latham, 2002). The one that we provide here is an eclectic adaptation of various models in the literature. If the learning goal is to have a good chance of being achieved and therefore initiated, the criteria outlined are to be considered with the learner. In order to take these criteria beyond abstract suggestions, we present a case from our experience to exemplify how the criteria can be applied.

Yolanda Scott-Machado, whose tribal affiliation is Makah, is a student in a research course. In order to learn more about a variety of skills and concepts, including research design, validity, reliability, sampling procedures, statistical analysis, and operationalization, she wants to design, conduct, and report a research study in an area of personal interest. Yolanda has questions about the concept of learning styles, especially as it is applied to American Indians. She wants to carry out a study to determine if urban Indian high school students, when compared to urban European American high school students, score significantly higher in the field-sensitive mode (a cognitive style in which patterns are perceived as wholes) as measured by the Witkin's Group Embedded Figures Test. This is an ambitious study for a new research student. We begin the goal-setting process by examining the criterion of achievability.

Achievability. Can the learner reach the learning goal with the skills and knowledge at hand? If not, is there any assistance available, and how dependable is that assistance?

Yolanda feels confident, and her competent completion of exercises in class substantiates that confidence. She is also a member of a class cooperative learning group and values her peers as knowledgeable resources. We work out a plan that includes a preliminary conference with peers to garner their support and a follow-up call to me. Is there enough time to reach the goal? If not, can more time be found, or should the goal be divided into smaller ones? This is a bit tricky. Yolanda will need at least fifty students in each of her comparison groups, which will mean involving two high schools at a minimum. Can she get the necessary permission? Who will do the testing, and when? This could drag on and complicate the study.

Measurability. How will the learner specifically gauge progress toward the goal and its achievement? In many circumstances, this can be done quantitatively, in terms of problems completed, pages read, or exercises finished, for example. To respect different conceptualizations of how to accomplish long-range goals, scheduling intervals to talk about evolving experience is important.

We decide the most important next step is for Yolanda to write a research proposal and bring it in for a meeting with me. Then we might work out a schedule for her study.

Desirability. Why is the goal important? The learner may have to do it or should do it, but does the learner want to do it? If not, then the satisfaction level and sense of self-determination for the learner will be less. Goal setting can be used for required tasks, but this is best handled if we are clear about it and admit to the learner the reality of the situation to avoid any sense of manipulation.

Yolanda wants to do this study. She believes certain teaching practices derived from learning-styles research may not apply to some Northwest Indian tribes or members of urban Indian communities. Because these methods are so often advocated by educators for teaching Indians, she believes more caution about their use may be necessary.

Focus (Optional). For some people, to avoid forgetting or procrastination, it is important to have a plan to keep the goal in the learner's awareness. For others, such an idea may seem oppressive. Possible reminders are outlines, chalkboard messages, and daily logs.

Yolanda found this option unnecessary.

Identifying Resources and Learning Processes. Engaging the learner in a dialogue about how she or he would like to reach the learning goal can be a creative process. This is the time to consider various talents and preferred ways of knowing. Will accomplishing the learning goal involve media, art, writing, or some other possibility? What form should it take: a story, a research project, a personal multimedia presentation? Identifying outside resources such as library materials, local experts, exemplary models, or films aid and sometimes inspire the entire learning process.

Yolanda decided to review the literature on learning styles, especially as it referred to American Indians and other native peoples. She also chose to interview a professor at another university and an Indian administrator at a local school district. She decided the format for reporting her study would be the conventional research thesis outline.

Commitment. A formal or informal gesture that indicates the learner's acceptance of the learning goal is a valuable part of the goal-setting process. It can range from a shared copy of notes taken at the meeting to a contract. This affirms the learner's self-determination and acknowledges the mutual agreement between the learner and the teacher, building trust, motivation, and cooperation for further work together.

Yolanda composed a contract that we agreed on at our next meeting.

Arranging a Goal Review Schedule. Some time for contact between the learner and the teacher to maintain progress and refine learning procedures is usually necessary. Because of the way time varies in its meaning and feeling to different people, contact can be at regular or irregular intervals. The main idea is that trust and support continue.

If progress has deteriorated, reexamine the criteria. Also, it may be helpful to search together for informative feedback (Brophy, 2004) with questions such as, "What's working and why?" and, "What needs to change (or improve) and how?"

We had three meetings at irregular intervals prior to Yolanda's completion of an excellent study. To find a large enough sample for her research, she eventually involved five high schools. Her research indicated that urban Indian high school students are more field independent than European American high school students, suggesting the possibility that previous research conducted on American Indian learning styles is far from conclusive across tribes and regions.

Learning Contracts

One of the fields most familiar with the use of learning contracts is adult education. Practitioners view learning contracts to be a significant means of accommodating cultural differences among students and fostering self-direction to enhance learning (Lemieux, 2001; Berger, Caffarella, and O'Donnell, 2004). They are an effective technique for helping learners pinpoint their learning interests, plan learning activities, identify resources that are relevant, and become skilled at self-assessment (Brookfield, 1986).

The ability to write contracts is a learned skill, and teachers may have to spend considerable time guiding learners to focus on realistic and manageable activities. Our experience as teachers in undergraduate programs and graduate school support Brookfield's observation: "Particularly in institutions where other departments and program areas conform to a more traditional mode, learners will often find it unsettling, inconvenient, and annoying to be asked to work as self-directed learning partners in some kind of negotiated learning project. Notwithstanding the fact that learners may ultimately express satisfaction with this experience, initially, at least, there may be substantial resistance. It is crucial, then, that learners be eased into this mode . . . and faculty must make explicit from the outset the rationale behind the adoption of these techniques" (pp. 82–83).

Learning contracts are used to personalize the learning process and provide maximum flexibility for content, pace, process, and outcome. They usually detail in writing what will be learned, how the learning will be accomplished, the period of time involved, and frequently the evaluation criteria for assessing the learning. Learners can construct all, most, or part of the contract depending on their and their teacher's knowledge of the subject matter, resources available, restrictions of the program, and so on. For example, what is learned (objective) may not be negotiable, but how it is learned may be wide open to individual discretion. The actual document is frequently divided into these categories (Berger, Cafarrella, and O'Donnell, 2004):

- The learning goal or objective. (What are you going to learn?)
- The choice of resources, strategies, and activities for learning. (How are you going to learn it?)
- The target date for completion.

- Evidence of accomplishment. (How are you going to demonstrate your learning?)
- Evaluation criteria for learning. (What criteria will you use to evaluate your learning, and who will participate in that evaluation process?)

Exhibits 3.1 through 3.3 are different types of learning contracts. Exhibit 3.1 applies to a specific skill to be accomplished in a short period of time in an undergraduate communication skills course. Exhibit 3.2 applies to a broad and comprehensive learning goal to be accomplished within a full semester in a graduate education program. Exhibit 3.3 is the contract that Yolanda Scott-Machado submitted. (Whether grades should be assigned to learning contracts is discussed in Chapter Five.)

Nancy Berger, Rosemary Caffarella, and Judith O'Donnell (2004) have some helpful ideas about the use of learning contracts with learners who are inexperienced or unfamiliar with them:

- Enlist the aid of learners more familiar with designing learning contracts to help those beginning this process.

Exhibit 3.1 Learning Contract for a Specific Skill

Learning goal: To apply paraphrasing skills to actual communication situations.

Learning resources and activities: View videotapes of paraphrasing scenarios. One hour of role playing paraphrasing situations with peers.

Target date: End of one week (date specified).

Evidence of accomplishment: Participate in a paraphrasing exercise under the teacher's supervision.

Evaluation for learning: Can contribute appropriate paraphrasing responses to 80 percent of the communicated messages. Validated by teacher.

Exhibit 3.2 Learning Contract for a Broad Goal

Learning goal: To learn about the effects of parent influence on student learning in school and to learn how to increase parent-school involvement in support of student learning activities.

Learning resources and activities: Conduct a computer search for relevant research from the Educational Resources Information Center. Read this literature, and attend a workshop on parent partnerships sponsored by the National Association for the Education of Young Children and the National Black Child Development Institute. Read books and articles by prominent parent involvement researchers and advocates, including Joyce Epstein, James Comer, Luis Moll, Norma Gonzales, and Angela Valenzuela. Interview three parents or custodial family members, three teachers, and three administrative leaders on this topic. If possible, interview parents or family members in their home to learn about the aspects of their lives that they might not think to mention in an interview but that are examples of skill and knowledge evident in their home. (Work with an interpreter so that it is possible to interview at least one family member who speaks a home language other than English.)

Target date: End of semester (date specified).

Evidence of accomplishment: Create a parent/family-teacher handbook containing the following sections: The Role of Parents and Family Members as Educators of Their Children; How to Develop School and Family Partnerships; Involving Families in Student Learning; Communication Between Family Members and School Personnel; and Suggestions for Successful Family-Teacher Conferences. Make a one-hour presentation on the topic of "Families and Schools: A Two-Way Commitment" to a local community group, and videotape the program. On completion, present the handbook, videotape, workshop participant evaluations, and self-evaluation. If possible, conduct a follow-up interview with a participant who is from a cultural background and linguistic group that is different from my own.

Evaluation for learning: Handbook will be clearly written for an audience of families, educators, and community members; will use examples consistent with the experiences of the intended audience and will contain recent research and references. Workshop evaluations will indicate the presentation was useful for learning new ways to strengthen teacher-parent collaboration. My self-evaluation will identify the value of what I learned from this entire process. My follow-up interview will include questions such as (1) In what ways did the presentation speak to you? (2) When were you most engaged? (3) When were you least engaged? (4) Are there ways in which my presentation made you want to learn more or try something new? (5) Is there something that you have learned from your experience or reading that I might want to include in future presentations?

Exhibit 3.3 Learning Contract for a Research Study

Learning goal: To conduct a research study to determine if American Indian high school students when compared to urban European American high school students have a significant perceptual difference as measured by the Witkin's Group Embedded Figures Test.

Learning resources and activities: Conduct a review of the literature on learning styles, especially as this concept relates to American Indians. Interview a professor at the University of Washington who specializes in the relation of learning styles to people of color. Also, interview a local American Indian school administrator who has responsibility for a number of projects involving American Indian students. Carry out the research in communication with my cooperative learning group and our instructor.

(continued)

Target date: Two weeks before the end of the semester, to allow for revisions.

Evidence of accomplishment: Completed research study according to the design agreed on by myself and my instructor.

Evaluation for learning: A self-evaluation indicating what I learned and why it was important to me. Validation by the instructor and an American Indian graduate student regarding the quality of my research design and analysis and the soundness of my discussion and conclusion as drawn from the research evidence. For this validation, my teacher and I will compare the elements and structure of my research report to the studies offered as excellent models of research at our first meeting.

- Give those with less experience more time to develop their plans.

- Allow less experienced learners to develop a minilearning plan and then complete a more in-depth one.

- Give learners clear guidelines for developing contracts. Supply a number of diverse samples to encourage a variety of learning processes and outcomes.

- Expect that the evaluation criteria for learning are likely to be the most challenging aspect of constructing the learning contract. Most students do not have much practice in creating criteria to evaluate their work and need support and encouragement.

In general, the use of learning contracts is often, like good writing, a process of revision and refinement. Remaining open to feedback from learners about their contracts and staying flexible and ready to make reasonable adjustments are ways to ensure their effective use.

Approaches Based on Multiple Intelligences Theory

We subscribe to the definition of intelligence, offered by Howard Gardner (2006), as the ability to solve problems or fashion products that are valued in one or more cultural or community settings. Problems may range from how to create an end to a mystical story to finding a physics equation that describes the interaction among subatomic particles. Products entail anything from making delicious bread to creating musical compositions to designing computer software. The range appears to be nearly infinite and highlights the realization that intelligence cannot be conceptualized apart from the context in which individuals live.

Gardner describes nine intelligences (see Table 3.2) and understands there are probably more. Each, however, makes no sense as an abstraction, as a biological entity (like the stomach), or

Table 3.2 Gardner's Multiple Intelligences

Intelligence	Example	Core Components
Linguistic	Novelist Journalist	Sensitivity to the sounds, rhythms, and meanings of words; sensitivity to the different functions of language, written and spoken
Logical	Mathematician Accountant	Sensitivity to and capacity to discern logical and numerical patterns; ability to handle long chains of inductive and deductive reasoning
Musical	Composer Guitarist	Abilities to produce and appreciate rhythm, tone, pitch, and timbre; appreciation of the forms of musical expressiveness

(Continued)

Table 3.2 Gardner's Multiple Intelligences (Continued)

Intelligence	Example	Core Components
Spatial	Designer Navigator	Capacities to perceive the visual-spatial world accurately and to perform transformations on one's initial perceptions and mental images
Bodily-Kinesthetic	Athlete Actor	Abilities to know and control one's body movements and handle objects skillfully
Interpersonal	Therapist Politician	Capacities to discern and respond appropriately and communicate the moods, temperaments, motivations, and desires of other people
Intrapersonal	Entrepreneur Spiritual leader	Access to one's own feelings and inner states of being with the ability to discriminate among them and draw on them to guide behavior; knowledge of one's own strengths, weaknesses, desires, and intelligences
Naturalist	Botanist Zoologist	Capacity to recognize and classify plants, animals, mineral, and objects or phenomena in nature
Existential[a]	Cosmologist Philosopher	Capacity to conceptualize phenomena and questions beyond sensory evidence, such as the infinite and the genesis of morality

[a]At the time of this writing, this intelligence has been provisionally identified by Gardner (2006).

Source: Adapted from Viens and Kallenbach (2004); Moran, Kornhaber, and Gardner (2006).

even as a psychological entity (such as emotion). There is always an interaction between biological proclivities and the opportunities for learning that exist in a culture (Kornhaber, Krechevsky, and Gardner, 1990). For example, a person might have the potential to be a great chess player, but if that person happened to be born in a culture without chess, that potential may never be realized. This individual's spatial or logical intelligence might distinguish him or her eventually as a navigator or a scientist, but it is just as possible this person might not excel in any way.

According to Gardner's analysis (2006), all human beings are capable of at least nine different ways of knowing the world— through language, logical-mathematical analysis, spatial representation, musical thinking, the use of the body to solve problems or to make things, an understanding of other individuals, an understanding of self, a capacity to distinguish phenomena in nature, and the ability to reflect on questions beyond sensory data, such as infinity (Moran, Kornhaber, and Gardner, 2006). Where people differ is in the strength of these intelligences—their profile of intelligences—and the ways in which such intelligences are invoked and combined to complete tasks, solve problems, and progress in diverse domains. Therefore, learners possess different kinds of minds and learn, remember, perform, and understand in different ways. All of these ways are inextricably bound to the interaction of a person's biological proclivities with the practices and assumptions of his or her culture.

There is considerable documentation that some people take a primarily linguistic approach to learning, while others favor a spatial or a quantitative tack. Some learners perform best when asked to manipulate symbols of various sorts, while others are better able to demonstrate their understanding through a hands-on process or through interaction with other individuals (Viens and Kallenbach, 2004). Another important implication of multiple intelligences theory is that the cultural tools, procedures, techniques, and social supports are part of one's intelligence, as well as how one demonstrates intelligence.

Without writing and its instruments, how would we know the genius of people such as Alice Walker or Gabriel García Márquez? The crucial question, then, is not, "How intelligent is one?" but, "How is one intelligent?"

In order to realize the potential of a multiple intelligences approach to instruction, we need to remember that each person's profile of intelligences consists of different strengths and weaknesses among the nine intelligences. An effective lawyer probably has a strong profile of linguistic, logical-mathematical, and interpersonal intelligences, but her profile of musical, spatial, and bodily-kinesthetic intelligences may be weaker than that of a professional dancer, and vice versa.

Today's postsecondary educational system largely operates in a way that assumes that everyone can learn the same materials in the same way using uniform measures to test learning. This system is heavily biased toward linguistic—and, to a lesser degree, logical quantitative—modes of instruction. Because people learn in ways that are identifiably distinctive, determined to a large extent by their profiles of intelligences and unique cultural persona, the broad spectrum of learners would be better served if learning involved "rich experiences in which students with different intelligence profiles can interact with materials and ideas using their particular combinations of strengths and weaknesses" (Moran, Kornhaber, and Gardner, 2006, p. 27).

Rich learning experiences are activities in which students personally engage with material rather than try to understand it in abstract and decontextualized ways such as a lecture. These activities usually include projects, research, and problem solving that are collaborative, allowing students to learn from each other's unique profiles of intelligences as well as their own. Using rich learning experiences means avoiding educational formats that ask learners to merely spew back what they have been taught and replacing them with opportunities to use concepts and skills in relevant contexts with their own words and analogies. For example, this could be a project in which students use sociological concepts to analyze and assess a local political campaign in which they participate. As they collaboratively study the financing (logical-mathematical and linguistic intelligences), strategizing (linguistic and interpersonal intelligences), and goals (intrapersonal and existential intelligences) of the campaign, they engage a variety of their profiles of intelligences.

The postsecondary system produces many needless casualties, dropouts, and labeled academic failures because of its inflexibility and resistance to accommodating learners who might exhibit understanding but cannot because the pathways of learning and teaching are restricted to verbal/written and logical/mathematical modes devoid of any context beyond a paper and pencil. For example, a significant student population lacks facility with formal examinations but can display relevant comprehension when problems arise in natural contexts. Teachers and medical educators bear witness to this phenomenon on a daily basis.

Howard Gardner (1993) and teachers/researchers (Viens and Kallenbach, 2004) using multiple intelligences theory to teach adult literacy propose that most topics can be approached through a variety of "entry points" (engagement activities) that roughly map onto the multiple intelligences listed in Table 3.2 and allow a range of learners relevant access. They advocate thinking of any topic as a room with at least five doors or entry points. We have used this approach in teaching and found that these entry points usually accommodate the wide range of cultural backgrounds and profiles of intelligences found among a diverse group of college students. Let us look at these five entry points one by one, considering how each might be used to approach a concept in the natural sciences (photosynthesis) and one in the social sciences (democracy).

A *narrational entry point* presents a story or narrative account about the concept in question. In the case of photosynthesis, a student might describe with appropriate vocabulary this process as it occurs among several plants or trees relevant to his or her environment, describing differences as they are noted. In the case of democracy, the student could trace its beginnings in ancient history and draw comparisons and contrasts with the early development of constitutional government in a selected nation.

A *logical-quantitative entry point* approaches the concept by invoking numerical considerations or deductive or inductive reasoning processes. Photosynthesis could be approached by creating a time line of the steps of photosynthesis and a chemical analysis of the process. In the case of democracy, a student could develop a time line of presidential mandates, congressional bills, constitutional amendments, and Supreme Court decisions that have broadened democratic principles among people in the United States, or analyze the arguments that relevant political leaders throughout history have used for and against democracy.

A *foundational entry point* explores the philosophical and terminological facets of a concept. This approach is appropriate for people who like to pose fundamental questions of the sort often associated with young children and philosophers. For example, a question like "What happens to a good idea if no one pays attention to it?" might be asked by a ten-year-old studying how things are invented or a graduate student studying ancient philosophy. A foundational corridor to photosynthesis might examine a transformative experience of oneself or a relevant individual, family, or institution and compare it with the actual process of photosynthesis assigning parallel roles as they fit (source of energy, catalyst, and so on). A foundational means of access to democracy could ponder the root meaning of the word, the relationship of democracy to other relevant forms of decision making and government, and the reasons one might prefer, or not prefer, a democratic rather than a social political philosophy.

With an *aesthetic entry point*, the emphasis falls on sensory or surface features that appeal to learners who favor an artistic approach to the experience of living. In the case of photosynthesis, the student could look for visual, musical, or literary transformations that imitate or parallel photosynthesis and represent them in artistic formats (for example, painting, dance, mime, video, cartooning, or a dramatic sketch). With reference to democracy, the student could experience and consider the variations of artistic performance that are characterized by group-oriented control versus individual control: a string quartet as compared to an orchestra, experimental modern dance compared to ballet, improvisational acting compared to a stage play, and so on.

The last entry point is an *experiential approach*. Some people learn best with a hands-on approach, dealing directly with the materials that embody or convey the concept. For photosynthesis, such individuals might carry out a series of experiments involving photosynthesis. The learners dealing with democracy might consider a recent relevant news issue and "enact" a democratic procedure—legislative, judicial, or executive; they might then enact another approach to the same issue, replicating a less democratic system from another country and finally compare their experience of the two diverse processes.

A teacher can open a number of doors on the same concept. Rather than presenting photosynthesis only by example or only in terms of quantitative considerations, the teacher makes available several entry points at the beginning or over time. In this way, there is a good chance that diverse learners with different ways of knowing and differing intelligence profiles will find a relevant and engaging way of learning. They may also suggest entry points of their own design. The use of technology such as the Internet can enhance these efforts. In Exhibit 3.4 we present an example of a concept with five entry points.

Multiple entry points are a powerful means for dealing with learner and teacher misconceptions, biases, and stereotypes. When only a single perspective is offered on a concept or problem, learners will understand it only in a limited and rigid fashion. By encouraging learners to develop multiple representations

Exhibit 3.4 Multiple Intelligences Learning Activities

Concept and Related Principle

Concept: All living things are essentially related.

Principle: All human behaviors affect the earth's land, water, and air.

Learning Entry Points

Narrational: Learners generate views of how they recognize the effects of human behavior taking place in other countries and from distant places. Identify behaviors according to whether they harm or benefit the planet. Based on interests generated, select relevant reading materials.

Logical-quantitative: Choose a harmful but controversial human systemic influence such as carbon emissions. After finding data that quantify the effects that result from this systemic influence, search for cultural, economic, and political factors (possibly from a country of interest) that inhibit or exacerbate this influence.

Foundational: Reflect on one's personal influence on the local environment. Consider behaviors that improve the environment and that pollute it. Examine the beliefs, assumptions, and values that appear critical to each set of these behaviors. Create a personal environmental philosophy. Sharing it in small groups is optional.

Aesthetic: Create a sketch, photo journal, video, or poem to depict relevant systemic relationships in one's own environment.

Experiential: Create mini-environments in local yards or terrariums (or both). Experiment according to relevant influences (for example, temperature, water, pollutants, pets, and traffic). Observe and report effects on various life forms.

and having them relate these representations to one another, we can move away from a correct-answer tyranny and arrive at a fuller understanding of our world. Most knowledgeable and innovative practitioners of any discipline are characterized by their capacity to access critical concepts through a variety of routes and apply them to a diversity of situations. In addition, this overall approach makes us colearners with our students and likely to take their views and ideas seriously, with all of us developing a more comprehensive understanding of the topic. Implementing this approach is an enormous challenge, but it is more than time, materials, or methods that may block progress toward teaching of this sort. These issues are manifestations of what we most value and believe. As Gardner (1991) states, "Whether we will choose to follow this route, to educate for understanding is a political issue rather than a scientific or pedagogical one" (p. 248).

Sensitivity and Pedagogical Flexibility Based on the Concept of Style

We are aware of how frequently the literature on teaching diverse learners refers to style (Nieto, 2004; Adams, Jones, and Tatum, 2007). With over twenty measures of learning style in existence, each with its own unique model to follow, the array of choices can be confusing. To the extent that we can, we would like to clarify what may seem to be an overwhelming number of educational imperatives.

Although learning style is a popular concept, there is no common definition of it and no unified theory to explain it (Cassidy, 2004; Desmedt and Valcke, 2004). Learning style is often conceptually lumped with cognitive style. However, cognitive style models are developed in laboratory and clinical settings. They refer to individual differences in cognitive processing—how people perceive, remember, think, and problem-solve (Messick, 1976). For example, some people tend to see and make sense of their world from a holistic perspective, while others approach it more analytically. While the latter persons would want the specifics, facts, and figures first to understand something, the former would request the whole story or picture to comprehend a situation. These preferences show a strong interdependence with personality. Although there is a great deal of research on cognitive styles, most of it has been done with children, and it is unclear how the findings translate to college students or adults and their educational settings (Bonham, 1988; Desmedt and Valcke, 2004).

Learning style concepts are constructed and applied in educational contexts to explain personal preferences and differences in learning (Desmedt and Valcke, 2004). Learning style research tends to emphasize the relationship of the learner to the learning situation versus the notion of how people perceive, remember, and organize information (Hiemstra and Sisco, 1990). For example, some people prefer to learn by doing, using their behavior and its outcomes to understand a theory, whereas others would rather understand the theory before practically applying its ideas. Although learning style models are generally described by their authors as relatively stable and consistent, these claims have no solid research base (Cassidy, 2004). Learning styles appear to vary across tasks and situations (Gardner, 1993). For example, in ethics, a person might prefer knowing a moral principle before applying it to his life circumstance but in the realm of education prefer using a particular teaching method and seeing its results before understanding the theory behind it. Cassidy (2004) concluded from his work on more than twenty learning style measures that further empirical research was needed to provide evidence regarding the validity of these models. As Roland Tharp (1989) has cautioned, we need to avoid the tendency to re-stereotype learners with uncritical or simplistic application of learning style models.

Because different ethnic or cultural groups have different histories, adaptive approaches to reality, and socialization practices, they are likely to differ in their characteristic ways of approaching learning. For example, for those who have learned to directly experience reality and engage in concrete tasks before considering theoretical abstractions, courses that require the comprehension of theory to precede application or laboratory exercises may undermine their best chances to learn. Although such a learning preference is not absolute or true for all content areas, it may be present for a proportion of students and we may need to adjust our teaching accordingly. As Anderson (1988) points out, teachers often view the writing and speaking styles of Mexican Americans, African Americans, and Puerto Rican Americans as too flowery, too subjective, involving an excessive use of metaphors, and using wrong verb tenses. What has been a valuable and valid communication process in their own cultural domain may be perceived as an example of linguistic deficiency in a postsecondary classroom.

A culturally based learning style orientation helps us to realize that these differences are not deficits for one group and indications of greater capability for another group (Adams, Jones, and Tatum, 2007). Understanding that there are cultural differences in how students may prefer to learn can help us as teachers acknowledge our own teaching style preferences (for example, analytical, verbal, and theoretical) and to plan creatively for curricular activities that are more congruent as well as challenging to a variety of students. The five entry points for multiple intelligences accommodate many cultural styles, as do the collaborative learning procedures discussed in Chapter Two. Our experience is that multiple intelligences theory generally provides a more effective and comprehensive instructional approach than any particular theory of learning styles for engaging culturally different learners. The Kolb model of learning, described next, is another broad procedure for incorporating a variety of ways of learning

Experiential Learning: The Kolb Model

Often among diverse learners for particular subjects of study there will be a lack of common experience or preexisting interest in the topic at hand. Relevance may have to emerge through immediate experience, and teachers need a flexible framework for lesson or course design that provides such experience while accommodating cultural and style differences among learners.

Kolb's experiential learning model (Smith and Kolb, 1986) affirms active learning and provides a theoretical configuration for selecting and organizing learning activities that can serve an array of culturally derived differences (Adams, Jones, and Tatum, 2007). This experiential learning theory (Kolb and Kolb, 2005) focuses on the process of learning and offers a constructivist model for designing learning activities that are well integrated. In fact, the model is comprehensive enough to allow a teacher to include Gardner's proposed five entry points (1993) within its learning cycle.

As shown in Figure 3.2, the cycle begins in clockwise movement with the learner's direct involvement in a concrete experience. The learner then uses the processes of observation and reflection, considering the experience from personal or multiple viewpoints, or both, to understand its meaning. Out of this reflection, the learner forms generalizations or abstract concepts. These may be generated with the aid of the theoretical constructs of peers and teachers. The resulting constructs are then, through decisions and actions, tested or experimented, leading to new concrete experiences and thereby starting the learning cycle anew.

Figure 3.2 The Experiential Learning Model

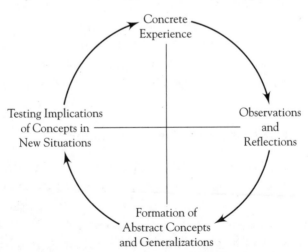

Source: Smith and Kolb, 1986. © Experience-Based Learning, Inc., 1981, revised 1985. Developed by David A. Kolb. Reprinted with permission from The Hay Group, Inc., 116 Huntington Ave., Boston, MA 02116. 617-425-4500.

Figure 3.2 also portrays two bipolar intersecting dimensions representing along the vertical axis, on a continuum from concrete to abstract, how we take in information and, along the horizontal axis, on a continuum from reflective observation to active testing—how we process information. Through learning sequences that allow movement through the full cycle, learners should be able to learn more comprehensively than they would with a single dimension. Yet each of the four aspects of this model can be understood to represent a learning style and a preferred entry point for learning for individual students. Although our suggestion for implementing this model is to begin with concrete experience for learning sequences and move through the entire cycle to ensure students a more balanced exposure to all four dimensions, there are many occasions when other entry points or use of fewer than all of the dimensions would be appropriate. An example is a graduate research seminar where abstract conceptualization (formulating hypotheses) leads to active experimentation (to test these hypotheses) and then to reflective observation (analysis of experiments and discussion) without the need for concrete experience to occur in the cycle. Another example is a history major who prefers to begin by hearing a lecture about a particular topic (abstract conceptualization), then moves on to reading original manuscripts about the topic (concrete experience), followed by writing a reflective paper (reflective observation). In this sequence there is no need for active experimentation.

Figure 3.3 (Svinicki and Dixon, 1987) offers learning activities representative of each of the four dimensions of the learning cycle. Interviews, field work, observations, reading primary sources, and so on give the learner concrete personal experiences with content. These processes could also easily be doorways for the Gardner's narrational and experiential entry points. Activities such as discussion and journaling help learners reflect on their own experiences and those of others. In addition, they are opportunities for the logical-quantitative and foundational entry points. Creating hypotheses, listening to lectures, and building models can evoke abstract conceptualization, again providing a doorway for the foundational and experiential entry points, and possibly the narrative too. Role playing, developing case studies, creating collages, and laboratory work can promote active experimentation. These activities lend themselves to all five of Gardner's entry points including the aesthetic. As we can see, Kolb's learning cycle and the five entry points of multiple intelligences theory are a creative combination for designing lessons. Chapter Five offers many more concrete suggestions for this promising partnership.

Typically to create a complete cycle, teachers and learners generate activities from each dimension and move through them

Figure 3.3 Sample Learning Activities for Dimensions of the Kolb Model

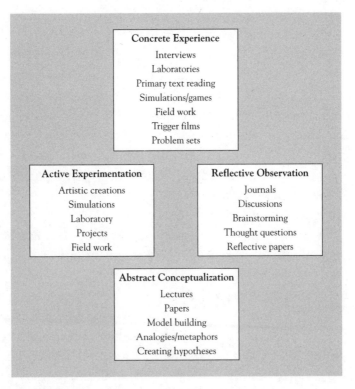

Concrete Experience
Interviews
Laboratories
Primary text reading
Simulations/games
Field work
Trigger films
Problem sets

Active Experimentation
Artistic creations
Simulations
Laboratory
Projects
Field work

Reflective Observation
Journals
Discussions
Brainstorming
Thought questions
Reflective papers

Abstract Conceptualization
Lectures
Papers
Model building
Analogies/metaphors
Creating hypotheses

Source: Adapted from Svinicki and Dixon (1987, p. 142).

in order (Svinicki and Dixon, 1987). For example, Figure 3.4, a unit designed for political science focusing on ethnic variables related to political attitudes, might begin with reading recent studies on this topic and conducting interviews in learner-selected neighborhoods (concrete experience).

Individual learners or collaborative groups of learners could categorize their observations and make initial speculations on differences among the ethnic groups represented (reflective observation). Then the class as a whole might pool its results and identify patterns among ethnic groups to generate hypotheses (abstract conceptualization) that predict how members of different ethnic groups are likely to respond to various political issues. Finally, the entire class could test its predictions by a follow-up questionnaire with members of the identified ethnic groups (active experimentation).

Figure 3.4 Learning Sequence According to the Kolb Model for a Political Science Course

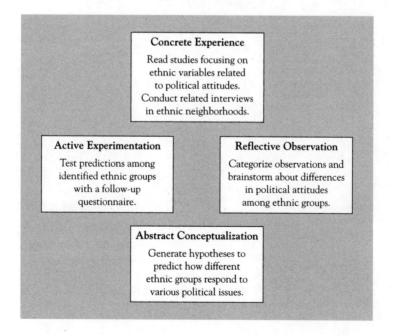

Concrete Experience

Read studies focusing on ethnic variables related to political attitudes. Conduct related interviews in ethnic neighborhoods.

Active Experimentation

Test predictions among identified ethnic groups with a follow-up questionnaire.

Reflective Observation

Categorize observations and brainstorm about differences in political attitudes among ethnic groups.

Abstract Conceptualization

Generate hypotheses to predict how different ethnic groups respond to various political issues.

A specific activity such as a laboratory experiment or conducting an interview may fit into more than one dimension depending on the learning goal. In the political science unit just discussed, interviewing was used twice: first as a concrete experience and then as an active experiment. In the first instance, this method was to "see what is" and in the second instance to verify a set of predictions based on various hypotheses. Thus, the functional purpose of the activity governs its selection and placement in the learning sequence. In practical use, reflective observation often becomes a form of examining, abstract conceptualization becomes a form of explaining, and active experimentation becomes a form of applying (Svinicki and Dixon, 1987).

Another way to use Kolb's model and to accommodate learner preferences is to vary the degree to which the learner is active or passive. Figure 3.5 illustrates such an improvisation. The activities at the outer edge of the ellipse most actively

Figure 3.5 Degree of Direct Student Involvement in Various Teaching Methods

Student as Actor

Direct experience
Recall of experience
In-class experience (Lab)
Simulations
Films/tapes
Lecture examples   Rhetorical
                        questions
Field work Projects Case studies Lecture | Student as | in lecture   Discussion   Logs
Labs   Homework Simulations Examples | Receiver | Thoughtful   Brainstorming Journals
                                          questions for
Lecture analogies   readings
descriptions

Text reading
Model critiques
Paper, project proposals
Model-building exercises

Source: Svinicki and Dixon (1987, p. 146). Reprinted with permission of the Helen Dwight Reid Educational Foundation. Published by Heldref Publications, 1319 Eighteenth St., N.W., Washington, D.C. 20036–1802. Copyright 1987.

engage the learner, while those closer to the center involve the learner far more passively. As an example, Introductory Science as conventionally taught is abstract, individually learned, and competitively tested (Rosenthal, 1997). With today's diverse learners, many students prefer a more experiential, collaborative, and project-based approach. Figure 3.5 allows both.

Others have substituted dimensions such as verbal and visual in a similar manner to extend this model to a greater range of students (Anderson and Adams, 1992). Almost playfully, the Kolb model not only allows a more systematic and broader selection of learning activities but centralizes the importance of experience in learning and flexibly accommodates some of the more important culturally derived differences among learners.

Teacher-Learner Conferences

A teacher-learner conference is often the first formal means of appeal or dissent for a learner. (We prefer the word *conference* to *meeting* because it is defined as the act of consulting together for the interchange of views, suggesting a more respected voice for the learner.) It is also frequently the only means for teachers and learners to cooperatively resolve issues and to personalize learning. Consider the following case:

Adrian Chan is a twenty-one-year-old Chinese American student in a public policy course made up of mostly African American and European American learners. The course is conducted as a roundtable discussion with case studies serving as stimuli for eliciting theory and opinion from the learners. On occasion, the teacher, Dr. Joshua Giles, an African American, uses role playing as a method of increasing perspective taking and of personifying some of the conflicting ideas that arise in class. In this typically lively setting, debate and expressions of strong feelings are common.

Dr. Giles has noticed that Adrian rarely participates. He has also observed that the one time Adrian's viewpoint was challenged, he became silent, and a tension quickly emerged in the group when Dr. Giles good-naturedly encouraged him to respond and he continued to remain quiet. Since that time, Adrian has appeared more withdrawn and even sullen in class. His last reaction paper was superficially completed, and Dr. Giles realizes he has begun to avoid calling on Adrian for class participation because of the discomfort that might arise. At the end of a recent class, Dr. Giles drew Adrian aside and asked him if anything was wrong. Adrian politely responded, "No, nothing is the matter," and quickly left.

This case brings up the following questions:

- What cultural influences may be affecting Adrian's behavior and manner of expressing himself?
- Should he and Dr. Giles have a conference?
- If so, how should Dr. Giles conduct the conference, and what should he say at the outset?
- Without a conference, should the course be adjusted to be more relevant and inclusive for Adrian? If so, in what ways?

As teachers we are probably more sensitive to attitudinal problems among our learners than we are to academic ones. Learners who are apparently sullen or uncooperative affect the mood of a class as well as get our attention. When these learners are also culturally different from ourselves, we are likely to be uncertain, even wary, about how to respond. How does one conduct a conference with culturally diverse learners?

We have found most postsecondary teachers have no training in how to conference with learners. We begin our teaching careers knowing we will post office hours for the explicit purpose of having conferences with learners. Yet rarely do we receive any formal training in this important process. What follows are nine guidelines for conferencing with diverse learners when attitude or other motivation and learning issues prompt us to use this more intimate way to understand:

■■

1. *The more that the conferencing process and goals are seen as appropriate by the learner, the more likely the meeting will be an effective and helpful one* (Sue and Sue, 1999). Conferencing parallels counseling in this sense. It means making the language and strategies used in the conference as consistent as possible with the learner's values, life experiences, and culturally conditioned ways of responding. It also means agreeing on goals that are preferred by and make sense to the learner. In the case of Adrian, he may not wish to discuss his feelings or how he emotionally reacts when he is challenged but may prefer to focus on academic issues. Forced self-disclosure to strangers may not be comfortable for Adrian if his cultural norm is to reserve expression of personal feelings for the intimacy of family. Creating optional learning activities that more fairly demonstrate his knowledge may be more helpful than finding ways to make him more comfortable in class.

A body of literature suggests that self-disclosure may be incompatible with the cultural values of Asian Americans, Latinos, and American Indians in particular. Many members of ethnic minority groups may prefer an active-directive approach to discussing academic problems to an ambiguous, nondirective approach filled with pauses, paraphrasing, and reflected feelings (Sue and Sue, 1999). However, groups and individuals differ from one another, so the rigid application of these generalizations to all situations is inappropriate.

In the area of diversity, consistency and flexibility can appear to be in conflict. Conferencing brings this to mind because so often the outcome is an adjustment in one's teaching or assessment practices to provide an equitable chance for learning for a particular student. Other students may resent such accommodation, deeming it preferential. Such confusion occurs through misunderstanding the distinction between the objectives of equal access and opportunity and those of equal treatment. For historically underserved learners to have equal opportunity to learn, it may be necessary to use a different approach. We believe that the mantle of equal treatment is too often a shield for discrimination. Using the same approach to learning for all students tends to favor groups socialized in dominant norms.

2. *Taking the role of an empathic and diplomatic teacher who follows the learner's lead is often a good beginning for a conference.* At the outset of a conference, this usually means listening without interruption to the student's reasons for requesting the conference. When the teacher has requested the conference, this means giving the student ample opportunity to respond to the teacher's stated reasons.

3. *Create a collaborative attitude that avoids blame.* Using descriptive language, avoiding labels, and showing authentic compassion help to build trust as well as focus on the issue at hand. If the teacher has requested the conference, he will have to state the reason initially—for example: "I've noticed your last two test scores have progressively declined. I'm concerned about this trend and how we might work together to turn it around. What's your opinion about this matter?" (more open ended) or, "Let's consider what might be done to improve things" (more directive). In the case of Adrian, Dr. Giles might say, "I'm beginning to wonder if the way we're conducting class is giving you the best chance to learn and demonstrate what you know. What's your opinion about this?" (more open ended) or, "If you agree, let's explore some ideas about what we could do to make this a better learning situation for you" (more directive).

4. *Although finding and mutually agreeing on the issue or problem is usually helpful, being lucid and in agreement about the goal of the conference is particularly significant.* Many people do not see the world in linear cause-and-effect terms. Probing for possible explanations may only add to the discomfort of the situation and stimulate further argument. Also, discussing possible reasons for conflict or difficulty may make some learners feel unsafe or embarrassed. This is why tone and demeanor are so important. One can convey empathy and care without being unnecessarily analytical. In the case of Adrian and Dr. Giles, it may be that they arrive at a common understanding that the way class is conducted is argumentative to a degree that diminishes Adrian's wish to participate. Or they may, after a short conversation that does not focus on specific reasons for Adrian's ostensible distress, agree to look for other acceptable ways for Adrian to learn and demonstrate his knowledge while in class.

5. *Flexibly consider specific goals or solutions.* Mutually agree on the selected ones. Such prompts as, "Let's take a look at the different approaches we might use," or, "Let's think about this and see what comes to mind," may be good starting points. Brainstorming may be used to generate possible strategies. In the beginning, all ideas are valid. After the ideas have been exhausted, they are evaluated for effectiveness. In Adrian's and Dr. Giles's situation, three possible alternatives can come into play: (1) Adrian is excused from any role-playing activities until he decides otherwise, (2) class is reconfigured to precede the roundtable discussions with small-group discussions after which only volunteer representatives of the small groups debate, or (3) Adrian corresponds in a journal with another student or Dr. Giles regarding his reactions to the issues debated in class.

When goals are complicated and involved, two strategies may be useful. In *means-ends analysis,* the goal is divided into a number of subgoals, and then a means of reaching each is worked out. For example, a learner wants to improve the quality of her next case study. The teacher and learner decide to break this task into several shorter objectives, each one allowing for feedback from the teacher, such as selecting a topic, locating sources of information, reading and organizing the information, visiting a field site and conducting observations, making an outline, and documenting and creating the case study. Depending on the situation, the learner and possibly the teacher can then develop a plan to accomplish each of these tasks.

The *working backward strategy* holds that some goals are best considered by looking first at the goal and moving back from it to see the order and timing of what needs to be done to reach it. Let's say a small group of learners wants to meet with the teacher for the purpose of improving their scores on the next exam. At the conference, they decided that they will collaboratively study, organize and share their notes, and receive a list of study questions from the teacher; they will also study individually. They might begin by looking at the date of the next exam, decide how much time they individually want to prepare the day before the test, figure out how much time they need to prepare and organize their notes, and then decide on a schedule to collaboratively consider the study questions, working backward from the day before the exam.

6. *Make a plan that both the teacher and learner record when desirable.* When the outcome of the conference is taking an action for which someone is responsible or on which a grade may be based, it is important to have a record to avoid possible confusion or disagreement. Also, when the goals and their procedures are complicated, organizing and writing them down improve clarity. This does not have to be a laborious or obsessive task. A simple review at the end of the conference, with both the learner and teacher taking the necessary notes, may suffice as well as bring a sense of closure to the meeting.

Plans and notes also give the learner and teacher a way of keeping track and revising or refining goals as desired. We suggest teachers keep a conference journal as an aid to memory and a means to make future and continuing conferences more constructive and focused.

7. *Encourage.* When the conference results in a learner goal or some kind of expected action on the part of the learner, this person benefits from knowing the teacher believes he or she can do it. Such encouragement also denotes higher expectations on the part of the teacher. A look or a gesture can sometimes be sufficient, or the teacher can provide a few words of appreciation or expectancy. In the case of Adrian, words as simple as, "I think we have some good ideas for better ways of working together. Thanks for coming," may suffice.

8. *Evaluate the results of the conference.* Has the goal been accomplished? Is the learner satisfied with the results? What has been learned? Should another conference be scheduled to refine or improve matters? In some ways, this is not as much evaluation or record keeping as it is caring. Reflective attention of this sort signifies to the learner that the conference made a difference to both parties. They took it seriously and organized themselves so things would change for the better.

9. *Use critical self-reflection throughout the entire conferencing process.* As Pam Hays (2001) recommends, we need to continuously think critically about our own assumptions in relation to the learner's communication. Even when we are well acquainted with the learner's cultural community, we are wise not to assume we know his personal experience and identity with that community. Our humility in such matters cannot be underestimated.

If we reconsider the case that began this chapter, we now see that Dr. Kubiak has at least one option that accommodates her perspective and Maria's need for relevance and volition. She could use a contract procedure that incorporates the necessary standards of performance and allows Maria more choice. Also, if she had an understanding of the influence of culture on interaction styles and profiles of intelligences and an awareness of the importance of relevance to learning, she would be more likely to provide greater flexibility in her assignments. She can do this through contracting, using problem-solving goals, and increasing entry points for projects.

Intuitively we know it is best for people to like what they must do. We want students to feel positive toward learning. However, exhorting, explaining, or cajoling seldom encourages attitudes that benefit learning. Such "talk," if you will, has little impact compared to an integrated set of educational norms and practices. When harmonious, these elements contribute to a shared ethos among diverse students that what they are learning is important and worth doing well.

4

ENHANCING MEANING

Come and stand in my heart, whoever you are, and
a whole river would cover your feet and rise higher
and take your knees in whirlpools, and draw you
down to itself, your whole body, your heart too.
                                        —*Eudora Welty*

What is meaning? And who determines it? What compels our
yearning to make sense of things, to risk the familiar for an idea
that is just barely visible in the dark, to imagine and communicate
beyond words? As Juana Ines de la Cruz wrote more than three cen-
turies ago, "Sorting the reasons to leave you or hold you, I find an
intangible one to love you, and many tangible ones to forego you."
Learning, like loving, cannot be simply rendered through verbal
intentions and explanations. In fact, at times, verbal explanations
contaminate significant moments, as this poignant recollection of
the Vietnam Memorial by Michael Ventura (1994) attests:

> Only when I step back to photograph the wall do I begin to
> appreciate the genius of its creator, Maya Ying Lin. For you can-
> not photograph it, not really. There is no angle through which
> you can see it whole through a lens unless you're standing so far
> off that the picture would be meaningless. Even with advanced
> equipment, if you're close enough to see that the names are
> inscribed, you're too close to contain the whole; if you contain
> the whole, you can't tell from the photograph alone what it
> really is. So the wall defies deconstruction and transmission by
> any other medium. You can't take it home with you. You have
> to experience it to know it, and you can keep only as much as
> you've experienced [pp. 5–6].

The realms of emotion, art, and spirituality are historically essential to human experience. They have incontestable meaning, often beyond words, and certainly stand outside the scope of modern measurement. We make such a declaration not because we doubt its acceptance by teachers but because we see such an absence of regard for these realms in so many postsecondary courses in spite of this awareness. The logical, the verbal, the explainable—the higher-order thinking, if you wish—reign supreme in higher education. We argue not against these ways of knowing but for the inclusion, acceptance, and respect of less "rational" approaches to sense making. Their absence during learning excludes the simultaneity of different systems of meaning making and perpetuates the boring, fear-driven, sterile, demotivating quality of many college classrooms. Since conformity to a verbal, abstract, scientifically reasoned world is so all-encompassing in higher education, and especially in graduate school, it is quite possible that a considerable number of people avoid experimenting with pedagogies because exhortation is a convenient and accepted convention. Vital engagement, a foundational aspect of enhancing meaning, requires a valued relationship to learning that stretches a person's capacities over time. To be under the direction of a teacher whose perception of consciousness does not allow the intuitive or the unexplainable and whose authority determines one's grade or promotion is for many as meaningless as it is daunting.

Although meaningful curriculum and instruction can take many forms, we offer an initial case study as one of several examples of a challenging and engaging learning experience:

As Lisa Zouari enters her first-semester math course at a four-year college in Houston, she is a bit apprehensive. Lisa enjoys math although, as an aspiring middle school teacher, she has heard that at the college level, it is often taught in ways that are very abstract. The first class was interesting, but at some point she wonders if it will become like so many others: cycles of lecture, then a bit of practice, then homework. While she finds a seat, she watches as Dr. West posts a life-size picture of Yao Ming, the seven-foot four-inch Houston Rockets basketball player from China, on the wall. Her curiosity is piqued.

What does Yao Ming have to do with today's assignment? How does Dr. West's review of metrics and customary systems of measurement connect to the poster?

After a brief welcome and overview of today's lesson, Dr. West asks his class of seventy students to partner with a neighbor to clarify basic definitions. On the whiteboard, he posts four questions for partners to discuss:

- What do you know about the metric system of measurement?
- What do you know about the customary system of measurement?
- List examples of items in this room that measure about one centimeter.
- List examples of items in this room that measure about one inch.

After ten minutes, Dr. West tells students that next, with the same partner, they will convert inches to centimeters by estimating, calculating, and comparing their own height in centimeters and inches to estimations and calculations of Yao Ming's height. He explains that he has selected Yao Ming as a model not only because he is one of the tallest players in the National Basketball Association, but because, like many local community members, he has demonstrated remarkable skill traversing the different worlds that are a part of his life. In some ways, says Dr. West, measuring Yao Ming can also be interpreted as a metaphor of what it means to take the measure of a human being. He explains that this is not a new idea. In fact, Stephen Gould's *The Mismeasure of Man* (1996) may be a familiar book to students who have had courses in the social sciences. But for today's purposes, he continues, the goal is to become more familiar with the ordinary mathematical metrics of measurement and conversion.

Students may use any approach they'd like, including the newsprint brought to class for those who wish to sketch. After twenty minutes, he will ask students to volunteer their approaches and findings for estimating and calculating height, first for themselves and then for Yao Ming. He will note their findings on the SMART Board and conclude class by asking students to examine patterns and quick-write in their math journals regarding patterns related to students' height in Math 101 compared to Yao Ming's height. He will also ask students to note any insights they have developed about the relationship between the customary system of measurement in the United States and the metric system, as well as insights into conversion strategies. Finally, he explains that for homework, along with preassigned reading, students will create a minimum of two problems related to fields they are interested in for their partner to solve. The problems will apply today's learning about converting U.S. measurement to the metric system. Dr. West also lets students know that tomorrow's class will begin with a conversation regarding the political implications of rejection of the metric system by the United States. At the conclusion of class, Dr. West provides an example of one way to approach the homework assignment and urges creativity.

As Lisa leaves the classroom, her head is spinning with ideas and concerns. Although she understands the mathematical concepts and appreciates Dr. West's interactive instructional practices, she wonders about what she will choose to enact as a teacher. How, for example, might seventh-grade boys feel about measuring themselves against Yao Ming? Would they be excited by the task or filled with anxiety? What would she do to adapt this learning experience to a very different context? Finally, how will Dr. West ensure that a university-level discussion about the U.S. rejection of the metric system will encourage a diverse group of students to deeply engage?

Meaning—to What End?

Meaning is a constant in learning and motivation. However, it is a concept difficult to define because any definition can become circular (Csikszentmihalyi, 1990). How do we address the meaning of meaning itself? There are a number of ways to unravel this word in a manner that enlightens how the motivation of diverse learners can be deepened. One way to understand this concept is to see it as the connections or patterns human beings create to link information to an important goal—something that matters to them (Sousa, 2006). The experience of such meaning intensifies motivation for people because there is obvious relevance and an emotional response. This kind of meaning can be understood on a more profound level and refers to whatever determines one's sense of purpose. This "deep meaning" accesses passionate feelings and can range from a basic sense of territoriality to an awareness of a strong and unified goal to an intuitive connection to something greater than our personal beings (Bohm, 1987; Csikszentmihalyi, 1997). This realm of meaning is also the domain of that which is extremely vital to us but that we may not be able to articulate, such as creative, artistic, and spiritual connections and expressions. Regardless of what we as teachers intend, these deeper meanings will contribute to learners' interpretations of learning activities. Culturally responsive teaching offers challenging and engaging learning experiences that connect with and elaborate on deeply personal meaning-making schemata.

Another way to understand meaning is as the ordering of information that gives identity and clarity, as when we say the word *citadel* to mean a refuge or sanctuary, or recognize our telephone number in a listing. This kind of meaning embraces facts, procedures, and behaviors that help us understand how things relate or operate or are defined but in a way that does not deeply touch our psyche. In the words of Whitehead (1979) this is "inert knowledge." In postsecondary education, much knowledge remains at the surface level. Too much of what passes for postsecondary education is constructed as and remains inert knowledge. Introductory textbooks are notorious for this.

Enhancing meaning refers to norms and practices that expand, refine, or increase the complexity of what is learned in a way that matters to learners, includes their values and purposes, and ideally contributes to a critical consciousness. The phrase "that matters to learners" refers to those processes beyond artic-ulation, such as the creative and the spiritual, as well as those processes involved with emerging relevance—when the act of learning creates its own meaning, as in the case of insight or confirmed prediction. Often, enhancing meaning will involve learners' using information, skills, or inert knowledge so that they acquire deeper meaning. In fact, one of the main goals that we advocate for postsecondary education, and therefore for any course within it, is to exalt what is significant in learners' lives, to assist them in realizing and enhancing that which is impor-tant in their world. As the philosopher Susanne Langer (1942) has posited, there is a basic and pervasive human need to invest meaning in one's world, to search for and find significance everywhere. Across many cultures, achieving purpose appears fundamental to a satisfying life (Csikszentmihalyi, 1988).

When an important goal is pursued with resolution, and all one's varied activities work together, consciousness becomes har-monious (Csikszentmihalyi, 1990). People who realize that their feelings, thoughts, and actions are congruent are in a euphoric state of being. Although their lives may offer enormous challenges, they are likely not to have felt their efforts wasted on doubt, regret, or fear. Ultimately, it seems, inner strength dwells within this realm. This realm, however, is not neutral to larger social and global concerns.

In education, we are obliged to simultaneously serve individual, cultural, and social purposes. To exalt the significance of students' individual interests or individual motivation in the absence of a local and global social justice framework is troubling. As with the overarching motivational framework, "enhancing meaning" relies on norms and practices rooted in a number of frameworks and traditions. These include experiential pioneers such as John Dewey (1938), David Kolb (1984), and Paulo Freire (1970). However, they also embrace contemporary race-conscious frameworks that explicitly speak to the need for allies in the struggle for justice (Reason, Broido, Davis, and Evans, 2005; Tatum, 1998; Aanerud, 1999), critical scholarship on hegemonic master narratives about race (Delgado, 1995; Kozol, 2005; Cochran-Smith, 2004; Gay, 2000), and extensions of critical race theory such as LatCrit, which offer perspectives of Latinos (Leonardo, 2005; Yosso, 2006) and tribal critical race theory, TribalCrit (Castagno and Lee, 2007). These latter theories confront the black-white binary understanding of race that fails to capture some important issues and nuances applicable to the experiences of other racialized groups and indigenous communities (Brayboy, 2005).

Combined, these theories invite a broad and deep conversation within higher education about the enduring legacy of racial oppression and the need for significant attention to social justice in curriculum, pedagogy, and institutional priorities. They remind us that greater racial equity and social justice will not be achieved within a liberal framework of individual property rights, a focus on equality in terms of sameness, and on color-blindness (Delgado and Stefancic, 2001; Dixson and Rousseau, 2006). While the motivational condition of enhancing meaning attempts to deepen learning in ways that matter to students—through experiential methods, interdisciplinary learning, and imaginative projects—these forms of engagement cannot be separated from clear commitments to social justice. A fundamental goal that is part of this condition is to teach against the grain (Cochran-Smith, 2004), which embodies social justice pedagogical practices rooted in the following ethic:

1. *Power awareness:* Knowing that society and history can be made and remade by organized groups; knowing who exercises dominant power in society, what their ends are, and how power is currently organized and used in society.

2. *Critical literacy:* Analytical habits of thinking, reading, writing, speaking, or discussing that go beneath surface impressions, dominant narratives, mere opinions, and routine clichés; understanding the social contexts and consequences of any subject matter; discovering the deep meaning of any event, text, technique, process, object, statement, image, or situation; applying that meaning to one's own context.

3. *Ongoing personal and professional transformation:* Recognizing and challenging one's own prejudicial myths, values, behaviors, and language learned; facilitating constructive social change, ideas, and projects.

Learning within an ethic of social justice allows students to gravitate toward deeper meaning. With this frame of reference, the motivational goal of enhancing meaning reveals a personal and global frontier, an exciting possibility for learning.

Engagement, Challenge, and Intrinsic Motivation

Although cognitive science and constructivism are popular theories in academia, college learning frequently remains superficial. Tests that assess students' low-level reproduction of large amounts of information sanction such surface learning, overshadowing the quality of students' thinking and diminishing their motivation. Too often their instruction features lecturing that covers vast swatches of content irrelevant to the daily lives of students or their immediate future. Students pass these courses, especially introductory ones, by memorizing soon-to-be-forgotten facts and using problem-solving recipes (Wieman, 2007). Many introductory courses are terminal courses; students seldom consider these subjects again. Rather than opportunities for learning, they tend to be gauntlets for students to run for the purpose of grades and test scores.

Learners who are less attracted to academic success that is signaled by grades and test scores will likely be less motivated to learn and perform according to superficial measures. Postsecondary science education offers an example of introductory courses where large groups of diverse students are disinterested and reluctant learners (Wieman, 2007). For decades, students have complained about how poorly their science courses have been taught, employing problems of little or no relevance, using a lecture format, and grading on a competitive basis (Rosenthal, 1997; Hrepic, Zollman, and Rebello, 2007). Yet the conventional wisdom, sometimes perpetuated by faculty themselves, is that lack of student ability and effort, rather than inadequate teaching, are the major causes of poor performance and negative attitudes in these courses. However, emerging research from science faculty offers insights as to why lecturing is often a poor format for instruction (Hrepic, Zollman, and Rebello, 2007) and how methods that promote engagement are particularly effective (Hake, 2002; Mazur, 1997; Wieman, 2007). This chapter and the next discuss and exemplify these methods in ways that have implications for a broad range of disciplines.

One issue in higher education, even with outcomes-based and performance-based instruction, is that starting with and focusing on how well something should be done can draw attention away from the subjective appeal of the learning process itself. Standards, writ large, take priority over the perspectives and values of the learners, making them seem frivolous. In courses, students may actually learn more and better but not be any more motivated to continue to learn or apply the particular course's content.

From the perspective of intrinsic motivation, a learning goal is significant because it allows learning to occur in a particularly challenging or fascinating way. Academic performance is crucial, but it is not the sole criterion of learning. You need the mountaintop not so much to reach it but because it creates the climb. The goal provides the routes, the journey, the challenge. We need the goal because its accomplishment to a large extent determines the means. That is where the deeper value of learning lies. Like the ending to a great novel, it is important because it helps to construct a compelling story, but in and of itself, it means less than how we arrived there. This is a critical understanding, because *the more we make the achievement of a specific goal the ultimate reason for learning, the less likely we are to provide learners with opportunities to enhance meaning as they proceed.*

With this understanding as a context, we can address the first criterion for enhancing meaning: learner engagement. Engagement is a multidimensional concept and at its most basic level a meaningful response to something on the part of the learner. The learner pays attention to some entity and is aware of the interaction. In this regard, seeing someone on the street, hearing thunder, and touching someone's hand can be brief but powerfully engaging. In teaching and learning, engagement is usually of much longer duration and includes involvement, participation, engrossment, and transcendence, as in involvement in an experiment, participation in a project, captivation in acting out roles, and transcendence of an ideological model. In engagement, the learner is active and might be searching, evaluating, constructing, creating, or organizing some kind of learning material into new or better ideas, memories, skills, values, feelings, understandings, solutions, or decisions. Often a product is created or a goal is reached. Frequently, concepts have been transformed, and mental, emotional, and physical energy has been exerted (Donovan, Bransford, and Pellegrino, 1999; Nakamura and Csikszentmihalyi, 2003).

The voices of the learner and the teacher in dialogue with one another are crucial to engagement. Both are heard, and their meanings are entwined as they define themselves as active authors of their worlds (Giroux and McLaren, 1986). Self-expression and dialogue affirm their identities and perspectives as they negotiate the meaning of their separate and mutual experiences. Such dialogue recognizes rather than negates the realities of both the teacher and the learner.

Since engagement so frequently implies a challenge, let us immediately discuss the second criterion for enhancing meaning. Challenge occurs when we have to apply current knowledge or skills to situations that require development or extension of them (Wlodkowski, 2008). This broad definition of challenge could encompass speaking with a friend, writing a letter, learning to ride a horse, reading a novel, or conducting an experiment. In this manner, a challenge may be seen as the available learning opportunity and engagement as the kind of action in which a person immerses herself. The challenge often has a goal-like quality to it. The form of engagement requires and contains some degree of capacity, skill, or knowledge on the part of the learner. We prefer the word *capacity* to *ability* because the latter concept so often refers to a genetically endowed, test-measured, fixed capability that is used to exclude learners. Also, the concept of capacity embraces the idea of multiple intelligences and culturally influenced ways of knowing, which the teacher has a responsibility to accommodate when planning learning experiences (challenges).

For example, an adult education student wants to investigate the influence of gender in the development of her field of study. She agrees with her teacher to conduct a historical research study, which is the challenge or learning opportunity. Although the student has never conducted a study and has scored below the average of the other graduate students in her program on both the math and verbal components of the Graduate Record Exam, she has the organizational skills to complete such an investigation and the capacity to effectively use primary and secondary resources, as well as to learn how to compose a survey with the support of her teacher. She also wants to conduct some oral interviews because of the qualitative information they can bring to this research. Her teacher accommodates this request. Carrying out the study—the reading, writing, organizing, surveying, and interviewing—comprises engagement.

A challenging learning experience in a flexible and highly engaging format about a relevant topic is intrinsically motivating because it increases the complexity of skill and knowledge required for learning and the range of connections to those interests, applications, and purposes that are important to the learner. This enhancement of meaning is at the core of learning and motivation, because human beings by their very nature need to maintain an ordered state of consciousness (Csikszentmihalyi, 1997) and seek integration and cohesion both within themselves and with others (Ryan and Deci, 2002).

Highly engaging and challenging learning activities often lead to the experience of *flow*, one of the most enjoyable forms of involvement possible in learning (Csikszentmihalyi, 1997). We have all had a flow experience outside an educational context. It is the feeling and concentration that sometimes emerge in a closely contested athletic competition, a challenging board game such as chess, or, more simply, reading a book that seems as if it were written just for us, or in the spontaneous exhilaration that accompanies a long, deep conversation with an old friend. In such activities we feel totally absorbed, with no time to worry about what might happen next and with a sense that we are fully participating with all the skills necessary at the moment. There is often a loss of self-awareness that results in a feeling of transcendence or a merging with the activity and the environment. Writers, dancers, therapists, surgeons, pilots, and teachers frequently report feelings of flow while they are working. Flow has been found to improve the quality of human experience in very different cultures across the world (Massimini, Csikszentmihalyi, and Delle Fave, 1988).

Learners can have flow experiences as well when they are engaged in meaningful learning. Studies across numerous cultural communities suggest four characteristics that create the conditions for this optimal experience (Nakamura and

Csikszentmihalyi, 2003). We present these on page 200 as a context for the practices in this chapter.

Norms for Enhancing Meaning

The essence of enhancing meaning is to create opportunities to accomplish work that learners find relevant. In this manner, they will become more effective at what they value, which is the core of personal competence (the motivational condition discussed in the next chapter). Central to this outcome from a culturally responsive perspective are learning processes that encourage people to think holistically and critically about their conditions, realize the dynamic relationship between critical thought and critical action, and feel empowered to make the changes needed. This kind of critical consciousness reflects one of the highest developments of thought and action possible among people (Freire, 1970). For postsecondary courses to advance this potential, the following norm is necessary: *Learners participate in challenging learning experiences involving deep reflection and critical inquiry that address relevant, real-world issues in an action-oriented manner.*

Included in this norm are consistent opportunities for learners to manipulate information and ideas in ways that transform their meaning and implications, such as when they combine data and concepts in order to synthesize, generalize, explain, hypothesize, create, or critique a conclusion or interpretation. If we were to observe learners at work, we would see adults clarifying distinctions, developing arguments, constructing explanations, creating hypotheses as well as artistic inventions, and dealing with complex understandings. We would also see people in dialogue, often with the condition of promoting collective understanding. It would be obvious that learners are frequently connecting their understanding to relevant, real-world issues in an effort to influence an audience beyond their immediate environment— for example, by communicating their ideas to others, promoting solutions to social problems, offering assistance to particular people or causes, or generating performances or outcomes with pragmatic political or aesthetic value (McLaren, 2006; Newmann and Wehlage, 1993). In general, learners are constructing their own evidence that they are moving significantly beyond what they knew and could do before they began the course.

A central question (Sheared, 1994) related to enhancing meaning is, "How are we as teachers to interact with course content in such a way that the discourse acknowledges all voices— the multiple ways in which people interpret and reflect their understanding of the world?" To enter into dialogue and uncover and acknowledge the voice of each student is necessary for understanding that whatever each of us offers is grounded in a political, social, historical, sexual, and economic context that is unique yet related to the cultures of others.

Since speech indicates position in school and society, the domination of the teacher's language, no matter what the learning activity, promotes a teacher-centered learning environment. To avoid undemocratic discourse and to enhance dialogue, mutual inquiry, and support for learners as knowledge builders we propose the second norm: *learner expression and language are joined with teacher expression and language to form a "third idiom" that enables the perspectives of all learners to be readily shared and included in the process of learning.* Learners' language brings a conversational and concrete quality to the frequently more abstract and conceptual nature of the teacher's language, offering both parties accessibility to the knowledge and realities of each other (Shor, 1992).

This language fusion of language fosters a democratic relationship between teachers and learners. The process is not formal; it occurs in an evolutionary manner as the teacher encourages learner expression and gradually uses and reflects back the learners' ways of communicating with attention to talking and lecturing less. The third idiom is vital to the democratic transformation of education to a construction that is more equitable and multicultural.

The third idiom is, of course, not a static language. With each new learning group, it is invented anew and reflects the particular learners, subject matter, and political climate of the school or community. Without speech to pose learning within the language and experience of students, it is impossible for everyone to speak as members of an authentic learning community.

Practices for Enhancing Meaning

As we consider the practices for enhancing meaning, we realize content is only as important as the learners' interaction with it. Since we accept multiple realities and differing profiles of intelligences, we need ways of creating knowledge that embodies these perspectives. Dealing with relevant and larger concepts while learning offers this possibility. Numerous disciplines, from critical literacy and constructivism to multiple intelligences theory and the neuroscience of learning, support this approach and, respectively advocate the use of deep conceptual understanding (Donovan, Bransford, and Pellegrino, 1999; Zull, 2006), key topics (Windschitl, 2002), and essential questions (Gardner and Boix-Mansilla, 1994). All of the latter terms are synonymous with broad conceptual themes that present issues or ideas of such magnitude, depth, and meaning that they provide a relevant focal point as well as elicit intrinsic motivation among diverse students. Broad conceptual themes also evoke relevant meanings within learners, kindling their desire to pursue personal learning goals. As an example, each of the following questions could be used to generate a broad conceptual theme among students:

- How could we find out if competition is necessary for learning to excel?
- What key concerns do the following words—*slum, environment, food, work, salary, vote, immigration, government,* and *wealth*—compel us to articulate?

- Why do the ideas of justice and conflict seem to so frequently be related to one another in personal life as well as in history?
- Which social systems do you belong to that do not rely on a hierarchy of authority for their operation?
- What keeps us healthy?

In the case of the last question, the themes of health care, illness, and prevention come to mind. All students could find a relevant and, perhaps, deeply personal perspective to bring to one or more of these themes.

The practices that follow are excellent ways to extract meaning from major conceptual themes. In most cases, instructors exercise the role of representing ideas and skills, engaging in dialogue with learners, and encouraging their reflection. To encourage knowledge building rather than authoritarian truths, we must allow different perspectives to coexist without unnecessarily placing them in competition with each other (Lather, 1991). In addition, as we consider dialogue to be a transformative exchange of voices where teachers and learners are involved in a colearning process, learner participation awakens insight into how students think and learn, helping teachers to successively deepen levels of thematic inquiry. To make authentic dialogue (Cranton, 2007; Shor, 1992) a constant process throughout these practices, we need to do the following:

- Analyze with learners' participation.
- Avoid jargon or esoteric references that intimidate learners into silence.
- Encourage learners to generate thought-provoking questions for discussion.
- Be patient in listening to learners and providing time for them to think on their feet.
- Invite learners to speak from experience, realizing that knowledge consists of everyday lived experiences, and integrating that material into social issues and academic themes.

- Include the narrative method, in which people tell their stories in print or by voice, allowing the whole to give meaning to the particular.

- Invite learners to suggest themes for study, and ask them to specify reading matter.

- Draw learners out with questions after they speak and a response from other students.

- Make resources such as the Internet and electronic libraries accessible so that perspectives and information relevant to learners can be infused in discussions and knowledge construction.

With this kind of dialogue as integral to the procedures that follow, learners have a reasonable opportunity to arrive at meaningful and conceptually coherent learning that is respectful of a multicultural perspective. Indispensable to this process is reflection—a chance to spend time considering experience in order to more fully grasp the implications and inferences. Reflection allows teachers and learners to be simultaneously open-minded and discerning, while still able to develop more complex understanding (Zull, 2002).

Schön (1987) makes a useful distinction between reflection-in-action and reflection-on-action. The former is on-the-spot analysis and dialogue, excellent for making sense of the variety and unpredictability inherent in such real situations as teaching, medical practice, experimenting, and computer work. The latter is a post hoc examination, often with feedback and dialogue, of what has transpired—what might be learned looking back in fields ranging from politics to music. Both of these forms of reflection imply the need for self-observation and openness to multiple perspectives. (In Chapter Five, the essential role of reflection for self-assessment is specifically addressed.)

Most of the practices that follow tend to be analytical. However, an excellent way to deepen meaning is through contemplation: placing ideas and experiences in the mind and observing them without any form of analysis or deliberation. Like patiently and calmly watching a child or remembering a dream without seeking to understand, patterns, insights, and perspectives can eventually emerge. Allowing learners time to look at a problem without trying to solve it or to move away from a project without the demand to map its completion may be the best way to nurture resolution. There is no formula for the optimal use of dialogue, reflection, and contemplation. Yet their integration with the procedures that follow is crucial to meaning making.

Cultivating Flow

Earlier we discussed the feeling of flow—the deeply satisfying experience of an intrinsically motivating activity. All of the procedures that follow have the potential to be flow occurrences for teachers and learners alike. As flow has been studied across cultures, it has been found to have remarkably similar characteristics or conditions for people to experience it (Nakamura and Csikszentmihalyi, 2003). When these elements are present in a learning process, students are likely to experience flow.

- *Goals are clear and compatible*. Playing games like chess, tennis, and poker induces flow, but so can playing a musical piece or designing computer software. As long as our intentions are clear and our emotions support them, we can concentrate even when the task is difficult. Knowing what we want to accomplish helps us to become immersed, as in the case of a challenging experiment or a worthwhile project. In such matters, cultural relevance is an inescapable necessity.
- *Feedback is immediate, continuous, and relevant as the activity unfolds*. We are clear about how well we are doing. Each

move of a game usually tells us whether we are advancing or retreating from our goal; as we read, we *flow* across lines and paragraphs and pages. In a good conversation, words, facial expressions, and gestures give immediate feedback. When we experience insight or agreement or think of deeper questions, we often feel a sense of accomplishment. In learning situations, there should be distinct information or signals that let us assess our work.

• *The challenge is in balance with our skills or knowledge but stretches existing capacities.* The challenge is manageable but pulls us toward further development of our knowledge or skill. Flow experiences usually occur when our ability to act and the available opportunity for action correspond closely. If challenges get significantly beyond our skills, we usually begin to worry; if they get too far away from what we are capable of doing, anxiety can emerge because we are in over our heads in a learning project, a job, a sport, or something else. Conversely, when the challenge is minimal, we feel apathetic even if we have the skills. (Busywork comes to mind.) When the challenge is reasonable but our skills still exceed it, we are likely to become bored. However, when the challenge is closely balanced with our capacity to act and just a bit beyond our skills or knowledge, we can become exhilarated as we meet it. Thus, a learning activity should have a range of challenges broad enough and flexible enough to engage learners with a variety of backgrounds and profiles of intelligences.

• *Vital engagement is when flow merges with meaning.* It is one of the highest forms of flow and a pinnacle of what living can be. This phenomenon occurs when there is enjoyable absorption in a valued, socially useful task such as work, teaching, or learning— for example, when a person sees her work as a calling and is joyfully immersed in it. Although such vital engagement can occur temporarily, such as during problem solving in a course, it is more likely to occur where there is a "felt conviction" that the task is part of something "inherently important" such as art, science, or education (Nakamura and Csikszentmihalyi, 2003, p. 100). A sense of community and purpose make vital engagement possible in a course.

■ ■

Flow itself is much more attainable for students and teachers than many instructors realize. One in five people have this experience as frequently as several times a day (Csikszentmihalyi, 1997). Because flow can be found across cultures, it may be a sense that humans have developed in order to recognize patterns of action that are worth preserving and transmitting over time (Massimini, Csikszentmihalyi, and Delle Fave, 1988). When it occurs as part of the process of learning, it makes learning an end in itself. Those who experience flow have not only a better chance of learning but also a better chance of wanting to learn more. Creating flow with learners regardless of ethnicity, gender, or class is the challenge embedded in every practice that follows.

Critical Questioning for Engaging Discussions

The first practice we address is critical questioning. If teachers and learners are to realistically engage in the co-construction of meaning, where everyone at times is a teacher and a learner, then they must frequently be co-inquirers mutually capable of thinking about information in ways that transform that material into new knowledge. Thought-provoking questions can prompt everyone to make connections as well as raise contradictions between what they already know and what is the presented "knowledge." Raising critical questions reveals individuals' differing perspectives on ideas and issues.

However, there is research to show that fewer than 5 percent of teacher questions are higher-order questions (requesting complex thinking) and that the frequency of student-generated questions is infinitesimally low, averaging 0.11 per hour per student in classrooms in several countries; of these student questions, most are factual (Dillon, 1988; Kerry, 1987). Often, even when students are working in collaborative groups, unless the teacher provides direct guidance, they tend to be more focused on "finding the right answer" than pursuing thoughtful interactions (King, 2002).

Most definitions of critical thinking directly or indirectly address the skills of analyzing, inferring, synthesizing, applying, evaluating, comparing, contrasting, verifying, substantiating, explaining, and hypothesizing. In addition, critical thinking is as much an operative philosophy and disposition as it is an isolated skill. Educators make a distinction between a make-sense orientation and a critical orientation (Perkins, Allen, and Hafner, 1983). In a make-sense orientation, the criteria for the validity of a statement are that it seems to hang together and connect with one's prior beliefs. If something appears self-evident and makes sense, there is no need to think anymore about it. In a critical orientation, it is not sufficient for the statement to hang together or match prior beliefs. There is still a need to examine the data and reasoning for inconsistencies, take alternative perspectives, construct counterarguments, and look for bias and overgeneralization. A critical orientation is socio-culturally constructive and allows us to include a wider human panorama and consider the social implications of any idea from different perspectives. As a process, it helps us to realize there is nothing inherently wrong with changing our minds on an issue.

Critical questioning fosters discussions that are exploratory, unpredictable, risky, and exciting. It is fundamental to critical reflection and democratic discussions that foster growth in one's capacity for learning and sensitivity to the same capacity in others (Brookfield and Preskill, 2005).

With the opportunity to use mindful questions, learners can affirm and extend the critical thinking they bring to postsecondary educational settings. Such occasions can also foster the deepening of those attitudes and beliefs that support critical thinking and critical consciousness. Alison King (1994, 2002) has developed and extensively tested an instructional procedure for teaching university learners to pose their own thought-provoking questions. She has found that once this procedure is learned, it becomes a thinking strategy that learners can use on their own or in groups.

In using this procedure, the teacher provides the learners with a written set of generic questions or such question starters as, "What do we already know about...?" "How do you think...would see the issue of...?" These questions encourage knowledge construction because they serve as prompts to induce more critical thinking on the part of learners and the teacher as well. Learners use these generic questions to guide them in formulating their own specific questions pertaining to the material to be discussed.

Exhibit 4.1 contains a list of thoughtful question stems that can be adapted for use by filling in the blanks with information relevant to the subject being covered. The critical thinking skills these questions elicit are also listed. When the teacher offers these question stems to students for their conversations, students can use their own information and examples to deepen the content of what is to be studied. In this manner, a bridge can be formed between the usually more academic language of the teacher and the everyday language of the learners who are progressing toward a more mutual language (third idiom) and increased dialogue.

To King's list we add the following examples of the five types of questions Paul (1990) associates with Socratic dialogue:

1. *Clarification:* "What do you mean by...? Could you give me an example?"

2. *Probing for assumptions:* "What are you assuming when you say...? What is underlying what you say?"

Exhibit 4.1 Guiding Thought-Provoking Questioning

Generic Questions	Specific Thinking Skills Induced
What is a new example of…?	Application
How could…be used to…?	Application
What would happen if…?	Prediction/hypothesizing
What are the implications of…?	Analysis/inference
What are the strengths and weaknesses of…?	Analysis/inference
What is…analogous to?	Identification and creation of analogies and metaphors
What do we already know about…?	Activation of prior knowledge
How does…affect…?	Analysis of relationship (cause and effect)
How does…tie in with what we learned before?	Activation of prior knowledge
Explain why…	Analysis
Explain how…	Analysis
What is the meaning of…?	Analysis
Why is…important?	Analysis of significance
What is the difference between…and…?	Comparison-contrast
How are…and…similar?	Comparison-contrast
How does…apply to everyday life?	Application to the real world
What is the counterargument for…?	Rebuttal argument
What is the best…, and why?	Evaluation and provision of evidence

(continued)

Generic Questions	Specific Thinking Skills Induced
What are some possible solutions to the problem of…?	Synthesis of ideas
Compare…and…with regard to…	Comparison-contrast
What do you think causes…? Why?	Analysis of relationship (cause-effect)
Do you agree or disagree with this statement:…? What evidence or research is there to support your answer?	Evaluation and provision
How do you think…would see the issue of…?	Taking other perspectives

Source: King, A. "Inquiry as a Tool in Critical Thinking." In D. F. Halpern and Associates (eds.), *Changing College Classrooms: New Teaching and Learning Strategies for an Increasingly Complex World.* San Francisco: Jossey-Bass, 1994. Reprinted with permission of John Wiley & Sons, Inc.

3. *Probing for reasons and evidence:* "How do you know that…? What are your reasons for saying…?"

4. *Other perspectives:* "What might someone say who believed that…? What is an alternative for…?"

5. *Probing for implications as consequences:* "What are you implying by…? Because of…, what might happen?"

For guided practice in the use of both of these lists of questions, a teacher could set up a "fishbowl" discussion. One-third of the class sits in a circle and discusses a relevant topic using the questions as prompts. The rest of the class, sitting in a circle around the others, listens and takes notes and then has a dialogue about the discussion.

In the individual or self-questioning version of King's instructional procedure, learners can use the question stems to guide them in generating their own critical questions following a presentation, a class, or a reading. We have found students' use of these question lattices enhances the composition of their journals and self-assessments.

Guided reciprocal peer questioning (King, 1994), the group version of this procedure, can be implemented in any course. After activities such as seeing a project presentation, listening to a short lecture, or reading agreed-on material, learners use the generic question stems and work independently to generate two or three questions based on the material. Next, in pairs or small groups, they engage in peer questioning, taking turns asking their questions of their partner or group and answering each other's questions in a reciprocal manner. This approach encourages deeper dialogue and helps learners to check their understanding as well as to gain other learners' perspectives.

Let us say my class and I have read Ralph Ellison's *Invisible Man*. We have agreed to each bring along two questions based on the list in Exhibit 4.1 regarding any aspect of the book that we find applicable to our lives. We break off into dyads, and my partner and I each place our two questions before us:

1. How does the last line of the book, "Who knows but that, on the lower frequencies, I speak for you?" apply to our everyday lives?

2. What is the Brotherhood analogous to in our own contemporary society?

3. The book, heralded as the greatest American novel of the second half of the twentieth century, has many strengths. From your perspective, what are its weaknesses?

4. What are examples of invisibility at this college?

With these queries, we have an opportunity to relate ideas from this novel to our own knowledge and experience. We can have an extensive discussion that may clarify some inadequacies in our comprehension, and each of us has a chance to some extent to guide the thinking that will occur. There is opportunity to infer, compare, evaluate, and explain, all of which can lead to better understanding, fuller awareness of social issues, and the possibility of modifying one's own thinking.

Sometimes there will be conflicting viewpoints that can be facilitated with linking questions. For example, asking, "Is there any connection between your conclusion and Abdul's last statement?" or "How does that observation fit with Seth's comment?" may open avenues of new insight or mutual regard. Questions of this sort join the knowledge of learners with other learners; promoting the understanding that discussion is a collaborative process in which each learner can make an important contribution to everyone's learning (Brookfield and Preskill, 2005).

Both teachers and students learn to pose critical questions; clarify, extend, and refine their thinking; and realize the social implications of any idea from different perspectives. As Perkins, Faraday, and Bushey (1991) point out, the meaning that we make is what constitutes our lives. Critical thinking, and therefore critical questioning, precede and abet critical consciousness. They can broaden the quality of our lives, allow us to include a wider human panorama, and ultimately they offer a means to more equitably influence what can be known. Please see Resource E for further suggestions for conducting equitable class discussions within a multicultural classroom.

Posing Problems: From Emerging Relevance to Relevance

In a very broad sense, a problem can be characterized as any situation where a person wants to achieve a goal for which an obstacle exists (Voss, 1989). If relevant and within the range of human capacity, problems by definition are challenging and engaging. Review of the research in the area of culture and cognitive development indicates that the use of concepts and processes for solving problems is to a significant extent learned within a cultural context (Hofstede, 1986; Gay, 2000). Perceptual differences, information processing, constraints in terms of social and ethical codes, and technical materials and procedures are all culturally influenced and affect how a problem may be conceived and approached. From building a home to settling a divorce, the variation across the world is extraordinary. The interesting and important issue here is that the enormous variety among humans in how problems are perceived, constructed, and resolved is extremely valuable to what can be learned inside and out of schools.

We distinguish between *problem posing* and *posing a problem* as procedures because the former term is synonymous with a model of Freirean pedagogy (Freire, 1970) that will be explicitly considered in the last section of this chapter. However, Shor (1992), an exponent of critical teaching and student-centered learning, offers a useful taxonomy for the kind of problems that may be presented (posed as a problem) during learning. These are problems identified as generative themes, topical themes, and academic themes. All of them may be offered as questions, as most problems usually are.

Generative themes grow out of the learners' culture. They express problematic conditions of daily life. Learners find them deeply meaningful because they directly relate to their anxieties, fears, and dreams. They are the unsettled intersections of personal life and society based on experiences such as voting, working, housing, and community activity (Shor, 1992). When learners see their own words and experiences in the problems constructed and considered, intellectual work becomes compelling and based in the diversity of the learners' present. Learner subjectivity initiates learning and is often the leading edge but not the end. There is eventually a synthesis between the teacher's knowing and the learners' knowing.

The beginning of posing a problem based on a generative theme is to draw attention to a personally relevant and substantial issue or situation. We offer the following composite example from the experience of one of the authors.

For a research course for adult learners, I begin with the question, "If you believed research could really help you, and you were able to conduct the study yourself or with your family, friends, or colleagues, what is a personally relevant issue or problem you would like to study?" I then ask the learners to think about the question for a few minutes, usually in silence. Then I ask them to free-write their response in a narrative form for five to ten minutes (for example: "A problem that comes to mind…," "I was just thinking the other day that I wish I knew…"). After they have completed their free writing, I ask them to break into triads and to read and discuss their compositions, acting as research colleagues to give support and feedback and to deepen their thinking about what has been shared. When these discussions are completed, I ask each learner to review and, if desired, revise the problem or issue into a statement or question and to copy it onto a four- by six-inch note card. All of these cards are then posted on a wall for everyone to read. After reading the cards, we look for three or four themes that might unite the various problems that have been posed—for example, children, work issues, or financial concerns. We then reassemble into three groups according to the theme that is of the most individual concern, with the purpose of surfacing a problem that all members of that group would find personally worthwhile to research. The three problems that emerge are:

1. How could I find out if my children's food is healthy, given the number of chemicals used in globally produced products?

2. How would I know if the way I teach students who are recent immigrants who are English language learners to use personal computers is as effective as it can be?

3. What are socially responsible ways to invest money?

Using each of these questions as a starting point and asking questions that elicit the learners' language and experience, I begin to teach them how to operationalize a question for research: What does *healthy* mean to you? How would you measure health? What do you mean by *globally produced?* and so on. We now have three generative themes to use in considering other elements of research design. If we decide to, we can stay with these problems for as much as a quarter of the entire course. Eventually we learn together about action research and carry out projects in our communities based on these or other generative themes. Some of the learners go on to publish their work in newsletters, magazines, and journals. Others come back to the next course to share their thinking and offer support to another community of learners. I doubt if any of these outcomes could have occurred without generative themes.

"The *topical theme* [our emphasis] is a social question of key importance locally, nationally, or globally that is not generated directly from the students' conversation. It is raised in class by the teacher" (Shor, 1992, p. 55). Topical themes are often introduced because learner conversation and thought may not include important issues in society. Frequently it is a problem the teacher presents based on her or his critical knowledge of the world at large and the learners' experiences in it. A topical theme can be a way to encourage learners to step into an area ignored or covered uncritically by the conventional curriculum and mass media. Commercial textbooks frequently diminish consideration of diverse opinions as well as people. Topical themes can offer original and thoughtful conversations and exploration of social issues not yet being discussed by learners in daily life.

However, in a critical-democratic class, the topical theme is open to rejection by learners because a "problem-posing" course is a negotiated experience with a mutual curriculum (Shor, 1992). Therefore, in more conventional courses, teachers ought to choose topical themes with a sensitive awareness of learner needs and perspectives to avoid subjecting them to personal, political, and social harangues. In either case, we agree with Shor (1992) that topical themes fit when they are relevant to work in progress, introduced as problems for collaborative study, and are in an idiom learners can understand. If these minimal criteria are not met, then topical themes subvert culturally responsive teaching and make it another teacher-dominated learning experience.

An example of a topical theme we used in an education course was school-corporate partnerships (Molnar, 1989–1990) as a pretext for corporate advertising and as an impetus for an extrinsic orientation to learning—for example, pizzas for reading books, T-shirts for solving math problems, and so on. For a psychology class, one of us introduced a topical question about self-regulated learning (Zimmerman and Kitsantas, 2005) as a system of mastering one's own learning processes that masks a self-reliant ideology and diverts attention from systematic inequality and forms of institutional discrimination based on race, ethnicity, and social class.

In general, topical themes should be introduced as participatory problems rather than as a lecture, so that the door is always open for learner voices to reflect, comment, or disagree. If learners are not interested in the problem or do not wish to discuss it, their position is to be respected. Culturally responsive teaching is not about indoctrinating students.

The third kind of problem is the *academic theme*, which represents a scholastic, professional, or technical body of knowledge that the teacher wants to present or has to put forward as a requirement (Shor, 1992). This material is usually drawn from a specific subject area, such as science, history, or nursing. Often it is a particular knowledge or skill from the teacher's field of study and not part of the learner's culture. Academic themes are generally unfamiliar to learners and are composed of their own jargon and sets of skills. Learners bring many of their own ideas about "scholarly topics" like math, science, and statistics, but they seldom call what they know "knowledge." (Although we have both taught research courses and baseball is a popular topic among many different learners, especially during the spring and summer months, we have yet to hear a single student say, "I wonder how much age accounts for the percentage of variance in number of home runs hit." Yet many learners would say a player is getting older and does not have the eye or the power to hit as many home runs as in younger years.) By presenting problems, often posed as questions, we can integrate what learners know with our academic themes to cocreate learning.

A heuristic way to consider academic themes as posed problems is to envision the following ways to frame the problem:

1. The academic theme is a relevant problem.
2. The academic theme solves a relevant problem.
3. The academic theme is made relevant by an intriguing problem.

The first possibility is to present the subject matter itself as the problem. The second is to pose a relevant problem from the experience of the learners that the academic theme may help to solve. The third is to identify a problem with little or no initial relevance that is nonetheless intriguing, where the academic theme is made relevant through teacher mediation. In all cases, we use learners' language, perspectives, and suppositions to contextualize and create the problem-solving process.

The Academic Theme Is a Relevant Problem. From the broadest to the most specific academic theme, we can incorporate learner perspectives, experiences, needs, and interests by sequential "what" and "how" questions. In an educational psychology course, we might ask: "In the broadest sense, what do we know about psychology? What do we want to know about psychology?" "How is psychology important in our daily lives?" "How has psychology helped or hindered people in our families?" In a narrower sense, "What do we know about learning disabilities? What do we want to know about learning disabilities?" "What does learning disability mean as we live our daily lives?" "How has the label *learning disability* helped or hindered people in our families?"

With writing, reflection, dialogue, critical incidents (Brookfield and Preskill, 2005), primary materials, and so on, we can take either of these topics and follow them along the path of learners' perspectives to create challenging problems to pursue for a day, a week, or perhaps the length of the course.

The Academic Theme Solves a Relevant Problem. When an academic theme solves a relevant problem, we are looking for situations that draw out learner concerns and interests. They need to understand the academic theme to resolve the issue, comprehend what action to take, find relevant insights, and so on. For example, one way to introduce multiple academic themes is to ask learners to take a role or a particular view to solve a relevant problem: the learner who distrusts a historical viewpoint and becomes a historian reading the primary material and writing her own historical account; the learner who finds a psychological interpretation too individualized and wants to offer a sociological analysis; or the learner who wants to take a systemic view of what is presented as a criminal problem. Most forms of research, creativity, and invention find their initial impetus in a relevant problem.

Another approach is to place the learner in a relevant problem. For courses in accounting, math, organizational planning, and so on, the problem might be stated: "You're the treasurer of a community organization, and you are losing X amount of money per month. With these assets, liabilities, dues, and so forth, what would you do?" For ethnic studies or courses on social policy or the law, the posed problem might be: "You are a twenty-one-year-old African American male; you have your first automobile accident, for which you are not at fault, and you have no other driving violations. But your insurance is cancelled. What recourse do you have to establish bias? You will need to understand actuarial records and predictive statistics to investigate this matter."

The Academic Theme Is Made Relevant by an Intriguing Problem. Human beings are rivers of curiosity. Every day we are challenged to bring order out of chaos and meaning from paradox. What is puzzling, bizarre, and surprising attracts our attention not so much because it is relevant but because it is intriguing. The same wonder that makes a beach a miracle of small astonishments for a child elicits amazement from an adult in the presence of a gifted magician. To some extent, our capacity for beguilement is beyond relevance, anchored in our need to remain alive. We anticipate to survive, whether to take a step or to enter traffic on a high-speed freeway. We make countless predictions as we live our lives. When the outcome is something unexpected, our reactions can range from a reflexive startle to an enduring fascination. Add to this our need for feedback about personal competence (Csikszentmihalyi, 1997), and we have the genesis of engaging and intriguing problems that can create emerging relevance for academic themes.

Central to the use of provocative problems in culturally responsive teaching is reciprocal interaction (Cummins, 1986), where there is a genuine dialogue between learners and teacher and the teacher evokes meaningful language use by the learners rather than merely employing gimmickry to foster attention and passive learning. Problems of emerging relevance (Brooks and Brooks, 1993) are basic to constructivist pedagogy, in which learning is understood to be a self-regulated process of resolving inner cognitive conflicts that usually become apparent through concrete experience, collaborative discourse, and reflection. Teacher mediation for problems of emerging relevance is used to elicit learner perspectives and hypotheses. Effective problem-solving situations of this sort usually ask learners to make predictions, are complex enough to evoke multiple responses, and can include group efforts to test hypotheses.

As a prototypical example of an academic theme made relevant by an intriguing problem, we offer the following example adopted from the work of Jacqueline Grennon Brooks and Martin Brooks (1993), which invites learners to better understand the concepts of momentum and energy.

The teacher presents a set of five hanging pendula (see Figure 4.1) with metal balls of equal size all touching each other in a resting position. By raising one ball and releasing it, the teacher allows the learners to note that one ball swings out on the other side. When two balls are raised and released, the learners observe that two balls swing out on the other side. Then raising three balls, the teacher asks the group to predict what will happen when the three balls are let go.

Figure 4.1 A Set of Five Hanging Pendula

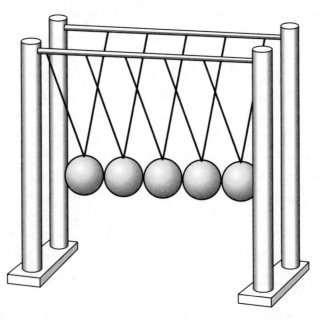

Source: Brooks, J. G., and Brooks, M. G. (1993). *In Search of Understanding: The Case for Constructivist Classrooms*, Set of Five Hanging Pendula Figure, p. 37. Reprinted with permission.

Having engaged diverse groups in this activity, Brooks and Brooks have found at least four of the following responses articulated by every group: (1) one ball will go out, but higher; (2) two balls will go out, but higher; (3) three balls will go out; (4) the balls will "go crazy"; (5) the balls will stop; and (6) the balls will swing together. They report they always ask learners to explain their responses, react to others' responses, and indicate whether they have changed their minds on hearing others' predictions. Because learners are given time to ponder the question, form their own responses, and share their thoughts in a manner that remains open to the opinions and questions of other learners and the teacher, interest develops in a context where immediate feedback by the apparatus itself can enlighten all possible responses. In fact, Brooks and Brooks write that within about half an hour, most groups demand the release of the three balls in order to test their theories.

Brooks and Brooks develop labs and experiences that focus explicitly on students' thinking. For example, those who claim the two balls will swing higher might examine the variables that influence the swing of a pendulum using balls of different weights and strings of different lengths to determine what gets a pendulum to swing higher. Further activities are developed based on learners' emerging interests and understandings.

Presenting learners with discrepant events and contradictory information is a corollary to this general method. For example, students may become more interested in the academic theme of heat transference when they have a chance to consider why the bottom of a paper cup does not burn from the flame of a lighter when the cup is filled with water. In fact, making academic themes relevant through learner engagement in intriguing problems is a process that relates to learner background and perspective. It requires instructors to know students well enough to understand what to do to encourage them to sincerely wonder about an important academic theme. But there must also be respect for learners' contributions—the reciprocal interaction that leads to a real dialogue with a view toward the social relevance of what is being learned. Without it, this method remains little more than an expedient trick to enliven conventional learning.

In a broad sense, most of the procedures that follow can also be characterized as problem-solving processes. Yet they possess sufficient differences to merit their own classifications as, for example, decision making or inquiry. In all instances, although we may offer guidelines and examples, we will not present precise or prescriptive steps for their use. We understand real-life problems as dialectical, where the ability to zig and zag between contradictory lines of reasoning, using each to critically evaluate the other, is necessary. Because culturally responsive pedagogy potentially embodies the social contexts and consequences of all learning, problem-solving processes do not lend themselves to technical or algorithmic sets of operations.

Decision Making

Decision making is a process used to arrive at a course of action, a policy, a plan, or a particular choice. It answers such questions as "What is the best way?" and "Which idea is most suitable?" The evidence generally includes estimated or imagined consequences, often arrived at through consideration of several options. Learners usually have to assemble information in the needed topic areas, compare advantages and disadvantages of alternative approaches, determine what additional information is needed, and justify their judgment of the most valued or effective response (Jimenez-Aleixandre and Pereiro-Munoz, 2002). Often the process includes the identification of criteria to determine the selection made.

Decision-making learning activities can be used in a wide variety of content areas. When based on learner interests, concerns, and perspectives, they can be used to address generative, topical, and academic themes. Because this process is well suited to real-life events and direct action, it is an excellent medium for the development of critical consciousness and intrinsic motivation.

The example we provide here could be used in almost any of the social sciences as well as courses in social and health policy, international studies, research, and statistics. The teacher asks the learners to form collaborative groups and to explore the Internet for any article whose topic deeply concerns them and that they see as relevant to the course. One group brings the article found in Exhibit 4.2.

Exhibit 4.2 Internet Article

No End in Sight for the Devastating Disease of HIV/AIDS

In the world today, approximately 33 million people have HIV/ AIDS. Last year, 2007, this ravaging illness took the lives of nearly 2.1 million, as estimated by UNAIDS, the Joint United Nations Programme on HIV/AIDS. With the World AIDS Day approaching, it is important to note that there has been medical progress in the detection and treatment of this disease. There is also much better access to medications in many African and Asian regions.

Nonetheless, globally, the number of women and young girls infected with this virus is rising. Those most poor among women are most at risk. Often, they live in cultures where prevention strategies are difficult to use because women have little autonomy. Sound practices such as the use of condoms and abstaining from high-risk sex are not available choices for them. Without human rights, especially for women, the means to combat HIV/ AIDS, *for men and women*, such as information and preventive practices are far less effective.

The World Health Organization (WHO) began World AIDS Day in 1988 to draw global attention to the devastating effects of this disease. The purpose of this day is to create unity in the

(continued)

world to combat HIV/AIDS, to use this day as reminder and a catalyst to fight this disease. However, without social change and greater social justice, continuing advances in the treatment and prevention of this virus have far less chance to be effective.

Source: Adapted from "HIV/AIDS: The Continuing Epidemic," *Everyday Health* (3). Retrieved February 19, 2008 from http://www.everydayhealth.com/ hiv/world-aids-day-feature/introduction.aspx.

After a dialogue about the meaning and ramifications of the information contained in the article, students and teacher agree to a project in which the learners will assume the role of a task force to further examine the materials and data used by UNAIDS, the Joint United Nations Programme on HIV/AIDS, to estimate the impact of this virus. Afterward, they will conduct their own study to arrive at a set of realistic and defensible recommendations regarding U.S. international policy and the AIDS epidemic. Students also want to collaborate to write an article based on these recommendations for the opinion column of the local newspaper. They have decided that central to this project is their mutual agreement about the criteria that will be used to create and select their recommendations. The report of their study will include explanations of why they chose these criteria and how well the recommendations meet them, along with a discussion of salient alternatives that may have failed to meet the criteria but remain worth consideration.

Authentic Research

Creative problem solving, research, and critical consciousness serve a number of similar functions. All three enhance meaning. All three question the status quo. All three use active-participatory methods. All three provide evidence that knowledge is not fixed but constantly changing. In fact, among some proponents of such research, the term *knowledge base* has been replaced with *knowledge dynamic* (English, 2005). And all three offer an opportunity to rethink experience and society.

In a general sense, research is an in-depth study of something. It involves detailed investigation and extensive explanation in order to understand, predict, apply, create, or evaluate some phenomenon. Much research also has an action agenda, with the researcher sharing results to have an impact on an audience, as in the case of a medical researcher submitting findings to health professionals. Although most people do research—for example, studying *Consumer Reports* and reading newspaper articles before shopping for a new car—the term is popularly associated with scholars, scientists, and graduate students. Also, to many learners, research is interpreted to mean the coerced ritual of writing a research paper using secondary sources to expound on a teacher-determined topic, resulting in dull encyclopedic information and a negative attitude.

Culturally responsive teaching advocates authentic research as a learning procedure in which learners actively investigate a problem or question of personal interest where there is no answer yet and use primary resources and real-world information and data to share results with people who might benefit from the findings or take action themselves based on these findings. Authentic research can be conducted in any discipline or across disciplines and used for generative, topical, or academic themes. As a procedure, it helps learners know that their questions and perspectives matter to acquire the skills and knowledge to pursue any interest in a competent and critical manner.

Authentic research also allows teachers to be co-researchers with their learners, acting as colleagues collaborating in the pursuit of knowledge. Because authentic research requires a researchable question of genuine interest to learners, it emphasizes, as most other culturally responsive teaching procedures do, the need for the teacher to know the concerns, cultural conditions, speech, and ways of learning represented among those in the class. Not surprisingly, encouraging learners to do authentic research means teachers must do a kind of research themselves about their learners, using learner-centered discourse and writing to arrive at questions and problems of mutual interest. In addition, brainstorming, concept mapping, and interviewing learners are other possible ways to find authentic research interests with learners.

In the rest of this section, we discuss five forms of authentic research. Each is distinct because of the type of investigation that is conducted. We have adapted four of the categorizations from the work of Robert Marzano (2007). This is not an exhaustive list, but it offers an exploration and exemplification of the range of possibilities.

Definitional Investigation. Definitional investigation involves clarifying or identifying the defining characteristics or important features of a concept, event, or situation for which such characteristics are unknown, in question, or not readily apparent (Marzano, 2007). Many evolving concepts and events have an emerging quality or debatable interpretation for which a definitional investigation could make important distinctions and lead to learner enlightenment, emancipation, or action of social consequence. For example, depending on the course, among the many current possible topics are abortion, sexual harassment, and bilingual education. What does each term mean? How do race, class, gender, and ethnicity affect how we understand the contemporary issues related to these terms and their defining characteristics? What personal concerns or experiences make any of these three terms more salient? A definitional investigation would research how any of these terms are commonly portrayed in the media or textbooks. Research tools would include primary source materials, direct studies, and interviews to explore less diluted information and data. Careful attention would be given to identifying contradictions, confusions, and misrepresentations. The process of students offering and justifying solutions or actions based on their definitional investigation becomes a preeminent motivational force for learning.

As a result of discourse, learners may offer their own conception of a situation or a generative theme for definitional investigation. This was the case for Daniel Solorzano (1989) at East Los Angeles College, who offered a course jointly listed by the sociology and Chicano studies departments to students who were mostly Chicanos from the local area.

In the late 1970s, when this class was first offered, gang violence was receiving much attention in the press and in the film industry. Just as the course began, the *Los Angeles Times* ran a three-part series on Chicanos in the mass media. By examining these texts and the theme of youth gangs, the students and their teacher engaged in a dialogue centering on the negative stereotypes of Chicanos and on the Chicano-white culture clash presented in Hollywood gang movies. After two weeks of discussion, Solorzano and his students arrived at two questions: Why are Chicanos portrayed negatively in the mass media? and Whose interests are served by these negative portrayals of Chicanos?

Based on these queries, extended research began with the class dividing itself into three research groups: (1) a library group to research contemporary and historical images of Chicanos in the media, using among their resources Hollywood trade papers, the *Readers' Guide to Periodical Literature*, *Sociological Abstracts*, the *Social Sciences Index*, the *Los Angeles Times Index*, and the *New York Times Index*; (2) a group to research public information data on youth gangs in East Los Angeles, using the area census on Chicanos, information from the sheriff's office and from the police department, sociological theories of gang and deviant behavior, and firsthand reports from gang members; and (3) a group to research the film industry, including representatives of Universal Pictures and Warner Brothers studios, Chicano community members and groups working as consultants to moviemakers, and groups that were beginning to challenge the negative images of Chicanos in the media.

Among the findings of the teams was that the gang problem was blown out of proportion, with the percentage of Chicano youths joining gangs not 10 percent as reported in the media but closer to 3 percent. Another finding was that in films and media, "Chicanos were stereotyped disproportionately in subordinate and demeaning occupational roles such as bandits, thieves, and gangsters" (Solorzano, 1989, p. 221). After analyzing and discussing their research, the learners more clearly realized how film companies were exploiting Chicano stereotypes to make a profit. Consequently, they organized a boycott and an informational picket against some of the films they found insulting. Collaborating with outside organizations for assistance led to the founding of the Gang Exploitation Committee. Solorzano reports that no new Chicano youth gang movies appeared in the decade after this class. Public protest and the mixed profitability of these films seem to have stopped their production. It was apparent to him that these learners developed commitment to and confidence in their own ideas and research and succeeded in doing something they considered important and positive.

Historical Investigation. Historical investigation involves determining, understanding, and evaluating past events in order to comprehend them, often with the purpose of clarifying present or future incidents and actions. This procedure is usually concerned with why or how something happened (Marzano, 2007). Every academic discipline has historical relevance, and questions can range from "Why did the dinosaurs die?" to "What was the crucial chain of events leading to the dismantling of apartheid in South Africa?" The history inherent in any subject area is often replete with contradictions and confusion. For this as well as other reasons, historical research can be an exciting and engrossing context for dialectical thinking. When we begin to ask whose interests are served by certain interpretations of historical events and whether particular actions were justified, we quickly move into the realm of multiple perspectives and critical consciousness (Sirotnik, 1990).

Students frequently have questions about the accuracy or authenticity of historical information. Working with them as actual historians and investigating primary sources of data such as original documents, diaries, journals, photo collections, letters, and oral histories can be a fascinating enterprise. The following example, adapted from Giroux (1978), offers a dialectical approach for conducting historical research that can be extended to numerous topical and academic themes. In this instance, the academic theme is immigration law, and the question is, "What was the argument for nineteenth-century U.S. immigration restriction legislation?" A way to initially proceed and develop a relevant context and a variety of perspectives is to ask learners to consider data from their own lives about the impact and fairness of immigration laws. Using this dialogue as a bridge, the teacher could present an overview on the passing of twentieth-century immigration laws to enhance the learners' awareness of a broader historical context.

At this point, learners could engage the concept of "frame of reference." This could be done by having the learners read two specific historical accounts from the nineteenth century, each covering the same subject and a similar set of information but arriving at two very different ideas:

- Immigrants played a pivotal role in the growth of U.S. cities and industries by providing valuable skills and labor.
- Immigrants displaced native workers from jobs by lowering wages and intensifying unemployment.

After students finish their readings, they discuss the possible frames of reference represented by these two ideas and the meaning of this exercise for themselves. With this background, they form historical research teams to investigate the primary materials (congressional records, newspaper accounts, and so forth) relevant to the restriction laws limiting immigration in the nineteenth century. Through facilitation by the teacher, they agree to pay attention in their research to the same set of possible historical influences, for example, political machines, racism, the growth of the Catholic church, anti-Semitism, and large-scale immigration from southeastern Europe. They also add some of their own information based on their team's frames of reference and possible findings. When they conclude their research, they draft a paper with a modified question: "Were nineteenth-century targeted legislative restrictions on immigration justified?" In their paper, they identify the information they selected, the frames of reference that emerged, what they were, and how they as practicing historians were influenced by them.

The research teams read each other's papers and meet with one another or as a whole group to compare and contrast the differences and similarities of ideas that resulted from their investigations. This dialogue leads to an individual reflection paper or some form of artistic expression that indicates the meaning and learning constructed by the learners from this entire experience. The possibility remains that the group continues with this theme and explores the rationalization of current restrictive immigration laws—for example, toward people from Mexico or Central America—with consideration of collective action based on learning.

Projective Investigation. Projective investigation is concerned with the hypothetical. It involves researching what will happen if certain circumstances continue or change or if some future event occurs (Marzano, 2007). Current concern about the severe global consequences of rain forest and old growth forest depletion is due in part to projective investigations. Another form of projective investigation is to predict the consequences if some past event had or had not occurred. For example, students predict the likely political outcomes if Nixon's presidency had continued beyond Watergate, or they estimate the potential agricultural production in the United States if the great floods of 1993 had not happened.

Again, learners research what is conventionally accepted about the topic, look at primary source material, collect data, identify contradictions and confusions, and seek to resolve them with justified solutions and actions. The following is an example of a projective investigation that might be conducted in courses ranging from sociology and public policy to economics and education.

For many, the stereotypical image of a homeless person is of a man sleeping in a city doorway or asking passersby for spare change. Although this depiction is inaccurate in many ways, until the early 1980s almost all homeless people were men (DeAngelis, 1994); now, families—typically women with two children under age five—make up about 50 percent of the homeless population. This percentage represents 600,000 families and 1.35 million children (National Alliance to End Homelessness, 2007). Whether urban, suburban, or rural, there are areas populated by homeless people throughout the United States, sleeping in shelters, cars, motels, and on the street. The most conclusive research indicates that lack of affordable housing is the primary cause of homelessness. For families and individuals struggling to pay the rent, a serious illness or disability can start a downward spiral into homelessness, beginning with a lost job, depletion of savings to pay for health care, and eventual eviction.

With this kind of background information and after considering their own experience, a class might begin to address the following questions:

- Can the rate of homelessness or the people who become homeless be predicted in a city or a local community?
- What are the relationships among such factors as gender, unemployment, health care, affordable housing for the poor, and homelessness?

- What are the historic trends or patterns among such factors, and how might they influence the future?
- What can be done politically to prevent or reduce homelessness?

In addition to viewing public and real estate records, interviewing key informants is essential. Informants include people who are homeless, shelter administrators and volunteers, religious leaders, community mental health workers, and police officers.

Through dialogue, students might identify aspects of homelessness they believe to be most important for a projective investigation. Research teams might then be divided across a number of possible ways to learn: students working with public records, conducting interviews with families, meeting with single women and men, contacting religious leaders, interviewing the police, and so forth. Tasks for the instructor and students would include structuring the interviews, organizing data, and analyzing findings. In addition to learning more about homelessness and what might be predicted in one's own community, the emotional and social impact of the process is significant. Journal writing and self-assessment procedures, detailed in the next chapter, might be used to support further learning. Eventually the teacher and students may be moved to ask, "Now that we know what we know, what can we do about it?" Action is a real possibility. The National Alliance to End Homelessness has a Web site (http://www.endhomelessness.org/section/action/actnow) with specific ideas and resources for reducing homelessness, including community education, political advocacy, volunteering, and donating. This organization may provide a venue for the actions that students want to carry out as a result of their learning and transformed perspectives."

Experimental Inquiry. Experimental inquiry approximates the conditions of a scientific experiment that seeks to explain something, better understand how or why something occurs, or explore if certain hypotheses can lead to specific predictions. In its most fundamental form, experimental inquiry involves observing phenomena, analyzing or generating explanations about those phenomena, making predictions based on one's analysis, then testing those predictions and reflecting on the results to arrive at insights and greater understanding (Marzano, 2007).

Most people have conducted experiments in science courses, but our purpose here is to bring this kind of inquiry to all content areas and across disciplines as an intrinsically motivating way of learning for both teachers and learners. Our experience is that experimental inquiry increases the validity of multiple perspectives and allows more challenging discourse regarding the status quo in many fields of study. We especially want to advocate its use on a spontaneous basis: "Given that observation, why don't we try an experiment?" and as a means for teachers to improve educational practice. With the latter goal in mind, we offer the following example from a shared experience.

- *Observation.* Having used films and videos for many years to illustrate various ideas and perspectives, we noticed that learners' enjoyment of humor regarding the content seemed to vary according to the guidelines we provided before watching the films. With one film—of a professor teaching physics—we observed that when there were no prior instructions, learners seemed to laugh more and react more strongly than when we would advise them, before the film began, to analyze scenes within the film. This was a film used to heighten student awareness of the impact of unpredictability rather than to teach a particular concept or skill.

- *Analysis.* One thought was that different groups have different senses of humor, and fate or randomness favored the groups without guidelines. Another thought, the one we preferred, was that humor is often a narrative and holistic experience, and analysis, as requested by the teacher, fragments humor and distracts attention from it. Because of our instructions, students were literally looking for something else.

• *Prediction.* Learning groups without prior instructions to analyze will experience and report greater enjoyment in response to the physics teacher film than learning groups receiving prior instructions regarding analysis.

• *Test.* We showed the film to eight groups of graduate students in teacher education courses. Four groups received no prior instructions and four received the same prior instructions to "look for the quality of unpredictability in the professor's examples of various principles of physics." We used the process of triangulation, collecting observations or accounts of a situation (or some aspect of it) from a variety of perspectives (Elliot, 1991) in order to gather sufficient evidence. We could then compare the data for possible support or contradiction. The three perspectives represented were those of one of the authors, a colleague, and students. After seeing the film, each group of students was asked to respond to the Likert scale shown in Exhibit 4.3. We observed each group and agreed to use evidence of attention, smiles, and laughter as indication of students' enjoyment and expressions of distraction, boredom, and discomfort as signs of the students not enjoying the film as we completed the Likert scale for each group.

• *Reflection on results.* For students' self-ratings, we decided to use "interest" as the descriptor because a group could appear to enjoy a film less than another group but be equally interested. Also, for purposes of learning, we believed interest was a more important distinction. The results of the experiment supported our prediction. Student groups without prior instructions had higher self-ratings of interest and were observed to enjoy the physics teacher film more than student groups receiving prior instructions to analyze the film.

■ ■

Exhibit 4.3 Likert Scales and Learners' and Teachers' Ratings

Learners' Self-Ratings
I found this film to be:

1	2	3	4	5	6	7
very dull						very interesting

Teachers' Ratings
The learners appeared to be:

1	2	3	4	5	6	7
not enjoying the film						enjoying the film

Ratings for Groups Receiving Instructions[a]

Learners	Colleague	Myself
5.2	4	4
5.9	6	5
5.6	5	5
5.5	5	5

(continued)

Ratings for Groups Not Receiving Instructions[a]

Learners	Colleague	Myself
6.5	6	6
6.5	6	7
6.6	7	6
6.4	6	6

[a]Ratings are mean scores.

A primary lesson was how subtle but powerful an orientation, or frame of mind, can be, how looking for one thing or having an analytical perspective may diffuse, diminish, or distract from realizing certain aspects or qualities of a given experience—in this case, humor in a film. Indirectly, this small experiment heightened our respect for the obviously more powerful effects of language, experience, and culture on perception. Specifically, it supported our intuitive notion that with regard to the particular film, student enjoyment is indicative of student interest; our directions probably detract from the students' total interest in the film. In general, it contributed to sensitizing us to how learners and teachers create a goal or frame of mind for a learning activity. And finally, for this film, the experiment informed our decision to abstain from providing students with instructions prior to viewing this film in the future.

Although the previous experiment was not technically rigorous, it did offer more information about a teaching practice. It also broadened an understanding of perspective and how it can influence what is eventually perceived. Experimental inquiry does not prove something or determine knowledge. It allows us to better understand something, improve something, and arrive at information in which we have more confidence and trust. It also helps us to understand the insufficiency of much research and the need for multiple perspectives to validate findings. Part of the fascination of research is that it is an endeavor that leads us to know more while constantly reminding us how little we know. With modest instruction and support, most learners are able to carry out intriguing forms of inquiry in any academic discipline.

Action Research

Action research is disciplined inquiry that has become increasingly common in organizations seeking to improve through local knowledge. It is a systematic cyclical process based on a presenting problem of practice, as the example in this section illustrates. Action research is often collaborative and includes a form of action or intervention with related evidence to support new insights, questions, and innovations applied to practice. Unlike conventional theoretical research, however, which attempts to make generalizable knowledge claims, action research feeds new insights into the context in which it is situated. The work of Kathryn Herr and Gary L. Anderson (2005), Peter Reason (2006), and Ernest Stringer (2007) is comprehensive and informative for educators with modest action research experience. We advocate that instructors using this book consider action research as a method to improve their own professional practice.

Although an extensive explanation of action research is beyond our scope in this book, we offer an example of it related to how a math instructor strengthened her instructional practice. The example includes (1) a problem of practice; (2) a cycle of inquiry that is rigorous, structured, and continuous based on a presenting problem of practice; (3) an action or set of actions to address the problem of practice; (4) systematic data collection; (5) analysis of data; and (6) reflection from which to pose new problems of practice or presenting questions. Inquiry that relies on local knowledge within a local context provides a way to enhance meaning in how we, as instructors, can continuously improve our practice.

Mathematics professor Allison Sloan wants to find new methods to teach an introductory math course more effectively. This course is a recent addition to the curriculum, designed as an alternative to the college algebra path. As course chair, Dr. Sloan has taught the course for two semesters and has identified four areas that need improvement: student attitude and lack of motivation to participate in what they saw as a "dead-end" math course, the apparent lack of connection between topics, students' difficulty in comprehending the material, and the students' perception that the course was irrelevant to their lives.

To address these problems of practice, Dr. Sloan decides to experiment with a set of new practices that she believes could strengthen collaborative learning and heighten the relevance of learning. She creates note packages with "holes" (incomplete statements) for students to fill in during class lectures to ensure attention to key concepts and improve comprehension. She periodically pauses and asks students to compare their responses with a partner, helping each other to complete their holes. Professor Sloan also uses a Web-based discussion board to promote communication among students outside class. Furthermore, she attempts to heighten relevance by asking students to choose a topic from their own major that could provide a context for exemplifying newly learned math concepts in action. Although students are reluctant to make the choices at first, by the end of the semester they appear to be deeply engaged in choosing personal topics for further illustrations.

To examine her perceptions about the ways in which her new set of pedagogical strategies influences student motivation and learning, she reserves an hour during the end of the quarter to conduct five-minute interviews with nine students, three of whom have been low performing, three of whom are performing along the mean, and three of whom are consistently high performing. In addition, she compares the quality of their culminating projects to the work of a subset of former students who were demographically similar and had similar reasons for taking the course.

An analysis of interview data reveals that the current class of students enjoyed class more and spent more time on their final papers than had students in the previous two courses. In addition, compared to her "control" group of former students, she notes a higher level of critical analysis and synthesis. This seems to correspond to her theory that making note taking more focused and content more personally relevant strengthens students' attention and influences the likelihood of deeper engagement with their math projects. In the summary of her personal journal notes, Dr. Sloan notes that the activities have helped her and her students connect with each other at a higher level than the previous class, elevating the opinions of each other, and, more important, strengthening student motivation and learning. Students have expressed an appreciation of the usefulness of mathematics to them in their majors and their lives, and Dr. Sloan notes that she is less likely to see "poor math students" who are avoiding algebra and more likely to see students who are successful in analyzing how mathematics fits in and supports their aspirations.

An unanticipated outcome is that students have brought questions for Dr. Sloan during class about using math in areas beyond the scope of this course of study. Using this challenge to continue her cycle of inquiry and related actions, she decides to seek assistance from colleagues outside her department to learn and experiment with ways to provide more helpful feedback to students when their questions exceed her own range of knowledge.

In this example of action research, the teacher enhances meaning for her own professional practice. Her collection and analysis of student reflections help her to identify new ways to make her course more engaging and relevant. She also sees the need for learning more advanced approaches to giving feed-back in her course. For a specific example of students learning about their own professional knowledge through action research, review the data-in-a-day action research project at the University of Washington (Ginsberg and Kimball, 2008).

Invention and Artistry

Invention and artistry are creative ways to express oneself, respond to a need or desire, react to an experience, and make connections between the known and the unknown, the concrete and the abstract, the worldly and the spiritual, and among different people, places, and things. With art and invention, people attempt to answer such questions as these:

- What do I want to express?
- What would I like to create?
- What is another way?
- What is a better way?
- What do I imagine?
- What do I wish to render?

We discuss invention and artistry together because the conceptual and subjective differences between them is difficult to discern and because we believe both ought to be integral to learning and not, as is so often the case with art, a separate entity or curriculum within education. Artistry can be considered embedding art in learning as opposed to a separate and frequently disenfranchised experience. As Jamake Highwater (1994) has said, "Knowledge is barren without the capacity for feeling and imagination." Art is a vivid sensibility within life and learning across all cultures throughout the world. The lack of meaning so frequently discerned in academic learning is due in part to its distillation of artistry from learning.

Although invention is more frequently associated with a specific product or technology, it is quite difficult to tell the difference internally between when one is being inventive and one is being artistic. Both processes can be used in every subject area. Both are open ended and kindle an awareness of creative possibility while considering generative, topical, and academic themes. For example, a former colleague, Michele Naylor, who taught a course in foundations of education, approached her learners with the question, "As educators in our communities, what are the things we most deeply want to contribute and accomplish?" The learners were asked to take an hour to reflect, write, and sketch their reactions to this question. Afterward they met in small groups to share their responses. This led to the mutual agreement to post their sketches and conduct a large-group conversation. From this activity, it was suggested that the group compose a mural depicting the theme of community and learning. Using poster paints, a large roll of paper, and masking tape, they collaborated, using their ideas and sketches to create a mural that covered the entire bottom six feet of the circumference of the classroom. This took about six hours and a Saturday of their time. Although the classroom was heavily used by other learners from other disciplines, the mural stood for approximately six months. During the creation of the mural, one of the students took photographs of the process and created a collage. Each student also wrote a reflective paper discussing the process of creating the mural and the ideas it represented. At the next class session, encircled by the mural they created, students summarized their reactions and made connections between this process and the work they do or intend to do in the community.

To exemplify invention, we recall a small cadre of learners who were struggling to comprehend systems theory and decided to invent a game, played according to systems theory, that could teach the fundamental concepts and principles of this theory to other learners in an enjoyable way. The game board was a narrow roll of cloth with simulated steps that, when extended, created a serpentine figure across the width of a small room. In order to be eligible to play the game, one had to have completed a "systems reader" identified by the learning group. The game could be played by teams or individuals. Along its path were several stations where players would be interviewed or asked to complete activities and draw graphic models of systemic processes. These stations were operated by the game's inventors. When players appeared confused about or unaware of systemic concepts, they could talk with the inventors, explore relevant examples, and find out about other references. The game was not competitive and had three objectives: (1) to comprehend systems theory, (2) to have an enjoyable learning experience, and (3) to improve the game itself. Because systems theory is a foundation for a number of disciplines at these students' university, the inventors had no difficulty finding players. Postgame interviews with each set of players provided formative feedback for ongoing revision. In order to maximize its use with other learners, the game was donated to the university library with a DVD video that included directions and explanations.

Our experience has been that learners across many cultures welcome the invitation to infuse their academic work with artwork such as sketches and poetry. We have also found that projects that include as a core or as an essential component works of film, photography, play writing, visual art, musical composition, songwriting, and performance art offer access to and legitimization of some of the most profound knowledge and understanding learners achieve.

Simulation, Role Playing, and Games

Simulation is defined by Meyers and Jones (1993) as an umbrella term for learning procedures that include role-playing and simulation exercises and games that allow students to practice and apply their learning in inauthentic yet sufficiently realistic contexts. When learners are able to experience perspectives, ideas, skills, and situations approximating authentic instances of life, they have an opportunity to enhance the meaning of what it is they are learning, as well as to become more proficient.

Role playing is acting out a possible situation by personifying another individual or by imagining another scene or set of circumstances. Simulation exercises refer to situations in which a whole class is involved, with learners assuming different roles as they act out a prescribed scenario. These scenarios allow participants to acquire or put into practice particular concepts or skills. Simulations often immerse students in another social reality to allow them to feel what might remain only abstract in textual materials—such concepts as power, privilege, stereotyping, and discrimination. Simulation games are similar to simulation exercises but are usually very structured and have a competitive win-lose quality. A simulation game that provides the opportunity for learners to immerse themselves in the dynamics of power and privilege is Star Power (Simulation Training Systems, 1993). However, we offer a note of caution: our experience is that because of their gamelike characteristics, simulations can feel contrived; they benefit from a teacher who maintains a serious and compassionate tone while learners participate. (One of several texts with useful ideas for role playing to enhance multicultural awareness is Pedersen, 2004.)

Since role playing has broad, cross-disciplinary applicability and allows the most flexible and learner-centered perspectives among simulation approaches, it can be a useful procedure for culturally responsive teaching. Role playing provides an opportunity to try out ideas, skills, and perspectives that have been introduced formally from textbooks and learning materials, as well as more informally from teachers and peers. Depending on the degree of prescriptiveness and formality of the scenario, role playing can blend into a simulation exercise. The main goal with either procedure is that the learner is genuinely involved with intellect, feeling, and physical senses so that the experience is substantive and realistic.

Role playing provides the opportunity to think in the moment, question one's perspectives, respond to novel or expected circumstances, and consider different ways of knowing. It can be used to practice a specific skill such as critical questioning, a collaborative skill such as collective bargaining, a problem-solving skill such as a computerized simulation of the procedure for a biochemistry experiment, or a synthesizing skill such as how to organize a learning plan using procedures from throughout this book. Role playing is also excellent for the development of empathy and validation, especially when students and instructors imagine the viewpoints and rationales of people from different backgrounds, as in the case of a European American rancher in southern Texas or a Mexican immigrant offering opinions about immigration policy. When there is a chance to reverse roles and act out roles from opposing or different perspectives (for example, labor and management) or from an unfamiliar or conflicting perspective (as in the case of a police officer taking on the role of a gang member or vice versa), learners have a chance to consider and feel from a position they may never have engaged before.

We have had extensive experience with role playing in academic and community settings when the perspectives of administrator, teacher, student, parent, and community member were in conflict. One of us also uses role playing as a way to build the confidence of prekindergarten to grade 12 teachers who are planning home visits with families who are recent immigrants to the United States. Beginning with a knock on the door and concluding with examples of how a family story or experience will be woven into curriculum, role playing helps teachers and interpreters practice ways to build relationships in a brief window of time (Cobbs and Ginsberg 2006).

Role playing is an excellent procedure for shifting perspectives, adding insights, and starting conversations that may have been unimaginable before the introduction of the simulation process. A unique use of this procedure by Loretta T. Johnson in history courses (Meyers and Jones, 1993) is to have learners create their own character at a particular time in history, giv-ing that person a series of characteristics related to, say, gender, religion, class, occupation, and ethnicity. Learners write out the character's personality and role in society. As history continues and historical events occur, whether the Hiroshima bombing in 1945 or the French Revolution, students describe their charac-ter's actions and reactions to circumstances of the times as they continue their reading and research. By consciously chronicling and imagining the effect of historical events on a realistic per-son in a context the learner has actively constructed, and also by understanding that person's impact on those events, learn-ers gather meaning from history and employ a level of analysis beyond textbook superficiality.

Using a scenario of a teacher and parent in conflict about a student's performance, we offer the following series of guidelines, adapted from the work of Meyers and Jones (1993), for creating effective simulations. If you have not done simulations before, observe a teacher you trust who uses them routinely so you can see the process firsthand with your own teaching situation in mind and are able to ask relevant questions before you begin:

• *Know where and how the simulation conforms to your teaching sit-uation.* Is it a good fit given who your students are, where learn-ing is headed, and what learners expect to do? It is possible and necessary to prevent a simulation that feels contrived or trivial-izes a significant issue or concept.

• *Plan well ahead.* Have some degree of confidence that your learners are familiar and proficient enough to use the con-cepts or skills to be practiced. Do they have a fair knowledge of or background about the cultural roles or personal roles they may assume? If they are uncomfortable, can learners excuse themselves or observe until they are more at ease to play a role? Simulations often benefit from a lead observer. This is a facilitation role students can play if they are initially reluctant to take part in the scenario. The observer in the role-playing process provides feedback and guides the discussion that follows.

• *Be relatively sure students understand the roles and the scenario before you begin the role play.* Allow questions and clarification. Often it is helpful to write out a script with students to describe roles, attitudes, experiences, and beliefs. Developing a script with students helps deepen their familiarity with the role. For example, after reading an article on "funds of knowledge" (Gonzalez, Moll, and Amanti, 2005), aspiring K–12 educators who were learning to conduct home visits collaborated to write a script that included a teacher, an interpreter, and a family member. An excerpt from the agreed-on script for the parent in the home visit role play included such statements as this one:

> I work two jobs and run a small business selling dinner to
> neighbors and friends. I am tired from the day but happy the
> teacher has taken time from her own work to meet with us.
> It is an honor to have her visit. Although I am usually confi-
> dent, including when I had to find reliable medical care when
> my child was ill, I am worried that at my own kitchen table I
> will not have a way to display my gratitude for the work of the
> school. I am also concerned that the stories that define our
> determination and that have long been a part of our family's
> history will be buried in superficial chatter. I do not want to be
> boastful, but I want to do everything I can to develop a strong
> and positive two-way relationship.

• *Set aside enough time for the simulation and the discussion that follows.* The discussion and analysis are as important as the simulation itself. What perspectives, reactions, and insights emerge? What has not been dealt with that needs attention? Have our goals for learning been accomplished? How do we know? What about the process itself? How can it be improved? This is the time to raise issues of critical consciousness, when impressions are fresh and resonant.

• *When role playing seems potentially embarrassing or threatening, it is often helpful for the teacher to model the first role play and discuss it.* This may alleviate some initial hesitation and allow learners to see how other reasonably competent adults use potential imperfections and mistakes to learn. In some cases, starting out slowly, with only learners who are interested in role playing serving as initial models, can help work up to exercises involving all learners.

• *Freeze the action during a role play when necessary.* A pause in action can serve many purposes, providing students with more time, for example, to critique a perspective, explore reactions to a poignant comment, make suggestions to the actors, and relieve the tension. Some people suggest ending a simulation at a high point so that discussion will be more enthusiastic and compelling. We believe this depends on the purpose and narrative of the role play because some issues may need to be further encountered to explore their depth and ramifications.

■■

For many students, simulation may be the only way to enter worlds apparently too distant or to try out actions initially too uncomfortable. In some instances, this procedure may not only enhance meaning, but also nurture courage and the capacity to act with new insight.

Case Study Method

A case study is a narrative of real events that presents provocative questions and undercurrents in a way that compels learners and teachers to analyze, deliberate, and advance informed judgments that integrate an array of perspectives and concepts (Shulman and others, 1990; Marsick, 2004). The hallmark of cases is their authenticity. With lifelike, concrete details and characters expressing a personal voice, they put flesh and blood on otherwise abstract and ambiguous concepts. Because cases present dilemmas and are open ended, they tend to stimulate extremely different reactions and propositions across a group.

The case study method enhances meaning and is ideal for teaching diverse learners because it fosters multiple interpretations. Yet it does so in a manner that permits students and teachers to be more open and less defensive, because the situation is someone else's (Hutchings, 1993). In addition, we can share our uncertainty as well as our knowledge and experience, because this is a knotty problem, not one given to glib resolution. When we face a relevant predicament with an opportunity to learn something important with others, an interesting form of solidarity often emerges. Although cases are sometimes viewed as being an exploratory tool, as opposed to a form of valid inquiry, they are used across disciplines to examine real-life situations, issues, and problems, often with imagination and vision.

As in our discussion of the previous procedures in this chapter, our goal is to be specific enough about the way to use case studies so that you can make use of this method in your own setting and offer guidelines general enough to allow your own creativity and situational conditions. Most practitioners are dogmatic about only one thing: having a thorough understanding of the case and its nuances before teaching it (Meyers and Jones, 1993; Marsick, 2004). By reading the case a few times, you can begin to see if it meets such criteria as relevance, authenticity, narrative strength, complexity, and so forth to merit selection for use. If it does, then rereading the case provides the opportunity to construct discussion notes and a possible outline for dialogue. These questions can be used to reflect on while reading a case:

- What is your first impression?
- What are different ways to interpret this case?
- What are the teaching and learning issues?
- What is culturally relevant in this case?

- Can students construct principles and applications from this case?

Keep these questions in mind as you read the case in Exhibit 4.4, which was originally composed for use by faculty for collaborative discussion about improving college teaching.

Exhibit 4.4 Case Study

"See You on Wednesday!"
by
Deanna Yameen,
Instructor and Critical-Thinking Specialist,
Massachusetts Bay Community College,
and
Elizabeth Fideler,
Recruiting New Teachers, Inc.

The first class meeting seemed to go smoothly enough. I went in, introduced myself, and reviewed the course syllabus and calendar. The students seemed pretty much like the students I taught at State U.—maybe a little older. They asked the same questions about how long the paper should be and which books to buy. They made no comments about the journal assignment for the next class. They readily filled out my survey, and class ended twenty minutes early.

I used the same survey I used at State U., with exactly the same directions: "I'm just looking for some information to get a feel for the class. Tell me (1) why you are taking the class, and (2) what you want me to know about you. Please be honest. You don't have to sign your name if you'd rather not." From reading their responses I know I'll have to reconsider what I am going to do on Wednesday. I can't assume that students have similar writing skills or academic goals to students at a state university. I may need to talk with someone more experienced with teaching students at this community college.

(continued)

Take a look at the responses for yourself:

I want to write very, very well.

I want you to know is that the main reason for me to learn, is because I wanna go to computer afterwards.

This is my first class in college. Since I graduated I wanted to try writing to see if I didn't have the ability.

I am an international student. Sometimes I don't speak or tell what I want to say well.

I want to how to use research information then write paper.

To enter nursing program, and have a good abilities.

You should know that I have a learning disable.

I have a Learning Disability in Reading and I think my writing is Poor.

I would like to prove to myself that I am now ready to be a serious student and that I can get an A in this class.

I failed out of school and it has taken me a long time to get the guts to try again. I really want to do well.

I have taken this course last semester and wrote three essay.

A lot of things come very easily to me but what does not I become easily frustrated which makes it that much harder. I have to read lips. I have trouble hearing.

I would like to learn how to get my thought down in an organized fashion.

I would like my writing to be impressive and express how I feel.

I would like to write a paper on my own that really makes sense.

I want to be able to write a good essay, or other papers I might have to write in my college days.

I want to be prepared for the other courses for my college education. I want to improve my writing skills.

> I'd like to read different kinds of books and I want to try to like writing.
>
> I want to learn to read and think about a situation or article and know what to write about.
>

It describes the first day of a course in which students will be working to improve their writing skills.

A practical first step is to be sure that learners comprehend the goals of the particular case study. In this instance, possible goals could include the following:

- Increase understanding of how to improve teaching and learning among diverse learners.
- Improve understanding of how bias, class, privilege, and disability present themselves and influence teaching and learning.
- Analyze and explore multiple perspectives of the issues found in the case.
- Learn how to find out more about learners at the beginning of a course so that teaching can be more effective and culturally responsive.

Discussion notes can be helpful in designing a plan for moving the learning group through the case: how to introduce the case, questions and probes for analysis, cues for taking the case to another stage, and what to ask if discussion stalls. However, we encourage flexibility with their use because it is not uncommon for learners to create perspectives and insights beyond the teacher's imagination. An initial and partial discussion outline for "See You on Wednesday!" follows (for those less familiar with teaching writing, a fine resource intended for secondary education but also applicable to postsecondary students is National Writing Project and Nagin, 2006):

Suggested Discussion Outline

1. Which items in this case stand out as significant teaching and learning issues?

   Probes: Which of these issues are you familiar with from your own teaching? Which of these issues have you had some success in resolving?

2. What kind of diversity is represented in this case?

   Probes: How might this kind of diversity be constructed as a greater opportunity for learning for everyone? Which issues of diversity in this case stir up apprehension? Why?

3. How effective is the assessment strategy used to find out about the learners?

   Probes: How might you improve this assessment strategy? What alternative assessment strategies would you suggest?

4. What does one do on Wednesday?

Depending on factors such as the focus of the case text and the experience, trust, and sense of community among the learners, cases can be examined in small groups or with a single larger group. Opening the discussion of the case in a manner that invites wide participation and relevant commentary is important. Some ways to start include:

- Ask learners to free-write for a couple of minutes after reading the case so they have something to offer based on reflection.
- Ask each learner to speak with a partner for a few minutes about key issues in the case before requesting individual responses.

- Ask a couple of learners to summarize the case before asking others to join in.

- Ask each learner to remark about one element she or he felt was important in the case and record these comments publicly. This lets everyone know there is a range of interpretations before discussion begins.

During the discussion, the kinds of questions the instructor asks can serve different purposes. Some questions, for example, further analysis, challenge an idea, mediate between conflicting views, and compel students to generate principles and concepts. For the teacher, the role is one of a facilitator who provides opportunities for everyone to contribute but who also has the responsibility to provoke and inform, cautiously avoiding the temptation to impose his or her own perspectives. At times, role-playing aspects of the case may be effective—for example, "Given your experience and discussion, how would you approach students on Wednesday? What would be your first remarks to students on Wednesday? What would you specifically do as their instructor?"

Other times it may be beneficial to record key information on the board or a chart. Direct quotes from the case can help focus the group. At times, playing devil's advocate may be a way to surface missing issues or counterpoints. Typically, after the case has been read, the pattern of learning moves incrementally from reflection and analysis to problem-solving hypotheses to application to one's own practices or social action. (You may recognize this sequence as the Kolb experiential learning model discussed in Chapter Three.)

Closing the case discussion well is critical. As Hutchings (1993) points out, there is disagreement among practitioners about the degree of closure appropriate to the case study method. This approach, more than some other procedures presented in the chapter, has a structure and style for which looking for "the answer" is not appropriate. However, it is possible and necessary to conclude the case study process in a satisfying manner. This might include the opportunity to reflect on what has been learned, synthesize or identify new understandings, air unresolved conflicts or questions, and make plans for making changes or taking action. The following list provides suggestions (Hutchings, 1993):

- Spend some time writing answers to such questions as these: "What new insights did you gain from this case study and its discussion?" "What are your lingering questions?" "What are some new ideas with which you would like to experiment?" "What resources would be useful to you?"
- Brainstorm in small groups or as a large group insights, personal changes in thinking or action, or new areas to explore as a result of the case study.
- Go around the group, and allow each student to provide one insight, question, lesson, change, or good that has emerged as a result of this process.

Using case studies in technical fields such as chemistry may require a more structured approach, but the challenge remains to employ this format in a manner that does not suppress the free flow of ideas and perspectives. Also, for generative, topical, and academic themes, learners, individually and collaboratively, are a rich resource for constructing cases for course study.

■ ■

Because of the complexity of these experiential and research practices and because of some students' unfamiliarity with them, students often need an opportunity to learn these approaches before they more independently apply them. Beyer (1988) offers the following set of guidelines, which we have adapted and found quite helpful:

1. Introduce the procedure by describing and demonstrating the steps of the process with a vivid relevant example,

clearly outlined on paper or overhead projector (even better when the example comes as a suggestion of the learners).

2. Have learners work in guided practice with a short and relevant process that captures the form of the procedure. For example, students can conduct brief experimental inquiry among themselves following an outline prepared by the teacher.

3. Have learners take notes on their reflections while they are involved in guided practice and discuss them collaboratively afterward (reflection-in-action).

4. As a result of this reflection-in-action, learners may make changes in the procedure to align with their cultural perspectives and intellectual strengths. If necessary, they may continue the inquiry cycle by experimenting with the modified procedure and again reflecting on the process.

When students are not familiar with a practice to enhance meaning and have had no chance for prior guided learning, teachers will need to coach them more closely through the process.

Projects

When a practice for enhancing meaning becomes one of the major involvements of a course, takes the better part of a semester to complete, and is formally noted as a legitimate option or requirement in the course's syllabus, it is probably a project. In the world outside education, *project* is often the term used to describe the major undertakings of businesses and institutions ("We're working on a new project," or, perhaps as a criticism, "This thing is turning into a project"). In education as well as in life, magnitude and complexity generally afford something the status of a project. From community service to dramatic presentations, projects offer the multiple parts, relationships, challenges, perspectives, meanings, and resolutions, bundled in a holistic framework, that make learning intrinsically motivating and capable of embracing cultural diversity. Because of their size and duration, projects provide the opportunity for active immersion across disciplines and the use of a wide range of profiles of intelligence. They can easily connect the concepts and skills of education with the lives and goals of learners to the world outside academe. The definitional investigation conducted by Daniel Solorzano (1989) and students (discussed earlier) is a good example of a collaborative project carried out with critical consciousness. In the same vein, the definitional investigation of learning style designed and executed by Yolanda Scott-Machado (also cited earlier) is a fine representation of an individual project.

The following guidelines are useful when creating and carrying out projects:

- Whether the project is individual or collaborative, it is ideal for students to be involved in its conception and planning.

- The creation of the project can involve the questions and procedural identifications found in the next list.

- Consider goal setting or some of its elements as a means to explore and plan the project.

- Request an outline of the project with some schedule of agreed-on documentation and a completion date.

- Arrange for the presentation of the project to a relevant audience who can offer authentic acknowledgment and feedback.

- Assess the project, including a thorough self-assessment (see Chapter Five), from numerous perspectives (Gardner, 2006), which may include project planning, execution, and presentation; the challenge level; creativity and originality; employment of resources; and what was learned. Include the evaluation of other learners and knowledgeable people outside of the course.

One way to begin creating projects is to reflect on the questions in the list that follows and identify relevant issues and their related procedures. For each selection, sketch and outline the actions and resources that would appear necessary to carry out the identified practice. Further reflection on what emerges from this process can lead to choosing a compelling issue with an appealing and reasonably challenging procedure:

Decision making: Is there an unresolved issue that learners find relevant that calls for a course of action, a policy, a plan, or a choice?

Definitional investigation: Is there an unresolved issue that learners find relevant that calls for clarifying or identifying the defining characteristics or important features of a concept, event, or situation for which such characteristics are unknown, in question, or not readily apparent?

Historical investigation: Is there an unresolved issue that learners find relevant that calls for determining, understanding, and evaluating past events?

Projective investigation: Is there an unresolved issue that learners find relevant that involves researching what will happen if certain circumstances continue or change or if some future event occurs?

Experimental inquiry: Is there an issue that learners find relevant for which conducting an experiment will provide greater understanding?

Action research: Is there a problem of practice where investigating a form of action or intervention and gathering related evidence could support new insights, questions, and innovations?

Invention and artistry: Is there something learners find relevant—a problem, an issue, a state of being—about which they want to deeply and artistically express themselves or create a conceptual or material invention?

Simulation or case study: Is there something relevant to be
learned for which the creation of a simulation or case
study affords learners the kind of authentic understanding or skill acquisition currently unavailable through
other academic procedures or direct experience?

The Problem-Posing Model

In theory and espoused practice, we view the problem-posing
model of teaching (Freire, 1970; Shor, 1992) as one of the most
consistently authentic forms of culturally responsive pedagogy. It
has crucially informed our teaching and our writing. When all
classroom discourse is situated in the learners' language, experience, perspective, and community life, the foundation of its
curriculum is students' cultural diversity. In the problem-posing
classroom, the learning process is negotiated with learners rather
than unilaterally imposed, the discourse is codeveloped rather
than teacher dominated, and knowledge is examined rather than
prescribed. Such significant differences as these make problem
posing a genuinely alternative structure for learning and authority in postsecondary education.

With such strong culture centeredness and a methodology
that immerses students in challenging questions and forms of
inquiry, this approach to teaching, if done well, elicits intrinsic
motivation. Problem-posing presents all subject matter as a historical product to be questioned rather than as a universal wisdom to be received. The current canons of knowledge and use
are not considered a common culture because they have largely
ignored the diverse themes, idioms, and achievements of such
nonelite groups as women, historically underserved ethnic and
linguistic communities, lesbians, and people who live in poverty
(Shor, 1992; hooks, 2003).

Although it is essential to scrutinize claims of academic
neutrality in any context, this orientation does not suggest
that prevalent knowledge within academic disciplines, whether

chemistry, mathematics, sociology, or education, has nothing to offer or that the expertise of the teacher counts for very little. As Shor (1992) states: "Formal bodies of knowledge, standard usage, and teacher's academic background all belong in the critical classroom. As long as existing knowledge is not presented as facts and doctrines to be absorbed without question, as long as existing bodies of knowledge are critiqued and balanced from a multicultural perspective, and as long as the students' own themes and idioms are valued along with standard usage, existing canons are part of critical education" (p. 35).

As a form of critical pedagogy, the problem-posing model of teaching recognizes that any current system of power, for example a large institution, corporation, or government, has a tendency to make its ideas part of the status quo and inevitably the equivalent of "common sense" (Kincheloe, 2005). One example might be that people should accept advances in technology or pharmacology when they provide advantages such as more efficient communication or reduction of a particular health problem. It just makes sense. According to such logic, however, consequent related issues such as pollution or reduced immunity may be overlooked or concealed. Critical pedagogy consistently asks, "Whose interests are being served?" Applying this orientation to computers, a problem-posing computer science teacher would likely integrate the following questions into the framework of her course: Who controls the design and marketing of computers? Which groups in society use them, and for what purposes? Which groups lack access to them? In which schools are they more accessible to learners? How could groups without access to computers use them? How do computers promote or diminish the rhetoric of democracy in school, at work, and in society?

Problem-posing teachers use lesson plans and predeveloped questions and materials, but they maintain flexibility, being open to exploring outside their plans based on what emerges from interactions with and among students. Although students have considerable flexibility, they do not have license to do whatever they wish. A problem-posing model for a term-long course might look like this:

1. Posing a generative, topical, or academic problem to students and facilitating a related dialogue
2. Asking students to write on the posed problem
3. Inviting peer group, collaborative editing, and discussion of the rough drafts
4. Conducting whole-class dialogue based on the essays
5. Questioning student responses and encouraging students to question each other
6. Posing a second-level problem based on the class dialogue
7. Following this posed problem with a second cycle of student writing, peer editing and discussion, and whole-class dialogue
8. Continuing these cycles as appropriate and integrating reading materials and other media along the way
9. Conducting an interim class evaluation and adjustment of the process
10. Offering a lecture (dialogic) based on the teacher's view and expertise concerning the currently identified problem
11. Hearing student feedback and challenges to the lecture
12. Discussing solutions and actions regarding the problem
13. Taking action if possible and reflecting on it
14. Posing a new problem based on action and reflection
15. Scrutinizing an end-term evaluation for opportunities to strengthen the learning experience

Problem posing is a creative process. As a way of teaching, it can be quite difficult to convey in outline form or with short declarative statements. It typically requires a lengthy narrative voice to flesh out its qualities of dialogue and reflection-in-action. (For practical examples of problem posing, we recommend Shor, 1992; Brookfield, 2005; and Adams, Bell, and Griffin, 2007.)

■■

As the problem-posing model and the other elements of this chapter have indicated, personal meaning is essential to learning and motivation. However, culturally responsive teaching does not impose meaning. The norms and practices offered in this chapter present a holistic means to bring a multicultural perspective to existing knowledge. In this process, the balanced interaction between teacher expertise and student experience integrates the authority of an academic discipline with the validity of a student's perspective. How to create this symmetry in the area of assessment of learning is in our opinion one of the critical challenges to genuinely implementing a culturally responsive pedagogy. We encounter this politically charged and often contentious educational responsibility in the next chapter.

5

ENGENDERING COMPETENCE

Nobody ever measured, not even poets, how much
the heart can hold.

—*Zelda Fitzgerald, writer*

The desire to be competent—effective at what we value—extends across all cultures. Yet this powerful human need resonates with something beyond feeling competent. It connects with our dreams, our will to matter, our sense of what makes life worth living. Competence is the nexus for our spiritual, moral, and pragmatic lives. And learning is its heartbeat—where it begins, where it finds energy and realization. But because competence is part of real life, gaining it comes with risk and challenge, and doubt and failure. With this in mind, we offer the following scenario:

As a graduate student, full-time educator, and father of two children, Edward Cobbs enjoyed the unconventional format of weekend courses and summer institutes. Most of the time, however, class time consisted of seatwork with occasional fifteen-minute breaks. That is why he was intrigued when he heard about a five-day summer course in which students would learn about research by conducting research.

Sitting with a group of other students on the first day of class, he listened as the instructor, Dr. Lee, explained that she had been working with a school that the school district had slated for closure. The school's staff and parent advisory council wanted to understand how this decision might affect families, most of whom were recent immigrants working two or three jobs. The goal for the week would be for students to investigate how members of linguistic minority communities are influenced by policy decisions such as school closure. She also indicated that in addition to learning about perspectives on policy, students would learn from each other about how home visits challenged (or not) their own assumptions regarding equitable communication and cultural awareness.

With the experience spanning five days, Dr. Lee explained that the first day was reserved to prepare, and the last day was reserved for presentations. To prepare, she explained, students would review literature on the topic of school closure and other studies written about visiting people in their homes. Preparation would also include how to take field notes and maintain a record of personal thoughts. In addition, the class would interview interpreters from the Somali, Mien, Spanish, Cambodian, and Ukrainian linguistic communities they would be visiting. Finally, Dr. Lee explained that she would solicit volunteers to participate in a simulation, so that the class could imagine, from start to finish, how it might feel to be both a guest and an interviewer in the home of a family. The simulation was also intended to provide a context, if vicarious, within which students could consider the influence of their power and the burden of responsibility for this kind of inquiry into someone else's life.

The following three days would provide students with the opportunity to visit members of linguistically diverse communities in their homes with an interpreter. In pairs, students would visit two homes from the same language group. In the first home, one student would ask interview questions, and the other would take field notes. In the second home, partners would reverse roles. The research questions that the students posed, although focused primarily on the topic of school closure, could be modified to include stories that families might want to share. Dr. Lee shared sample interview questions and explained that the class would ultimately determine which ones to ask or modify.

Finally, Dr. Lee took out a folder of student work from a previous course. She used the folder's table of contents and samples of work to show how, throughout the week-long experience, in addition to visiting homes, students would prepare a portfolio. Smiling, she explained that when the first class conducted field research of this sort, they were relieved to see that she had done a mockup of a sample portfolio such as those that students would create in language-specific groups of approximately four people. She acknowledged that this approach had a lot of dimensions and explained that one portfolio group, for example, would consist of all of the students who visited Cambodian American homes. Another group would be students who visited only Latino homes. The common campus location that students shared while not visiting homes would provide wireless Internet access so that teams could research and submit a brief bibliography related to their focus.

To Edward, this sounded like a lot of work. At the same time, Dr. Lee's clear overview of final products made a group portfolio seem within reach. Over the course of the week, the students would engage with a variety of material:

- A review of literature related to the week-long experience.
- Ethnographic field notes and field note analysis with a set of emerging themes and questions. Field notes described the experience in its entirety, including travel to and from each home with an interpreter.
- A graphic organizer to make visually explicit various forms of knowledge and expertise found in each family (Moll, Saez, and Dworin, 2001). For example, one chart from a previous class listed multilingualism, household management, fabric design, immigration policy and practices, building social networks, cross-cultural knowledge, survival skills, and problem solving.
- A poem entitled "Where I'm From," imagined from the perspective of a child in one of the families and informed by field notes (Christensen, 1997).
- Personal reflections.

Although Dr. Lee was cautious about not explaining too much that might influence the class's own perspectives, she read one example from a former student:

> Visiting families from Mountain Vista Elementary allowed us to experience, first hand, how to conduct interviews with parents who speak a language other than English and to work with a translator and meet people in their home. I learned the most in regard to my interviewing and research skills. Taking field notes was not an easy task. Maintaining descriptive writing from the interview without inserting bias and opinion was difficult. It made me realize how I slip in and out of personal opinion and bias. During the debriefing from the first interview, my partner and I [a fellow student] compared our recollection of some of the interview information. It was interesting how we recalled parts of the interview differently. As part of the interview analysis, my partner and I debated what was descriptive from the mother's perspective and what was biased opinion from the interpreter. I recognize the importance of careful questioning during the interview, specific note taking, and careful analysis during the debriefing and writing of field notes.

Edward could imagine participating effectively and in ways he valued. Although he had a lot to learn, he had reason to believe that his experiences in this class would lead him toward a culminating product that would be a reasonable assessment of his competence as a novice researcher.

He was ready to begin!

In college, as in the rest of life, the desire for competence is a constant. Across cultural groups, human beings desire to be effective in authentic and valuable ways. From the beginning, this extraordinary force in life is observable in infants. Within the first two months of life, activities involving manipulation and exploration often provide satisfaction to babies because they are instinctual ways to become effective in one's environment. Researchers have demonstrated that infants as young as eight weeks old can learn particular responses to connect with their environment. In one such study, infants were placed in cribs with a mobile above each of their heads (Watson and Ramey, 1972). By turning their head to the right, they activated an electrical apparatus in their pillow that caused the mobile to move. Not only did these children learn to move the mobile, but they displayed more positive emotions (smiling, cooing) than infants for whom the mobile movement was controlled by a researcher. Similarly, when learners can sense their insights and progress or accomplishment, their motivation is enhanced. Although culture largely determines what is worth accomplishing, motivation is evoked across cultures by the desire to be effective at what one values.

With this understanding of the powerful motivational influence of competence, we propose that the essential purpose of assessment is *to engender competence*. Assessment provides evidence of learning and proficiency. By honoring the origin of this word, that is, *assidere*, or "to sit beside," we as teachers should, figuratively and sometimes literally, seat ourselves with students to collaboratively understand what has been learned, how that has come to be, and how to proceed to inspire further intellectual growth.

There is clear evidence that teacher assessment, more than any other action, validates student competence (Elliot and Dweck, 2005; Hattie and Timperley, 2007). However, teacher judgment is vulnerable to subtle forms of bias. From personal experience, most of us are aware that teachers make subjective judgments about such affective qualities of learners as effort, initiative, and commitment. We also know that these judgments can influence expectations of learners and consequent grades. Research at Northwest Regional Laboratory suggests, for example, that there may be a tendency for teachers to unduly reward white male students who appear attentive and aggressive during class. The implication is that students who are most prepared culturally to fit the stereotype of "learning" may be disproportionately rewarded through higher grades (Stiggins, 1988).

In this chapter, we introduce norms and practices that are less likely to disguise bias and are consistent with the best we know about intrinsic motivation. Our emphasis is on practices that engender competence through clearly negotiated processes that illuminate and support students' authority, strength, and sense of cultural and academic identity. These processes also reveal authentic information about what has been learned and how that has occurred. We share the belief that assessment ought to be used to enhance learning as opposed to simply auditing it.

Authenticity, Effectiveness, and Intrinsic Motivation

Assessment that engenders competence meets two primary criteria: authenticity and effectiveness. We begin with an examination of the meaning and relevance of authenticity.

As students, most of us spent a good deal of time feeling right or wrong, smart or dumb, expecting that the teacher held the truth about where we fit among our peers and why this was so. The measures of our learning were often quizzes, tests, and examinations, most structured around specific chunks of information. To persevere or simply get by, we did not generally dwell on how measures of our learning could sustain our motivation, apply to our real lives, or help us to understand our strengths as learners.

Assessment has authenticity when it is connected to the students' life circumstances, frames of reference, and values (Wlodkowski, 2008). For example, authenticity within assessment, as well as in learning, requires students to solve problems that have an equivalent in their real world or their future work lives, involving use of resources, consulting with other people, integrating skills, and so forth. This kind of assessment explores factors that have contributed to or impaired learning and emphasizes relationships that have developed within a learning context in a manner akin to an apprenticeship or at least a trusting relationship (Gardner, 2006).

Authentic assessment supports intrinsic motivation because it makes the act of learning and the application of relevant knowledge primary within a realistic context to reveal how the students' knowledge and skills can be strengthened. For example, it is likely that students would be more interested in understanding why certain actions may be ineffective in resolving a case study based on real problems in their community than the nuanced differences between isolated definitions or facts on a multiple-choice exam.

For these reasons, as well as those of the added burdens of cultural marginality, displacement from personal experiences and values, and—at times—significant financial debt, a one-dimensional means-ends orientation to assessment can seriously impair the motivation of students within and across demographic groups. The overarching value of authentic assessment is to support intrinsic motivation. Intrinsic motivation is supported when learners see the locus of causality for learning within themselves, when the act of learning and application of knowledge are considered primary, and when the learning context is examined for ways in which the capacities and talents of all learners can be strengthened.

While authentic assessment seeks a broader, more realistic picture of student learning, it requires a genuinely supportive environment, an issue we examined in Chapter Two. Nonetheless, it is important to emphasize once again that activity and innovation can produce the same kind of isolation, fear, and boredom as can homogenized routines, memorization, and competitive grading. It is essential to demonstrate a sincere spirit of support and responsiveness to the needs, interests, and orientations of learners. At times, this requires a critical shift in authority where distinctions between "teacher" and "learner" converge for mutual reward. The instructor does not abdicate responsibility for establishing and maintaining reasonable and strong expectations. Rather, there is heightened sensitivity to students as individuals in ways that value autonomous thinking and initiative and respect the reasons some learners may prefer caution, deference, or the appearance of conformity, so that instructors are willing to engage in personal and professional dialogue but respect the reasons for silence and privacy and affirm and encourage, with a willingness to live with contradictions—our own as well as those of others.

From a practical as well as a culturally responsive perspective, effectiveness is the learners' awareness of their command or accomplishment of something they find to be important in the process of learning or as an outcome of their learning. Therefore, both the process and the result of learning are important forms of information for learners. The questions, "How well are we doing?" and "How well did this turn out?" are significant to any learning activity. Intrinsic motivation is elicited when people know they are competently performing an activity that leads to a valued goal. This affirms the innate need to relate adequately to an environment. The process and the goal are reciprocal and, to our way of thinking, indivisible—one gives meaning to the other.

If someone wants to learn how to use a new digital program because it is a valued skill and increases his or her range of occupational opportunities, that awareness will evoke motivation. The progress and competence gained while learning will influence the motivational value of the original goal. In other words, becoming more effective often increases the value of the goal. With increased competence, skill with technology and related occupational opportunities acquire even greater value for the learner.

The interactions that inform learners of their effectiveness may crucially affect their motivation. These events can be seen as informational or controlling (Deci and Ryan, 1991).

Informational transactions communicate about effectiveness and support a sense of self-determination for learning. In contrast, controlling transactions tend to undermine a student's self-determination by making learner behavior appear to be dependent on forces that demand, coerce, or seduce one's compliance. They encourage students to believe the reason for learning is some external condition, such as a reward or pressure. When these conditions are verbally communicated, they often contain imperative locutions such as *should* and *must*. For example, a teacher might say to a student in an informational transaction, "Your performance was clearly presented and relevant to your intended audience; your written information was well organized and vivid. I appreciate how well you supported your rationale with facts and anecdotes. Your audience appeared to be fully engaged." A teacher in a controlling transaction might say, "Your performance was excellent. You did exactly what I had hoped." The difference between these two statements is important. The former encourages self-determination, while the latter places the emphasis for learning in the direction of the teacher's control. The following practices for engendering competence emphasize the informational approach, which encourages empowerment and is more likely to be culturally responsive.

Norms for Engendering Competence

The norms that foster authenticity and effectiveness rely on the necessity for each instructor to become more conscious of his or her "assessment philosophy." An understanding of how new approaches to assessment fit with our overarching beliefs about learning helps us achieve greater consistency in actions and intentions. Our recommendations for developing an assessment philosophy are straightforward: (1) decide what sorts of information and skills are really needed, how often they are needed, and to what end; (2) examine assessment procedures for bias and for their consistency with how you teach; and (3) consider the relevance of high standards for compassion and cooperation as well as academic work.

We advocate the following assessment norms:

■■

1. *The assessment process is connected to students' worlds, frames of reference, and values.* As discussed in Chapters Two and Three, relevance strongly influences the extent to which human beings feel part of something. This applies to assessment just as it does to all other aspects of learning. Pragmatically, this has two important implications: (1) assessment ought to be contextualized in ways that hold meaning for students given their experiences, frames of reference, and values, and (2) assessment ought to allow personal interpretations of "truth"—linkages between traditional academic perspectives and personal experiences and the generation of valid alternative perspectives to conventionally held beliefs.

Real and significant contexts to demonstrate understanding enhance the relevance of learning, the responsibility for learning, and the coherence of learning. These are motivationally powerful conditions. Undergirding these conditions, and a key to motivation, is affirmation of one's own experiences (McLaren, 2006). When we standardize approaches to and judgments about assessment, we tend to constrict connections to students' experiences. This tends to constrain the relevance of an assessment process and generally requires conformity and subordination.

The issue of contextualized assessment resides alongside the debate about opportunities for personal interpretations of truth. We acknowledge the important tension between helping students understand theoretical traditions and allowing personal interpretation. Assessment that allows individual interpretations of truth, rather than fixed ideas about reality, validates the cultural lenses through which human beings view the world—in addition to expanding understanding beyond the dualistic "right" and "wrong" (Butler, 1993; Sternberg, 2003). This can be especially significant to students whose opinions and ways of understanding have been subjugated to dominant norms. Many learners from historically underserved groups are well aware that their instructors' opinions and ways of understanding conform to dominant norms. Assessment experiences that reward students who best conform to the instructor's norms and values serve as additional evidence of cultural bias. An obvious question to pose when developing assessment instruments is, "To what extent does this assessment promote quality and diversity simultaneously? To what extent might it perpetuate the idea that the conventions of my discipline are immutable, and how can I allow for interrogation of conventional ideas and representation of a partiality?" On a biology test, for example, there is an enormous difference between the necessity to solve a problem with a predetermined algorithm and the necessity to comply with a teacher's conceptual model of an illness.

The knowledge of external authorities can be used to encourage passivity and dependence—or it can provide a rationale for developing assessment procedures that, to the degree possible, create opportunities for well-substantiated alternative points of view. That is, as teachers, we can choose to ignore or acknowledge the ways in which our systems of belief are culturally mediated. The latter choice provides a window for promoting the emergence of multiple perspectives. This does not suggest that anything goes or that there are not valuable lessons from rigorous intellectual pathways. It is a reminder that the personal construction of knowledge is a salient feature in motivation to learn (Belenky, Clinchy, Goldberger, and Tarule, 1986; Walvoord, 2004) in addition to being essential to the overarching goal of creating a just and pluralistic society (Gilligan, 1982; Lather, 1991; Takaki, 1993). The science of certainty has a hierarchical structure that is rooted in a set of methodological and linguistic assumptions that are influenced by, as Freire (1998) suggests, the verticalization of power.

2. Demonstration of learning includes multiple ways to represent knowledge and skill. This is a value that has been consistently advocated in research on assessment and evaluation (Gardner, 2006; Walvoord, 2004). Nonetheless we appreciate that it is a value against which many educators vigorously defend. The vast amount of time devoted to the task of assessment is already daunting, and expanding one's assessment repertoire to more adequately guide, develop, and account for learning is complicated by other professional responsibilities.

Yet what could be more defeating to a student than to realize that critical judgments about learning are based on vague or superficial criteria, inadequate communication about academic expectations, insufficient opportunities to learn from mistakes, and dismissal of alternative indicators of accomplishment given the motivational limits of grades (Black and others, 2003; Dweck, 2007)? As we move from the once popular view that intelligence or ability is a single, fixed capacity to intelligence theories that stress the existence of a variety of human talents and capabilities (Sternberg and others, 2000; Gardner, 2006), we are further compelled to find ways in which learners can engage their potential.

3. Self-assessment is essential to the overall assessment process. All learning is about change. This can create confusion as well as opportunity. In this light, posing one's own learning as a problem to be solved has the potential to compel new learning. Self-assessment allows students to gain perspective into themselves as learners, knowers, apprentices in a discipline, and citizens in a complicated and paradoxical world (Brookfield and Preskill, 2005). With adequate guidance, self-assessment provides an opportunity to identify growth in ways that nurture respect for oneself as a learner and for the learning process. As students become more aware of their individual metacognitive processes, they are able to more deliberately access strategies that stimulate internal questions and self-monitoring, both of which are associated with intrinsic motivation and learning.

Interestingly, several studies in higher education provide evidence that undergraduate women consistently underestimate their abilities and that men overestimate theirs (Astin, Green, and Korn, 1987; Light, 1990). Self-assessment offers students a way to make well-reasoned connections between their actions and present learning opportunities (Brookfield and Preskill, 2005). Self-reflection about learning also allows students to validate their authenticity as learners. This is especially important for historically underserved students who may feel at times like impostors in the culturally isolated, often competitive, lonely, and disconnected universe of academia. Thus, in a larger sense, self-assessment provides an opportunity for students to develop new ways of understanding community, or lack thereof, and to gain insight into the contexts and conditions outside themselves that inhibit or promote learning and beliefs about their identity.

Based on his studies, Vincent Tinto (1998) addresses the learner's need for validation and connectedness. His research indicates that unless a student finds a place in a new cultural setting and feels connected to it, he or she will often "give up" and leave that culture. When we are able to tell our own story and receive credit for it in a new cultural setting, the validation assists us with finding a sense of place (Waluconis, 1994). The positive motivational implications of realizing this new cultural connection are profound.

Our discussion of self-assessment would be incomplete without consideration of possible sources of cultural discomfort, given expectations of self-disclosure and candor. Requests for self-disclosure may feel intrusive to some learners. Many students of color, as well as members of other historically underserved communities, intentionally reserve their confidences to family and other close relationships. It is important for instructors to be respectful of this and to collaborate with students to negotiate the content of the self-assessment. Choice and confidentiality are essential. With the best of intentions, instructors can create an irreparable gulf between unilateral expectations of openness and a student's right to privacy.

A second consideration is the impact of personal recognition on the individual. Some learners may view personalized claims of academic accomplishment as self-aggrandizing, whether they emanate privately from themselves or emerge from other forms of discourse. For some students, if a person stands out, it is because the community recognizes the individual (Plaut and Markus, 2005). Although self-assessment can provide a platform for self-definition, we encourage instructors to respect the value of community over individual accomplishment and consider ways for students to circumvent the need for psychologically intimate narratives about self. We offer suggestions for this purpose in the next section.

Practices for Engendering Competence

Practices for engendering competence are categorized as follows: feedback, alternatives to paper-and-pencil tests, well-constructed paper-and-pencil tests, and student self-assessment. Each of these categories and their related approaches encompass criteria and norms discussed earlier in this chapter. Although they may appear prescriptive, our goal is clarity. We invite readers to contextualize strategies to work within their own professional milieu and set of responsibilities. We also encourage multiple measures or instruments as well as longitudinal approaches to develop reliable perspectives on academic accomplishment. Students generally need a range of opportunities and approaches to demonstrate what they know. The most authentic forms of assessment involve long-term programs of study, activity, and practice while simultaneously enhancing learners' understanding of themselves in relation to others. However, short-term generation of products and activities that are associated with authentic or performance assessment may be more practical to implement. Also, many courses today are in accelerated or intensive formats, possibly as short as four weeks and with less than twenty-four teacher contact hours (Wlodkowski and Kasworm, 2003). We advise against basing judgments on one or two high-stakes testing occasions or one particular kind of assessment task. This can seriously skew generalizations about student accomplishment, especially with learners whose experiences, behaviors, beliefs, and values challenge an instructor's ways of understanding.

Feedback

Feedback is information that students receive about the quality of their work. Knowledge about the learning process and results, comments about emerging skills, notes on a written assignment, and graphic records are forms of feedback that teachers and learners use. Feedback appears to enhance student motivation because individuals are able to evaluate their progress, locate performance within a framework of understanding, maintain efforts toward realistic goals, correct errors efficiently, and receive encouragement from teachers and other learners.

Although most of the research has been done with youth (Hattie and Timperley, 2007), our experience with college students confirms that feedback is probably the most powerful process that teachers and other learners can regularly use to affect a learner's competence. Research and experience suggest that the following types and characteristics of feedback work together to engender competence:

• *Feedback that is informational rather than controlling.* Students tend to be motivated by feedback that provides information related to their increased effectiveness, creativity, and self-determination—for example: "You've identified three critical areas of concern. Your writing is well organized with vivid examples. I appreciate how well you have supported your rationale with facts and anecdotes," rather than, "I am pleased to see that you are making progress on the writing standards in this course. Keep up the good work."

- *Feedback that is based on agreed-upon standards.* When feedback provides evidence of the learner's effect relative to intent, it is often because there have been agreed-upon standards, models, and criteria for success. The closer that standards and criteria, including those represented by rubrics, come to students' own words, the better. In the case of models, students can compare their work against good and not-yet-good examples of others' work. They are then in a position to determine what makes a product good and the "not-yet" ones inadequate. This information more accurately guides effort, practice, and performance and contributes to the notion that self-assessment leads to self-adjustment. Clear criteria for success are especially important for learners for whom ambiguous learning criteria are one more unknown barrier to success—for example: "We agreed that any project containing more than six errors would be returned for revision. I've indicated where those errors are located as well as some examples and references that may be helpful. As always, please feel free to draw on whatever resources you have found in your own search for related literature."

- *Feedback that is specific and constructive.* It is difficult for a person to improve performance when she can realize only in general terms how well she has done (Brophy, 2004). Most people prefer specific information and realistic suggestions for how to improve, as in this example: "I found your insights on government spending compelling. To emphasize your conclusion, you might consider restating your initial premise in your last paragraph." In a similar vein, when students have done something well, they often like to know why from a teacher they respect:

"Your eloquent passage about your experiences in Central America brought your memoir to life for me."

• *Feedback that is quantitative.* In some areas (athletics, for example), quantitative feedback has definite advantages. It is precise and can provide evidence of small improvements, which can have long-range effects. One way to understand learning is by rate, which is to indicate how often something occurs over a fixed time. For example, students may be told they completed thirty laps during a one-hour swimming practice. Another way is to decide what percentage of learning performance is correct or appropriate. Percentages are calculated by dividing the number of times the learning performance occurs correctly by the total number of times the performance opportunity occurs, as in batting averages and field goal percentages. Another common form of quantitative feedback relates to duration: how long it takes a learning performance to be completed. For example, an environmental science student might receive feedback on how long it takes her to complete a practice analysis of a particular ecosystem, given that she will eventually perform the analysis under potentially adverse conditions. Whenever progress on learning a skill appears to be slow or difficult to ascertain, quantitative feedback may be a realistic and relevant means to enhance learner motivation.

• *Feedback that is prompt.* Promptness characterizes feedback that is provided as the situation demands, which may not be immediately. Sometimes a moderate delay in feedback enhances learning, because the delay is culturally sensitive or polite. For example, some learners may experience discomfort with direct mention of specific performance judgments shortly after the occasion. Also, a short wait may allow learners to more easily forget incorrect responses and reduce their anxiety, as in the case of a public performance. In general, it is best to be quick with feedback but to pay careful attention to whether any delay might be beneficial.

- *Feedback that is frequent.* Frequent feedback is probably most helpful when new learning is occurring. In general, we suggest providing feedback when improvement is most possible. Once errors have accumulated, learners may see improvements as more difficult to accomplish. Also, once multiple errors become established, the new learning encouraged through feedback may seem overwhelming and confusing to learners, making further progress seem even more remote.

- *Feedback that is positive.* Positive feedback places emphasis on improvements and progress rather than on deficiencies and mistakes. It is an excellent form of feedback because it increases the learner's intrinsic motivation, feeling of well-being, sense of competence, and positive attitude toward the source of the information. Negative feedback, an emphasis on errors and deficiencies, can be discouraging. Even when learners are prone toward mistakes, the instructor can point out any decrease in errors as positive feedback. Also, positive feedback can be given with constructive feedback. For example, an instructor might note, "You've been able to solve most of this problem. Let's take a look at what's left and see if we can understand why you are getting stuck."

- *Feedback that is personal and differential.* Differential feedback focuses on the increment of personal improvement that has occurred since the last time the learning activity was performed. In skill or procedural learning, such as writing, operating a machine, or learning a particular sport, emphasizing small steps of progress can be quite encouraging. The time allowed before such differential feedback is provided can be quite important. For example, learners are able to see larger gains and feel a greater sense of accomplishment when improvement is noted according to a daily or weekly schedule rather than after each performance. Portfolios and videos are excellent for this type of feedback because each can offer students a comparison to earlier work after significant time and practice. Students are able to ask questions of themselves such as, "How has my work changed?" What am I doing differently or to a greater or lesser extent?" "How do I see myself becoming more accomplished within a particular discipline or vocation?"

■ ■

In addition to the specific characteristics of feedback, some refinements in the composition and delivery of feedback may be helpful. For many skills, graphing or charting feedback can be encouraging to learner motivation because it makes progress more concrete and shows a record of increasing improvement. Asking learners what they would like feedback on is a strategy that should be considered. Their needs and concerns may be different from ours as teachers, and the knowledge gained from such discussion can make the feedback more relevant and motivating. Learner readiness to receive feedback is also important. If people are not ready to hear, they are not likely to learn. This may mean holding off on feedback until a personal conference can be arranged or until students are more comfortable with the learning situation. There are times when checking to make sure our feedback was understood can be important. This is certainly true for complex feedback or situations in which the student is an English language learner.

Everything that has been said about feedback thus far could also apply to group feedback. Whether it is a team, a collaborative group, or an entire class, feedback on total performance can affect each individual and contribute to group cohesiveness and morale. This is because group feedback has the potential to consolidate mutual identification. Please see Resource G for suggestions for how to use written feedback to promote diversity and respond to bias in student writing. Sometimes, however, the best form of feedback is simply to encourage learners to move forward to the next learning challenge. Too much comment by teachers tends to emphasize the teacher's authority and can contradict the norm that we are, in many ways, colearners. This is true in class discussion as well. When educators respond to every comment, the implication may be that a perspective is incomplete if it does not include the instructor's perspective. In addition to the obvious arrogance this conveys, a running commentary by the instructor can silence others and disrupt opportunities for students to consider and validate each other's perspectives. In the absence of other student-generated comments, a simple acknowledgment in the form of a sincere "thank you" for a person's participation is often appreciated. This is especially true when working with adults who have uncomfortable histories of encounters with teachers who believe that the opinions of learners need to be confirmed or elaborated on by someone who is supposed to have a superior knowledge base. Although there are times when additional information from instructors is necessary, we urge moderation. There is a disturbing contradiction in claiming to respect diverse opinions and ways of knowing and simultaneously positioning oneself as the ultimate authority. In addition, instructors need feedback as well. Please see Resource K for a form that can be used at the end of a class or course to receive feedback from students that is aligned with the four conditions of the motivational framework.

Overall, Carol Kasworm and Catherine Marienau (1997) remind us, learners of all ages become more competent, feel more confident, and look forward to assessment when these procedures are:

1. Related to goals they understand

2. Reflective of growth in learning

3. Indicative of clear ways to improve learning without penalty

4. Expected

5. Returned promptly

6. Permeated with instructor or peer comments that are informative and supportive

7. Used to encourage new challenges in learning

Alternatives to Pencil-and-Paper Tests: Assessment with Authentic Performance Tasks

Authentic performance tasks are one of the oldest forms of assessment. They have been extensively field-tested, particularly in community college settings, and have proven powerful tools for focusing faculty attention on what constitutes good learning (Ewell, 1991). Today we have a more sophisticated understanding of these procedures and their central idea: that assessment should resemble as closely as possible the ways students will apply in their real lives what they have learned (Woolfolk, 2007). Thus, if students are learning college math, we might assess their learning by asking them to solve or create math word problems that reflect compelling current challenges related to their community, their environment, the local economy, or relevant tax legislation.

The closer that assessment procedures come to allowing learners to demonstrate what they have learned in the areas where they will eventually use that learning, the greater will be their motivation to do well and the more they can understand their competence and feel the self-confidence that emerges from effective performance.

Providing the opportunity for learners to complete an authentic task is one of the best ways to conclude a learning activity because it promotes transfer of learning, enhances motivation for related work, and clarifies learner competence. An authentic task directly meets the human need to use what has been learned for more effective daily living.

According to Wiggins (1998), an assessment task is authentic if it has the following characteristics:

- *Is realistic.* The task replicates how people's knowledge and capacities are "tested" in their real world.
- *Requires judgment and innovation.* People have to use knowledge wisely to solve unstructured problems, as a director of a film or play must do more than follow a routine procedure.
- *Asks the learners to "do" the subject.* Rather than recite or demonstrate what they have been taught or what is already known, the learners have to explore and work within the discipline, as when they demonstrate their competence for a history course by writing history from the perspective of particular people in an actual historical situation.
- *Replicates or simulates the contexts that learners find in their workplace, community, or personal life.* These contexts involve specific situations and their demands. For example, aspiring business majors learning conflict resolution skills could apply them to their situations, ranging from part-time work to volunteer activities, with consideration of the personalities and responsibilities involved.
- *Assesses the learners' ability to use an integration of knowledge and skill to negotiate a complex task effectively.* Learners have to put their knowledge and skills together to meet real-life challenges. This is analogous to the difference between taking a few shots in a warm-up drill and taking shots in a real basketball game, or between writing a paper on a particular law and writing a real proposal to appropriate legislators to change the law.
- *Allows appropriate opportunities to rehearse, practice, consult resources, and get feedback on and refine performances and products.* Learning and, consequently, assessment are not one-shot enterprises. Almost all learning is formative, whether one is learning how to write a publishable article or bake a pie. We put out our first attempt and see how it reads or tastes. We repeatedly move through a cycle of perform, get feedback,

revise, perform. That's how most high-quality products and performances are attained, especially in real life. We must use assessment procedures that contribute to the improvement of student performance and learning over time. Doing so means that some of the time assessment is separated from grading processes to assure learners that their mistakes are not counted against them but are a legitimate part of the learning process. In this regard, we may assign credit for completion of such tasks or make them part of the requirements for the course.

Authentic performance tasks avoid asking, "Do you know this material?" and instead ask, "What do you know?" Because students are invited to exhibit what they have internalized and learned through application (Brooks and Brooks, 1993), this process extends—rather than merely tests—learning. For example, focused dialectical notes (a collection of student-written agreements, disagreements, questions, and so forth) provide an opportunity for learners to create a critical dialogue around statements encountered in assigned reading in order to practice critical thinking skills. One-sentence summaries ask students to reorganize a particular concept in a single grammatical sentence (Cross and Angelo, 1988). These techniques encourage learners to apply their understanding and analysis of information rather than regurgitate narrowly defined "correct answers." Such strategies have been extensively field-tested, particularly in community college settings, and have proven to be powerful tools for focusing faculty attention on what constitutes good learning (Ewell, 1991).

Comparing Personal Assessment Values with Actual Assessment Practice. Exhibit 5.1 lists key qualities and characteristics of authentic assessment tasks. It provides an opportunity to compare assessment-related values to actual practices. With the insights provided by this exercise, you can consider possible changes and suggestions as they are discussed in the rest of this chapter. We want to emphasize the importance of two

Exhibit 5.1 Considerations for Authentic Performance Tasks

Circle your own assessment (on a scale of 1 to 5, from weak to strong) of your personal values and practices for engendering competence. Compare your values with your practices to determine areas in which to focus your attention for improvement.

| Your Value | | | | | "Test" Components | Your Actual Practice | | | | |
Weak				Strong		Weak				Strong
1	2	3	4	5	Convincing evidence that students can use their new knowledge and skills effectively and creatively.	1	2	3	4	5
1	2	3	4	5	Simulations or real-life challenges where new academic knowledge or skill is required.	1	2	3	4	5
1	2	3	4	5	Tasks where a multifaceted repertoire of knowledge and skill must be applied with good judgment. Simple recall is insufficient for performing well.	1	2	3	4	5
1	2	3	4	5	A chance to produce a quality product or performance.	1	2	3	4	5
1	2	3	4	5	Demystified criteria and standards that allow students to thoroughly prepare, self-assess, and self-adjust with the resources that are available.	1	2	3	4	5
1	2	3	4	5	Opportunities for students to learn from the experience itself and to improve before the course or class has ended.	1	2	3	4	5
1	2	3	4	5	Reasonable chances to learn from mistakes without any penalty.	1	2	3	4	5

| Your Value | | | | | | Your Actual Practice | | | | |
Weak			Strong		"Test" Components	Weak			Strong	
1	2	3	4	5	Opportunities for students to justify their answers, choices, or plans.	1	2	3	4	5
1	2	3	4	5	Evidence of the pattern and consistency of student work.	1	2	3	4	5
1	2	3	4	5	Opportunities for teachers to learn new things with their students.	1	2	3	4	5

Source: Adapted from materials provided by the Center on Learning, Assessment, and School Structure.

of the items in the exercise: (1) using simulations or real-life challenges where new academic knowledge or skill is required and (2) producing a quality product or performance.

An implicit goal of each item is, whenever possible, to use assessment as yet another opportunity to bridge the learner's home community and the institutional context. Consider, for example, the enhanced meanings and intellectual value of a student-generated questionnaire on unemployment and immigration for a research, sociology, or statistics class. Imagine the motivational worth of a student-designed workshop on cultural respect and communication patterns for a speech class. In addition, they offer classmates and teachers invaluable opportunities to deepen their understanding of critical sociocultural issues.

Assessments with Options Based on Multiple Intelligences.
When students have the opportunity to select an assessment process that reflects their intellectual strengths, it should encourage their participation and enthusiasm for demonstrating their competence. The following menu of assessment options, adapted from *Multiple Intelligences and Adult Literacy* (Viens and

Kallenbach, 2004) and *Teaching and Learning Through Multiple Intelligences* (Campbell, Campbell, and Dickinson, 2004), is categorized by each intelligence:

Linguistic

- Tell or write a short story to explain...
- Keep a journal to illustrate...
- Write a poem, myth, play, or editorial about...
- Create a debate to discuss...
- Create an advertising campaign to depict...
- Create a talk show about...
- Write a culminating essay to review...

Logical-Mathematical

- Complete a cost-benefit analysis of...
- Write a computer program for...
- Design and conduct an experiment to...
- Create story problems for...
- Conduct a mock trial to...
- Induce or deduce a set of principles on...
- Create a time line for...
- Create a crossword puzzle for...

Musical

- Create a song that explains or expresses...
- Revise lyrics of a known song to...
- Collect a collage of music and songs to...
- Create a dance to illustrate...
- Create a music video to illustrate...
- Create an advertisement to...

Spatial

- Create a piece of art that demonstrates...
- Create a poster to...
- Create a videotape, collage, or photo album of...
- Create a chart, concept map, or graph to illustrate...
- Design a flag or logo to express...
- Create a scale model of...
- Create a mobile to...

Bodily-Kinesthetic

- Perform a play on...
- Invent or revise a game to...
- Role-play or simulate...
- Use puppets to explore...
- Create a sequence of...
- Create a scavenger hunt to...
- Create movements to explain...
- Create a poster session or exhibition to...

Interpersonal

- Participate in a service project that will...
- Offer multiple perspectives of...
- Collaborate to resolve a local problem by...
- Teach a group to...
- Use what you have learned to change or influence...
- Conduct an interview or a discussion to...

Intrapersonal

- Create a personal philosophy about...
- Discern what is essential in...

- Explain your intuitive hunches about...
- Explain your emotions about...
- Explain your assumptions in a critical incident...
- Keep a reflective journal to...

Naturalist

- Discover and describe the patterns in...
- Create a typology for...
- Relate and describe the interdependence of...
- Observe and describe...
- Use a field trip to analyze...
- Based on observation and field notes, describe your learning about...

The assessment options in this menu will need criteria for students (and instructors) to judge the quality of their learning and performance. As an example, creating an advertisement, a poster, or an exhibition might require criteria such as knowledge of the topic, creativity of delivery, supporting evidence, and organization of the format. (For further consideration of criteria and how to construct them please, see the section in this chapter on rubrics.)

In addition to accommodating multiple intelligences, this assessment menu offers a range of learning and performance that require deep understanding—*design, teach, discern, explain, analyze, write, create,* and the like. For example, a student in a science course might design an experiment to analyze the chemicals in the local water supply and write an editorial based on the results for the local paper. These assessments provide opportunities for imaginative experiences that allow students to use their perspectives, preferences, and strengths. Furthermore, these assessments make it possible for students to develop deeper relationships between new learning and significant personal or cultural values.

Assessments with Exhibitions and Poster Conferences.
In recent years, exhibitions of learning have received favorable attention as a means of revealing competence and performance across curricular areas. Science and technology students have demonstrated the use of scientific methodology (for example, conducting and documenting an experiment) as well as demonstrating awareness of how science is used in contemporary society (for example, staging a debate or conducting research on a scientific development by analyzing social costs and benefits). Mathematics students have developed and displayed projects that use various numerical calculations for political, civic, or consumer purposes (for example, collecting and analyzing demographic statistics, generating and analyzing polling data, and evaluating architectural projects).

One efficient and interactive method for reviewing exhibitions is the poster conference. Poster conferences allow an entire class to simultaneously display and discuss information. A typical format allows 50 percent of the class to display and discuss its visual and written material as the rest of the class interacts with the presenters at their poster sites. This process can be informal, with students spontaneously selecting displays to visit and independently determining topics of discussion. The alternative is a formalized review process in which peers are assigned to review specific displays, perhaps in roundtable groups, and are expected to submit as supporting evidence of their peer review such documents as resource lists, questionnaires, and semistructured interviews that are consistent with preestablished criteria for excellence.

Exhibitions can also be presented formally to a committee of peers, instructors, and community members (or any combination thereof) serving as "critical friends" who record their perspectives and offer responses in round-robin fashion at the conclusion of the presentation. Critical friends can be assisted with their documentation by the creation of a matrix that identifies assessment criteria and space in which to organize both warm and cool responses. Warm responses are taken from a believing, supportive, and appreciative perspective, and cool responses are taken from a constructively critical, doubting, and discerning perspective (McDonald, Mohr, Dichter, and McDonald, 2003). These two perspectives combine to support the socioemotional and academic-professional aspects of informative feedback.

Assessments with Portfolios. A portfolio is a sample of a person's work or learning. It documents evidence of learning that spans a longer period of time than a single test. A portfolio with examples of actual work such as written products, visual media, and self-assessments can contribute to a deep and comprehensive understanding of learning. When used in a formative manner, with regular intervals to examine accomplishments and challenges, portfolios promote continuous reflection on personal work that exemplifies course goals. The organizing schema is also a metacognitive process that can serve as an advanced organizer for anticipated learning.

The contents of a portfolio and the assessment criteria used to evaluate depend on the portfolio's purpose. Following is a list of some of the possible ways a portfolio can be used (Wiggins, 1998):

- As a display of the learner's best work, chosen by the learner, the instructor, or both
- As a display of the learner's interests and goals
- As a display of the learner's growth or progress
- As documentation of self-assessment, self-adjustment, self-direction, and learning
- As evidence for professional assessment of student performance

Based to some extent on the work of his colleagues (Krechevsky and Seidel, 1998), Howard Gardner (2006) offers five dimensions for assessing projects and portfolios:

1. *Individual profile:* Intellectual strengths and weaknesses, disposition to take risks and persevere, exhibited profile of intelligences such as intrapersonal, musical, and linguistic
2. *Mastery of facts, skills, and concepts:* The student's knowledge and skills as they represent the course objectives and curriculum
3. *Quality of work:* The relevant criteria that may apply, such as writing skill, application of knowledge, and critical thinking
4. *Communication:* The effectiveness of a student's work as it communicates with a wider audience that may include peers, teachers, and the community
5. *Reflection:* The capacity to review, critique, change, correct, and create one's work through self-reflection as it progresses

A portfolio can be a powerful tool for responding to the interests and concerns of diverse learners. Here are guidelines to consider when working with portfolios:

1. Involve students in the composition and selection of what makes up the portfolio.
   - Students may want to explore different aspects of a particular discipline. In a research course, for example, a student might design an ethnographic study and an experimental study for her portfolio.
   - Students may choose among categories, such as most difficult problem, best work, most valued work, most improved work, a spiritual experience, and so forth.

2. Include information in the portfolio that shows the student's self-reflection and self-assessment.

- Students may include a rationale for their selections.

- Students may create a guide for their portfolio, offering interpretations, commentary, critique, and matters of contextual importance.

- Students may include self- and peer assessments indicating strengths, areas for improvement, and relationships between earlier and later work.

3. Be clear about the purpose of the portfolio.

- Learners should be able to relate their goals for learning to the contents of the portfolios.

- Learners should be able to provide a fair representation of their work.

- Rubrics and their models for assessing portfolio contents should be clearly understood and available.

4. Exploit the portfolio as a process to show growth.

- Learners may submit the original, the improved, and the final copy or draft of their creation or performance.

- Using specific works, students may make a history of their movement along certain dimensions in their growth.

- Students may include feedback from outside experts or descriptions of outside activities that reflect the growth illustrated in the portfolio.

5. Teach students how to create and use portfolios.

- Offer models of excellent portfolios for learners to examine, but stress that each portfolio is an individual creation.

- Review portfolios regularly, and give feedback to learners about them, especially early in the term or year when learners are initially constructing their portfolios.

Overall assessments of the content of a portfolio often include applied checklists, rating scales, and rubrics with a particular sensitivity to learning improvement and progress. For example, a student's early writing displays numerous grammatical errors, but his later compositions exhibit stronger proficiency in the use of grammar. His most recent creations would receive greater or maximum weight for an evaluation, assuming the grading policy is intended to reflect what students know and can do. Although there is less quantitative precision, portfolios are likely to obtain a richer and more valid understanding of what students have learned. They make learning more obvious to students and teachers alike because they allow revisiting a repository of work, which more clearly reveals actual development of the student's skills and knowledge. Digital portfolios are rapidly growing as a creative and accommodating means of assessment, professional competence, and record keeping (Hartnell-Young and Morriss, 2007).

Rubrics: A Supplement to Alternative Assessment. Although many college instructors do not use rubrics formally, they do use them on an intuitive basis. They make evaluations of a learner's work based on experience and knowledge, but often without explicit language. For example, an instructor might say, "This writing is excellent, insightful, and entertaining," without specifically saying why or what made that writing so. Barbara Walvoord's definition (2004, p. 19) speaks well to a rubric's advantage and limitation: "A rubric articulates in writing the various criteria and standards" that an instructor "uses to evaluate" a learner's work. "It translates informed professional judgment into numerical ratings on a scale. Something is always lost in the translation, but the advantage is that these ratings can now be communicated and compared."

Grades or scores may be assigned and recorded according to a rubric for evaluation procedures such as authentic assessments and portfolios. As a set of scoring guidelines for evaluating a student's work, a rubric strongly directs learning. To perform this service proficiently, (Wiggins, 1998, p. 154) a rubric should answer the following questions:

- By what *criteria* should performance be judged?
- What should we look for to *judge performance success*?
- What does the *range in quality of performance* look like?
- How do we determine *validly*, *reliably*, and *fairly* what score should be given and what that score should mean?
- How should the *different levels of quality* be described and distinguished from one another?

Rubrics can be a concrete, specific, and telling antidote to the various contexts and experiences that students bring to the classroom. For many learners, the simplest performance can be a puzzle. Rubrics provide a way to answer a question that counts for many students: "What are you going to use to judge me?" If rubrics are fair, clear, reliable, and valid and get at the essentials of performance, students are in a better position to self-assess their performance before it is evaluated. Applied in this way, rubrics enhance motivation because they significantly increase the probability that students will achieve competence.

However, rubrics need models and indicators to make each level of quality concretely understandable. If they are to be culturally sensitive, they need to be created or revised with input from students. For example, if we use *smiles frequently* as one indicator for a *very good* presentation style, we penalize someone who is droll but is from a cultural background where smiling is more an indication of anxiety than of ease. Excellent rubrics are valuable, if flawed, assistants in evaluating learning—flawed because language at best renders, but never duplicates, experience.

Let's look at a straightforward rubric (Exhibit 5.2) for evaluating the recognition of alternative points of view in an

Exhibit 5.2 A Rubric for Recognizing Alternative Points of View

Rating	Descriptor with Indicators
Exemplary = 4	Acknowledges at least two alternative points of view expressed in the required readings. Summarizes them thoroughly and reasonably indicates why he has chosen his point of view in preference to the others.
Competent = 3	Acknowledges at least one alternative point of view expressed in the required readings. Summarizes it thoroughly, and reasonably indicates why he prefers his point of view.
Acceptable with flaws = 2	Acknowledges at least one alternative point of view expressed in the required readings. Summarizes it well, but does not indicate or unreasonably indicates why he prefers his point of view.
Needs revision = 1	Does not acknowledge any alternative points of view in the required readings. Or if he does, they are summarized poorly and he does not indicate or unreasonably indicates why he prefers his point of view.

Source: Adapted from Walvoord (2004, p. 89).

essay. (Other rubrics would be necessary for evaluating other dimensions of performance in the essay, such as critical thinking or writing skills.) This rubric provides an example for applying Grant Wiggins's guidelines (1998) for creating effective rubrics.

Evaluating a set of essays with this rubric (and a model, such as former essay with an exemplar for the descriptor of each level of performance) should enable the student and the teacher to:

- Use the rubric to accurately discriminate among the essential features of performance within each essay for recognizing alternative points of view. The goal is to make each rubric valid and guide successful learning and performance.

- Rely on the rubric's descriptive language (what the quality or its absence looks like), as opposed to relying on merely evaluative language, such as "excellent writing," to discriminate the levels of quality. This characteristic also contributes to the rubric's validity and usefulness as a guide for successful learning and performance.

- Use the rubric to consistently make fine discriminations across a range of four levels of performance. When a rubric can be repeatedly used to make the same discriminations with the same sample of performances, it is reliable. To maintain reliability, rubrics seldom have more than six levels of performance.

- Make sure that the rubric and its descriptors (and models) for each level of performance can be used to accurately judge the quality of performance and (students) to self-correct work.

- See that the rubric is parallel in structure. Each descriptor generally matches the others in terms of criteria language used.

- See that the rubric is coherent. The rubric focuses on the same criteria throughout.

- See that the rubric is continuous. The degree of difference between each descriptor (level of performance) tends to be equal. This characteristic contributes to making the rubric fair.

There are many books in higher education about how to write rubrics. At this time, we find most of these books to be quite sequential and not culturally sensitive. However, they are helpful for understanding the creative variety of rubrics and for deepening awareness about the uses, value, and possible harm of rubrics. A Web site (http://altec.org/index.php) we have found informative for creating rubrics (in Spanish or English) is sponsored by The Advanced Learning Technologies Project (ALTEC) at the University of Kansas Center for Research on Learning. In general, in the next section of this chapter, the guidelines for avoiding cultural bias apply to rubrics as well.

Well-Constructed Paper-and-Pencil Tests

Tests can be intrinsically motivating (Wlodkowski, 2008). The critical issue is how to construct tests so that they are worth taking. In this section, we discuss some of the limitations of tests as well as useful ideas on how to create substantively better assessments. This discussion should make it possible to critique and revise testing decisions within a culturally responsive and comprehensive framework of understanding.

Avoiding Cultural Bias. With respect to cultural diversity, discussion of the limitations of tests and rubrics must include cultural bias. As Ovando and Collier (1998) contend, it is virtually inevitable that any test that uses language as a means of assessment will have accompanying cultural content. The most common type of bias identified is item content that favors one cultural frame of reference over another (Kornhaber, 2004). These issues often relate to ethnicity and gender. For example, items about baseball averages tend to give males an edge, whereas an item of similar difficulty but focusing on child care may favor females (Pearlman, 1987). An item such as, "Bananas are (a) black, (b) yellow, (c) red, or (d) green," is clearly invalid to anyone who has traveled south of the United States and knows that all of the answers are correct depending on what kind of banana one is talking about (Ovando and Collier, 1998). Although these examples oversimplify the issue, they are a reminder to examine the assumptions embedded in the items created or selected for classroom use. As with all other curricular materials, it is important to consider the following when you select or construct test items and rubrics:

- *Invisibility:* Is there a significant omission of women and minority groups in testing materials? (This implies that certain groups are of less value, importance, and significance in our society.)

- *Stereotyping:* When groups or members of groups are mentioned in tests, are they assigned traditional or rigid roles that deny diversity and complexity within different groups? (When stereotypes occur repeatedly in print and other media, learners' perceptions are gradually distorted until stereotypes and myths about women and minorities are accepted.)

- *Selectivity:* Is bias perpetuated by offering only one interpretation—or allowing only one interpretation—of an issue, situation, or group of people? (This fails to tap the knowledge of learners regarding varied perspectives.)

- *Unreality:* Do your test items lack a historical context that acknowledges—when relevant—prejudice and discrimination? (Glossing over painful or controversial issues obstructs authenticity and creates a sense of unreality.)

- *Fragmentation:* Are issues about women or minorities separate from the main body of the test material? (This implies that these issues are less important than issues of the dominant culture.)

- *Linguistic bias:* Do materials reflect bias in language through the dominance of masculine terms and pronouns? (The implication of invisibility devalues the importance and significance of women and minorities.)

Even directions for tests can constitute a form of bias. This is especially true for language-minority students. English language learners of all ages can benefit from test instructions that are direct and simplified. Whenever possible, instructors ought to avoid the passive voice and ambiguous comments. In addition, test instructions should be in short sentences.

Ovando and Collier (1998) also remind us that the testing situation itself can manifest cultural bias. The discomfort that is familiar to many students can be especially devastating for students who have less experience in such situations or for whom such situations serve as reminders of feelings of alienation or inadequacy. Norms and ground rules for testing should be clear and explicit. There also ought to be adequate processing time for questions and directions to be understood.

Although learners of English do not have a disability, they are often at a disadvantage when taking tests. Just as it is fair and reasonable to provide assessment accommodations for learners with disabilities, adaptations are also sometimes necessary for English language learners (Kornhaber, 2004). For example, English learners may need to participate in a small group or individually. Modifications might include extra time to complete tests, presentation of assessment materials (in audio or video), and allowances for responding, such as dictation or the assistance of an interpreter. (One of several Web sites that can be helpful on this and other issues related to cultural fairness is http://www.bellevuecollege.edu/bias/.)

Avoiding the Imposition of Limitations on Knowledge. Paper-and-pencil tests can take the form of product assessments such as essays, stories, poems, and critiques. They can also be constructed-response or selected-response items. When many of us think of paper-and-pencil tests, we think of constructed-response items: filling in a blank, solving a mathematics problem, labeling a diagram or map, responding to short-answer questions, and so forth. Although these tests generally allow for application of a broader and deeper range of knowledge

(Woolfolk, 2007) than selected-response tests (multiple choice, true-false, and matching), constructed-response items can still have limitations:

- The content may be limited in its breadth and depth. The consequence is that imaginative and challenging problem solving is negotiated out of the test content domain (Shepard, 1989).
- The content may not cover the full range of important instructional objectives. The consequence is that instructors may end up teaching two curricula: one that promotes mastery of the content to be tested and the other that involves creative classroom pursuits that are often seen as tangential to measurable success and therefore less important (Popham, 1987).
- Tests may be limited in terms of format. For example, a short-answer question restricts the amount of knowledge students can convey. Therefore, students may not have an opportunity to demonstrate knowledge or, more important, how they might use that knowledge because the format does not allow it (Nitko and Brookhart, 2006).

Bear in mind these limitations as you consider ways to create tests that are fair and equitable and provide opportunities for the application of knowledge. Constructed-item responses are only one of many ways in which learning can be measured. Multiple forms of assessment yield more authentic and reliable information about learning experiences and ways of making meaning from those experiences: constructed-response tests, product assessments (essays, stories, research reports, writing portfolios, projects, and so forth), performance assessments (music, dance, dramatic performance, exhibitions, science lab demonstrations, debate, experiments, action research, and so forth), and process-focused assessments (oral questioning, interviews, learning logs, process folios, journals, observation, and so on). In addition, we know that learners are most likely to gain understanding when they construct their own cognitive maps of interconnections among concepts and facts. Relying only on decontextualized paper-and-pencil testing practices can cheapen teaching and undermine the authenticity of scores as measures of what learners really know.

Well-Constructed Paper-and-Pencil Tests. To the extent possible, design tests to resemble real learning tasks that have instructional value. This is one of the reasons that we prefer open-ended paper-and-pencil tests over multiple-choice tests. An example of a real learning situation that can be represented on paper is an item on an introductory bilingual education midterm that asks learners to outline a letter to the school board explaining the short-term and long-range benefits of bilingual education programs for learners.

Tests should require complex and challenging mental processes (Donovan, Bransford, and Pellegrino, 1999). For example, in an introductory course on organizational culture, a test item might require learners to create and present their reasoning for five interview questions that would help to determine which individuals are best suited for working effectively within a culturally diverse workplace.

Tests should acknowledge more than one approach or right answer. For example, in a course on culture and psychology, students might be asked to select and respond to one of the following two items:

Construct a map or schematic chart that illustrates seven to ten key social-political-cultural influences on the psychological well-being of members of culturally diverse groups.

■ ■

Which of the fifteen social-political-cultural influences that Don Locke (1992) uses to describe culturally diverse groups are most important in your work or everyday life? Why? Which seem least important to you? Why? Please select at least two influences for most important and at least two influences of least importance.

And perhaps most important, *tests should be meaningful to learners* (Eisner, 1999). This is likely to occur when students see tests as an opportunity for self-enhancement and meaning. Designing tests to fit a range of student interests and perceived needs supports the awareness that they have to understand and act in this world. Furthermore, whenever learners are able to make deliberate connections between what is new and what is known, the more likely they are to see learning as a fascinating elaboration on their lives.

Tests that are meaningful usually foster a sense of high challenge with low threat. Sometimes referred to as *relaxed alertness*, this is the optimal state of mind for expanding knowledge. We know from language acquisition studies, for example, that people learn language most easily when they are relaxed and the emphasis is on communication rather than error. Being calm and alert allows us to access what we know, think creatively, and more easily pay attention (Zull, 2002). When tests are meaningful, when the topics instructors choose matter to students and are even somewhat playful, students are less fearful and better able to engage their talents in even the most challenging processes.

As college graduates and educators, many instructors have been educated and socialized to believe that ability or intelligence is the major determinant of learner success and failure. The best of what we know about assessment reminds us that the systems in which we work and the practices we perpetuate are frequently not matched to the needs, interests, or experiences of the learners with whom we work. Students often see tests as exercises in trivia or a form of forced compliance to receive a grade. Such experiences can easily diminish a student's motivation for academic success. The limitations of popular testing practices and related recommendations are relevant not only to students of color and other historically underserved learners. Recent assessment theory and practice applies to everyone.

There are more significant criticisms than easy answers to questions of fairness, accountability, and how to revise testing practices in ways that promote consistently accurate judgments of learning among culturally diverse students (Stobart, 2005). In the high-stakes realm of grading student work, questioning past practices is difficult. Referring to doubt in general, Pulitzer Prize winner John Patrick Shanley might as well have been talking about assessment when he wrote (2007, p. 6): "Doubt requires more courage than conviction does, and more energy; because conviction is a resting place and doubt is infinite.... You may want to be sure. Look down on that feeling.... We've got to learn to live with a full measure of uncertainty. There is no last word."

Facing this challenge, we have to be aware that the language we use, the values we reflect, the environments we create, and the quality of the tests we select or design demonstrate our fidelity to both equity and excellence.

Self-Assessment

Self-assessment is a reflective process for gaining perspective on how we understand ourselves as learners, knowers, apprentices in a discipline, and citizens in a complex and paradoxical world. It requires us to observe, analyze, and develop insight into how we might improve personal performance relative to a set of academic standards. Self-assessment also allows a person to validate his or her authenticity as a learner and cultural being. It can help weave important relationships and meanings between academic or technical information and, in doing so, discover important connections.

In addition to locating one's own perspectives relative to academic work, self-assessment can provide an opportunity for students from all backgrounds to reflect on and more clearly negotiate the tension between personal orientations and dominant norms. For example, an instructor might ask students in a computer science course to visit two corporate settings to observe the ways in which technological skills are used and to develop insight into corporate norms and expectations. Prior to the field experience, students construct a brief set of semi-structured interview questions through which to access the assumptions of three workers in each corporate setting about the meaning and nature of work. Subsequent to the visits, students share their interview findings and draft a brief essay on the potential value conflicts that they as individual workers might experience in one of the settings. From these essays, the instructor demonstrates how to identify problems of practices for further study. Finally, she and her students explore ways to access digital resources for continued learning.

According to social theorists, the exploration of values is a complex process—and at times a lonely one (Jackson and Hardiman, 1988; Tatum, 1992). Within and across social groups, there are diverse epistemologies and perspectives. Creating opportunities to make frames of reference explicit is basic to intrinsic motivation. By exposing surprises, puzzlements, and hunches, structured self-reflection experiences can enhance motivation to make sense of things we might otherwise bury (Mezirow, 2000).

For each of the approaches that follow, we recommend that instructors carefully structure opportunities for learners to engage in personal reflection as a process of self-discovery and self-determination, even when self-assessment is primarily intended as a simple record of learning or a moment of accountability. In order to make this feasible, we encourage, when needed, developing agreements for mutual respect, focusing on confidentiality, honesty, nonconfrontation, speaking for oneself, and maximum opportunity for sense making. This invites the expansion and deepening of knowledge and helps to avoid cliché or culturally biased "truths."

A word of caution: too much ambiguity can overwhelm beginning students. To the extent possible, we encourage instructors to try to clearly identify what students are expected to focus on and learn in the process and what the instructor would like to learn as well. It is important for students to know how an instructor will evaluate or respond to self-assessments. Not surprisingly, students generally appreciate and are encouraged by a teacher's personal interest and timely feedback to their self-assessments. Although not everything needs to be read and commented on, learners are more likely to strengthen their reflective skills if they receive expected, sincere, specific, supportive, and timely feedback.

Self-assessment can be superficial when it is appended to a class as a single episode at the end of the term. To develop a habit or point of view about learning, MacGregor (1994) advises instructors to build self-assessment into the course as an ongoing process through such activities as learning journals, portfolio development, or classroom assessment strategies. Familiarity with shorter processes helps learners develop ease and confidence with long-term forms of self-assessment.

There are several approaches that can be used throughout a course for "micro" purposes or aggregated together and summarized for a long-term perspective. In our opinion, some of the most effective are student-invented dialogues, focused reflection, postwrites, journals, closure techniques, and summarizing questions.

Student-Invented Dialogues. Student-invented dialogues are a learning and performance task that involve using academic content to write an interactive narrative. For example, an instructor might ask students to create a conversation with major intellectuals or leaders to derive new meanings from course content. Consider a learner in dialogue with the secretary of defense about military spending (for a U.S. political science course) or perhaps in dialogue with a theoretical biologist on confusion about what the structure of DNA means for scientific research (for a biology course). The possibilities are endless. As part of a culminating project through which the instructor wanted students to clarify their learning as a gainful process, for example, one instructor asked students to create an autobiographical conversation, not to exceed two pages, between themselves as a learner at the beginning and at the end of the course. A short two- to three-sentence summary of insights gleaned was also part of the assignment.

Focused Reflection. In focused reflection, teachers ask students to write a five-minute reflection prior to the end of class. Topics can range from issues related to group participation to personalizing the meaning of academic course work. For example, teachers might ask learners to identify whether, how much, and what kinds of prejudices operated in how learners listened to each other. With respect to content, learners might be asked to identify something new and significant that was learned and why it is of interest or value. This technique has also been termed *five-minute writes* (Waluconis, 1994) or *quick writes* (Kingore, 2003). Students write answers to such questions as, "What is the most significant thing that you learned today?" "What question is uppermost on your mind at the conclusion of this course session?" These questions have obvious value for an instructor who wishes to build on the interests and needs of learners. They also help learners clarify the personal significance of their experiences and more fully understand their responsibility for conceptualizing what may need to be done for enhanced meaning.

Although five-minute writes and quick writes have value, they may be difficult for students who are in the process of learning English or are unaccustomed to shifts of authority in which they are asked to evaluate their own experiences. In addition, these brief exercises may trivialize opportunities for self-assessment and self-expression by reduction to "sound bites" of information. They may constrict awareness rather than expand it. With this in mind, you may want to consider extending the time allotted for reflection or allowing time outside class for students who would like more time or would like to create partnerships for responding to questions. Self-reflection becomes a natural condition for learning when there is diminished self-consciousness.

Postwrites. Michael Allen and Barbara Roswell (1989) have coined the term *postwrites* as reflection that encourages students to analyze a particular piece of work. Here is an example of how this might be presented to the class:

> Now that you have finished your essay, please answer the following questions. There are no right or wrong answers. We are interested in your analysis of your experience writing this essay. Questions might include the following:
>
> 1. What problems did you face in the writing of this essay?
> 2. What solutions did you find for these problems?
> 3. Imagine you had more time to write this essay. What would you do if you were to continue working on it?
> 4. Has your thinking changed in any way as a result of writing this essay? If so, briefly describe that change.

It is easy to imagine ways in which this technique could be applied across disciplines. In a science or math class, an instructor might redesign these questions to allow learners to identify and reflect on a problem that posed a particular challenge. Asking students to pay attention to problems and strategies for solving them changes the essential meaning of assessment from the assessment of a product to the assessment of learning.

Journals. Journals can take a number of forms. Consider, for example, a journal that is used in a science course to synthesize lab notes, address the quality of the work, examine the processes on which work is based, and address emerging interests and concerns. Journals are an informative complement to more conventional forms of assessment. They can preserve risks, experimentation with ideas, and self-expression.

With respect to sensitivity to cultural differences and encouraging critical awareness of the origins and meanings of subject-specific knowledge, journals can be used in every course to address the following questions (Meier, 1995).

1. From whose viewpoint are we seeing [or reading or hearing]?

2. From what angle or perspective?

3. How do we know what we know?

4. What is the evidence, and how reliable is it?

5. How are things, events, or people connected to each other? Is there a cause and effect?

6. So what? Why does it matter? What does it mean? Who cares?

Journals can address interests, ideas, and issues related to course material and processes, recurring problems, responses to instructor-generated questions, responses to learner-generated questions, and important connections that are being made. Important connections might refer to learner observations within the classroom. But optimally, connections are meanings that emerge through the application of course work to past, present, and future life experiences.

If we wish to promote this level of reflection, we must make the classroom a place where this can happen. Providing time in class for students to respond in their journals to readings, discussions, and significant questions builds community around the journal process and sends the message that the classroom is a place in which the skills of insight and personal meaning are valued.

Powerful journals require time and effort. For some students, journals are initially a difficult exercise. Although journals are common in many K–12 classrooms, students' experiences at times can range from poorly defined to uncomfortably intrusive. Some do not see a purpose for writing personal thoughts. For others, the lack of explicit criteria for success that is generally absent from journal assignments makes it difficult to proceed with confidence. It is often best to begin by clarifying the purpose and audience for journal writing and to ask students to pay less attention initially to the mechanics and organization and to simply try to get their thoughts down on paper so that they can learn from them.

If an instructor uses journals as a part of a writing course, she or he might want students to discuss the following:

- Your journal is a conversation with yourself. Trust your own voice.
- If you cannot respond to a prompt for writing in your journal, try to explain why not.
- From time to time, I will ask you to submit a summary of your journal. You will choose what you would like me to read from your journal and you would like me to know about something that has been written.
- Toward the end of the course, we will create a class anthology with at least one submission or summary from each person's journal. You will be asked to submit, along with your contribution, a brief preface indicating why you selected the material you submitted.
- In the back of your journal, keep a section for words, concepts, and phrases you are learning that can help your writing to become abundant.

Instructors may also want to consider eliciting student perspectives on the topic of guidelines for journal entries. It has been helpful for us to provide note cards and request that students note the guidelines that they would prefer or want to suggest. This process often allows the students to find a greater level of comfort with writing journals.

Closure Techniques. *Closure* is a term that implies an ending. For those of us who believe that arbitrary ending points are insufficient markers for learning, the concept of closure can be problematic. Our preference is to define closure activities as opportunities for formative synthesis—to broadly or selectively examine some of what we have learned, identify emerging thoughts or feelings, discern themes, construct meaning, and so forth. Essentially learners are encouraged to articulate their subjective relationship with course material as an active, ongoing process. For example, we might ask learners to formulate a question that they can take away with them for further consideration. Closure, then, becomes a way of building coherence between the classroom and personal experience. At other times, we might use closure as an opportunity for learners to pose their own learning as a problem to be solved. For example, students identify one obstacle they must still overcome to feel effective at a particular learning goal. Additional suggestions for positive and constructive closure follow.

Thematic Problematizing. Ask each learner to identify on a three-by-five card one issue, challenge, or concern that has emerged as a consequence of the previously completed learning experience. Anonymity is protected by asking learners not to put their names on their cards. With masking tape or push-pins, we post all of the cards and work together as a group to organize the cards into thematic categories for collective exploration. For example, in a graduate-level course on designing curricula for cultural diversity, we asked learners at the end of a lesson on alternative approaches to assessment to write down one fear they have that relates to making changes in their usual approach. We then posted their fears and, as we reviewed them, organized them according to themes that seemed to be emerging. Subsequently we broke into consultancy groups to explore and problem-solve the issues contained within each theme or category. An example of a category that emerged was "fear of making a mistake in evaluating someone." This category contained all of the cards that identified a particular way in which a mistake might be made or the various perceived consequences of making such mistakes (for example, an unfair grade, lowered motivation, or personal conflict).

Head, Heart, Hand. Another closure activity that learners often enjoy as a focus for reflection is "head, heart, hand." For "head," learners are asked to identify something they are thinking about as a consequence of the learning experience. For "heart," they are asked to identify a consequent feeling. And for "hand," they are asked to identify an action as a logical next step in the learning process. An option we offer is for students to select one of the three prompts. Those who prefer a more open approach to sense making appreciate this choice.

Note-Taking Pairs. Closure note-taking pairs (Johnson, Johnson, and Smith, 1991) can be used intermittently during a lecture or as a culminating activity. Either way, two students work together to review, add to, or modify their notes. This is an opportunity to cooperatively reflect on a lesson, review major concepts and pertinent information, and illuminate unresolved issues or concerns. Note-taking pairs are especially beneficial when there has been a lecture. Many learners, including but certainly not limited to students who speak English as a second language, benefit by summarizing their lecture notes to another person or vice versa. Students may ask each other such questions as these:

"What have you got in your notes about this particular item?"
"What are three key points the instructor made?"

"What is the most surprising thing the instructor said today?"

"What is something that you are feeling uncertain about?"

Summarizing Questions. The following examples come from *Embracing Contraries: Explorations in Learning and Teaching* by Peter Elbow (1986) and *Discussion as a Way of Teaching* by Stephen Brookfield and Stephen Preskill (2005):

- How do you feel now at the end? Why?
- What are you proud of?
- Compare your accomplishments with what you had hoped for and expected at the start.
- Which kinds of things were difficult or frustrating? Which were easy?
- What is the most important thing you did this period?
- Think of some important moments from this learning period: your best moments, typical moments, crises or turning points. Tell five or six of these in a sentence or two for each.
- What can you learn or did you learn from each of these moments?
- Who is the person you studied that you cared the most about? Be that person, and write that person's letter to you, telling you whatever it is he or she has to tell you.
- What did you learn throughout? What were the skills and ideas? What was the most important thing? What idea or skill was hardest to really understand? What crucial idea or skill came naturally?
- Describe this period of time as a journey. Where did the journey take you? What was the terrain like? Was it a complete trip or part of a longer one?

- You learned something crucial that you won't discover for a while. Guess it now.
- Tell a few ways you could have done a better job.
- What advice would some friends in the class give you if they spoke with 100 percent honesty and caring?
- What perspectives different from your own did you gain from this course that you now appreciate?
- As a result of this program, is there any way that you will act differently? If so, describe it.

Many students at first omit the "self" in self-assessment, writing instead about the teacher or the course or using vague and abstract language. For some, it takes time, practice, and feedback to build the confidence and skill to narrate their experiences with learning. It is a process that can carry personal risk. Yet the mastery of content is but a single challenge of academe.

Self-assessment creates a reciprocal reflection opportunity for learners and teachers. Instructors can gain critical insight into the selection of topics, materials, and approaches to teaching. We can also gain insight into some of our own assumptions about who we are culturally and are able to question our assumptions about students. As difficult as this unpredictable and unexpected learning can be, when we are willing to use authentic ways to learn from and with our students, they indeed are colearners, as opposed to audiences and critics. In this manner, self-assessment also contributes to building community in classrooms.

Self-assessment can be a powerful learning tool across contexts. Examples of the ways in which digital media are being used as a means for students and teachers to see their progress over time are numerous and exceed the scope of this book. We offer two that we have encountered: one that focuses on student work over time and one that allows educators to self-assess. The first example is the Averno Community College diagnostic digital portfolio (DDP). It guides and sorts proto-cols to make it possible for students, faculty, and advisors to use selected student work samples, criteria, student self-assessment records, and assessor feedback across disciplines and by skill (see www.ddp.alverno.edu). As at many other postsecondary institutions, a goal is to help students reflect on their learning development at critical intervals and set forth a plan for future learning.

The rapidly expanding repertoire of formats and media for educators to learn from one another also adds an interest-ing dimension to self-assessment. Although most of the Web sites, videos, and other media that afford opportunities for critical and collaborative self-assessment are K–12 focused, they can be easily adapted to other contexts. An informative anthology, *Going Public with Our Teaching* (Hatch and others, 2005), provides particularly inspiring ways in which educators can use technology to publicly examine their own teaching practice and the practice of education as a whole (see www.carnegiefoundation.org/castl/k-12/). On her interactive page, for example, Mississippi high school teacher Renee Moore, asks others to help her consider "some effective, culturally engaged approaches to teaching English with African-American stu-dents." Her imaginative archives engage external audiences through clear descriptions, photographs, and video regarding context, teaching practices, and student work. If for no other reason, it behooves us, as postsecondary instructors, to know how students such as Brandon and his friends describe their lives ten years after high school graduation in letters they com-pose to their teacher (http://www.goingpublicwithteaching.org/rmoore/).

The perfect assessment process has yet to be found. Our path as professional learners committed to enhancing motivation among diverse learners is to set reasonable and fair assessment goals, use multiple approaches, and learn from them as we go along.

Effective Grading

Although grades do not accurately predict educational or occupational achievement, they nevertheless have high status in U.S. society. Low grades often threaten and stigmatize students, doing more to diminish their motivation to learn than to enhance it. Because grades and grade point averages construct a historical record of academic performance, they create a legacy throughout students' lives, determining, often to a large extent, opportunities for graduate school, professional occupations, and scholarships and grants.

In four-year selective colleges, there are concerns that grades are too high. This inflationary trend probably spans several decades (Young, 2003). It is estimated that the average grade in college is now a B (Rojstaczur, 2002). There is compelling evidence that the source of this problem is the lack of validity of grades. Nonetheless, grades legitimize teacher power and control over students, and most people continue to believe that grades are an objective indicator of learning. As instructors, we need to realize the authority that grading gives us and understand that students may restrict their critique of our teaching and assessment practices out of fear that such criticism will lower their grades. Student course evaluations are only one of several indicators of instructional competence.

Quantification of the GPA does not necessarily indicate accuracy or objectivity. So many factors and forces enter into grading that ranking students based on grades from different subject areas, different teachers, and often different institutions is not a sufficiently valid process. The "meaning of a grade is socially determined" (Walvoord and Anderson, 1998, p. 102). It is interpreted in the society we inhabit, more specifically in the college and department in which we teach. Those standards are relative and usually based on the norms and perspectives of the faculty within the given department. Yet this lack of validity is symptomatic of a deeper issue: that a single grade for a single course cannot accurately represent all the variables in performance and progress of learning over time. As Ohmer Milton, Howard Pollio, and James Eison (1986, p. 212) observed, "The lone letter symbol is a conglomerate which specifies none of its contents."

If we graded only a single essay rather than all the compositions in a writing course, the variables we might consider for evaluation are vocabulary, phrasing, exemplification, quality of ideas and analysis, cohesiveness, depth of understanding, how much the student had to learn to write the essay, how this essay compares with the student's previous essay, how this essay compares with other students' essays, how this essay demonstrates the student's progress in quality of writing, and so forth. In many ways, it is preposterous to imagine that a single grade can adequately represent the complicated interactions of a written assignment, much less an entire course.

Our response to this conundrum is not to look at grades per se but to look at grading practices: how we arrive at a grade and what those practices do to support learning and motivation. No matter what the scale (for example, A to F), grades should be clearly specified and based on reasonable standards that students can use to guide their learning. Not surprisingly, at the top of our list, grading practices should sustain and encourage intrinsic motivation to learn. The most academically beneficial grading practices offer accurate, specific, timely feedback that improves student learning (Marzano, 2007).

We will begin with what to avoid. Douglas Reeves (2008) identifies three practices for grading that are so ineffective that they can be considered toxic. The first is to use a number system, such as 100 points, and to assign zero credit for a missing assignment. This is essentially a punitive practice that dramatically lowers a student's chance for a higher grade. In such a case, when the real thing that benefits learning is completing the assignment, this practice diminishes student motivation and does little to improve learning. Finding ways to coach or collaborate (Chapter Two) with learners to support completion is much more beneficial.

The second practice is averaging all scores throughout a semester or quarter to arrive at the final grade. This practice infers that all learning is equal and that performance early in the course is as important as performance later in the course. Since so much complex learning is developmental, sequential, and the result of practice and revision, this approach to grading is typically reductive and unfair. Students' first papers, early tests, and beginning projects are the means by which they learn their errors and make improvements based on feedback and guidance. It is also the way the real world works: we construct and then refine a product to achieve quality, or learn and then practice a skill to become proficient. This is one of reasons for the common belief that learning follows a curve and why editors, managers, and coaches do not evaluate on the basis of initial or even midlevel performance. In general, authentic performance at the end of a course is likely to be more accurate than throughout the course.

The third precarious practice is the single test, assignment, or project that is so high stakes that it determines almost all of the student's grade but is based on approximately a quarter of the course's duration. An example of this is a project that determines 80 percent of a student's grade but takes only about four weeks out of a sixteen-week semester to complete; or a final paper-and-pencil test that determines 60 percent or more of a student's grade. In the project example, unless there have been successive opportunities for feedback, revision, and development over the semester, such a grading practice undermines the learning that preceded it. In the case of a test, an intrinsically motivating and valid representation of learning would include a series of formative and related assessments, covering similar content and with specific, relevant feedback that allows self-correction.

Another grading practice about which we urge caution is to strictly ascertain grades through quantification. Understandably, because we have to "give grades," we want to be objective. Using numbers such as scores may seem to easily offer this possibility. We try to remember, however, that when we assign a number as a value for a component of an assessment or a test, it influences the construction of that element and consequently what students will study and learn. A common example is the use of multiple-choice tests as formative assessments. Because they are easy to score and average, many instructors are attracted to the format of multiple-choice, true-false, and short-answer tests. However, if these formats are to assess *and* encourage learning, they must be carefully constructed. A common pitfall is to rely on factual recall at the expense of intricate thought (Woolfolk, 2007).

Poorly constructed or overly simplified "objective" tests promote cramming because superficial information can be rapidly covered and retained for a short period of time. In a few days, the information is gone, but the grade has been captured. To avoid such complicity, many postsecondary educators are moving toward grading practices that use authentic assessments. These are presented to students with graded exemplary models (see Chapter Three) that include relevant specific criteria introduced early in the learning cycle. Contracts and rubrics strengthen this approach.

Contracts (see Chapter Three) have a structure that allows mutual understanding and agreement, as well as dialogue about the content, process, criteria, and outcomes. For culturally diverse students, especially those who are learning English, the negotiation of a contract can be clarifying and reassuring. Contracts also have the benefit of targeting a particular grade and removing some of the insecurity that tests can engender regarding which grade will be attained. Negotiating a contract for a particular grade ought to be a democratic process between an instructor and a student, but not a permissive one, or the integrity of the learning experience will be in question.

Rubrics have their limitations. However, when clearly written, they can be scaled to accommodate grades and offer students an understanding of what needs to be accomplished for a particular grade. In the example of the rubric in Exhibit 5.2 each descriptor (Exemplary, Competent, and so forth) could also be assigned a letter grade (A, B, and so forth) and a number (4, 3, 2, 1), allowing for averaging among the rubrics used for a particular assignment and its ultimate grade. Because rubrics tend to become easily reified, we want to again emphasize the importance of giving students the opportunity to discuss the criteria within rubrics with openness to receiving their input for constructing the final criteria.

Our experience with faculty who teach both adult learners and younger, traditional-age students indicates that they perceive a difference in attitudes toward grading between these two groups. Discussions with these faculty have generated the following perceptions. (We caution that these generalizations are not the result of rigorous research, but we offer them as possible insights for consideration when grading.)

- Adults who are first generation college students are more likely to regard grades as a reflection of their capabilities than are younger, traditional-age students. Adults, especially when older, are less familiar with how the system of college grading works and may perceive their grades as truer reflections of their talents.
- Employers of adults often use grade averages to determine tuition support. Higher grades mean a higher percentage of financial support. For this reason, grading policies may seem to provoke more anxiety among adult learners.

Following are some ideas that have been aggregated to suggest practices and policies that are generally considered equitable and informative. While not all of the suggestions will fit within the pragmatic limits of different contexts, these ideas can contribute to conversations with colleagues about personal grading philosophies and approaches:

- *Limit the attributes measured by grades to individual achievement.* Such things as effort, participation, or attitude should be reported separately, which may require an extended assessment format. Avoid using your assessment policy for things that ought to be addressed through separate attendance and participation agreements.

- *Sample student performance.* Do not mark everything students do, and do not include all marks in the final grades. Provide feedback through formative assessments and include only summative assessments in grade calculations.

- *Grade in pencil.* Emphasize the most recent information when grading progress. For example, it makes little sense to average the marks of a student in the first week and the last week of a digital simulation class; the most recent marks should offer the best assessment of the student's skill. When possible, offer opportunities to improve grades. This does not mean instructors have to offer unlimited chances to pass a test or improve a paper. Some instructors, for example, require students who want to retake a test or revise an assignment to demonstrate that they have done additional work that increases the chance that they will do better the second time around.

- *Relate grading procedures to the intended learning goal.* The emphasis given to different topics or skills in a class should be reflected in the weight they have in determining the final grade. (A typical method that often does not stress particular topics or skills is to determine final grades by simply allotting 40 percent to tests and quizzes, 20 percent to homework, 20 percent to class participation, and so on.)

- *Use care "crunching" numbers.* One of the biggest quandaries is what to do when a student gets a zero on an assignment. If scores on all assignments are simply averaged, a single zero can yield a grade that does not reflect the student's performance. Instructors might consider using students' median score. If a student earns a zero or a very low score on a major assignment, is there a chance to revise the work? If not, can a future assignment demonstrate new learning and count for additional credit?

- *Use criterion-referenced standards to distribute grades.* In addition to other problems, grading on a curve does not allow all students to see how close they are coming to high standards of performance. If all students reach the standard, it is okay for all to reach the highest grade.

- *Discuss assessment and grading with students at the beginning of instruction.* The criteria for quality work should not be a mystery to students. It is extremely helpful for students to see the grading schemes and rubrics that will be used to judge performance as well as a model of superior performance. It is even better if grading schemes and rubrics are cocreated with students.

Below are some additional considerations for effective grading practices.

- In entry-level courses, consider working with students to compose a letter to family or friends that outlines what is being studied, the performance standards to which the student aspires, and the percentage of the grade that different standards will be designated. For example, one standard might be that an effective oral presentation will be 10 percent of the final grade. This process can be clarifying as well as further connect families to the learning experiences of their young adults.

- Consider agreed-on common writing rubrics that help students across disciplines develop their language skills. Many disciplines have a specific vocabulary and organizing schema. However, there are also common writing conventions across the course spectrum. In recent years, high schools have begun to share responsibility for teaching reading, writing, speaking, and listening. This is a need throughout higher education contexts as well. Vocabulary tends to be one of the strongest predictors of overall success on any achievement measure, and speaking well is the first way into a good job.

- Bring in experts from the community to work with you and your students to ensure that tasks and scoring systems are authentic. For example, an editor of a local paper might help create a scoring rubric based on what she or he looks for in well-prepared article. Students might interview a panel of community experts to discuss assessment criteria that might fit with a range of perspectives.

- In early college years, consider a dissertation and defense model where students create inquiry-based projects with support of a committee with another instructor, peer, parent, and community representation.

- With major projects, have students engage peers in dialogue about an aspect of their work. A roundtable format is especially suited to this form of interaction.

- Educators at all levels should model for students and for the community their own interest in personal growth through learning. Find ways to share things that you are learning and that matter to you.

■■

This chapter has presented fundamental norms and practices for engendering competence. Assessment that is culturally responsive illuminates the nature of human learning—the connection between knowledge as others have defined it and meaning that is relevant to individual experiences and belief systems.

Change and adaptation to new ways of working with assessment is a multidimensional, interpersonal, and intrapersonal negotiation. Our decisions are mediated by standards of quality and excellence that are defined by individuals, institutions, communities, and cultural agreements. We believe that the unique spirit and meanings that motivate us as learners and teachers can be affirmed even amid the confusion of competing expectations and policies. When assessment is conveyed and sanctioned as a trusted medium for understanding learning, it is not something one simply practices or performs. It is an ethical process and one of our most profound responsibilities as educators.

6

IMPLEMENTING A CULTURALLY RESPONSIVE PEDAGOGY

> We have a choice in this country. We can accept
> a politics that breeds division, and conflict, and
> cynicism. We can tackle race only as spectacle...
> or as fodder for nightly news.... That is one option.
> Or, at this moment... we can come together and
> say, "Not this time." This time we want to reject
> the cynicism that tells us... those kids who don't
> look like us are somebody else's problem. The
> children of America are not those kids, they are our
> kids, and we will not let them fall behind in a 21st
> century economy. Not this time.
>
> —*Barack Obama*

Many colleges and universities seek to address issues of social justice through curricula, recruitment of larger numbers of faculty and students of color, and more inclusive educational environments. Yet college teaching—how courses are organized and taught on a daily basis—is particularly slow to change. This is not for lack of theoretically solid and pragmatic advice from a range of disciplines.

Historians, philosophers, and systems theorists continue to remind us that oppression is a complicated and dynamic phenomenon and that educational innovation requires humility. This extensive body of literature is complemented by neuroscientists and cognitive theorists who challenge outdated beliefs about fixed intelligence with compelling evidence regarding the desire and capacity for learning throughout one's life span. Adult learning scholars provide an array of methods to diversify teaching, including approaches for experiential, transformational, and contemplative learning.

As the previous chapter highlighted, evaluation and assessment scholars are leading a revolution to change narrow and exclusive assessment standards and practices. With such an array of perspectives on teaching and learning, the prospect of significant instructional improvement ought to be hopeful. Yet one thing we know with some certainty regarding change is that overly precise models tend to neglect the importance of political will and local imagination. Veteran faculty are well aware that instructional directives are typically dismissed. Telling teachers, "What the research says…" as a reason for change is abstract and questionable. Certainly research can illuminate understanding, but it does not settle the argument. The implications of this awareness for any number of learning contexts—professional development through higher education—are as relevant now as they were for the early champions of multicultural education. This is also true for students.

Granted, there are many who believe that educators are having a discussion when what is needed is a revolution (Anyon, 2005). Yet we believe that transformation among people is cumulative in its progression. Like the movement of the hour hand of a clock, pedagogical innovation may be imperceptible but quite dramatic over time. People do change: how we vote, how we confront injustice, how we educate our youth, how we alter our own teaching practices.

Yet asking educators to change within the vacuum of their classrooms is likely to be ineffective. Innovative pedagogies require collaboration, if for no other reason than that they require support for the discomfort that new risks impose. Change theorists remind us that if we are truly doing something different, we will experience an "implementation dip" and, in all likelihood, expose personal flaws and contradictions (Fullan,

2004). Yet when adults experience something that is relevant and unsettling, and have the time and support to gain insight into the experience, they are at the portal of a new perspective.

This chapter offers ideas about how to apply a motivational framework to a lesson or a course. It also provides ideas for instructors who are interested in sequencing content and more effectively responding to the needs of English learners. Examples of professional collaboration that support experimentation and inquiry into practice are included throughout the chapter, as are suggestions for personal reflection on practice.

The Example of a Single Course

In this section, we illustrate how the motivational framework for culturally responsive teaching might look in practice by applying it to a course that sought to support students' personal transformation. Beverly Daniel Tatum's course on the psychology of racism serves as a context for this example. It is emblematic of the philosophy and approach that an educator seeking to implement a well-aligned set of intrinsically motivating instructional practices could use to construct a complex and challenging learning experience. We use italics to identify which of the four conditions of the motivational framework are addressed through various aspects of Dr. Tatum's course. You will notice that the motivational framework is a not a sequential heuristic. The four motivational conditions are often mutually supportive and tend to overlap. Yet when we map a course, we can usually associate different aspects of the course with a primary motivational condition.

When Dr. Tatum taught this course, class size averaged twenty-four students; most were white European Americans and ranged in socioeconomic background from very poor to very wealthy. The course was designed "to provide students with an understanding of the psychological causes and emotional reality of racism as it appears in every day life" (Tatum, 1992, p. 2).

Beyond the reading material and media used in the course, Dr. Tatum created opportunities for learners to experience situations where the realities of racism might exist and be witnessed first hand (*two motivational conditions: developing a positive attitude through relevance and choice and enhancing meaning through challenge and engagement*). These experiences included visiting supermarkets in different racially composed neighborhoods to compare costs and quality of goods and services and going apartment hunting as mixed-racial partners. Students kept journals for critical reflection of their experiences using their writing as an opportunity to examine their own underlying beliefs and assumptions and to generate their own sense of these experiences (*motivational condition: engendering competence through authentic ways to make sense and become more effective in learning something of value*).

Furthermore, there was an opportunity following the experience for reflective discourse. Stated differently, there was a chance to engage in dialogue with peers and to search for a clearer understanding and interpretation of experience (*motivational condition: engendering competence*). With such self-generated knowledge (generated by the students, not told to them by the professor), learners were inclined to explore possibilities for change and ways to take effective action (*motivational condition: developing a positive attitude through volition and relevance*).

Students could work collaboratively in small groups to develop realistic action plans to interrupt racism (*motivational condition: establishing inclusion through respect and connectedness*). They also had the opportunity to privately tape an interview of themselves regarding their racial views and understanding at the beginning of the course and at the end of the course. After reviewing these two tapes, they wrote about their perceived changes in racial understanding (*motivational condition: engendering competence*).

Dr. Tatum accepted the validity of students' experiences, thinking, and judgments, and, with context and meaning making as central components, constructed learning in a way that was a transforming process: at the conclusion of the course, students acted with new awareness and self-understanding.

If Dr. Tatum were to have mapped this course using the framework, she might have approached it as follows:

Motivational Framework Lesson Plan

Please see Resource D for a structure in which this lesson plan would fit neatly.

Establishing Inclusion: Respect and Connectedness

How can this learning experience help students feel respected by and connected to other students and to the teacher?

- Develop explicit norms for group discussion to ensure equitable opportunities for public discourse.

- Use peer collaboration for community visits and journals.

Developing a Positive Attitude: Volition and Personal Relevance

How can this learning experience promote volition and greater personal relevance?

- Provide choices such as generating forms of action and knowledge through personal experience in the community and determining what to share in journals and class discussion.

Enhancing Meaning: Challenge and Engagement

How can this learning experience engage students in challenges that include their perspectives and values?

- Use multiple modes of instruction and learning opportunities: reading, discussion, community engagement in authentic settings, storytelling, critical questions, allowing for emotion in order to render deeper meaning.

Engendering Competence: Authenticity and Effectiveness

How can this learning experience enhance students' understanding that they are becoming more effective in authentic learning they value?

- Create frequent opportunities for sense making through journals, discussion, and ongoing additional forms of personal and group reflection.
- Provide ongoing instructor and peer feedback.
- Use literature to explicitly anchor and illuminate personal experiences.
- Provide for pre- and post-taped interviews for documentation of changes in racial understanding

Planning with this motivational framework is a dynamic process. The purpose of the framework is to guide the likelihood that a course or an individual lesson will address all four motivational conditions in culturally relevant ways. Dr. Tatum's example illustrates using the framework for constructing and aligning significant learning experiences in a course. Later in this chapter, we address using the framework for individual lessons.

Content Considerations

In this book, we advocate following a motivation framework to teach content in a way that evokes intrinsic motivation to learn among diverse postsecondary learners. We suggest teaching any significant learning goal in a course or professional learning context using specific norms and practices to create the conditions of inclusion, attitude, meaning and competence. However, once a learning experience has started, it does not typically proceed in a sequential way. There are many unexpected but important twists and turns. This is why we refer to the motivational framework as more of a compass than a map. In addition, there are some general guidelines for organizing and presenting content.

Many instructors are also concerned with how to effectively organize and present content for learning in general. On this topic, we offer some technical suggestions from the field of instructional design (Tracey, 1992; Dick, Carey, and Carey, 2004). These suggestions are valuable as part of any pedagogical repertoire and are supportive of English language learners:

- Start the sequence with materials that are familiar to learners, and then proceed to new materials, interrelating the familiar with the new.
- Provide a context or framework to use in organizing what students will learn.
- Place easy-to-learn tasks early in the sequence.
- Introduce broad concepts and technical terms that have application throughout the instructional process early in the sequence.
- Place practical application of concepts and principles close to the point of the initial discussion of the concepts and principles in a just-in-time manner.
- Place prerequisite knowledge and skills in the sequence before they must be combined with subsequent knowledge and skills.
- Provide time for practice and review of skills and knowledge that are essential parts of tasks to be introduced later in the activity.
- Introduce a concept or skill in the task in which it is most frequently used.

- Cluster learning goals in closely related, self-contained groups.
- Avoid overloading any task with elements that are difficult to learn.
- Place complex or cumulative skills late in the sequence.
- Provide support or coaching for practice of related skills, concepts, and principles in areas where transfer is likely to occur.

Authentic Roles and Practices

A pluralistic community is always a community in the making. As such, teaching requires orchestration of multiple social, creative, and academic interests with attention to existing flaws and willingness to envision new possibilities. Leading an ethical professional life often means trespassing—not in the sense of a moral transgression, but to infringe on the status quo, to question unexamined assumptions or media that demean or exclude the experience of those who are underserved and disenfranchised (Bensimon, 1994).

This means starting with ourselves and our own course content, syllabi, and materials, being willing to cross the border from what we know to what we need to know. In our opinion, this is the first requisite for culturally responsive teaching: a sincere sense of self-scrutiny, not to induce guilt or knee-jerk responses but to deepen sensitivity to the range of ways educators are complicitous with the inequitable treatment of others and to open ourselves to knowing the limitations of our own perspectives and our need for those of others.

We must also consider students. Their histories and experiences are critical to how we create with them the kind of learning where trust, equal participation, and inquiry are normal ways of proceeding. Our experience and that of other practitioners (Adams, Jones, and Tatum, 2007; Anderson, 2008) in the field of multiculturalism is that many learners are uncomfortable with the topics, methods, and changing roles of its pedagogy. Students may resist learning procedures that require active engagement with other learners, faculty, or course materials. Constructing and critiquing their own and other's knowledge may contradict their experience and the paradigm that knowledge is something the teacher possesses at the beginning and transmits to students during the course, and that students demonstrate as their own private possession on a test. Dialogue can make students feel provoked, exposed, or even used, as well as sometimes frustrated when other students talk too much or too little. As we indicated in Chapter One, culturally responsive teaching may violate the unspoken norms of many conventional college classrooms. In some ways, the resistance of learners may very well mirror our own.

We have addressed student and teacher resistance at the beginning and end of this book because we respect the enormity of the challenge not only to assist learners to construct and acquire knowledge but to raise their critical consciousness about social justice. Culturally responsive teaching often places marginalized views and issues of social inequity in the foreground. This means teachers and learners at times will grapple with altering long-held viewpoints as they begin to understand and accommodate other perspectives. Therefore, teaching in a culturally responsive way may require considerable transformation. Being skilled, prepared, and willing to deal with some of the tensions and difficulties that accompany this pedagogy is an essential part of the experience. In this regard, emerging literature related to cultural and intercultural competence is informative (Connerly and Pedersen, 2005; Ancis and Ali, 2005). Many people who take up residence in a culture different from their own are eventually able to develop an understanding of and respect for the perceptions, experiences, and values of the other culture. Initially, however, there is a period when sojourners feel dissonance and emotions ranging from fear to exhilaration as they experience the incongruities between their host community and their primary cultural group. Through actively observing, socializing, and developing friendships within the host community, they eventually arrive at a more integrated perspective. Very few of us are able to do this without some period of uneasiness. As practitioners evolving toward a more culturally responsive pedagogy we offer the following guidelines:

- Proceed gradually and with care.
- Build on your strengths.
- Examine a syllabus for a course.
- Create a reasonably safe climate in which to learn.
- Learn with others.
- Identify new roles as they emerge.
- Create action plans.
- Acknowledge doubt and anxiety as signs of change and potential for growth.
- Recognize the power of self-generated knowledge.
- Share your work with others.

For our discussion of the previous suggestions, Exhibit 6.1 outlines the summary of norms and practices of a motivational framework for culturally responsive teaching. The recommendations that follow the exhibit are for consideration by faculty who seek to become more competent as culturally responsive teachers. The ideas we offer are heuristics rather than prescriptions, designed to stimulate additional possibilities about how to move one's professional practice in a culturally relevant direction. As is evident from multiple intelligences theory and literature on cultural differences, there are many places to begin, with an array of possible directions and dimensions. The entry point that an instructor selects for the purposes of planning a lesson or a unit is less relevant than care to include all four motivational conditions. That said, at certain points in a course, certain conditions of the framework may seem more important than others. For example, the motivational condition of establishing inclusion through respect and connectedness is a particularly important focus at the beginning of a course or new learning experience. However, throughout the course, in large- and small-group formats, instructors will want to help a class recall and, at times, strengthen, agreements for equitable discussion.

Exhibit 6.1 Norms and Practices of a Motivational Framework for Culturally Responsive Teaching

Norms

Establishing Inclusion (Criteria: Respect and connectedness)

1. *Human purpose:* Course work emphasizes the human purpose of what is being learned and its relationship to the learners' personal experiences and contemporary situations.
2. *Constructivist approach:* Teachers use a constructivist approach to create knowledge.
3. *Collaboration:* Collaboration and cooperation are the expected ways of proceeding and learning.
4. *Hopeful view:* Course perspectives assume a nonblameful and realistically hopeful view of people and their capacity to change.
5. *Equitable treatment:* There is equitable treatment of all learners with an invitation to point out behaviors, practices, and policies that discriminate.

Developing Attitude (Criteria: Relevance and volition)

6. *Learners' experience:* Teaching and learning activities are contextualized in the learners' experience or previous knowledge and are accessible through their current thinking and ways of knowing.
7. *Volition:* The entire academic process of learning, from content selection to accomplishment and assessment of competencies, encourages learners to make choices based on their experiences, values, needs, and strengths.

(continued)

Enhancing Meaning (Criteria: Engagement and challenge)

8. *Challenge:* Learners participate in challenging learning experiences involving deep reflection and critical inquiry that address relevant, real-world issues in an action-oriented manner.

9. *"Third idiom":* Learner expression and language are joined with teacher expression and language to form a "third idiom" that enables the perspectives of all learners to be readily shared and included in the process of learning.

Engendering Competence (Criteria: Authenticity and effectiveness)

10. *Relevant assessment:* The assessment process is connected to the learner's world, frames of reference, and values.

11. *Multiple ways:* Demonstration of learning includes multiple ways to represent knowledge and skill.

12. *Self-assessment:* Self-assessment is essential to the overall assessment process.

Practices

Establishing Inclusion

1. Introductions
2. Collaborative and Cooperative learning
3. Writing groups
4. Peer teaching
5. Opportunities for multidimensional sharing
6. Focus groups
7. Reframing
8. Participation agreements
9. Learning communities
10. Cooperative base groups

Developing Attitude

11. Learning goal procedures
    a. Clearly defined goals

   b. Problem-solving goals

   c. Expressive outcomes

12. Fair and clear assessment criteria

13. Relevant learning models

14. Goal setting

15. Learning contracts

16. Approaches based on multiple intelligences theory

17. Sensitivity and pedagogical flexibility based on the concept of style

18. Experiential learning—the Kolb model

19. Teacher-learner conferences

Enhancing Meaning

20. Critical questioning for engaging discussions

21. Posing problems

22. Decision making

23. Authentic research

   a. Definitional investigation

   b. Historical investigation

   c. Projective investigation

   d. Experimental inquiry

   e. Action research

24. Invention and artistry

25. Simulations, role playing, and games

26. Case study method

27. Projects

28. Problem-posing model

Engendering Competence

29. Feedback

30. Alternatives to pencil-and-paper tests: authentic performance tasks

   a. Comparing personal assessment values with actual assessment practice

(continued)

> b. Assessment with options based on multiple intelligences
> c. Assessments with exhibitions and poster conferences
> d. Assessments with portfolios
> 31. Well-constructed paper-and-pencil tests
> 32. Self-assessment
> 33. Effective grading

Proceed Gradually and with Care

As we suggested earlier in this chapter, the majority of faculty and students are a product of conventional postsecondary experience. Developing new roles such as colearners in the classroom and using unique ways of learning and assessing will often initially feel awkward. Stepping into a class on the first day is akin to walking into a theater of strangers: we have a vague mutual goal, but there is no sense of personal attachment and little expectancy of developing a relationship. Rarely are most learners seeking social change or coming with a transformative agenda. As Goodlad (1990) has observed, most students are largely passive, because it best fits the nature of school. There is also the reality that when we change the way we teach, we are not just going to learn from this experience; we are going to learn in it, acting in the situation and being acted on by it (Wlodkowski, 2008). A negative and difficult initial teaching experience, even with a positive attitude and new methods, can distort an otherwise positive process. Therefore, to proceed gradually and carefully offers a better chance to negotiate challenges as they emerge. Rather than choosing rigidly and exclusively between conventional and culturally responsive forms of pedagogy, it may be more reasonable to focus on how to move the course gradually toward more culturally responsive norms and practices.

In addition, our experience is that unless significant alterations in course norms and practices are explicitly named and discussed with learners, learners are likely to be confused and resistant.

As you proceed through the suggestions that follow, it may be beneficial to review our idea of culturally responsive pedagogy. It (1) respects diversity; (2) engages the motivation of all learners; (3) creates a safe, inclusive, and respectful environment; (4) derives teaching practices from principles that cross disciplines and cultures; and (5) promotes justice and equity in the broader community and beyond. For explicit teaching about social justice, we draw from Adams, Bell, and Griffin's ideas about social justice education (2007, p. 58): "Social justice requires an understanding of the social power dynamics and societal inequality that result in some social groups having privilege, status, and access, whereas other groups are disadvantaged, oppressed, and denied access. It illuminates how social power allows access to resources that enhance one's chances of getting what one needs or influencing others in pursuit of a safe, productive, and fulfilling life."

Build on Your Strengths

One way to begin to access the materials and information in this book is to review Exhibit 6.1, this time checking off all the norms and practices that you currently use when composing your courses. This will affirm what you do and may give you some ideas about what you would like to do next. Another immediate possibility is to check your syllabus and materials for bias. Making changes here can profoundly affect the learning process and clarify how the knowledge of the course is constructed.

Examine a Syllabus for a Course

To begin, you might take a syllabus for a course you regularly teach and scan the entire composition for the norms it reflects and how it integrates the various practices. After this careful consideration, you might reflect on how you would like to revise or remodel the course to be more culturally responsive, using Exhibit 6.1 as a suggestion map. To exemplify this process, and as a point of departure and critique, we have provided in Exhibit 6.2 the syllabus for Introduction to Research, a course that one of us has taught. The four representative questions that follow it might be used to examine where a syllabus is consistent with the norms and practices of culturally responsive teaching and to find areas for possible improvement from a culturally responsive perspective.

Composing a course syllabus is similar to making a map for a particular terrain. It creates definite directions, expectations, and boundaries. Along with the people in class, the course syllabus probably creates the strongest impression at a course's initial meeting. Writing a course syllabus that can reassure students about the value of a course as well as evoke their motivation to learn is a considerable challenge:

Exhibit 6.2 Introduction to Research

Introduction

Welcome to *Introduction to Research*. The type of thinking and requirements for a course of this nature may appear formidable. Research has a jargon and set of symbols that can seem strange, difficult, and rigid. Yet it is a way of knowing that can be helpful and very creative.

As a graduate student, I came to research with a sense of inadequacy and trepidation, and after having worked over twenty years as a psychologist and educator, and using and conducting research on a regular basis, I still feel those two emotions about research. They are more tempered now, however, because I am also more familiar with research as a discipline and as a way to understand the world and our experience in it.

Research as a means of knowing dominates our society. It influences every aspect of our life, from the purity of the water we drink to the size of the federal budget. It has an authoritative influence on educational and social policy. To understand research and to know how to critique it is a valuable asset in the pursuit of personal and social goals. Thus, this course aims to increase conversational and critical skills in the use of research. As the syllabus indicates, we are going to use research for purposes we value.

Please access the texts as soon as possible, and do the required reading. Most of the course activities are guided practice in the application of knowledge about research. No one has to be expert, but if you have not done the necessary reading, the experience will be confusing. In addition, you will not be able to participate in discussions, which are essential to our shared learning. The first few classes will be much like a clinic. We will find out what we know and what we need and want to know about research.

Course Intention

The purpose of this course is to develop an understanding of the primary assumptions, perspectives, and methods that guide research in the social sciences. This course also provides a framework and literacy for understanding and evaluating research studies found in professional journals and reports. Because of the nature of education, action research is offered as a research method to be learned at a level of useful proficiency.

Learning Goals

1. Understanding, with an inclusive orientation to the culture and diversity, the usefulness, limitations, advantages, and assumptions of research approaches and practices represented by the following topics:

    a. The nature of human inquiry and the scientific method
    b. Inductive and deductive theory
    c. Correlation and causality
    d. Research designs for exploration, description, and explanation
    e. Reliability and validity

(*continued*)

    f. Questionnaire formats

    g. Sampling design

    h. Experimental designs

    i. Survey research

    j. Ethnographic research

    k. Unobtrusive research

    l. Evaluative research

    m. Action research

    n. The ethics of research

2. To effectively interpret and critique research articles published in such education and social science periodicals as the *Journal of Teacher Education*, *Equity and Excellence*, and *Anthropology and Education Quarterly*.

3. To effectively construct and apply an action research method to know what happens as a result of specific educational practices and interventions.

Anticipated Learning Experiences and Class Outline

1. General introduction.

2. Overview of current issues in educational research.

3. Reaction panels to controversial articles in education and social science. A number of small cooperative groups will be formed. Each will find a different research article that deals with a topic of a controversial nature (for example, educational myths based on neuroscience research, retaining teachers in high-poverty schools, using college entrance exams to predict academic performance). Each group will have a chance to publicly critique the article based on its knowledge of research methods.

4. Designing an action research project to better understand current issues in education. Using a small-group format, participants will create or choose a specific description of an important issue in education (for example, parent and community

involvement, supporting language learning among students who are recent immigrants, using data to improve instructional practice). Each group will design a study to develop a better understanding of the issue. These designs will be presented to the rest of the class and open to further refinement.

5. Freewheeling. Each participant suggests one social or educational problem about which he or she feels genuine concern. The participant describes it in approximately 100 words on newsprint. These descriptions will be posted, and the class will select one or more for a research study to be designed (in class) to provide information to better understand and respond to the problem. Carrying out this study will be optional.

6. Formative test. Each participant will receive a formative test to evaluate his or her knowledge of general research methods. Each participant will receive immediate feedback regarding the accuracy of his or her responses. This feedback will be private. After the evaluation, there will be time for discussion, clarification, and refinement of understanding.

7. Conducting research among ourselves. Using ourselves as a database, we will conduct a number of studies using survey and interview methods. Participants will be divided into research teams and will have the opportunity to generate their own research questions and methods of investigation. The work of research teams will include information about the ethnic/racial community(ies) of the people they interview as well as their perceptions of possible discrimination or privilege and its relationship to the findings of their research. Results of the studies will be reported back to the class.

8. Overview of action research.

9. Discussion of models of action research.

10. Discussion and exercises for analysis of data.

11. Guidance in the development of an action research project.

(continued)

Guidelines for problem definition, literature review, and action research designs will be offered. Participants will bring their ideas for potential research projects to class. The class and instructor will act as a sounding and advisory board in response to participant research ideas. This will give all participants a good chance for a solid beginning in their research work as well as another chance to apply their knowledge in the area of action research.

Demonstration and Assessment of Learning

1. Unless otherwise negotiated, full attendance and active participation. Note: On the first day of class, a rubric will be distributed to understand how participation in this course could be assessed. The final criteria for this rubric will be decided among us.

2. Completion of critiques of two personally selected research articles; competent analysis and discussion (two to four pages in length) of the research indicated in the article. Note: Models of excellent and unsatisfactory critiques by former students of this course will be provided to offer examples for discussion of assessment criteria.

3. Competent completion of one action research proposal.

Some scholars (Herr and Anderson, 2005, p. 49) have described the criteria for judging action research as an "ongoing conversation" because it is flexible and context generated. We will have excellent and unsatisfactory models of action research proposals from former students. With these, we will consider five possible criteria for assessment (Herr and Anderson, 2005): (1) connection to existing scholarship, (2) achievement of action-oriented outcomes, (3) education of research and participants, (4) relevance to the local setting, and (5) soundness of research methodology.

1. *Which culturally responsive teaching norms are clearly embedded in the context of this syllabus?* Norm one (human purpose) is reflected in the introduction (discusses the influence of research on society and its connection to learners' experience) and in potential learning experiences numbers four (designing research to understand current issues), five (freewheeling), seven (conducting research among ourselves), and eleven (development of an action research project).

Norm three (collaboration) is reflected in potential learning experiences numbers three (reaction panels), four (designing research to understand current issues), seven (conducting research among ourselves), and eleven (development of an action research project).

Norm six (volition) is reflected in potential learning experiences numbers three (reaction panels), four (designing research to understand current issues), five (freewheeling), seven (conducting research among ourselves), and eleven (development of an action research project); and assessment of learning number two (critique of research articles).

Norm seven (challenge) is reflected in potential learning experiences numbers three (reaction panels), four (designing research to understand current issues), five (freewheeling), seven (conducting research among ourselves), and eleven (development of an action research project).

Norm nine (relevant assessment) is reflected in assessment of learning numbers two (critiques of research articles) and three (an action research proposal).

2. *Which culturally responsive teaching norms are obviously absent from the context of this syllabus?* I found norm numbers four (hopeful view) and eight ("third idiom") difficult to specifically state in my syllabus, although I would hope to behave

in a way that would reflect them. These are norms I continue to consciously work on for improvement. Norm ten (multiple ways) has a chance to come about in activities where learners generate their own methods of investigation, such as qualitative or quantitative research approaches. Clearly, norm eleven (self-assessment) is missing. For norm eleven, I will make a definite change using the summarizing questions of self-assessment (see Chapter Five), including them with the required research proposal and using instructions such as, "Compare your accomplishment with what you had hoped for and expected at the start of this course."

3. *Which culturally responsive teaching practices are clearly found in this syllabus?*

Practice two (cooperative learning) is reflected in potential learning experiences numbers three (reaction panels), four (designing research to understand current issues), and seven (conducting research among ourselves).

Practice eleven (a) (clearly defined goals) is reflected in *assessment of learning* number two (critiques of research articles).

Practice eleven (b) (problem-solving goals) is reflected in assessment of learning number three (action research proposal).

Practice seventeen (pedagogical flexibility) is reflected in potential learning experiences number seven (conducting research among ourselves).

Practice eighteen (the Kolb model) is reflected in potential learning experiences number five (freewheeling)—for example, concrete experience (the 100-word problem), reflective observation (class selection and discussion of problem), abstract conceptualization (creating a research design), and active experimentation (carrying out research).

Practice twenty (critical questioning) is reflected in potential learning experiences numbers three (reaction panels), four (designing research to understand current issues), five (free-wheeling), and seven (conducting research among ourselves).

Practice twenty-three (c) (projective investigation) and (d) (experimental inquiry) are both possible with potential learning experiences numbers nine (conducting an action of research) and eleven (development of an action research project).

Practice twenty-three (e) (action research) is obviously potential learning experience number eleven (development of an action research project)

Practice twenty-nine (feedback) is reflected in potential learning experiences numbers six (formative test) and eleven (development of an action of research project).

Practice thirty (alternative to paper-and-pencil tests) is reflected in the three assessments of learning. Procedure thirty-one (paper-and-pencil test) is reflected in potential learning experiences number six (formative test).

From exploring my syllabus, I realized I would like to develop more pedagogical flexibility and use multiple intelligences theory to design an activity in which different research designs emanate from learners who explore a concern or question from such different entry points as foundational, aesthetic, and narrational. An example would be if learners were to write a short story (narrational) about how a particular problem is resolved and then design a study that would be likely to inform that process of resolution. I further noted that although it might not be clear in the syllabus, generative and topical themes are likely to be embedded in the problems posed by learners during potential learning experiences numbers four and five.

■■

The university where I taught this course used narrative evaluations. My approach to assessment was to begin by providing the class with models of research article critiques and action research proposals from the work of former students who took the class. To offer a contrast of how the quality of criteria might vary, I gave students some models that were a satisfactory level of performance and others that I considered excellent. After reviewing the models and how they related to the assessment criteria, I asked the class to divide into small discussion groups to examine from their perspectives why these models might be considered satisfactory or excellent.

Students also reflected on other approaches and ways to compose these outcomes that might vary from the examples offered and still be laudable. During a whole-group discussion, we listed both sets of these qualities on the chalkboard. Although the assessment was not bound by these criteria, I asked a volunteer to record this information to illuminate important considerations for later application. If I had to give grades, I would still use a similar process, compose a contracting system (see Chapter Five for contracting examples) based on it, and bring it to the next class session for mutual agreement.

Transforming courses into the kind of educational settings where learners share responsibility and authority for their learning is an evolving process for them as well as for instructors. It means arriving at class with a well-considered plan while being willing to reinvent some of that structure according to the learners and situation there. Creating a safe climate is essential to easing doubts and cushioning the risks inherent in any group that may undergo this process.

Create a Reasonably Safe Climate in Which to Learn

Creating a safe climate begins with respect—for ourselves and for students. Such respect means that we plan to ensure their success and minimize any possible negative consequences before we attempt any new approach or change. We can also use student focus groups to test ideas before we put them into action.

A nonblameful orientation to being experimental supports a greater likelihood that the risk we are taking to develop our craft is not a final judgment of our own or our students' skills and character but information to reflect on for further improvement. Quick writes, postwrites, and surveys help instructors learn from students and gain insight into how to refine new methods before negative consequences become entrenched. In addition and where appropriate, it is helpful to directly inform students about the rationale, purpose, and process of the change we are initiating and our intention to request their perspectives as we proceed. Finally, our professional colleagues often provide invaluable counsel. In addition to being enjoyable, learning new teaching approaches with peers contributes to our own sense of efficacy and safety.

Learn with Others

There's an old saying that no one can avoid pain but that most people can escape suffering. One of the key aspects of this adage is "not going it alone," that is, sharing the burden or the challenge, whichever it may be. Taking on something a bit daring alone is often considered risky. Add a few people to the same venture, and it could easily be called a sport. The literature on professional learning is unanimous in declaring that educators are most likely to effectively change teaching practices with support and feedback from other faculty (Joyce and Showers, 2002). As theorists Smith, MacGregor, Matthews, and Gabelnick (2004) have found, faculty collaboration in the development of learning community programs is a powerful means for educators to build their repertoires and confidence.

Collaborative approaches to sharing local knowledge about teaching and learning are not new. Over the years, shared learning among faculty and staff has been referred to as communities of practice (Senge, 1990; Wenger, 1998), discussion groups (Brookfield and Preskill, 2005), cooperative groups (Johnson, Johnson, and Smith, 1991), critical friends' groups (Sizer, 1984;

Meier, 1995), and others. Whatever the label and particular focus of a learning team, the main idea is that complex challenges of teaching and learning deserve and require forms of ongoing, inquiry-focused, and peer-mediated discourse within productive and authentic contexts.

While there is reason to guard against forms of contrived collaboration, there are a number of productive ways to create serious collaborative learning environments within formal education boundaries (Johnson, Johnson, and Smith, 1998). In the following section, we outline practical approaches to cooperative group work, reciprocal coaching, lesson study, book study, and structured classroom visits to the classrooms of colleagues. Although cynics abound, we agree with Sloterdijk (1988) that the ideology of pessimism and over-critique renders people powerless. Although there is hard work to be done beyond classrooms, for example, linking the micro to the macro, the subject to the structure, the culture to the economy, and the local to the global (Cho, 2002), it is entirely possible that the consciousness of postsecondary instructors who resist change is more naive than that of their students who remain optimistic about what their world is capable of doing.

Cooperative Learning

Cooperative learning among a group of faculty colleagues, modeled after the work of Johnson, Johnson, and Smith (1998), would include the principles of positive interdependence, individual accountability, promotive interaction, social skills, and group processing. Each of these attributes is discussed in Chapter Two under cooperative learning groups and applies in this situation as well. A goal in professional learning is to create the same conditions for ourselves, as faculty, that we seek for students. To apply the ideas in this book regarding motivation and culturally responsive teaching, the purpose of forming a cooperative learning group (or groups) among faculty would be to:

1. Provide the help, assistance, support, and encouragement each member needs to improve in the use of culturally responsive teaching practices.

2. Serve as an informal support group for sharing and discussing challenges connected with implementing culturally responsive teaching practices.

3. Serve as a base for faculty experienced in the use of culturally responsive teaching practices to teach others how to use these approaches.

4. Create a context in which friendship and shared success occur and are celebrated.

Collegial groups should be organized to ensure active participation by faculty, developing such concrete outcomes as syllabi, lesson plans, and learning activities and sharing articles, books, media, and other resources. Once members have established rapport with each other and are ready to deepen their work together, they might experiment with a modified coaching process.

Reciprocal Coaching

There are several ways to approach reciprocal coaching that involve observing each other's teaching. Many faculty have had positive experiences with this set of guidelines:

1. Observation partners confer with each other to decide whether to focus on student responses, use of critical questions, how problems are posed, or some other aspect of the learning procedure.

2. The feedback is on what occurs and the procedures used, not on teacher competence.

3. The observer provides information the teacher requests and does not impose unsolicited advice, opinions, or suggestions.

4. Information regarding observation and insights is confidential and nonevaluative.

5. The observer provides support and participates in the collaborative solution of problems posed by the educator being observed.

6. The observer is also a learner watching for practices and materials to discuss and consider for her or his professional use.

7. The tone of the entire process is one of respect and trust.

Because of the reciprocity and shared experience, coaching often deepens relationships and generates new teaching practices in collegial cooperative groups. Fenwick (2003) found that the practice of evolving methods in an authentic context with peer support has a significant impact on the ability to effectively transfer and maintain new ways of teaching. In general, the more authentic the setting, the more likely we will retain and use what we have competently applied.

Our own experience, including a survey completed by faculty at the British Columbia Institute of Technology, suggests that instructors who have training in peer coaching typically report an improved attitude toward their role as a teacher, as well as toward their students and colleagues. The ability to transfer new skills to one's own setting with an increased positive attitude toward instruction and students is an expected outcome of effective reciprocal coaching.

Coaching Protocol to Examine Student Work with the Motivational Framework

The discussion of reciprocal coaching illustrates how colleagues might provide support for effective implementation of specific teaching strategies. The following protocol serves at least two additional purposes. One is to enhance awareness of the four conditions of the motivational framework through application to a coaching experience. The second is to enhance awareness of the influence of instructional practice on student learning by examining student work. Examining student work requires the generation of work samples by the conclusion of a class period or by whatever other time coaching partners have agreed to meet for a follow-up conversation. However, with a bit of advance planning, this is easily accomplished. Educators who use this approach to improve teaching and learning often find ways to modify it for a manageable time frame or to eliminate aspects of collaboration that are unnecessary given existing relationships and experience with this sort of protocol. To eliminate confusion, we use a male pronoun for the coach and a female pronoun for the presenting instructor.

The rubrics found in Resource J may be helpful for identifying attributes of the lesson that correspond to each of the four conditions of the motivational framework. For example, a coach might first mention some of the attributes of the lesson associated with "establishing inclusion." Then he might do the same for "developing a positive attitude," "enhancing meaning," and "engendering competence." In addition, Resource I offers an observation chart with rubrics for each of the four motivational conditions. The primary goal with Step One is to establish the intention to build on strengths.

Step One: The colleague in the role of coach thanks the instructor for allowing him to learn by watching. He shares his notes regarding positive aspects of the lesson (*motivational condition for the presenting instructor:* **establishing inclusion** *through respect and connectedness*).

Step Two: The colleague in the role of coach asks his peer about her own perception of the lesson and allows time for a brief discussion.

Step Three: The colleague in the role of coach asks the instructor to organize student work from the lesson into three piles: proficient, almost proficient, and needs improvement. The coach asks the teacher to select the work of a student from the "needs improvement" pile to serve as a focus for brainstorming (*motivational condition for the teacher:* **developing a positive attitude** *through choice and personal relevance*).

Step Four: The colleague in the role of coach and the teacher work together to reflect on the learning context to consider ways to enhance the quality of this particular student's work by:

- *Establishing inclusion:* making it "safer" for that student to learn

- *Developing a positive attitude:* creating opportunities for students to make decisions or enhancing the relevance of the lesson

- *Enhancing meaning:* setting up opportunities for greater student engagement

- *Engendering competence:* providing concrete information to students about expectations for success in ways that are valued by the student (*motivational condition for the teacher:* **enhancing meaning** *through problem solving*)

Step Five: The presenting instructor thinks through options based on notes from the conversation. Often the coach will give the presenting instructor feedback based on "wows and wonders" from her notes. (Please see Resource A.) She sets specific implementation goals and identifies a way she will share related follow-up experiences with the coach or another colleague (*motivational condition for the teacher:* **engendering competence** *through clear criteria for success that the teacher values*).

Step Six: The person in the role of coach repeats Step Four, applying insights and ideas to his own teaching (or advising) practice and sharing these with the instructor (*motivational condition for the coach:* **engendering competence** *through clear criteria for success that the coach values*).

Step Seven: The presenting instructor and the coach share final comments. These might include feelings, thoughts, or ideas to support future collaboration (*motivational conditions: inclusion, attitude, meaning, and competence*).

Lesson Study

Another way to develop practice that is personal and collaborative is through research lessons, a central part of the lesson study approach. Lesson study, referred to in Japanese as *jugyokenku*, has been central to Japanese professional development for many years and has become the focus of considerable research in the United States (Lewis, Perry, and Murata, 2006; Hiebert, Gallimore, and Stigler, 2002). In recent years, it has captured the attention of higher education in the United States—staff and faculty. Essentially it is a process of planning, observing, and making sense of student learning with colleagues.

There are several galleries of protocols, examples, and insights about lesson study on the web. The Web site of the Lesson Study Group at Mills College (www.lessonresearch. net) is particularly informative and features an interview with Catherine Lewis, a scholar of the lesson study process. The conversation highlights some of the possibilities and challenges for faculty in higher education. Regardless of context, higher education or prekindergarten through twelfth grade, Lewis cautions educators about the illusion of premature expertise and suggests a process that carefully develops collegial skills, observation skills, knowledge of content, and pedagogy resources beyond those of the group.

One of the challenges of lesson study in higher education is its feasibility within the competing demands of instructors' schedules. For adjunct faculty at commuter colleges, efficiency is a particular concern. The following overview is intended as a brief illustration of the process, including the way in which we use the motivational framework as a guide. Although we do not specify ways to develop collegial relationships and understandings so that feedback is rich and supportive of taking pedagogical risks, Chapter Two is a resource for developing a foundation of respect and trust among participants. The coaching protocol earlier in this chapter is a resource that encourages collegial instructional conversations focused on motivation and student learning.

Lesson Study Overview. The goal of lesson study is to improve instructional practice by collaboratively planning, teaching, and debriefing a lesson. Educators come together as an interdisciplinary or subject-specific team to plan a specific lesson for a particular student group. The team then moves directly (or within a reasonable period of time) into a classroom, where one member of the team teaches the planned lesson, while the other members observe. The process concludes with the group debriefing about the observed lesson, including its influence on student learning. All participants set goals for themselves and for a continuous cycle of developing, observing, and making sense of research lessons in others' classes.

As a strategy to systematically design, teach, observe, debrief, and build a professional community of educators, the experiences stimulate a discussion of authentic issues from a teaching experience in ways that allow clear examples from shared experience. Furthermore, one of its strongest attributes is generating awareness of the variety of shared instructional knowledge that resides among a group of educators.

The process is not an evaluation of teaching practices where the critique is personal, comparative, and high stakes. Nor is it intended as a depository of unbounded knowledge. Listening is as much a part of the process as sharing observations, wonders, and ideas.

Considerations for Higher Education. The potential of the process is vast. Lesson study can be a vehicle for cross-campus or even cross-site and national learning. At association meetings and conferences, for example, digital research lessons have been examined by hundreds of people. Although large contexts generally strengthen awareness of what participants in a lesson study process might see and discuss, these opportunities exemplify different conceptions of inquiry and problem solving. These forums also provide ideas for ways to accelerate the process, including Web-based lessons. Across contexts, however, Catherine Lewis, Rebecca Perry, and Aki Murata (2006) suggest the following questions as a way to assess the influence of the process:

1. What did I learn about teaching, the subject matter, instructional resources, and student learning?

2. Did the lesson study work affect my sense of efficacy as a teacher, that is, my sense that instruction can be improved in ways that make a difference for students?

3. Did my lesson study work affect my relationships with colleagues—for example, my interest in informal or formal collaboration with them in the future?

4. Did the lesson study work leave a residue in my course materials—in syllabus, course content, activities, and so forth?

In addition to previous ideas for developing and sharing research lessons, advocates of lesson study cycles in higher education might want to pose the following questions among themselves, their departments, and systemwide policymakers as a way to work within time constraints:

- How can lesson study be designed so that it helps take some other requirements off the plate of busy faculty?

- How can lesson study reports fulfill the "service to university" requirement or be published to support academic advancement?

- How can study of student work be fed into assessment and grading?
- How can lesson study work be combined with faculty mentoring programs or other existing commitments?
- How can we elicit support for Web-based videos and communication to promote an active and ongoing conversation across disciplines and campuses based on research lessons?

For working with ideas of intrinsic motivation, the following tools can help plan and implement a lesson study in a reasonable period of time.

- Motivational Framework (Resource C)
- Peer Coaching Rubric (Resource J)
- Charting Insights from Lesson Study (Resource A)

Procedure. A priority before beginning this process is to create a collegial environment in which to plan and examine a lesson. This allows more authentic and in-depth discussion of teaching practices. Following are some ways to experiment with the process include:

1. *Gather a team of educators* for a half-day, on-site professional development. Or carve out time in a day to plan a lesson (a half-hour or more), observe the lesson (a half-hour or more), and then examine the lesson (a half-hour or more). Although the approach is quite brief, it provides an initial way to experiment within conventional time constraints.

2. *Identify an academic discipline* within which the team seeks to design a lesson.

3. *Plan the lesson* with the motivational framework as a template (Resource D) by using either specific student data—when available—or a previous or future lesson that is of genuine concern to participants. In some instances, teams

may want to share preplanned draft lessons that other team members can review and modify. Although this approach to lesson design is efficient, there are a number of reasons to collaborate on initial lesson design. One of the primary sacrifices of precreated, independently designed lessons is that they tend to inhibit a full examination of the research lesson during the debriefing phase.

4. *Teach the lesson* in a designated learning environment. The instructor or a combination of instructors may want to work together. Other team members observe the lesson and refer to motivational framework rubrics to record pedagogical interactions for later recall. (An alternative is to take field notes on the learning experience as a whole and make connections to principles of intrinsic motivation once the lesson has been completed.)

5. *Debrief the lesson* as a team. Using the motivational framework to guide the conversation, discuss the strengths and areas of challenge (which we refer to as "wonders" and more fully explain under caveats at the end of this section) for each of the four conditions. Although all team members record notes, one person publicly scribes for the group.

6. Discuss how the lesson study process has affected each individual's view of teaching and student learning. *Set individual goals and team goals for future work.*

To summarize, the three phases that are commonly associated with a research lesson are the planning phase, research lesson implementation, and lesson colloquium. As delineated, the planning phase provides an opportunity for team members to identify instructional foci, study existing curricula (when time permits), choose a topic for the research lesson, discuss learning goals or targets for the specific research lesson, and design a research lesson that maps onto the motivational framework.

The second part of the process is the research lesson implementation phase. This is when an instructor teaches the lesson with attending teachers observing, using observation rubrics (one for each condition of the motivational framework).

The third phase is the lesson colloquium, during which team members discuss notes and data collected while observing the lesson. For this part of the process, one team member creates a chart to capture insights for later reference. Prior to concluding, the team discusses how to report on the process and summarize what was learned. They also select a new focus of study or refine and reteach the lesson, reflect on the lesson study process, and set individual goals based on collective insights.

A *caveat:* When providing feedback, it is often more comfortable to focus on the strengths of a lesson. While this is generally a good starting point, providing supportive feedback that allows team members to challenge instructional practice is the primary goal. A nonthreatening approach to such feedback is to begin sentences with a "wonder" or question of possibility—for example, "What do you think might have happened if...?" or "I wonder what might have happened if you had provided an opportunity for students to write down their thoughts prior to public comment." Or, "I wonder if you have had a chance to work with students on ways to distribute responsibility when they are working in small discussion groups." This form of "cool" or collegial feedback is respectful and allows the team to use its full range of knowledge and imagination without indicting another person. This is essential because the answers to some of our most puzzling instructional challenges reside among ourselves. Respectfully implemented, lesson study allows faculty to recall this simple but easily overlooked fact.

Collaborative Text Annotation

Collaborative text annotation is an idea that has been handed down through so many sources that it is difficult to attribute to a single person. It is an efficient way to allow faculty study groups to inform their practice with new ideas and research. This strategy for reading a piece of text in the moment provides a way for study groups to stay focused and begin a conversation that can be shared with others. The reading material is relatively short: a passage or summary that can be read in ten to fifteen minutes. The following protocol can be applied to any number of purposes, literature genres, or time frames. We are introducing it here as a way for a study group to read and generate initial comment on a portion of a text. For example, we might ask group members to read pages 48–55 from Chapter One—Fear, Conflict, and Resistance—with the following protocol.

Protocol for Article Review.

1. As a group, select a facilitator to lead the group process and keep time.

2. As a group, briefly review the layout of the article, and discuss how it appears to be organized.

3. As individuals, read the selected text for approximately ten minutes. As you read, jot annotations in the margins as a response to the text. For example, your annotations might include notes about connections you are making, as well as remarks, questions, or observations. Some people prefer to underline meaningful passages or circle significant phrases.

4. After approximately ten minutes of reading and annotating, pass your article with annotations to a group member.

5. Skim over the same text and your group member's annotations, and add new remarks, questions, or observations to your group member's page.

6. If time permits, pass again and repeat.

7. Be sure to save some time as a group to compare and draw conclusions from comments (approximately seven to eight minutes).

A Protocol for Reading from Various Perspectives. This approach to sharing text is one of several ways to consider different perspectives within a faculty study group. Introduced to us by Rachel Johnson, a high school language arts teacher, it has been adapted for use in a number of high schools and colleges seeking ways to encourage multiple perspectives on a piece of literature. We suggest it here as a way to imagine how to implement ideas from this text to address the needs of four different students in their second year at a four-year college.

1. Divide up perspectives, allowing time to collectively clarify details. Examples of roles follow:

   a. One person reads the passage as an instructor who is concerned about a student who is an English language learner, is the first in her family to attend college, and is highly motivated to succeed even though her median grade point average is a C+.

   b. One person reads the passage as an instructor who is concerned about a low-performing student who is the first in his family to attend college and is on the verge of dropping out even though his prose has been published in widely respected magazine.

   c. One person reads the passage as an instructor who is concerned about a student who is adequately performing although not pushing herself beyond the basics that are required for a B.

   d. One person reads the passage as an instructor who is concerned about a high-performing, academically driven student with an individualistic, means-end orientation to getting an A.

2. With the motivational framework as a guide, read the text selection, and underline any aspects of it that stand out, given the vantage point from which you are reading. For example, if you are reading the previous section about lesson

study from the perspective of an instructor who is concerned about a student who is not sufficiently challenging himself, you might consider what kind of a lesson you would design to maximize the positive influence of peers (*motivational condition: establishing inclusion*) or perhaps to structure an interesting project that requires analytical skill (*motivational conditions: developing a positive attitude and enhancing meaning*).

3. When you are through reading the selected text, consider how your reading may have been influenced by the lens you used.

4. As in a role play, remain in character as you record the thoughts your character might have after reading the passage.

   a. What information stood out to him or her?

   b. What will she do with that information?

5. Reflect as a group on how these various people might have different perspectives from yours and what new understanding you can take away from this passage as a result of considering their different perspectives.

Book Study to Introduce the Text. There are many ways to approach a book study. This particular protocol can be useful as an introduction to this text and is easily modified for the time frame within which faculty are working.

- In a large group, review the layout of the book, using the Contents page and selected practices to provide examples of how these strategies are organized in each of the four chapters related to the motivational conditions (Chapters Two through Five).

- In a large group, review the index, noting the range of topics (pair-share).

- Divide into groups of four. Select a group facilitator and a timekeeper.

- Each member of the group identifies a chapter to examine. Limit yourselves to Chapters Two through Five so that collectively, your group has these four chapters covered.

- Read Chapter One, the introduction. (Everyone reads this chapter.) Then read the designated chapter for which you have volunteered, and peruse the headings. Find a practice that is relevant to you. Read this section twice: first for general understanding and second to apply an idea to your own work.

- Develop a ten-minute presentation for your small group that:

  - Provides an introduction to your chapter.

  - Lists some of the topics within the chapter that caught your attention.

  - Involves your group in examining one practice or topic that appears to be particularly relevant or interesting. Reserve time for comment on the presentations.

Identify New Roles

Identity is a powerful influence on motivation. We do things we would otherwise not do because we adhere to certain roles—teacher, parent, friend. Identities confine as well as expand our lives and the lives of those around us. We reward, we encourage, we prevent or undermine others because of who we think we are. To change one's identity is to change one's entire motivational system. Those who claim to be reborn or to have reinvented themselves have also reidentified themselves. "Coming out" is a public embracing of one's identity. In higher education, one of the greatest challenges to change is our investment in and identity with teaching techniques we may have used for years, as well as our strong identities as experts of content knowledge in a particular area of study.

One of the largest impediments to transforming teaching in colleges and universities is faculty identity—and identity resists change. We are professors. We are scholars and researchers. The amount of time we will devote to teaching and the position we believe we should maintain relative to students are in many ways controlled by those identities. Many faculty teach the way they do not because of the way they were taught but because of whom they identified with when they were taught. With respect to teaching, the brilliant theoretician, the renowned researcher, and the mesmerizing lecturer are academic clichés that have often imprisoned even those among us who speak of the need for instructional emancipation.

Thus, an important question is: How do you see yourself professionally? What do the words *professor, faculty, instructor, teacher,* and *teacher assistant* mean to you? Which college teachers have influenced your teaching and in what ways? How have they taught you by example to use your power as a teacher? As Jim Cummins (1986) states, "In the absence of individual and collective educator role redefinitions, schools will continue to reproduce, in these interactions, the power relations that characterize the wider society and make minority students' academic failure inevitable" (p. 33).

Culturally responsive teaching recedes from identities that are authoritarian, elitist, or directive and gravitates toward roles that are collaborative, egalitarian, and consultative. Primary to this pedagogy is the identification of oneself as a colearner. How could a colearner lecture for an entire period? How could a colearner ignore another learner's perspective? How could a colearner completely avoid collaboration? The identity of being a colearner makes many forms of conventional teaching so incongruous as to be humorous or, at the very least, uncomfortable. With the active, cooperative, and critical nature of culturally responsive teaching, there are more than a few nontraditional educational roles that may surface from this approach, such as mediator, advocate, orchestrator, arbiter, and archivist (Bensimon, 1994). In addition, some of the quite conventional provinces of teaching still hold and are necessary. There must continue to be someone to guide, consult, and facilitate—and, less often than many of us might believe, offer expert knowledge and skills. To begin to reference oneself with these roles while thinking or talking about teaching encourages the conscientious evolution of teaching practice and, we believe, supports the will to enlist a culturally responsive pedagogical orientation.

Create Action Plans

Earlier in this section we discussed and exemplified a number of ways one might revise a syllabus to reflect a more culturally responsive pedagogy. We began this way because it illustrated a holistic orientation toward an entire course. However, many instructors want to try changes on a smaller scale or experiment with a particular norm or procedure before formally revising their course. In all cases, an action plan, also known as an action agenda, can help to organize and facilitate the use of new teaching approaches. Action agendas work a lot like goal-setting strategies: they clarify what we want to do and illuminate how to organize and emotionally prepare for making changes. They increase our chances for optimal implementation and help us avoid the kind of utopian ignorance that undermines success and dampens future experimentation.

In Exhibit 6.3, we provide an action plan for applying the use of the case study method to a research course. A short discussion follows to model our thinking and to discuss how the plan was conceptualized.

Some recommendations for proceeding with each stage of the action plan are as follows:

Goal: Although there are exceptions to this (see the discussion of problem-solving goals and expressive outcomes in Chapter Three), most often it is beneficial to start with what you want to do and what you imagine students will learn and how you will understand or assess this learning.

Exhibit 6.3 Action Plan

Goals(s): To have learners develop a critical understanding of ethical issues in research—specifically informed consent, right to privacy, and protection from harm—through the analysis of a case study in which gay adults were uninformed subjects.

Actions to be taken: (1) Write a realistic and complex narrative based on research in the manner of the study of Laud Humphreys (1970) that resulted in the publication of the book *Tearoom Trade*. (2) Create a discussion outline. (3) Decide how to begin the case study (free writing and discussion with a partner) and how to end the case study (go around the group, with each learner providing an insight, goal, and so forth).

Potential obstacles: None that are apparent.

Needed support: Have a couple of my colleagues (gay and straight) critique the case before I use it.

Criteria for success: High learner involvement; discussion that references ethical issues, analyzes the historical variables, and allows multiple interpretations.

Postimplementation assessment: Discussion initially very tentative and somewhat self-righteous and accusatory. Discourse became more integrated and inclusive when we dealt with how research ethics historically reflect what the broader society will condone. For example, use and treatment of animals in experiments has been changing due to activism of animal rights organizations and greater public awareness. After this point in the discussion, there was high involvement. Ending activity revealed a variety of critical insights. I need to revise the discussion outline. I learned some of the ways scientific method and the research process can engender *mistrust among people in general and students in particular.*

Source: Action plan format adapted from Cheek and Campbell (1994).

Sensitivity to the teaching practice and its connection to what is learned is critical to assessing its value.

Actions to be taken: Writing a narrative of the steps that will make the teaching practice a reality ensures a better chance it will be effective.

Potential obstacles: If there are any obstacles, it is best to know what they are and plan for them.

Needed support: This can be crucial to uncovering or resolving problems with the plan. What if the written case was inadvertently sexist, homophobic, or otherwise offensive?

Criteria for success: Sometimes there are surprises, but if we know what we are looking for, we are more likely to understand when it occurs. Knowing the criteria should support its assessment and add consistency to our learning goal.

Postimplementation assessment: This stage is essential to refining the teaching practice or, in some cases, to rejecting it. Many first experiences with a new teaching approach are somewhat awkward, and reflection at this time can be immensely helpful for finding ways to improve. The discussion outline needed a more sensitive and less inflammatory beginning.

Acknowledging and including what the teacher learned is important validation of a pedagogy based on the premise that the teacher is a colearner. Action plans can be immensely useful to collegial cooperative groups. They create anticipation, focus the group on concrete teaching, assist reciprocal coaching, and can be enjoyable to collaboratively create and assess.

Acknowledge Doubt and Anxiety as Signs of Change and Potential Professional and Personal Growth

As we have mentioned a number of times, colearning—using critical analysis, adapting to local conditions, reshaping course content, sharing authority, and trying new teaching practices—complicates and enriches a teacher's life. All of this takes time to learn and practice. Feelings of confusion and disorientation are common. However, doubt and anxiety are often invitations to probe a bit further and to realize that we may need to change or are changing and it will not feel comfortable for a while. Collegial support, a sense of purpose, and being aware of the results of one's work help, but they don't completely free us of these emotions.

Recognize the Power of Self-Generated Knowledge

Who speaks in class and how often? How much of the time is the teacher speaking? Do learners talk to one another during class discussions? How pluralistic are the examples or perspectives given throughout the course? Who gets the highest test scores and best-graded papers? Are lessons connected to the students' communities and aspirations? Do students explain themselves in a number of sentences and with reference to concepts or principles?

These are just some of the questions that we can use to concretely understand how culturally responsive our teaching really is. We can answer a number of these questions ourselves, and for the others we can enlist the assistance of a colleague or learner to observe and record. If you have doubts or question the validity of a particular norm or procedure, you might create an observational process, a survey, or a classroom study (preferably with a colleague) for further inquiry.

Self-generated knowledge is also a significant way to integrate and refine new teaching practices. In addition to action plans, some of the self-assessment procedures in Chapter Five, such as postwrites, journals, and summarizing questions, can deepen our understanding of the changes we are making. Also, we highly recommend action research (Herr and Anderson, 2005) and experimental inquiry (Chapter Four) as a means to generate knowledge about one's teaching.

Share Your Work with Others

Sharing your work with others is critical to continuing the dialogue and evolution of culturally responsive pedagogy. We learn from and with each other. The voices of the many teachers in this book—Beverly Daniel Tatum, Luis Moll, Paulo Freire, Gerald Weinstein, Maurianne Adams, and Linda Marchesani—have informed and inspired us. We also need to communicate about our own work, because—for the sake of historically underserved students as well as our society—we need to move it from the margins to regular practice. Institutional transformation occurs when dynamic change evolves on both the inside and the outside of its structure. By writing about our work in newsletters and within digital networks as well as in books and journals, by bringing our ideas to brown-bag lunches as well as to conferences and seminars, by forming collegial cooperative groups as well as national networks and organizations, we can more effectively respond to shifts in student populations that are occurring in this country and across the world at this moment. We also normalize culturally responsive pedagogy. As James Banks (Brandt, 1994) said of instructors devoted to cultural pluralism, "we make a strong, unequivocal commitment to democracy, to basic American values of justice and equality" (p. 31). In philosophy and intent, culturally responsive pedagogy is relevant and essential to a diverse society and global community.

Faculty Development

Our experience with the topic of cultural diversity in the area of professional development is that within faculty groups, there is often apprehension, an idea at the outset by some that they may be doing something wrong or are guilty of perpetuating some form of "ism." Not surprisingly, culturally responsive teaching approaches tend to work well for faculty development. Transformation comes from finding language and means to help faculty examine their values, creating a safe and respectful learning climate, and responding to concerns and needs for pragmatic and effective procedures.

Based on our work and the writing and expertise of colleagues (Adams, Bell, and Griffin, 2007; Hays, 2001; Tatum, 1998) and a review of the discussion among faculty and institutions focusing their efforts to better serve students (Branche, Mullennix, and Cohn, 2007; Anderson, 2008; Kuh and Associates, 2005; Schmitz, Paul, and Greenberg, 1992), we find that the following practices in faculty development are instructive guidelines:

- Collaborate with faculty from the beginning to plan and design a high-quality program. This is motivationally significant, and faculty have a right to shape a program that will vitally affect their teaching.

- Infuse within the program measures (including disaggregating data) that will assess its goals—such as retention, degree completion, course completion, program selection, and changes in students' GPA.

- To save planning time, reduce initial errors, and encourage confidence among faculty and administrators, examine programs that have worked well on other campuses with similar demographics and curricula.

- Consider having one or two outside consultants participate in planning, instruction, and assessment. Because of internal politics, administration and faculty are sometimes more open to viewpoints and expertise that has minimal connection to their campus.

- Use media and technology to record and communicate important meetings, teaching methods, and student reactions. An internal library can facilitate communication and help to educate new and adjunct faculty.

- Assess the developmental needs and strengths of faculty. Continuously assess perspectives and attitudes toward the faculty development process. Recognition of early errors as well as competencies can strengthen the development program and add to its transparency and authenticity.

- With administrative support, set clear expectations for faculty participation and outcomes at each stage of the process.

- Design specific activities for faculty development with opportunities for modeling and peer coaching. At the very least, create opportunities for classroom visits with follow-up discussions among faculty.

- Pilot the implementation and assessment phases of the program with opportunity for revisions when needed.

- Use expertise available among faculty members at the institution, as well as outside experts.

- Faculty need both practical and theoretical components in the program. Most adults are more open-minded as learners when they know why as well as how and what.

- Consider the culture and expectations placed on faculty. These contribute to their boundaries for work and motivation.

- Make specifically clear to faculty that the program is of concrete benefit to students, the institution, and their own professional learning.

- Provide resources to compensate faculty for the amount and kind of work expected of them. This may include stipends, release time, course reassignments, travel, and so forth. These matters are usually related to how faculty have previously been rewarded for service and professional development.

Although we have not addressed curricular reform, we agree the task is daunting and want to emphasize how important it is to consider how inseparable content and pedagogy really are. The kind of culturally responsive procedures available to a research course may be quite different from those accessible to a language course. Also, even if the same procedures were to be used in both disciplines, their form and texture might markedly vary. Faculty appreciate development programs that are sensitive to and inclusive of the content of their disciplines.

Both reports from the literature and past experience indicate that few faculty development programs will be successful without support from senior leadership and distributed leadership from all sectors of the campus (Anderson, 2008; Kuh and Associates, 2005). What Schmitz, Paul, and Greenberg indicated in 1992 still holds true: "The ideal level of support includes an institutional mission statement that emphasizes the creation of a multicultural campus community, financial resources to set up permanent programs for faculty and TA development (including resources for permanent staff), a faculty culture that values professional development and teaching improvement and endorses the need for a positive multicultural environment, and student support for improved intergroup actions, on campus and in the classroom" (p. 82). Because each institution is unique, we know that change strategies will vary. More ideas are found in the references cited in this section. The resources at the end of this book provide additional ideas and materials.

All of the activities described in this chapter have been used successfully in professional development sessions in a variety of settings. They have helped others to create shared understanding and plan specific applications of motivating instruction and culturally responsive pedagogy. In addition, they have helped us to scrutinize our own beliefs and teaching, learning from the range and style of discourse that this work evokes. Although we have created more agendas than would be useful to share, we have never found scripts or formulas that allowed us to overlook the intricacies of human behavior. Even with a very thoughtful plan, there simply is no substitute for comparison and imagination.

There Is More to Higher Education Than We Have Yet Imagined

After completing the second edition of this book, we continue to believe, based on experience and scholarship, that pedagogy in higher education must be inseparable from human concerns within and across cultures. Although change in an entire college is more complicated than planning a learning experience and asking hard questions about it, what we do as educators through instructional practices has a real influence on human beings and consequent global structures. As essential as it is for all of society to imagine utopian alternatives to the aggressions of globalization and the local politics of sorting potential students with standardized tests and exorbitant fees, the path to political action is political action itself. In classrooms, agency and consciousness are center stage, whether by intention or default.

We propose that an intrinsic theory of motivation more adequately represents and serves the interests of all people, within and across cultural groups, in educational settings. We have presented four conditions and documented eight criteria as essential to creating situations that elicit any person's intrinsic motivation to learn. When people feel *respected* and *connected* in the learning setting, when people *endorse or determine* learning they find *relevant*, and when people *engage* in *challenging* and *authentic* experiences that enhance their *effectiveness* in what they value, people learn. Because the authority of the teacher must be shared to some extent and because knowledge must be constructed from multiple cultural perspectives, this is a complex and subtle way to teach. Yet this kind of pedagogy is the only approach that we have found that heralds our common endowment as human beings, respects the cultures from which we come, and acknowledges the ways in which each of us is an individual. To think that increasing developmental skills and creating more of an attitude and preparation for conventional college learning are adequate strategies for diverse, low-income, and first-generation college students is far short of what is necessary and possible. Today, perhaps more than ever before, extrinsic rewards such as grades and rankings are not sufficient for many, if not most, students.

We are part of a world ravaged by divisive interests. How can higher education be structured so that its graduates directly contribute to a society in which more people are compassionate with one another and serve their collective interests? As we reflect on this question, we realize how rare it is to be in a college course and among diverse learners who have dialogues of respect and who feel neither victim nor oppressor but sincerely and critically curious. Most of us have memories of challenges in which we have not been heroic or courageous. We have not had much guidance in learning to be open and critical at the same time, in having honest and respectful conversations about cultural issues that threaten us, in seeking and telling our own truth knowing there are other truths for other people, and in knowing that as a pluralistic society, we can explore and create a future together.

To live such experiences so that we can imagine them with others, colleges must become places where inquiry, reflection, respect, and equal participation among diverse people are the norm. Although this ideal is more vivid in our imaginations than on the campuses of this country, it is widely shared.

As an institution, higher education enjoys remarkable status and influence locally and around the world. It can change the consciousness of society, serving as an agent of genuine social and economic improvement, or it can perpetuate the pretense of equity in an increasingly unequal world. For those of us who teach, we live out one of life's oldest stories: to have compelling work to do in the world and to learn about the world from doing it well. To this we owe fidelity.

Resource A

CHARTING INSIGHTS FROM LESSON STUDY

The following guidelines and definitions are useful for peer coaching and feedback during the lesson study process.

Strengths (WOWS)

Participants in a research lesson comment on the strengths of the lesson, using the motivational framework as a common tool from which to base comments. *Strengths* are those observations that clearly demonstrate where conditions of the motivational framework are effectively addressed in teaching and learning. Team members provide specific instructional examples as well as examples of students' responses to illustrate important points.

Wonders

Team members comment on the *Wonders* of the lesson. What might the presenting instructor have done to produce deeper understanding? What might be included next time to deepen the quality of student work or responses?

Debrief

Colleagues reflect as a group on the set of Strengths and Wonders for each of the four conditions of the motivational framework with their own practice in mind. They set individual goals before discussing team goals that support improved instructional practice.

Relationships (Inclusion)	Relevance (Attitude)
Strengths	Strengths
Wonders	Wonders
Results (Competence)	Rigor (Meaning)
Strengths	Strengths
Wonders	Wonders

Resource B

WORKING WITH A FACULTY TEAM TO INTRODUCE THE MOTIVATIONAL FRAMEWORK

The following agendas illustrate a process through which faculty design and cofacilitate an institute with a professional development expert from within the institution or outside. This process can be a bit intimidating to faculty who are not yet familiar with the motivational framework and have not participated in teaching peers in a professional learning institute. That is why no one is asked to do anything that they do not wish to do. Some faculty members, for example, provide extra support for developing materials or working with small groups. Others enjoy facilitating as long as they do so with another person.

Cofacilitation of an initial institute opens many doors. It symbolically establishes the institution's own faculty as expert learners in motivating instructional practice. In addition, it allows follow-up, job-embedded learning through such methods as lesson study and peer coaching. Faculty members who have participated in these kinds of activities consistently report that cofacilitating deepens their own learning, contributes to effective use of the motivational framework within their own courses, and provides perspectives on adult learning that are invaluable.

Generally the first whole-school institute focuses primarily on the motivational framework for culturally responsive teaching and related strategies that educators can immediately use. This kind of pragmatism contributes to deepening trust and developing a positive attitude for staff and faculty to eventually grapple with often controversial issues that accompany change.

A sample agenda for a planning session to cocreate and collaboratively facilitate a campus institute follows, after which we provide a sample two-day agenda for college faculty. Both of these can be modified to fit the context and audience.

Sample One-Day Agenda for Planning an Institute with a Small Team

Participants: A team of five to seven faculty with a representative from student services and perhaps an administrative-level volunteer

Goals: To strengthen and develop an understanding of the motivational framework; to plan a campus-based institute that reflects the institution's strengths and challenges as they relate to student motivation and learning; to enhance the leadership capacity of the institution for ongoing application of a motivational approach to culturally responsive teaching.

8:30–8:45: Welcome, introduction, goals
8:45–9:15: Building community

Activity: Quick-write a personal and professional reason for interest in this opportunity, followed by round-robin sharing that includes each person's name and professional focus.

9:15–9:30: Informal dialogue

Purpose: To touch base on previous campus improvement efforts and discuss how a one-day institute might connect to previous work and contribute to campus goals.

9:30–10:15 Overview of the text

Activity: Each person reads the Preface for *Diversity and Motivation* and teaches the rest of the group about a specific chapter (see book study p. 361 to develop a protocol).

10:15–10:30: Break

10:30–11:30: Book study sharing and review of a sample agenda for the campus institute (see following example on p. 380).

Activity: On an overhead or large piece of newsprint, use suggestions and ideas from the previous activity to outline a one- or two-day agenda. Be very specific. For example, start with 8:30–9:00, and so forth. Ask participants not to worry about who will do what. No one will be asked to do anything that they would prefer not to do. Also, the primary facilitator will provide the theoretical underpinnings. The group, as individuals or collectively, may want to facilitate specific activities or be willing to video their own practice as a context for examining instructional practice for applying the motivational framework rubrics.

11:30–12:30: Lunch

12:30–1:30: Individual and collective commitments

Activity: Group discussion from which volunteers emerge so that there is a clear sense of who will do what. Then review materials and resources needed for the institute.

1:30–1:45: Break

1:45–3:00: Practice and preparation

Activity: Ask participants to outline their approach and identify materials they will need and support needed.

3:00–3:15: Suggestions and reminders

a. During the institute, keep a list of what has been accomplished on a posted sheet of newsprint for everyone to see.

b. At the conclusion of an activity, always remember to ask, "How could you adapt this activity to your specific context?"

c. If someone would like to add to or clarify what the facilitator of an activity is saying, he or she joins the facilitator (as opposed to calling out from somewhere in the room).

d. The anticipated times allotted for activities are approximations. It is best to distribute an agenda to participants at the institute that specifies the exact times only for breaks and lunch.

3:15–3:30: Closure

Round-robin: How will we know if we have been successful? (List responses)

Closing quote: "The road was new to me, as roads always are, going back."—Sarah Orne Jewett

Sample Two-Day Institute to Introduce the Motivational Framework: Designing Lessons That Support the Motivation of All Students

Institute participants: Faculty, advisors, administrative leadership

Goals: To examine the purpose and potential of the motivational framework for culturally responsive teaching, to apply the framework to lesson design, to develop awareness about some of the reasons for academic disparity among student groups and what can be done within the pedagogical sphere of influence.

Distribute three- by five-inch cards, and at an appropriate time, indicate that the cards provide an opportunity for anonymous questions that can be placed in a box by the door and will be addressed at the following intervals: after morning break, after lunch, and prior to closure each day.

Day 1

8:30–8:45: Welcome, goals, overview
8:45–9:00: Getting acquainted (*motivational condition: establishing inclusion through respect and connectedness*)

Activity: Round-robin: In table groups or with a partner, introduce yourself and respond to the following question: What is one thing an outsider might not know about your college [or instructional focus] at first glance?

9:00–9:30: Introduction to the concept of culture

Activity: Venn diagram (discussed and exemplified in Chapter Two) (*motivational condition: establishing inclusion*)

9:30–10:15: Introduction to the motivational framework for culturally responsive teaching

Activity: Mini-lecture with volunteers summarizing important information or insights to the entire group during and at the end of the lecture (*motivational condition: developing a positive attitude through relevance and volition*)

10:15–10:30: Break
10:30–11:00: Reflection on mini-lecture

Activities: Note sharing and dialogue with a partner to identify two or three of the most important points and then large-group comments and questions (*motivational condition: engendering competence through authentic ways to identify learning*)

11:00–11:45: Applying the motivational framework to a sample lesson

Activities: Instructors describe a motivating lesson that they regularly teach. Four colleagues listen, each one representing a motivational condition. After the description of the lesson each reports back to the instructor how he carried out that condition in his lesson. All four conditions may not have been illustrated. The group discusses possible ways to instructionally insert the missing conditions in a future lesson (*motivational condition: enhancing meaning through challenge and engagement*) and KWL Strategy (Ogle, 1986) to guide afternoon foci

11:45–12:00: Review of the morning and preview of the afternoon

Activity: Door passes: The question to which participants respond individually on a three- by five-inch note card is: "Given our work together this morning, what is something that most surprises you?" The cards are collected as the instructors leave for lunch.

12:00–1:15: Lunch

1:15–2:00: Establishing inclusion

Activities: Facilitator selects two or three of the following to use with participants, who are then asked to apply them to their own practice:

Participation agreements (Chapter Two)

Dialogue journals to plan and reflect on teaching (Chapter Five)

Debrief: Pair-share: Select a teaching practice and tell a partner how you will use it and how you will gauge its effect.

2:00–2:15: Break

2:15–3:00: Developing a positive attitude

Practices (facilitator selects one to examine as a group): carousel graffiti (Ginsberg and Wlodkowski, 2000) or approaches based on multiple intelligences theory (Chapter Three)

Free writing: Write about how you will adapt this strategy to classroom use; if time permits, post your idea on the designated reading wall for gallery-style review.

3:00–3:30: Review of the day, preview of day 2, closing comments.

Day 2

8:30–8:45: Welcome, review, overview

8:45–9:15: Building community

Activity: Annotated reading: Interview with Beverly Daniel Tatum (http://www.pbs.org/race/000_About/002_04-background-03-04.htm)

9:15–10:15: Enhancing meaning

Activity: Lesson study simulation (p. 356) with video segments of a teaching experience from various departments; use strengths and wonders process (Resource A)

Protocol to apply the rubrics in Resource J to a video segment: After viewing the video, (1) in small groups, participants identify the lesson's strengths; (2) small groups discuss questions they might pose to help the instructor improve his or her teaching based on the motivational framework; (3) the large group comes back together and interacts with the facilitator as if she was the instructor on the videotape; (4) the facilitator responds as she imagines an actual teacher might who is receiving "helpful" feedback; (5) the group creates a set of guidelines for a peer support during similar (hypothetical, at this point) future opportunities.

10:15–10:30: Break

10:30–11:15: Enhancing meaning (continued)

Activity: Personal applications of critical questions (Chapter Four). One person presents an instructional challenge about which he or she is concerned. Group members check for clarity. Once the problem is well understood, a round of questions follows based on sentence starters (p. 104). The person sharing his or her challenge records questions and ideas for personal application.

11:15–11:45: Review of the morning, preview of the afternoon

Activity: Head, Heart, Hand (Chapter Five)

11:45–1:00: Lunch

1:00–2:00: Engendering competence activity: Examining grading policies and practices (mini-lecture guided by personal and then small group reflection)

2:00–2:15: Break

2:15–4:00: Engendering competence (continued)

Activity: Using the motivational framework for lesson design.

Activity: Demonstration with design of the two-day institute; discipline-specific design teams with the option to create individual lessons; conclude with volunteers who are willing to share examples of lessons.

4:00–4:30: Overview of the text

See Chapter Six for suggestions regarding an introductory book study. Because of time, the book study protocol will need to be modified.

4:30–4:45: Review of the two-day institute

Activity: Personal goal setting (Chapter Three) that includes follow-up with an implementation partner from this session or another trusted colleague.

4:45–5:00: Final comments, future direction

Resource C

THE MOTIVATIONAL FRAMEWORK

Source: Copyright © 2004 by Margery B. Ginsberg.

Resource D

MOTIVATIONAL FRAMEWORK LESSON PLAN

This two-dimensional model may be used to facilitate lesson planning with the Motivational Framework for Culturally Responsive Teaching.

Class: Date:

Learning Goals:

How does this learning experience . . .

. . . contribute to developing as a community of learners who feel respected by and connected to one another and to the teacher? **Establishing Inclusion:** **Respect and Connectedness**	. . . offer meaningful choices and promote personal relevance to contribute to a positive attitude? **Developing a Positive Attitude:** **Volition and Personal Relevance**
. . . create students' understanding that they are becoming more effective in authentic learning they value? **Engendering Competence:** **Authenticity and Effectiveness**	. . . engage students in challenging learning that has social merit? **Enhancing Meaning:** **Challenge and Engagement**

Resource E

FACILITATING EQUITABLE DISCUSSIONS WITHIN A MULTICULTURAL CLASSROOM

Topically focused class discussions potentially offer English learners rich exposure to new vocabulary and use, along with opportunities to interact in a variety of academic situations—reporting information, summarizing, synthesizing, and debating. Frequently, however, members of linguistic minority groups remain silent participants in whole-class discussions for varied reasons, including lack of confidence in their listening comprehension, pronunciation, word choice, and culturally loaded interactional strategies. Instructors who lead carefully orchestrated class discussions that provide language-promoting assistance and facilitate more active participation for English learners often use the following strategies:

1. Create a supportive classroom environment for less confident English learners by encouraging all students to talk in turn, to listen well while others talk, and, when appropriate, to offer assistance with respect for the ability for classmates to speak two languages.

2. Demonstrate your desire and expectation for participation among all students in oral activities by consistently inviting every member of the class to participate. For example, an instructor might say, "Let's hear from some of the people who have not yet had an opportunity to comment."

3. Allow students to first share and rehearse their responses to a key question or comments on a topic with a partner to

increase learning, confidence, and motivation to contribute to a unified class discussion.

4. Be sensitive to the linguistic and conceptual demands of discussion questions and activities. Don't inhibit participation by pushing students to communicate too far beyond their current level of English proficiency.

5. The easiest content for less proficient English learners to grapple with is often related to everyday life and activity. Make a concerted effort to build in opportunities for language-minority students to share information about their cultures, communities, families, and special interests.

6. Pair less proficient English users with a respectful classmate who can clarify concepts, vocabulary, and instructions in the primary language and also coach the classmate in responding.

7. Attempt to activate students' background knowledge on topics, and provide through "schema"-building activities (such as brainstorming, mapping, and advance organizers) requisite linguistic, conceptual, and cultural information that would otherwise distract from active learning and participation.

8. Move purposefully around the room to enable as many students as possible to enjoy having close proximity to the teacher. This has the added advantage of encouraging students to stay alert, ask questions, and take response risks.

9. Do not constantly pose questions to the group at large, allowing a minority of more confident or impulsive students to dominate the discussion.

10. Ask a question before naming the respondent to encourage active learning by allowing all students to "attend" and decide how they would answer.

11. Draw students with less oral confidence by asking them to respond to an open-ended question after they have heard a variety of responses from their classmates.

12. Call on English learners to answer not only safe yes/no questions but also more challenging, open-ended questions that provide opportunities for thoughtful and extended English use.

13. Increase wait time (three to nine seconds) after asking a question to allow adequate time for students to successfully process the question and formulate a thoughtful response.

14. When calling on a specific student who is learning English, it often helps to first pose the question and make eye contact with the student while stating his or her name; then pause a few seconds, and restate the question verbatim.

15. Discourage classmates from blurting out responses and intimidating less confident English users from taking communication risks.

16. Do not interrupt a student's thought processes after asking an initial question by immediately posing one or more follow-up questions; these tandem questions confuse rather than assist English learners, who may not realize that the teacher is actually rephrasing the same question.

17. Encourage students to talk through nonverbal means, such as waiting comfortably, smiling, and nodding in approval.

18. Make any corrections indirectly by mirroring in correct form what the student has said. For example, suppose a student says, "Majority immigrants San Francisco from Pacific Rim." You can repeat, "That is correct. A majority of the immigrants in San Francisco come from the Pacific Rim."

19. Use these conversational features regularly, and in so doing model for your students how to use them in class discussions, lectures, and small-group work:

    Confirmation checks—"Is this what you are saying?" "So you believe that ..."

Clarification requests—"Will you explain your point so that I can be sure I understand?" "Could you give me an example of that?"

Comprehension checks (best to do this privately)—"Is my use of language understandable to you?"

Interrupting—"Excuse me, but ..." "Sorry for interrupting, but ..."

Source: Kinsella (1993, p. 16). Used by permission.

Resource F

EFFECTIVE LECTURING WITHIN A MULTICULTURAL CLASSROOM

Although occasionally necessary, lectures present particular challenges for students who are in the process of acquiring full English proficiency and who may be largely unfamiliar with the specialized terminology of academic disciplines and effective note-taking strategies.

Content area instructors may want to use the following strategies while presenting critical information orally during lessons to facilitate listening comprehension, engagement, and note-taking skills for nonnative speakers of English and other students who may not have a strong auditory learning modality:

1. Begin the lecture with a brief review of the main ideas covered in the previous class session. You can also ask students to summarize the main points of the previous lesson first in pairs, then as a class.

2. Early in the semester, teach your students a manageable note-taking system that is particularly useful for your content area. Spend adequate time modeling this system and sharing examples of well-written notes.

3. Encourage English-dominant students or fluent bilingual students who take effective, comprehensible notes to share them with English learners.

4. Provide a partially completed outline of the lecture following the system that you have taught to lighten the listening load for students who are learning English. Use a handout for

lengthy presentations of information, and the board or digital media for simpler outlines that students may easily copy.

5. Build in accountability for taking effective lecture notes by randomly collecting and commenting on them and allowing students to use their notes during exams.

6. Clarify the topic and key objectives of your lecture at the very beginning.

7. Write as legibly as possible on the board or use electronic equipment, keeping in mind that students educated abroad may be unfamiliar with cursive writing.

8. Allow students to record your lectures and class discussions so that they can listen to them as many times as they need to comprehend and retain information.

9. Before and during the lecture, identify key terms, and write all important vocabulary and points on the board, overhead transparency, or handout.

10. Modify your normal conversational style to make your delivery as comprehensible as possible: use a slightly slower speech rate, enunciate clearly, limit idiomatic expressions, and pause adequately at the end of a statement to allow time for thought processing and note taking.

11. Follow an orderly progression of ideas and stick to your outline, thereby enabling English learners to readily identify essential lesson information and reduce potential "linguistic clutter."

12. Complement challenging information relayed orally with visual aids: illustrations, charts, advance organizers, concept maps, demonstrations.

13. Use many concrete examples and analogies so that students can conceptualize concepts within a more familiar context, and also elicit relevant examples from student volunteers.

14. Build in considerable redundancy with repetitions, examples, anecdotes, expansions, and paraphrases.

15. Relate information to assigned readings whenever possible and give the precise place within the text or selection, enabling students to write these page numbers in their notes and find the information later for study or review.

16. Highlight major points and transitions with broad gestures, facial expressions, purposeful movement, exaggerated intonation, and obvious verbal signals.

17. Focus your students' listening and note taking by using consistent verbal signals or cues (for example, *furthermore, in summary*) that indicate the structure and progression of ideas in your lecture. Distribute a chart with transitional expressions organized by function that are commonly used in formal speaking and writing in university classes and professional settings.

18. Make regular eye contact with all your students.

19. Check for comprehension regularly rather than at the end of the lecture. Predetermine critical transitions and ask students to summarize key points, first in pairs, then as a class. You can also ask students to review their notes up to that point and write down any questions they would like answered.

20. Try to answer all questions that the students ask, but avoid overly detailed explanation, which may further confuse them. Simple answers that get right to the point will be understood best, particularly if you use relevant visual aids and examples or demonstrate actions to help get the meaning across.

21. Save adequate time at the end to clarify the main points of the lecture.

22. Allow students to compare their notes in small groups or pairs, and then formulate any additional questions for the instructor that they could not answer within their group.

Source: Kinsella, (1993, p. 13). Used by permission.

Resource G

PROVIDING WRITTEN FEEDBACK TO STUDENTS IN A MULTICULTURAL CLASSROOM

Suggestions for how to use written feedback to promote diversity and respond to bias in student writing follow:

1. Ask for concrete examples, clarifications, illustrations, and details.
2. Provide additional information that corrects misinformation or fills in missing information.
3. Ask about feelings associated with a situation. If they have described feeling a certain way, ask more about the situation that prompted those feelings.
4. Inquire about how students act on their beliefs.
5. Provide students with different perspectives—other ways of looking at the same situation—and invite them to try on a different perspective.
6. Provide students with a broader context (historical or global) with which to think about issues.
7. Point out the "loops" in their thinking (changing their views from one statement to the next).
8. Paraphrase your understanding of the intent of their remarks, and ask if you are understanding their intentions and arguments correctly.
9. Support indications of new awareness, growth, and risk-taking behavior.

10. Provide suggestions for how to take the next step and explore topics further by suggesting books, resources, films, and cultural events.

11. Acknowledge the emotional aspects of dealing with these issues.

12. Introduce students to concepts that can help them make sense of their personal experience.

13. Affirm students' willingness to engage with issues.

14. Share examples of your own experience with students.

15. Let them know you've been there too!

Source: Created by Linda Marchesani. Reprinted with permission.

Resource H

COOPERATIVE LESSON WORKSHEET

Step 1   Select an activity and desired outcome(s).

_____

_____

Step 2   Make decisions:

    a. Group size: _____

    b. Assignment to groups: _____

    _____

    c. Room arrangement: _____

    _____

    d. Materials needed for each group: _____

    _____

    e. Roles: _____

    _____

Step 3   State the learning component in language your students understand.

    a. Task: _____

    _____

    b. Positive interdependence: _____

    _____

c. Individual accountability: _____

_____

d. Criteria for success: _____

_____

e Specific behaviors to encourage: _____

_____

Step 4   Monitor progress.

a. Evidence of cooperative and encouraged
    behaviors: _____

_____

b. Task assistance needed: _____

_____

Step 5   Evaluate outcomes.

a. Task achievement: _____

_____

b. Group functioning: _____

_____

c. Notes on individuals: _____

_____

d. Feedback to give: _____

_____

e. Suggestions for next time: _____

_____

_____

Source: Adapted from Johnson, Johnson, and Smith (1991).

Resource I

INCLUSION, ATTITUDE, MEANING, AND COMPETENCE RUBRICS

Inclusion: Respect and Connectedness

Yes/Obvious	Yes, But	Not Seen This Visit	Ideas
Routines and rituals are present that contribute to respectful learning (for example, ground rules, cooperative learning).			
Students comfortably and respectfully interact with each other.			
Students comfortably and respectfully interact with teacher (for example, students share their perspectives).			
Teacher treats all students respectfully and fairly.			
General Information/Comments			

Attitude: Volition and Personal/Cultural Relevance

Yes/Obvious	Yes, But	Not Seen This Visit	Ideas
Classes are taught with students' experiences, concerns, or interests in mind.			
Students make choices related to learning that include experiences, values, needs, and strengths.			
Students are able to voice their opinions.			
Teacher varies how students learn (discussion, music, film, personal interaction).			

General Information/Comments

Meaning: Challenge and Engagement

Yes/Obvious	Yes, But	Not Seen This Visit	Ideas
Students actively participate in challenging ways (for example, engaging in investigations, projects, art, simulations, case study).			
Teacher asks questions that go beyond facts and encourages students to learn from different points of view.			
Teacher helps students recall what they know and build on it.			
Teacher respectfully encourages high-quality responses.			

General Information/Comments

Competence: Authenticity and Effectiveness

Yes/Obvious	Yes, But	Not Seen This Visit	Ideas
Teacher shares or develops with students clear criteria for success (for example, rubrics, personal conferences).			
Grading policies are fair to all students (for example, students can learn from mistakes and the grades reflect what students know and can do).			
There are demonstrations or exhibitions of learning with real world connections.			
Assessment includes student values (for example, students self-assess and there are multiple ways to demonstrate learning).			

General Information/Comments

Resource J

PEER COACHING RUBRICS

Date and time:
Brief description of the lesson:

Learning Goals

Establishing Inclusion

How does the learning experience contribute to developing as a community of learners who feel respected and connected to one another?

Routines and rituals are visible and understood by all

_____ Rituals are in place that help everyone feel that they belong in the class.

_____ Students and teacher(s) have opportunities to learn about each other.

_____ Students and teachers(s) have opportunities to learn about each others' unique backgrounds.

_____ Classroom agreements/rules and consequences for violating agreements are negotiated.

Evidence:

All students equitably and actively participating and interacting

_____ Teacher directs attention equitably.

_____ Teacher interacts respectfully with all students.

_____ Teacher demonstrates to all students that he or she cares about them.

_____ Students talk to or with a partner or small group.

_____ Students respond to lesson by writing.

_____ Students know what to do, especially when making choices.

_____ Students help each other.

_____ Student work is displayed.

Evidence:

Developing a Positive Attitude

How does this learning experience use learners' volition and promote personal relevance to contribute to a positive attitude?

Teacher works with students to personalize the relevance of course content

_____ Students' experiences, concerns, and interests are used to develop course content.

_____ Students' experiences, concerns, and interests are addressed in responses to questions.

_____ Students' prior knowledge and learning experiences are explicitly linked to course content and questions.

_____ Teacher encourages students to understand, develop, and express different points of view.

_____ Teacher encourages students to clarify their interests and set goals.

_____ Teacher maintains flexibility in pursuit of teachable moments and emerging interests.

Evidence:

Teacher encourages students to make real choices such as

_____ How to learn (multiple intelligences)

_____ What to learn

_____ Where to learn

_____ When a learning experience will be considered to be complete

_____ How learning will be assessed

_____ With whom to learn

_____ How to solve emerging problems

Evidence:

Enhancing Meaning

How does this learning experience engage participants in challenging learning?

The teacher encourages all students to learn, apply, create, and communicate knowledge

_____ Teacher helps students to activate prior knowledge and to use it as a guide to learning.

_____ Teacher, in concert with students, creates opportunities for inquiry, investigation, and projects.

_____ Teacher provides opportunities for students to actively participate in challenging ways when not involved in sedentary activities such as reflecting, reading, and writing.

_____ Teachers asks higher-order questions of all students throughout a lesson.

_____ Teacher elicits high-quality responses from all students.

_____ Teacher uses multiple safety nets to ensure student success (for example, not grading all assignments, working with a partner, cooperative learning).

Evidence:

Engendering Competence

How does this learning experience create an understanding that participants are becoming more effective in learning they value and perceive as authentic to real world experience?

> _There is information, consequence, or product that supports students in valuing and identifying learning:_

_____ Teacher clearly communicates the purpose of the lesson.

_____ Teacher clearly communicates criteria for excellent final products.

_____ Teacher provides opportunities for a diversity of competencies to be demonstrated in a variety of ways.

_____ Teacher helps all students to concretely identify accomplishments.

_____ Teacher assesses different students differently.

_____ Teacher assesses progress continually in order to provide feedback on individual growth and progress.

_____ Teacher creates opportunities for students to make explicit connections between new and prior learning.

_____ Teacher creates opportunities for students to make explicit connections between their learning and the real world.

_____ Teacher provides opportunities for students to self-assess learning in order to reflect on their growth as learners.

_____ Teacher provides opportunities for students to self-assess their personal responsibility for contributing to the classroom as a learning community.

Evidence:

Resource K

EVALUATING THE MOTIVATIONAL CONDITIONS OF A CLASS

Please give us feedback on this evaluation by indicating your insights regarding your personal learning experiences and ways in which students and faculty can create increasingly compelling and equitable learning experiences. Also, please rate the following questions using a scale of 1 to 5 (1 as low and 5 as high) and write that number on the line in front of each item.

_____ 1. The learning environment was respectful. (motivational condition: establishing inclusion)

_____ 2. The learning environment promoted a sense of connectedness among ourselves and with faculty. (motivational condition: establishing inclusion)

_____ 3. The opinions and ideas of others were encouraged. (motivational condition: developing a positive attitude)

_____ 4. The ways in which we learned included some of my strengths. (motivational condition: developing a positive attitude)

_____ 5. I was challenged to think deeply about issues that have social and political merit. (motivational condition: enhancing meaning)

_____ 6. Most of the time I felt engaged in what was going on. (enhancing meaning)

_____ 7. I have learned things that help me to be effective at what I value. (motivational condition: engendering competence)

_____ 8. I will use the knowledge and skills that I am learning. (engendering competence)

References

Aanerud, R. "Now More Than Ever: James Baldwin and the Critique of White Liberalism." In E. D. McBride (ed.), *James Baldwin Now*. New York: New York University Press, 1999.

Adams, M. "Cultural Inclusion in the American College Classroom." In L. L. B. Border and N. Van Note Chism (eds.), *Teaching for Diversity*. New Directions for Teaching and Learning, no. 49. San Francisco: Jossey-Bass, 1992.

Adams, M. "Pedagogical Frameworks for Social Justice Education." In M. Adams, L. A. Bell, and P. Griffin (eds.), *Teaching for Diversity and Social Justice*. (2nd ed.). New York: Routledge, 2007.

Adams, M., Bell, L. A., and Griffin, P. (eds.). *Teaching for Diversity and Social Justice*. (2nd ed.) New York: Routledge, 2007.

Adams, M., Jones, J., and Tatum, B. D. "Knowing Our Students." In M. Adams, L. A. Bell, and P. Griffin (eds.), *Teaching for Diversity and Social Justice*. (2nd ed.) New York: Routledge, 2007.

Adams, M., and Marchesani, L. S. "Curricular Innovations: Social Diversity as Course Content." In M. Adams (ed.), *Promoting Diversity in College Classrooms: Innovative Responses for the Curriculum, Faculty, and Institutions*. New Directions for Teaching and Learning, no. 52. San Francisco: Jossey-Bass, 1992.

Adams, G., and Markus, H. R. "Toward a Conception of Culture Suitable for a Social Psychology of Culture." In M. Schaller and C. S. Crandall (eds.), *The Psychological Foundations of Culture*. Mahwah, N.J.: Erlbaum, 2004.

Alfassi, M. "Reading to Learn: Effects of Combined Strategy Instruction." *Theory into Practice*, 2004, 39(4), 237–247.

Allen, A. "Portray Me in Silence: Teaching for Justice." In R. A. Pena, K. Guest, and L. Y. Matsuda (eds.), Community and Difference: Teaching, Pluralism, and Social Justice. New York: Peter Lang, 2005.

Allen, M. S., and Roswell, B. S. "Self-Evaluation as Holistic Assessment." Paper presented at the annual meeting of the Conference on College Composition and Communication, March 1989. (ED 303 809)

Ancis, J. R., and Ali, R. "Multicultural Counseling Training Approaches: Implications for Pedagogy." In C. Z. Enns and A. L. Sinacore (eds.), Teaching and Social Justice: Integrating Multicultural and Feminist Theories in the Classroom. Washington, D.C.: American Psychological Association, 2005.

Andersen, P. A., and Wang, H. "Unraveling Cultural Cues: Dimensions of Nonverbal Communication Across Cultures." In L. A. Samovar, R. E. Porter, and E. R. McDaniel (eds.), *Intercultural Communication*. (11th ed.) Belmont, Calif.: Thomson Wadsworth, 2006.

Anderson, J. "Cognitive Styles and Multicultural Populations." *Journal of Teacher Education*, 1988, 39(1), 2–9.

Anderson, J. A., and Adams, M. "Acknowledging the Learning Styles of Diverse Student Populations: Implications for Instructional Design." In L. L. B. Border and N. Van Note Chism (eds.), *Teaching for Diversity.* New Directions for Teaching and Learning, no. 49. San Francisco: Jossey-Bass, 1992.

Anderson, R. A. *Driving Change Through Diversity and Globalization: Transformative Leadership in the Academy.* Sterling, Va.: Stylus, 2008.

Anyon, J. "Social Class and the Hidden Curriculum of Work." *Journal of Education*, 1980, 162, 67–92.

Anyon, J. *Radical Possibilities.* New York: Routledge, 2005.

Anzaldua, G. *Borderlands/la Frontera: The New Mestiza.* San Francisco: Ante Lute Press, 1987.

Apple, M. *Education and Power.* London: Routledge, 1982.

Aronson, E., and others. *The Jigsaw Classroom.* Newbury Park, CA: Sage, 1978.

Aronson, J., and Steele, C. M. "Stereotypes and the Fragility of Academic Competence, Motivation, and Self-Concept." In A. J. Elliot and C. S. Dweck (eds.), *Handbook of Competence and Motivation.* New York: Guilford Press, 2005.

Aslanian, C. B. *Adult Students Today.* New York: College Board, 2001.

Astin, A. W. "The Future of Higher Education: Competition or Cooperation." *Cooperative Learning*, 1993a, 13(3), 2–5.

Astin, A. W. *What Matters in College? Four Critical Years Revisited.* San Francisco: Jossey-Bass, 1993b.

Astin, A. W. *What Matters in College? Four Critical Years Revisited.* San Francisco: Jossey-Bass, 1997.

Astin, A. W., Green, K. C., and Korn, W. S. *The American Freshman: Twenty-Year Trends 1966–1985.* Los Angeles: Higher Education Research Institute, Graduate School of Education, University of California, 1987.

Attewell, P., and Lavin, D. E. "Distorted Statistics and Graduation Rates." *Chronicle of Higher Education*, July 6, 2007, p. B16.

Attewell, P., Lavin, D. E., Domina, T., and Levey, T. *Passing the Torch: Does Higher Education for the Disadvantaged Pay Off Across the Generations?* New York: Russell Sage Foundation, 2007.

Auletta, G. S., and Jones, T. "Unmasking the Myths of Racism." In D. F. Halpern and Associates (eds.), *Changing College Classrooms: New Teaching and Learning Strategies for an Increasingly Complex World.* San Francisco: Jossey-Bass, 1994.

Bandura, A. *Self-Efficacy: The Exercise of Control.* New York: Freeman, 1997.

Banks, J. A. *Cultural Diversity and Education: Foundations, Curriculum, and Teaching.* Boston: Pearson, Allyn & Bacon, 2001.

Banks, J. A. *Race, Culture, and Education: The Selected Works of James A. Banks.* New York: Routledge, 2006.

Banks, J. A., and McGee Banks, C. A. (eds.), *Multicultural Education: Issues and Perspectives.* (2nd ed.) Needham Heights, Mass.: Allyn & Bacon, 1993.

Baptiste, S. E. *Problem-Based Learning: A Self-Directed Journey.* Thorofare, N.J.: SLACK, 2003.

Barkley, E. F., Cross, K. P., and Major, C. H. *Collaborative Learning Techniques: A Handbook for College Faculty.* San Francisco: Jossey-Bass, 2005.

Belenky, M., Clinchy, B., Goldberger, N., and Tarule, J. *Women's Ways of Knowing: The Development of Self, Voice, and Mind.* New York: Basic Books, 1986.

Bensimon, E. M. (ed.). *Multicultural Teaching and Learning.* University Park: National Center on Postsecondary Teaching, Learning, and Assessment, Pennsylvania State University, 1994.

Berger, N. O., Caffarella, R. S., and O'Donnell, J. M. "Learning Contracts." In M. W. Galbraith (ed.), *Adult Learning Methods: A Guide for Effective Instruction.* (3rd ed.) Malabar, Fla.: Krieger, 2004.

Beyer, B. K. *Developing a Thinking Skills Program.* Needham Heights, Mass.: Allyn & Bacon, 1988.

Black, P., and others. "The Nature and Value of Formative Assessment for Learning." Paper presented at the National AERA Conference, Chicago, Apr. 2003.

Blanc, R. A., DeBuhr, L. E., and Martin, D. C. "Breaking the Attrition Cycle." *Journal of Higher Education,* 1983, 54(1), 80–89.

Blum, E. J. *Reforging the White Republic: Race, Religion, and American Nationalism, 1865–1898.* Baton Rouge: Louisiana State University Press, 2005.

Bohm, D. *Unfolding Meanings: A Weekend of Dialogue with David Bohm.* London: Ark Paperbacks, 1987.

Bonham, L. A. "Learning Style Use: In Need of a Perspective." *Lifelong Learning,* 1988, 11(5), 14–17.

Bonilla-Silva, E. *Racism Without Racists: Color Blind Racism and the Persistence of Inequality in the United States.* Lanham, Md.: Rowman & Littlefield, 2003.

Bonsangue, M. "Long Term Effects of the Calculus Workshop Model." *Cooperative Learning,* 1993, 13(3), 19–20.

Boud, D., Cohen, R., and Sampson, J. *Peer Learning in Higher Education: Learning from and with Each Other.* London: Kogan Page, 2001.

Bourdieu, P. "The Forms of Capital." In J. Richardson (ed.), *Handbook of Theory and Research for the Sociology of Education.* Westport, Conn.: Greenwood Press, 1986.

Branche, J., Mullennix, J., and Cohn, E. R. (eds.). *Diversity Across the Curriculum: A Guide for Faculty of Higher Education.* Bolton, Mass.: Anker, 2007.

Brandt, R. "On Educating for Diversity: A Conversation with James A. Banks." *Educational Leadership,* 1994, 51(8), 28–31.

Brayboy, B. M. "Toward a Tribal Critical Race Theory in Education." *Urban Review,* 2005, 37(5), 425–446.

Brookfield, S. D. *Understanding and Facilitating Adult Learning: A Comprehensive Analysis of Principles and Effective Practices.* San Francisco: Jossey-Bass, 1986.

Brookfield, S. D. *The Power of Critical Theory: Liberating Adult Learning and Teaching.* San Francisco: Jossey-Bass, 2005.

Brookfield, S. D. *The Skillful Teacher: On Technique, Trust, and Responsiveness in the Classroom.* (2nd ed.) San Francisco: Jossey-Bass, 2006.

Brookfield, S. D., and Preskill, S. *Discussion as a Way of Teaching: Tools and Techniques for Democratic Classrooms.* San Francisco: Jossey-Bass, 2005.

Brooks, J. G., and Brooks, M. G. *The Case for Constructivist Classrooms.* Alexandria, Va.: Association for Supervision and Curriculum Development, 1993.

Brophy, J. *Motivating Students to Learn.* (2nd ed.) Mahwah, N.J.: Erlbaum, 2004.

Brothers, L. "The Social Brain: A Project for Integrating Primate Behavior and Neurophysiology in a New Domain." In J. Cacioppo and others (eds.), *Foundations in Social Neuroscience.* Cambridge, Mass.: MIT Press, 2000.

Bruffee, K. A. "Sharing our Toys: Cooperative Learning Versus Collaborative Learning." *Change,* 1995, 27(1), 12–18.

Butler, J. E. "Transforming the Curriculum: Teaching About Women of Color." In J. A. Banks and C. A. Banks (eds.), *Multicultural Education: Issues and Perspectives.* (2nd ed.) Needham Heights, Mass.: Allyn & Bacon, 1993.

Caffarella, R. S. *Planning Programs for Adult Learners: A Practical Guide for Educators, Trainers, and Staff Developers.* (2nd ed.) San Francisco: Jossey-Bass, 2002.

Campbell, L., Campbell, B., and Dickinson, D. *Teaching and Learning Through Multiple Intelligences.* (3rd ed.) Boston: Pearson, 2004.

Cassidy, S. "Learning Styles: An Overview of Theories, Models, and Measures." *Educational Psychology,* 2004, 24(4), 419–444.

Castagno, A. E., and Lee, S. J. "Native Mascots and Ethnic Fraud in Higher Education: Using Tribal Critical Race Theory and the Interest Convergence Principle as an Analytic Tool." *Equity and Excellence in Education,* 2007, 40(1), 3–13.

Center for Academic Development. *Supplemental Instruction: Review of Research Concerning the Effectiveness of SI from the University of Missouri–Kansas City and Other Institutions from Across the United States.* Kansas City: University of Missouri, 1991.

Cheek, G. D., and Campbell, C. "The Transfer of Learning Process: Before, During, and After Educational Programs." *Adult Learning,* 1994, 5(4), 27–28.

Chirkov, V., Kim, Y., Ryan, R. M., and Kaplan, U. "Differentiating Autonomy from Individualism and Independence: A Self-Determination Theory Perspective on Internalization of Cultural Orientations and Well-Being." *Journal of Personality and Social Psychology,* 2003, 84, 97–110.

Chiu, C., and Hong, Y. "Cultural Competence: Dynamic Processes." In A. J. Elliot and C. S. Dweck (eds.), *Handbook of Competence and Motivation.* New York: Guilford Press, 2005.

Cho, D. "The Connection Between Self-Directed Learning and the Learning Organization." *Human Resource Development Quarterly,* 2002, 13(4), 467–470.

Christensen, L. "Where I'm From." *Rethinking Schools,* 1997, 12(2), 22–23.

Clifford, J. "Introduction: Partial Truths." In J. Clifford and G. E. Marcus (eds.), *Writing Culture: The Poetics and Politics of Ethnography.* Berkeley: University of California Press, 1986.

Cobbs, B. J., and Ginsberg, M. B. "Learning to Listen Through Home Visits with Somali, Mien, Cambodian, Vietnamese and Latino Families." Jan. 2006. http://home.blarg.net/~building/strategies/multicultural/cobbs%20ginsberg.htm.

Cochran-Smith, M. *Walking the Road: Race, Diversity, and Social Justice in Teacher Education.* New York: Teachers College Press, 2004.

Cohen, E. G. *Designing Groupwork: Strategies for Heterogeneous Classrooms.* (Rev. ed.). New York: Teachers College Press, 1994.

Comer, J. "Creating Learning Communities: The Comer Process." Experimental session of the annual conference of the Association for Supervision and Curriculum Development, Washington, D.C., 1993.

Cones, J. H., Janha, D., and Noonan, J. F. "Exploring Racial Assumptions with Faculty." In J. H. Cones, J. F. Noonan, and D. Janha (eds.), *Teaching Minority Students.* New Directions for Teaching and Learning, no. 16. San Francisco: Jossey-Bass, 1983.

Connerley, M. L., and Pedersen, P. B. *Leadership in a Diverse and Multicultural Environment: Developing Awareness, Knowledge, and Skills.* Thousand Oaks, Calif.: Sage, 2005.

Constitutional Rights Foundation. *Current Issues of Immigration, 2006.* Los Angeles: CRF Publications, 2006.

Cranton, P. "Types of Group Learning." In S. Imel (ed.), *Learning in Groups: Fundamental Principles, New Uses, and Emerging Opportunities.* New Directions for Adult and Continuing Education, no. 71. San Francisco: Jossey-Bass, 1996.

Cranton, P. "Educator Authenticity: A Longitudinal Study." In *Proceedings of the Joint International Conference of the Adult Education Research Conference and the Canadian Association for the Study of Adult Education.* Halifax, Nova Scotia: Mt. St. Vincent University, 2007.

Cross, K. P., and Angelo, T. A. *Classroom Assessment Techniques: A Handbook for Faculty.* Ann Arbor: National Center for Research to Improve Post-Secondary Teaching and Learning, University of Michigan, 1988.

Cross, W. E., Jr. *Shades of Black: Diversity in African-American Identity.* Philadelphia: Temple University Press, 1991.

Csikszentmihalyi, M. "The Flow Experience and Its Significance for Human Psychology." In M. Csikszentmihalyi and I. S. Csikszentmihalyi (eds.), *Optimal Experience: Psychological Studies of Flow in Consciousness.* Cambridge: Cambridge University Press, 1988.

Csikszentmihalyi, M. *Flow: The Psychology of Optimal Experience.* New York: HarperCollins, 1990.

Csikszentmihalyi, M. *Finding Flow: The Psychology of Engagement with Everyday Life.* New York: Basic Books, 1997.

Cummins, J. "The Role of Primary Language Development in Promoting Educational Success for Language Minority Students." In California Office of Bilingual Bicultural Education, *Schooling and Language Minority Students: A Theoretical Framework.* Sacramento: California Department of Education, 1981.

Cummins, J. "Empowering Minority Students: A Framework for Intervention." *Harvard Educational Review,* 1986, 56(1), 18–36.

Cummins, J., Brown, K., and Sayers, D. *Literacy, Technology, and Diversity: Teaching for Success in Changing Times.* Boston: Allyn & Bacon, 2006.

Cuseo, J. "Cooperative Learning: A Pedagogy for Diversity." *Cooperative Learning,* 1993, 13(3), 6–9.

DeAngelis, T. "Homeless Families: Stark Reality of the 90's." *APA Monitor,* 1994, 25(5), pp. 1, 38.

Deci, E. L., and Ryan, R. M. "A Motivational Approach to Self: Integration in Personality." In R. Dienstbier (ed.), *Nebraska Symposium on Motivation,* Vol. 38: *Perspectives on Motivators.* Lincoln: University of Nebraska Press, 1991.

Deci, E. L., Vallerand, R. J., Pelletier, L. C., and Ryan, R. M. "Motivation and Education: The Self-Determination Perspective." *Educational Psychologist,* 1991, 26(3, 4), 325–346.

Delgado, R. (ed.). *Critical Race Theory: The Cutting Edge.* Philadelphia: Temple University Press, 1995.

Delgado, R., and Stefancic, J. *Critical Race Theory: An Introduction.* New York: New York University Press, 2001.

Delpit, L. D. "The Silenced Dialogue: Power and Pedagogy in Educating Other People's Children." *Harvard Educational Review,* 1988, 58(3), 280–298.

Desmedt, E., and Valcke, M. "Mapping the Learning Styles "Jungle": An Overview of the Literature Based on Citation Analysis." *Educational Psychology,* 2004, 24(4), 446–464.

Dewey, J. *Ethics.* New York: Holt, 1932.

Dewey, J. *How We Think*. (Rev. ed.) Lexington, Mass.: Heath, 1933.

Dewey, J. *Experience and Education*. New York: Collier, 1938.

Dewey, J. *John Dewey: His Contribution to the American Tradition*. Indianapolis: Bobbs-Merrill, 1955.

Dick, W. O., Carey, L., and Carey, J. O. *The Systematic Design of Instruction*. (6th ed.) Needham Heights, Mass.: Allyn & Bacon, 2004.

Dillon, J. T. *Questioning and Teaching: A Manual of Practice*. New York: Teachers College Press, 1988.

Dixson, A. D., and Rousseau, C. K. (eds.). *Critical Race Theory in Education: All God's Children Got a Song*. New York: Routledge, 2006.

Donovan, M. S., Bransford, J. D., and Pellegrino, J. W. (eds.). *How People Learn: Bridging Research and Practice*. Washington, D.C.: National Academy Press, 1999.

DuBois, W. E. B. *The Souls of Black Folk*. New York: Pocket Books, 2005. (Originally published in 1903)

Dweck, C. S. "The Perils and Promises of Praise." *Educational Leadership*, 2007, 65(2), 34–39.

Dweck, C. S., and Molden, D. C. "Self-Theories: Their Impact on Competence Motivation and Acquisition." In A. J. Elliot and C. S. Dweck (eds.), *Handbook of Competence and Motivation*. New York: Guilford Press, 2005.

Edelsky, C., and others. "Semilingualism and Language Deficit." *Applied Linguistics*, 1983, 4, 1–22

Eisner, E. W. *The Educational Imagination*. (2nd ed.) Old Tappan, N.J.: Macmillan, 1985.

Eisner, E. W. "The Uses and Limits of Performance Assessments." *Phi Delta Kappan*, 1999, 80, 658–660.

Eisner, E. W. *The Arts and the Creation of Mind*. New Haven, Conn.: Yale University Press, 2002.

Elbow, P. *Embracing Contraries: Explorations in Learning and Teaching*. New York: Oxford University Press, 1986.

Elliot, J. *Action Research for Educational Change*. Philadelphia: Open University Press, 1991.

Elliot, A. J., and Dweck, C. S. (eds.). *Handbook of Competence and Motivation*. New York: Guilford Press, 2005.

Engell, J., and Dangerfield, A. *Saving Higher Education in the Age of Money*. Charlottesville: University of Virginia Press, 2005.

English, L. M. *International Enclyclopedia of Adult Education*. New York: Palgrave Macmillan, 2005.

Enns, C. Z., and Sinacore, A. L. (eds.). *Teaching and Social Justice: Integrating Multicultural and Feminist Theories in the Classroom*. Washington, D.C.: American Psychological Association, 2004.

EPE Research Center, *Annual State Policy Survey*. 2007. www.edweek.org/ew/articles/2007/01/04/17sos-s1.h26.html.

Everyday Health. "HIV/AIDS: The Continuing Epidemic." Feb. 19, 2008. http://www.everydayhealth.com/hiv/world-aids-day-feature/introduction.aspx.

Ewell, P. T. "To Capture the Ineffable: New Forms of Assessment in Higher Education." *Review of Research in Education*, 1991, 17, 75–127.

Fenwick, T. *Learning Through Experience: Troubling Orthodoxies and Intersecting Questions*. Malabar, Fla.: Krieger, 2003.

Fisher, C., and others. "Teaching Behaviors, Academic Learning Time, and Student Achievement: An Overview." In C. Denham and A. Lieberman (eds.), *Time to Learn*. Washington, D.C.: National Institute of Education, 1980.

Fogarty, J., and others. *Learning Communities and Community Colleges.* Olympia, Wash.: Evergreen State College, Washington Center for Improving the Quality of Undergraduate Education, with the American Association for Higher Education, 2003.

Foner, N., and Frederickson, G. M. (eds.). *Not Just Black and White.* New York: Russell Sage Foundation, 2004.

Foucault, M. "Truth and Power." In C. Gordon (ed.), *Power and Knowledge: Selected Interviews and Other Writings, 1972–1977.* New York: Pantheon Books, 1980.

Frankenberg, R. *White Women, Race Matters: The Social Construction of Whiteness.* Minneapolis: University of Minnesota Press, 1993.

Frederick-Recascino, C. M. "Self-Determination Theory and Participation Motivation Research in the Sport and Exercise Domain." In E. L. Deci and R. M. Ryan (eds.), *Handbook of Self-Determination Research.* Rochester, N.Y.: University of Rochester Press, 2002.

Freire, P. *Pedagogy of the Oppressed.* New York: Continuum, 1970/1994.

Freire, P., and Macedo, D. *Literacy: Reading the Word and the World.* Westport, Conn.: Bergin & Garvey, 1987.

Fuligni, A. J. "The Academic Achievement of Adolescents from Immigrant Families: The Roles of Family Background, Attitudes, and Behavior." *Child Development,* 1997, 68, 351–363.

Fullan, M. *Leadership and Sustainability: System Thinkers in Action.* Thousand Oaks, Calif.: Corwin Press, 2004.

Galston, W. *Ethical Dimension of Global Development.* Totowa, N.J.: Rowman & Littlefield, 2006.

Gardner, H. *The Unschooled Mind.* New York: Basic Books, 1991.

Gardner, H. *Multiple Intelligences: The Theory in Practice.* New York: Basic Books, 1993.

Gardner, H. *Multiple Intelligences: New Horizons.* New York: Basic Books, 2006.

Gardner, H., and Boix-Mansilla, V. "Teaching for Understanding—Within and Across Disciplines." *Educational Leadership,* 1994, 51(5), 14–18.

Gardner, J. W. *On Leadership.* New York: Free Press, 1990.

Gay, G. *Culturally Responsive Teaching: Theory, Research, and Practice.* New York: Teachers College Press, 2000.

Geertz, C. *The Interpretation of Cultures.* New York: Basic Books, 1973.

Geismar, K., and Nicoleau, G. (eds.). "Teaching for Change: Addressing Issues of Difference in the College Classroom." *Harvard Educational Review,* Reprint Series, no. 25, 1993.

Gilligan, C. *In a Different Voice: Psychological Theory and Women's Development.* Cambridge, Mass.: Harvard University Press, 1982.

Ginsberg, M. B. "By the Numbers: Data-in-a-Day Technique Provides a Snapshot of Teaching That Motivates" *Journal of Staff Development,* 2001, 22(2), 44–47.

Ginsberg, M. B., and Kimball, K. "Data-in-a-Day: A New Tool for Principal Preparation." *Principal,* 2008, 87(3), 40–43.

Ginsberg, M. B., and Wlodkowski, R. J. *Creating Highly Motivating Classrooms for All Students: A Schoolwide Approach to Powerful Teaching with Diverse Learners.* San Francisco: Jossey-Bass, 2000.

Giroux, H. A. "Writing and Critical Thinking in the Social Studies." *Curriculum Inquiry,* 1978, 8, 291–310.

Giroux, H. A. *Border Crossings: Cultural Workers and the Politics of Education.* New York: Routledge, 1992.

Giroux, H. A., and McLaren, P. "Teacher Education and the Politics of Engagement: The Case for Democratic Schooling." *Harvard Educational Review*, 1986, 56(3), 213–238.

Goldin-Meadow, S. *Hearing Gestures.* Cambridge, Mass.: Belknap Press of Harvard University, 2003.

Goldschmidt, H., and McAlister, E. (eds.). *Race, Nation, and Religion in the Americas.* New York: Oxford University Press, 2004.

Gonzalez, N., Moll, L. C., and Amanti, C. (eds.). *Funds of Knowledge: Theorizing Practices in Households and Classrooms.* Mahwah, N.J.: Erlbaum, 2005.

Goodlad, J. *Teachers for Our Nation's Schools.* San Francisco: Jossey-Bass, 1990.

Gould, S. J. *The Mismeasure of Man.* New York: Norton, 1996.

Griffin, P. "Introductory Modules." In M. Adams, L. A. Bell, and P. Griffin (eds.), *Teaching for Diversity and Social Justice.* (2nd ed.) New York: Routledge, 2007.

Gudykunst, W. B., and Kim, Y. Y. *Communicating with Strangers: An Approach to Intercultural Communication.* New York: Random House, 1992.

Gutman, H. G. *Slavery and the Numbers Game: A Critique of "Time on the Cross."* Champaign: University of Illinois Press, 2003.

Hake, R. R. "Lessons from the Physics Education Reform Effort." *Conservation Ecology,* 2002, 5(2), 28.

Hardiman, R., and Jackson, B. W. "Racial Identity Development: Understanding Racial Dynamics in College Classrooms on Campus." In M. Adams (ed.), *Promoting Diversity in College Classrooms.* New Directions for Teaching and Learning, no. 52. San Francisco: Jossey-Bass, 1992.

Hardiman, R., and Jackson, B. W. "Conceptual Foundations for Social Justice Courses." In M. Adams, L. A. Bell, and P. Griffin (eds.), *Teaching for Diversity and Social Justice: A Sourcebook.* New York: Routledge, 1997.

Hartnell-Young, E., and Morriss, M. *Digital Portfolios: Powerful Tools for Promoting Professional Growth and Reflection.* (2nd ed.) Thousand Oaks, Calif.: Corwin Press, 2007.

Hatch, T., and others. (eds.). *Going Public with Our Teaching: An Anthology of Practice.* New York: Teachers College Press, 2005.

Hattie, J., and Timperley, H. "The Power of Feedback." *Review of Educational Research,* 2007, 77(1), 81–112.

Hayes, E., and Flannery, D. D. *Women as Learners: The Significance of Gender in Adult Learning.* San Francisco: Jossey-Bass, 2000.

Hays, P. *Addressing Cultural Complexities in Practice: A Framework for Clinicians and Counselors.* Washington, DC: American Psychological Association, 2001.

Hebel, S. "The Graduation Gap." *Chronicle of Higher Education,* Mar. 23, 2007, pp. A20–A21.

Helms, J. E. *Black and White Racial Identity: Theory, Research and Practice.* Westport, Conn.: Greenwood Press, 1990.

Hernandez, D. J., Denton, N. A., and Macartney, S. E. "Family Circumstances of Children in Immigrant Familias: Looking to the Future of America." In J. E. Lansford, K. Deater-Deckard, and M. H. Bornstein (eds.), *Immigrant Families in Contemporary Society.* New York: The Guilford Press, 2007.

Herr, K., and Anderson, G. L. *The Action Research Dissertation: A Guide for Students and Faculty.* Thousand Oaks, Calif.: Sage, 2005.

Herrington, A. J., and Curtis, M. *Persons in Process: Four Stories of Writing and Personal Development in College.* Urbana, Ill.: National Council of Teachers of English, 2000.

Hiebert, J., Gallimore, R., & Stigler, J. W. "A Knowledge-Base for the Teaching Profession: What It Would Look Like and How Can We Get One?" *Educational Researcher*, 2002, 31(5), 3–15.

Hiemstra, R., and Sisco, B. *Individualizing Instruction: Making Learning Personal, Empowering, and Successful*. San Francisco: Jossey-Bass, 1990.

Highwater, J. "Imagination as a Political Force." General session address given at the annual conference of the Association for Supervision and Curriculum Development, Chicago, March 1994.

Hill, P. J. "Multiculturalism: The Crucial Philosophical and Organizational Issues." *Change*, July–Aug. 1991, pp. 38–47.

Hillocks, G. "What Works in Teaching Composition: A Meta-Analysis of Experimental Treatment Studies." *American Journal of Education*, 1984, 93(1), 133–170.

Hmelo Silver, C. E. "Problem-Based Learning: What and How Do Students Learn?" *Educational Psychology Review*, 2004, 16, 235–266.

Hodgins, H. S., and Knee, C. R. "The Integrating Self and Conscious Experience." In E. L. Deci and R. M. Ryan (eds.), *Handbook of Self-Determination Research*. Rochester, N.Y.: University of Rochester Press, 2002.

Hofstede, G. "Cultural Differences in Teaching and Learning." *International Journal of Intercultural Relations*, 1986, 10(3), 301–320.

hooks, b. *Teaching to Transgress: Education as the Practice of Freedom*. New York: Routledge, 1994.

hooks, b. *Teaching Community: A Pedagogy of Hope*. New York: Routledge, 2003.

Hrepic, Z., Zollman, D. A., and Rebello, N. S. "Comparing Students' and Experts' Understanding of the Content of a Lecture." *Journal of Science Education and Technology*, 2007, 16(3), 213–224.

Humphreys, L. *Tearoom Trade: Impersonal Sex in Public Places*. Chicago: Aldine, 1970.

Hutchings, P. *Using Cases to Improve College Teaching: A Guide to More Reflective Practice*. Washington, D.C.: American Association for Higher Education, 1993.

Jackson, B. W. "Black Identity Development: Further Analysis and Elaboration." In C. Wijeyesinghe and Jackson B. W. (eds.), *New Perspectives on Racial Identity Development: A Theoretical and Practical Anthology*. New York: New York University Press, 2001.

Jackson, B. W. "The Theory and Practice of Multicultural Organization Development in Education." In M. L Ouellett (ed.), *Teaching Inclusively: Resources for Course, Department, and Institutional Change in Higher Education*. Stillwater, Okla.: New Forums, 2005.

Jackson, B. W., and Hardiman, R. "Oppression: Conceptual and Developmental Analysis." In M. Adams and L. S. Marchesani (eds.), *Radical and Cultural Diversity, Curriculae Content, and Classroom Dynamics: A Manual for College Teachers*. Amherst: University of Massachusetts, 1988.

Jimenez-Aleixandre, M., and Pereiro-Munoz, C. "Knowledge Producers or Knowledge Consumers? Argumentation and Decision Making About Environmental Management." *International Journal of Science Education*, 2002, 24(11), 1171–1190.

Johnson, D. W. "Social Interdependence: The Interrelationships Among Theory, Research, and Practice." *American Psychologist*, 2003, 58, 931–945.

Johnson, D. W., and Johnson, F. P. "Student Motivation in Cooperative Groups: Social Interdependence Theory." In R. Gillies and A. Ashman (eds.), *Cooperative Learning: The Social and Intellectual Outcomes of Learning in Groups*. London: Routledge-Falmer, 2003.

Johnson, D. W., and Johnson, F. P. *Joining Together: Group Theory and Group Skills*. (9th ed.) Boston: Pearson Education, 2006.

Johnson, D. W., and Johnson, R. T. "What We Know About Cooperative Learning at the College Level." *Cooperative Learning*, 1993, 13(3), 17–18.

Johnson, D. W., Johnson, R. T., and Smith, K. A. *Active Learning: Cooperation in the College Classroom*. Edina, Minn.: Interaction, 1991.

Johnson, D. W., Johnson, R., and Smith, K. *Active Learning: Cooperation in the College Classroom*. (2nd ed.) Edina, Minn.: Interaction Book Company, 1998.

Johnson McDougal, E. "The Double Task: The Struggle of Negro Women for Sex and Race Emancipation." *Survey*, Mar. 1, 1925, pp. 689–691.

Jonassen, D. H. "Objectivism Versus Constructivism: Do We Need a New Philosophical Paradigm?" *Educational Training and Development*, 1992, 39(3), 5–14.

Joyce, B. J., and Showers, B. *Student Achievement Through Staff Development*. (3rd ed.) Alexandria, Va.: Association for Supervision and Curriculum Development, 2002.

Kasworm, C. E., and Marienau, C. A. "Principles of Assessment for Adult Learning." In A. D. Rose and M. A. Leahy (eds.), *Assessing Adult Learning in Diverse Settings: Current Issues and Approaches*. New Directions for Adult and Continuing Education, no. 75. San Francisco: Jossey-Bass, 1997.

Katz, J. "White Faculty Struggling with the Effects of Racism." In J. H. Cones, J. F. Noonan, and D. Janha (eds.), *Teaching Minority Students*. New Directions for Teaching and Learning, no. 16. San Francisco: Jossey-Bass, 1983.

Katz, L., and Williams, A. "Pioneering the Electronic School by Using Focus Groups for Planning." *Journal of Computer Assisted Learning*, 2001, 18, 320–329.

Katznelson, I. *When Affirmative Action Was White: An Untold Story of Racial Inequality in the Twentieth Century*. New York: Norton, 2005.

Kerry, T. "Classroom Questioning in England." *Questioning Exchange*, 1987, 1(1), 32–33.

Kincheloe, J. L. *Critical Pedagogy Primer*. New York: Peter Lang, 2005.

King, A. "Inquiry as a Tool in Critical Thinking." In D. F. Halpern and Associates (eds.), *Changing College Classrooms: New Teaching and Learning Strategies for an Increasingly Complex World*. San Francisco: Jossey-Bass, 1994.

King, A. "Structuring Peer Interaction to Promote High-Level Cognitive Processing." *Theory into Practice*, 2002, 41(1), 33–39.

King, M. L. Jr. *Why We Can't Wait*. New York: New American Library, 1964.

Kingore, B. *Literature Celebrations: Catalysts to High-Level Book Responses*. (2nd ed.) Austin, Tex.: Professional Associates Publishing, 2003.

Kinsella, K. "Instructional Strategies Which Promote Participation and Learning for Non-Native Speakers of English in University Classes." *Exchanges*, 1993, 5(1), p. 12.

Kitano, M. K. "What a Course Will Look Like After Multicultural Change." In A. I. Morey and M. K. Kitano (eds.), *Multicultural Course Transformation in Higher Education*. Needham Heights, Mass.: Allyn & Bacon, 1997.

Kitayama, S., and Markus, H. R. (eds.). *Emotion and Culture: Empirical Studies of Mutual Influence*. Washington, D.C.: American Psychological Association, 1994.

Kohn, A. *The Brighter Side of Human Nature; Altruism and Empathy in Everyday Life*. New York: Basic Books, 1990.

Kohn, A. *Punished by Rewards: The Trouble with Gold Stars, Incentive Plans, A's, Praise, and Other Bribes*. Boston: Houghton Mifflin, 1999.

Kolb, A. Y., and Kolb, D. A. "Learning Styles and Learning Spaces: Enhancing Experiential Learning in Higher Education." *Academy of Management Learning and Education*, 2005, 4(2), 193–212.

Kolb, D. A. *Experiential Learning; Experience as the Source of Learning and Development.* Upper Saddle River, N.J.: Prentice Hall, 1984.

Kornhaber, M. L. "Assessment, Standards, and Equity." In J. A. Banks and C. A. M. Banks (eds.), *Handbook on Research in Multicultural Education.* (2nd ed.) San Francisco: Jossey-Bass, 2004.

Kornhaber, M., Krechevsky, M., and Gardner, H. "Engaging Intelligence." *Educational Psychologist*, 1990, 25(3,4), 177–199.

Kozol, J. *The Shame of the Nation: The Restoration of Apartheid Schooling in America.* New York: Crown, 2005.

Krechevsky, M., and Seidel, S. "Minds at Work: Applying Multiple Intelligences in the Classroom." In R. J. Sternberg and W. M. Williams (eds.), *Intelligence, Instruction, and Assessment: Theory into Practice.* Mahwah, N.J.: Erlbaum, 1998.

Kuh, G. D., and Associates. *Student Success in College: Creating Conditions That Matter.* San Francisco: Jossey-Bass, 2005.

Ladson-Billings, G. "Silence as Weapons: Challenges of a Black Professor Teaching White Students." *Theory into Practice*, 1996, 35(2), 79–85.

Lander, D. A. "Writing," In L. M. English (ed.), *International Encyclopedia of Adult Education.* New York: Palgrave Macmillan, 2005.

Langer, S. *Philosophy in a New Key.* Cambridge, Mass.: Harvard University Press, 1942.

Lardner, E. D. "Approaching Diversity Through Learning Communities." Occasional Paper, Winter 2003, no. 2, Washington Center for Improving Undergraduate Education.

Larimore, J. A., and McClellan, G. S. "Native American Student Retention in U.S. Postsecondary Education." In N. J. Tippeconnic Fox, S. C. Lowe, and G. S. McClellan (eds.), *Serving Native American Students.* New Directions for Student Services, no. 109. San Francisco: Jossey-Bass, 2005.

Lather, P. *Getting Smart: Feminist Research and Pedagogy within the Post Modern.* New York: Routledge, 1991.

Lave, J. "The Culture of Acquisition and the Practice of Understanding." In D. Kirshner and J. A. Whitson (eds.), *Situated Cognition: Social, Semiotic, and Psychological Perspectives.* Mahwah, N.J.: Erlbaum, 1997.

Lee, J., and Bean, F. D. "America's Changing Color Lines: Immigration, Race/ Ethnicity, and Multiracial Identification." *Annual Review of Sociology*, 2003, 30, 221–242.

Lee, V. E., and Burkham, D. T. *Inequality at the Starting Gate.* Washington, D.C.: Economic Policy Institute, 2002.

Lemieux, C. M. "Learning Contracts in the Classroom: Tools for Empowerment and Accountability." *Social Work Education*, 2001, 20(2), 263–276.

Leonardo, Z. (ed.). *Critical Pedagogy and Race.* Malden, Mass.: Blackwell, 2005.

Lewis, C., Perry, R., and Murata, A. "How Should Research Contribute to Instructional Improvement?" *Educational Researcher*, 2006, 35(3), 3–14.

Light, R. *The Harvard Assessment Seminars: Explorations with Students and Faculty about Teaching, Learning, and Student Life, First Report.* Cambridge, Mass.: Harvard University School of Education, 1990.

Lipsitz, G. *The Possessive Investment in Whiteness: How White People Profit from Identity Politics.* Philadelphia: Temple University Press, 1998.

Lipsitz, G. *The Possessive Investment in Whiteness: How White People Profit from Identity Politics.* (Rev. ed.) Philadelphia: Temple University Press, 2006.

Lobo, S., and Peters, K. (eds.). *American Indians and the Urban Experience.* Walnut Creek, Calif.: Altamira Press, 2001.

Locke, D. C. *Increasing Multicultural Understanding: A Comprehensive Model.* Thousand Oaks, Calif.: Sage, 1992.

Locke, E., and Latham, G. "Building a Practically Useful Theory of Goal Setting and Task Motivation." *American Psychologist,* 2002, 57, 705–717.

Luke, A. *The Social Construction of Literacy in the Classroom.* New York: Macmillan, 1994.

Lyons, N. "Two Perspectives on Self, Relationships and Morality." *Harvard Educational Review,* 1983, 53, 125–145.

MacGregor, J. "What Differences Do Learning Communities Make?" *Washington Center News,* 1991, 6(1), 4–9.

MacGregor, J. "Learning Self-Evaluation: Challenges for Students." In J. MacGregor (ed.), *Student Self-Evaluation: Fostering Reflective Learning.* New Directions for Teaching and Learning, no. 56. San Francisco: Jossey-Bass, 1994.

Marable, M. *The Crisis of Color and Democracy: Essays on Race, Class and Power.* Monroe, Md.: Common Courage Press, 1992.

Marable, M. *The Great Wells of Democracy: The Meaning of Race in American Life.* New York: Basic Books, 2002.

Marchesani, L. S., and Adams, M. "Dynamics of Diversity in the Teaching-Learning Process: A Faculty Development Model for Analysis and Action." In M. Adams (ed.), *Promoting Diversity in College Classrooms.* New Directions for Teaching and Learning, no. 51. San Francisco: Jossey-Bass, 1992.

Marsick, V. J. "Case Study." In M. W. Galbraith (ed.), *Adult Learning Methods: A Guide for Effective Instruction.* (3rd ed.) Malabar, Fla.: Krieger, 2004.

Marzano, R. J. *The Art and Science of Teaching: A Comprehensive Framework for Effective Instruction.* Alexandria, Va.: Association for Supervision and Curriculum Development, 2007.

Massimini, F., Csikszentmihalyi, M., and Delle Fave, A. "Flow and Biocultural Evolution." In M. Csikszentmihalyi and I. S. Csikszentmihalyi (eds.), *Optimal Experience: Psychological Studies of Flow in Consciousness.* New York: Cambridge University Press, 1988.

Mazur, E. *Peer Instruction: A User's Manual.* Upper Saddle River, N.J.: Prentice Hall, 1997.

McCombs, B. L., and others. *Learner-Centered Psychological Principles: Guidelines for School Design and Reform.* Washington, D.C.: American Psychological Association and Mid-continent Regional Educational Laboratory, 1993.

McDonald, J. P., Mohr, N., Dichter, A., and McDonald, E. C. *The Power of Protocols: An Educator's Guide to Better Practice.* New York: Teachers College Press, 2003.

McIntosh, P. "Curricular Re-Vision: The New Knowledge for a New Age." In C. S. Pearson, D. L. Shavlick, and J. G. Touchton (eds.), *Educating the Majority: Women Challenge Tradition in Higher Education.* New York: American Council on Education/Macmillan, 1989.

McLaren, P. "White Terror and Oppositional Agency: Towards a Critical Multiculturalism." In D. T. Goldberg (ed.), *Multiculturalism: A Critical Reader.* Cambridge, Mass.: Blackwell, 1994.

McLaren, P. *Life in Schools: An Introduction to Critical Pedagogy in the Foundations of Education.* (5th ed.) Needham, Mass.: Allyn & Bacon, 2006.

McLaren, P., and Leonard, P. (eds.). *Paulo Freire: A Critical Encounter*. New York: Routledge, 1993.

Meier, D. *The Power of Their Ideas: Lessons for America from a Small School in Harlem*. Boston: Beacon Press, 1995.

Merriam, S. B., and Associates. *Non-Western Perspectives on Learning and Knowing*. Melbourne, Fla.: Krieger, 2007.

Merriam, S. B., Caffarella, R. S., and Baumgartner, L. M. *Learning in Adulthood: A Comprehensive Guide*. (3rd ed.) San Francisco: Jossey-Bass, 2007.

Messick, S. "Personality Consistencies in Cognition and Creativity." In S. Messick and Associates, *Individuality in Learning: Implications of Cognitive Styles and Creativity in Human Development*. San Francisco: Jossey-Bass, 1976.

Meyers, C., and Jones, T. B. *Promoting Active Learning: Strategies for the College Classroom*. San Francisco: Jossey-Bass, 1993.

Mezirow, J. "Learning to Think Like an Adult: Core Concepts of Transformation Theory." In J. Mezirow and Associates, *Learning as Transformation: Critical Perspectives on a Theory in Progress*. San Francisco: Jossey-Bass, 2000.

Mills, R. C. "A New Understanding of Self: The Role of Affect, State of Mind, Self-Understanding and Intrinsic Motivation." *Journal of Experimental Education*, 1991, 60, 67–81.

Milton, O., Pollio, H. R., and Eison, J. A. *Making Sense of College Grades*. San Francisco: Jossey-Bass, 1986.

Minh-ha, T. T. *Woman, Native, Other: Writing Postcoloniality and Feminism*. Bloomington: Indiana University Press, 1989.

Moll, L. C., Saez, R., and Dworin, J. "Exploring Biliteracy." *Elementary School Journal*, 2001, 101(4), 435–449.

Molnar, A. "Guidelines for Business Involvement in the Schools." *Educational Leadership*, 1989–1990, pp. 84–86.

Molnar, A., and Lindquist, B. *Changing Problem Behavior in Schools*. San Francisco: Jossey-Bass, 1989.

Moore Howard, R. "Collaborative Pedagogy." In G. Tate, A. Rupiper and K. Schick (eds.), *A Guide to Composition Pedagogies*. New York: Oxford University Press, 2000.

Moran, S., Kornhaber, M., and Gardner, H. "Orchestrating Multiple Intelligences." *Educational Leadership*, 2006, 64(1), 22–27.

Nakamura, J., and Csikszentmihalyi, M. "The Construction of Meaning Through Vital Engagement." In C. Keyes and J. Haidt (eds.), *Flourishing: Positive Psychology and the Life Well-Lived*. Washington, D.C.: American Psychological Association, 2003.

National Alliance to End Homelessness. "Family Homelessness." In *Fact Checker: Accurate Statistics on Homelessness*. Feb. 2007. http://www.endhomelessness. org/content/article/detail/ 1525.

National Center for Educational Statistics, U.S. Department of Education. *Digest of Educational Statistics: 2002*. Washington, D.C.: National Center for Educational Statistics, 2002.

National Survey of Student Engagement. *2006 Annual Report: Engaged Learning: Fostering Success for All Students*. Jan. 2006. http://nsse.iub.edu/NSSE_2006_ Annual_Report/index.cfm.

National Writing Project, and Nagin, C. *Because Writing Matters: Improving Student Writing in Our Schools*. (Rev. ed.) San Francisco: Jossey-Bass, 2006.

Newmann, F. M., and Wehlage, G. C. "Five Standards of Authentic Instruction." *Educational Leadership*, 1993, 50(7), 8–12.

Nieto, S. *Affirming Diversity: The Sociopolitical Context of Multicultural Education*. (4th ed.) White Plains, N.Y.: Longman, 2004.

Nitko, A. J., and Brookhart, S. M. *Educational Assessment of Students.* (5th ed.) Upper Saddle River, N.J.: Merrill Prentice Hall, 2006.

Noonan, J. F. "Discussing Racial Topics in Class." In M. Adams and L. Marchensan (eds.), *Racial and Cultural Diversity, Curricular Content, and Classroom Dynamics: A Manual for College Teachers.* Amherst: University of Massachusetts, 1988.

Northwest Regional Educational Laboratory. "Listening to Student Voices Tools: Data in a Day." 2008. http://www.nwrel.org/csdi/services/lsv/diad.php.

Obama, B. "A More Perfect Union." Speech delivered in Philadelphia, March 18, 2008.

Ogbu, J. U. "Variability in Minority School Performance: A Problem in Search of an Explanation." *Anthropology and Education Quarterly*, 1987, 18, 312–335.

Ogle, D. "The K-W-L: A Teaching Model That Develops Active Reading of Expository Text." *The Reading Teacher*, 1986, 39, 564–576.

Oishi, S., and Diener, E. "Culture and Well-Being: The Cycle of Action, Evaluation, and Decision." *Personality and Social Psychology Bulletin*, 2003, 29, 1–11.

Olson, L. "What Does 'Ready' Mean?" *Education Week*, June 2007, 40, 7–12.

Orfield, G., Marin, P., and Horn, C. *Higher Education and the Color Line.* Cambridge, Mass.: Harvard University Press, 2005.

Ouellett, M. *Teaching Inclusively: Resources for Course, Department, and Institutional Change in Higher Education.* Stillwater, Okla.: New Forums, 2005.

Ovando, C. J., and Collier, V. P. *Bilingual and ESL Classrooms: Teaching in Multicultural Contexts.* (2nd ed.) New York: McGraw-Hill, 1998.

Passel, J., and Suro, R. *Rise, Peak and Decline: Trends in U.S. Immigration 1992–2004.* Washington, D.C.: Pew Hispanic Center, 2005.

Paul, R. "Socratic Questioning." In R. Paul (ed.), *Critical Thinking: What Every Person Needs to Survive in a Rapidly Changing World.* Rohnert Park, Calif.: Center for Critical Thinking and Moral Critique, Sonoma State University, 1990.

Pearlman, M. "Trends in Women's Total Score and Item Performance on Verbal Measures." Paper presented at the annual meeting of the American Educational Research Associates, Washington, D.C., Apr. 1987.

Pedersen, P. *A Handbook for Developing Multicultural Awareness.* (2nd ed.) Alexandria, Va.: American Counseling Association, 1994.

Pedersen, P. B. *110 Experiences for Multicultural Learning.* Washington, D.C.: American Psychological Association, 2004.

Perkins, D. N., Allen, R., and Hafner, J. "Differences in Everyday Reasoning." In W. Maxwell (ed.), *Thinking: The Frontier Expands.* Hillsdale, N.J.: Erlbaum, 1983.

Perkins, D. N., Faraday, M., and Bushey, B. "Everyday Reasoning and the Roots of Intelligence." In J. F. Voss, D. N. Perkins, and J. W. Segal (eds.), *Informal Reasoning and Education.* Hillsdale, N. J.: Erlbaum, 1991.

Perry, W. G. *Forms of Intellectual and Ethical Development in the College Years.* New York: Holt, 1970.

Phinney, J. S. "Ethnic Identity in Adolescents and Adults: Review of Research." *Psychological Bulletin*, 1990, 108(3), 499–514.

Plaut, V. C., & Markus, H. R. "The 'Inside' Story: A Cultural-Historical Analysis of Being Smart and Motivated, American Style." In Elliot, A. J., and Dweck, C. S. (eds.), *Handbook of Competence of Competence and Motivation.* New York: Guilford Press, 2005.

Popham, W. J. "The Merits of Measurement Driven Instruction." *Phi Delta Kappan*, 1987, 68, 679–682.

Prentice, D. A., and Carranza, E. "Sustaining Cultural Beliefs in the Face of Their Violation: The Case of Gender Stereotypes." In M. Schaller and C. Crandall (eds.), *The Psychological Foundations of Culture*. Mahwah, N.J.: Erlbaum, 2003.

Putnam, R. D. "E Pluribus Unum: Diversity and Community in the Twenty-First Century." *Scandinavian Political Studies*, 2007, 30(2), 137–165.

Ratey, J. J. *A User's Guide to the Brain: Perception, Attention, and the Four Theatres of the Brain*. New York: Pantheon, 2001.

Reason, P. (ed.). *Handbook of Action Research: Concise Paperback Edition*. Thousand Oaks, Calif.: Sage, 2006.

Reason, R. D., Broido, E. M., Davis, T. L., and Evans, N. J. (eds.). *Developing Social Justice Allies*. New Directions for Student Services, no. 110. San Francisco: Jossey-Bass, 2005.

Reeves, D. B. "Effective Grading Practices." *Educational Leadership*, 2008, 65(5), 85–87.

Remland, M. S. *Nonverbal Communication in Everyday Life*. Boston: Houghton Mifflin, 2000.

Rendon, L. "Validating Culturally Diverse Students: Toward a New Model of Learning and Student Development." *Innovative Higher Education*, 1994, 9(1), 33–52.

Rendon, L. I., Garcia, M., and Person, D. (eds.). *Transforming the First Year of College for Students of Color*. Columbia, S.C.: Center for the First-Year Experience and Students in Transition, 2004.

Rogoff, B. *Apprenticeship in Thinking*. New York: Oxford University Press, 1990.

Rogoff, B. "Culture and Learning." Address to the National Academy of Science Workshop, Committee on Research in Education, Washington, D.C., June 30, 2003.

Rojstaczur, S. "Grade Inflation at American Colleges and Universities." 2002. http://gradeinflation.com/.

Rosenthal, J. W. "Multicultural Science: Focus on the Biological and Environmental Sciences." In A. I. Morey and M. K. Kitano (eds.), *Multicultural Course Transformation in Higher Education*. Needham Heights, Mass.: Allyn and Bacon, 1997.

Ryan, R. M., and Deci, E. L. "Overview of Self-Determination Theory: An Organismic Dialectical Perspective." In E. L. Deci and R. M. Ryan (eds.), *Handbook of Self-Determination Research*. Rochester, N.Y.: University of Rochester Press, 2002.

Ryan, R., and others. "The American Dream in Russia: Extrinsic Aspirations and Well-Being in Two Cultures." *Personality and Social Psychology Bulletin*, 1999, 25, 1509–1524.

Sadker, M. and Sadker, D. "Confronting Sexism in the College Classroom." In S. Gabriel and S. Smithson (eds.), *Gender in the Classroom*. Champaign: University of Illinois Press, 1990.

Sadker, M., and Sadker, D. "Ensuring Equitable Participation in College Classes." In L. L. B. Border and N. Van Note Chism (eds.), *Teaching for Diversity*. New Directions for Teaching and Learning, no. 49. San Francisco: Jossey-Bass, 1992.

Sadker, M., and Sadker, D. *Failing at Fairness: How America's Schools Cheat Girls*. New York: Scribner's, 1994.

Said, E. W. *Culture and Imperialism*. New York: Knopf, 1993.

Sanlo, R. "Lesbian, Gay, and Bisexual College Students: Risk, Resiliency, and Retention." *Journal of College Student Retention Research Theory and Practice*, 2004, 6(1), 97–110.

Schein, E. H. *Organizational Culture and Leadership*. San Francisco: Jossey-Bass, 1992.

Scherer, K. R. "Unconscious Processes in Emotion: The Bulk of the Iceberg." In L. S. Barrett, P. M. Niedenthal, and P. Winkielman (eds.), *Emotion and Consciousness*. New York: Guilford Press, 2005.

Schlossberg, N. "Marginality and Mattering: Key Issues in Building Community." In D. C. Roberts (ed.), *Designing Campus Activities to Foster a Sense of Community*. New Directions for Student Services, no. 48, San Francisco: Jossey-Bass, 1989.

Schmitz, B., Paul, S. P., and Greenberg, J. D. "Creating Multicultural Classrooms: An Experience Derived Faculty Development Program." In L. L. B. Border and N. Van Note Chism (eds.), *Teaching for Diversity*. New Directions for Teaching and Learning, no. 49. San Francisco: Jossey-Bass, 1992.

Schön, D. A. *Educating the Reflective Practitioner: Toward a New Design for Teaching and Learning in the Professions*. San Francisco: Jossey-Bass, 1987.

Senge, P. M. *The Fifth Discipline: The Art and Practice of the Learning Organization*. New York: Doubleday/Currency, 1990.

Senge, P. M. *The Fifth Discipline: The Art and Practice of the Learning Organization*. (Rev ed.) New York: Doubleday, 2006.

Shanley, J. P. "Director's Notes." *Playbill for Doubt*, November 2007, 5–6.

Sheared, V. "Giving Voice: An Inclusive Model of Instruction—A Womanist Perspective." In E. Hayes and S. A. J. Colin III (eds.), *Confronting Racism and Sexism*. New Directions for Teaching and Learning, no. 61. San Francisco: Jossey-Bass, 1994.

Shepard, L. A. "Why We Need Better Assessments." *Educational Leadership*, 1989, 46(7), 4–9.

Shor, I. *Empowering Education: Critical Teaching for Social Change*. Chicago: University of Chicago Press, 1992.

Shor, I. "Education Is Politics: Paulo Freire's Critical Pedagogy." In P. McLaren and P. Leonard (eds.), *Paulo Freire: A Critical Encounter*. New York: Routledge & Kegan Paul, 1993.

Shulman, J. H., and others. "Case Writing as a Site for Collaboration." *Teacher Education Quarterly*, Winter 1990, pp. 63–78.

Simulation Training Systems. *Star Power*. Del Mar, Calif.: Simulation Training Systems, 1993.

Sirotnik, K. A. "Society, Schooling, Teaching, and Preparing to Teach." In J. I. Goodlad, R. Soder, and K. A. Sirotnik (eds.), *The Moral Dimensions of Teaching*. San Francisco: Jossey-Bass, 1990.

Sizer, T. R. *Horace's Compromise: The Dilemma of the American High School*. Boston: Houghton Mifflin, 1984.

Sloterdijk, P. *Critique of Cynical Reason*. Theory and History of Literature, Vol. 40. Minneapolis: University of Minnesota Press, 1988.

Smith, B. L., and MacGregor, J. T. "What Is Collaborative Learning?" In A. Goodsell, M. Maher, and V. Tinto (eds.), *Collaborative Learning: A Sourcebook for Higher Education*. University Park: National Center on Postsecondary Teaching, Learning, and Assessment, Pennsylvania State University, 1992.

Smith, B. L., MacGregor, R., Matthews, R., and Gabelnick, F. *Learning Communities: Reforming Undergraduate Education*. San Francisco: Jossey-Bass, 2004.

Smith, D. M., and Kolb, D. *User's Guide for the Learning Styles Inventory: A Manual for Teachers and Trainers*. Boston: McBer, 1986.

Solorzano, D. "Teaching and Social Change: Reflections on a Freirean Approach in a College Classroom." Teaching Sociology, 1989, 17, 218–225.

Sousa, D. A. How the Brain Learns. (3rd ed.) Thousand Oaks, Calif.: Corwin, 2006.

Sternberg, R. J. "The Rainbow Project: What's Wrong with College Admissions and How Psychology Can Fix It." Address at the annual convention of the American Psychological Association, Toronto, 2003.

Sternberg, R. J., and Grigorenko, E. L. (eds.). Culture and Competence: Contexts of Life Success. Washington, D.C.: American Psychological Association, 2004.

Sternberg, R. J., and others. Practical Intelligence in Everyday Life. Cambridge: Cambridge University Press, 2000.

Stiggins, R. J. "Revitalizing Classroom Assessment: The Highest Instructional Priority." Phi Delta Kappan, Jan. 1988, pp. 363–368.

Stobart, G. "Fairness in Multicultural Assessment Systems." Assessment in Education: Principles, Policy, and Practice, 2005, 12(3), 275–287.

Stringer, E. T. Action Research. (3rd ed.) Thousand Oaks, Calif.: Sage, 2007.

Suarez-Orozco, C., and Suarez-Orozco, M. M. Children of Immigration. Cambridge, Mass.: Harvard University Press, 2002.

Sue, D. W., and Sue, D. Counseling the Culturally Different: Theory and Practice. (3rd ed.) Hoboken, N.J.: Wiley, 1999.

Sue, S. "Ethnicity and Culture in Psychological Research and Practice." In J. D. Goodchilds (ed.), Psychological Perspectives on Human Diversity in America. Washington, D.C.: American Psychological Association, 1991.

Sung, L. "Stages of Racialized and Ethnic Identity Development." 2002. http://www.ivcf.org/glw/cfw/kog02/kog3_pkg_racial_&_ethnic_identity_charts.pdf.

Svinicki, M. D., and Dixon, N. M. "The Kolb Model Modified for Classroom Activities." College Teaching, 1987, 35(4), 141–146.

Tagg, J. The Learning Paradigm College. Bolton, Mass.: Anker, 2003.

Takaki, R. A Different Mirror: A History of Multicultural America. New York: Little, Brown, 1993.

Tannen, D. "Teachers' Classroom Strategies Should Recognize That Men and Women Use Language Differently." Chronicle of Higher Education, June 19, 1991, pp. B-1–B-3.

Tatum, B. D. "Talking About Race, Learning About Racism: The Application of Racial Identity Development Theory in the Classroom." Harvard Educational Review, 1992, 62(1), 1–24.

Tatum, B. D. "What Do You Do When They Call You a Racist?" National Association of Secondary School Principals Bulletin, 1998, 82(602), 43–48.

Tatum, B. D. Why Are All the Black Kids Sitting Together in the Cafeteria? And Other Conversations About Race. New York: Basic Books, 2003.

Tatum, B. D. Can We Talk About Race? And Other Conversations in an Era of School Resegregation. Boston: Beacon Press, 2007.

Taylor, E. W. "Intercultural Competency: A Transformative Learning Process." Adult Education Quarterly, 1994, 44(3), 154–174.

Taylor, E. W. "Making Meaning of the Varied and Contested Perspectives of Transformative Learning Theory." In D. Vlosak, G. Kielbaso, and J. Radford (eds.), Proceedings of the 6th International Conference on Transformative Learning. East Lansing: Michigan State University, 2005.

Tharp, R. G. "Psychocultural Variables and Constants: Effects on Teaching and Learning in Schools." American Psychologist, 1989, 44(2), 349–359.

Tinto, V. Leaving College: Rethinking the Causes and Cures for Student Attrition. Chicago: University of Chicago Press, 1987.

Tinto, V. "Colleges as Communities: Taking Research on Student Persistence Seriously." *Review of Higher Education*, 1998, *21*(2), 167–177.

Tippeconnic Fox, M. J., Lowe, S. C., and McClellan, G. S. (eds.). *Serving Native American Students*. New Directions for Student Services, no. 109. San Francisco: Jossey-Bass, 2005.

Tracey, W. R. *Designing Training and Development Systems*. (3rd ed.) New York: AMACOM, 1992.

Treisman, U. "A Study of the Mathematics Performance of Black Students at the University of California, Berkeley." Unpublished doctoral dissertation, Department of Mathematics, University of California, Berkeley, 1985.

Treisman, U. "Studying Students Studying Calculus: A Look at the Lives of Minority Mathematics Students in College." *College Mathematics Journal*, 1992, *23*(5), 362–372.

Treuba, H., and Delgado-Gaitan, C. "Socialization of Mexican Children for Cooperation and Competition: Sharing and Copying." *Journal of Educational Equity and Leadership*, 1985, *5*(3), 189–204.

Uguroglu, M., and Walberg, H. J. "Motivation and Achievement: A Quantitative Synthesis." *American Educational Research Journal*, 1979, *16*, 375–389.

U.S. Census Bureau. Census 2000 Redistricting Summary File. Washington, D.C.: Government Printing Office, 2002.

Valenzuela, A. *Subtractive Schooling: U.S.-Mexican Youth and the Politics of Caring*. Albany: State University of New York Press, 1999.

Vansteenkiste, M., Lens, W., and Deci, E. L. "Intrinsic Versus Extrinsic Goal Contents in Self-Determination Theory: Another Look at the Quality of Academic Motivation." *Educational Psychologist*, 2006, *41*(1), 19–31.

Ventura, M. "Standing at the Wall." *The Sun*, Mar. 1994, pp. 4–6.

Viens, J., and Kallenbach, S. *Multiple Intelligences and Adult Literacy: A Sourcebook for Practitioners*. New York: Teachers College Press, 2004.

Voss, J. F. "Problem Solving and the Educational Process." In A. Lesgold and R. Glaser (eds.), *Foundations for a Psychology of Education*. Hillsdale, N.J.: Erlbaum, 1989.

Waluconis, C. J. "Self-Evaluation: Settings and Uses." In J. MacGregor (ed.), *Student Self-Evaluation: Fostering Reflective Learning*. New Directions for Teaching and Learning, no. 56. San Francisco: Jossey-Bass, 1994.

Walvoord, B. E. *Assessment Clear and Simple: A Practical Guide for Institutions, Departments, and General Education*. San Francisco: Jossey-Bass, 2004.

Walvoord, B. E., and Anderson, V. J. *Effective Grading: A Tool for Learning and Assessment*. San Francisco: Jossey-Bass, 1998.

Watson, J. S., and Ramey, C. G. "Reactions to Response Contingent Stimulation in Early Infancy." *Merrill Palmer Quarterly*, 1972, *18*, 219–228.

Weaver, F. S. *Liberal Education: Critical Essays on Professions, Pedagogy, and Structure*. New York: Teachers College Press, 1991.

Weinstein, G., and Obear, K. "Bias Issues in the Classroom: Encounters with the Teaching Self." In M. Adams (ed.), *Promoting Diversity in College Classrooms: Innovative Responses for the Curriculum, Faculty, and Institutions*. New Directions for Teaching and Learning, no. 52. San Francisco: Jossey-Bass, 1992.

Wenger, E. *Communities of Practice: Learning, Meaning, and Identity*. Cambridge: Cambridge University Press, 1998.

Wetherell, M., and Potter, J. *Mapping the Language of Racism: Discourse and the Legitimation of Exploitation*. London: Harvester Wheatsheaf, 1992.

Whitehead, A. N. *Process and Reality*. New York: Free Press, 1979.

Whitman, N. *Peer Teaching: To Teach Is to Learn Twice.* ASHE-ERIC Higher Education Report, no. 4. Washington, D.C.: ERIC Clearinghouse on Higher Education, 1988.

Wieman, C. "Why Not Try a Scientific Approach to Science Education?" *Change,* Sept.–Oct. 2007, pp. 9–15.

Wiggins, G. *Educative Assessment: Designing Assessments to Inform and Improve Student Performance.* San Francisco: Jossey-Bass, 1998.

Wiley, T. *Literacy and Language Diversity in the United States.* McHenry, Ill.: Center for Applied Linguistics and Delta Systems, 1996.

Williams, R. M., Jr. *American Society: A Sociological Interpretation.* (3rd ed.) New York: Knopf, 1970.

Wilson, A. L., and Hayes, E. R. *Handbook of Adult and Continuing Education.* San Francisco: Jossey-Bass, 2000.

Winant, H. *The New Politics of Race: Globalism, Difference, Justice.* Minneapolis: University of Minnesota Press, 2004.

Windschitl, M. "Framing Constructivism in Practice as the Negotiation of Dilemmas: An Analysis of the Conceptual, Pedagogical, Cultural, and Political Challenges Facing Teachers." *Review of Educational Research,* 2002, 72, 131–175.

Winkielman, P., Berridge, K. C., and Wilbarger, J. L. "Emotion, Behavior, and Conscious Experience: Once More Without Feeling." In L. S. Barrett, P. M. Niedenthal, and P. Winkielman (eds.), *Emotion and Consciousness.* New York: Guilford Press, 2005.

Wlodkowski, R. J. *Enhancing Adult Motivation to Learn: A Comprehensive Guide for Teaching All Adults.* (3rd ed.) San Francisco: Jossey-Bass, 2008.

Wlodkowski, R. J., and Ginsberg, M. B. *Diversity and Motivation: Culturally Responsive Teaching.* San Francisco: Jossey-Bass, 1995.

Wlodkowski, R. J., and Kasworm, C. K. (eds.). *Accelerated Learning for Adults: The Promise and Practice of Intensive Educational Formats.* New Directions for Adult and Continuing Education, no. 97. San Francisco: Jossey-Bass, 2003.

Woolfolk, A. *Educational Psychology.* (10th ed.) Boston: Pearson, 2007.

Yosso, T. J. "Whose Culture Has Capital? A Critical Race Theory Discussion of Community Cultural Wealth." *Race, Ethnicity, and Education,* 2005, 8(1), 69–91.

Yosso, T. J. *Critical Race Counterstories Along the Chicana/Chicano Educational Pipeline.* New York: Routledge, 2006.

Young, C. "Grade Inflation in Higher Education." *ERIC Digest,* 2003. http://www.ericdigests.org/2005-1/grade.htm.

Young, R. *White Mythologies: Writing History and the West.* London: Routledge, 1990.

Zimmerman, B. J., and Kitsantas, A. "The Hidden Dimension of Personal Competence: Self-Regulated Learning and Practice." In A. J. Elliot and C. S. Dweck (eds.), *Handbook of Competence and Motivation.* New York: Guilford Press, 2005.

Zull, J. E. *The Art of Changing the Brain: Enriching the Practice of Teaching by Exploring the Biology of Learning.* Sterling, Va.: Stylus, 2002.

Zull, J. E. "Key Aspects of How the Brain Learns." In S. Johnson and K. Taylor (eds.), *The Neuroscience of Adult Learning.* New Directions for Adult and Continuing Education, no. 110. San Francisco: Jossey-Bass, 2006.

Name Index

Subject Index

Page references followed by *fig* indicate an illustrated figure; followed by *t* indicate a table; followed by *e* indicate an exhibit.

A

Abstract conceptualization: degree of direct student involvement in, 174*fig*; experiential learning model role of, 170*fig*; learning sequence role of, 173*fig*; sample learning activities for, 172*fig*

Academic theme. *See* Topical themes

Accountability, 99–100

Action plans: description of, 364; example of, 365*e*; recommendations for developing, 366–367

Action research: process of, 233–236; reflecting on projects and related issue of, 253

Active experimentation: degree of direct student involvement in, 174*fig*; experiential learning model role of, 170*fig*; learning sequence role of, 173*fig*; sample learning activities for, 172*fig*

Active Learning (Johnson, Johnson, and Smith), 102

The Advanced Learning Technologies Project (ALTEC), 295

Aesthetic entry point, 164–165, 166*e*

American Indian, 133

Anxiety/doubt, 367

Artistry and invention, 236–238, 253

Aspirational capital, 30

Assessment. *See* Student assessment

Attitude. *See* Developing attitude

Authenticity: culturally responsive teaching norm of, 334*e*; culturally responsive teaching role and practice, 330–346; engendering competence component of, 264–266; motivational framework lesson plan inclusion of, 328

Authentic performance tasks: assessment through use of, 279; based on multiple intelligences, 283–286; characteristics of, 280–281; exhibitions and poster conferences, 287–288; personal assessment values with practice of, 281–283; portfolios, 288–291; rubrics used to assess, 291–295

Authentic research: definitional investigation using, 222–224; description and issues related to, 220–222; experimental inquiry using, 228–229; historical investigation using, 224–226; learning activities related to, 229–233; projective investigation using, 226–228

B

Basic dualism, 61

Belief systems: cultural themes reflecting, 14–17; Eurocentric, 27–28; regarding learning, 10; representing different perspectives, 64–66. *See also* Values

Bias: constructing tests that avoid cultural, 295–297; contextualized assessment and issue of, 268–269; cues and triggers of, 53, 54;